H.L. Nash   5.00

P9-CDH-738

Cambridge Historical Series

THE REVOLUTIONARY AND NAPOLEONIC ERA.

CAMBRIDGE UNIVERSITY PRESS

LONDON : FETTER LANE, E.C.4

NEW YORK : THE MACMILLAN CO.
BOMBAY
CALCUTTA } MACMILLAN AND CO., LTD.
MADRAS
TORONTO : THE MACMILLAN CO.
OF CANADA, LTD.
TOKYO : MARUZEN-KABUSHIKI-KAISHA

ALL RIGHTS RESERVED

THE
REVOLUTIONARY
AND
NAPOLEONIC ERA
1789—1815

BY

J. HOLLAND ROSE, Litt.D.

AUTHOR OF "THE LIFE OF NAPOLEON I," "NAPOLEONIC STUDIES,"
"THE DEVELOPMENT OF THE EUROPEAN NATIONS."

SIXTH EDITION, REVISED

CAMBRIDGE
AT THE UNIVERSITY PRESS
1925

First Edition 1894
Revised Edition 1895.   *Reprinted* 1898, 1901, 1904
Sixth Edition, Revised 1907
Reprinted 1911, 1919, 1925

Printed in Great Britain
by Turnbull & Spears, Edinburgh

PREFACE.

The dramatic intensity of many phases of the French Revolution has, until recently, so absorbed the attention of students as to obscure its relation to the European Revolution. It is the chief aim of this little work to show this inter-dependence, and to explain the influence of French ideas and policy on Europe. Though this plan somewhat restricts the arena of personal achievement and romance, it will, I trust, ensure a corresponding gain in historical interest; for the European nations were then first brought into close contact, not merely by dynastic interests, but by their own conscious aspirations or antipathies. My object has been to exhibit the influences in France and Europe tending to overthrow the old systems of government and society, to trace, even amidst the apparent chaos of the French Revolution, the growth of forces which tended towards a strongly centralised government and autocracy, to describe Napoleon's work of destruction and reconstruction, and finally to analyse the character of the new national impulses which overthrew his domination. Passing over unimportant details, I have everywhere endeavoured to concentrate attention on those events and crises which exercised most influence on the formation of the European system, and to show the connection, too often ignored, between the earlier and later phases of the French Revolution. To study the intricate strifes of French parties in 1789—1795, apart from the reorganisation effected by Bonaparte, appears to me as unprofitable as to master the enunciation and construction of a geometrical problem without proceeding to its solution.

The present time is singularly favourable to an attempt at reviewing the features of this momentous era. The researches

of MM. Sorel, Aulard, Vandal and others have added largely
to our knowledge of the epoch, especially that portion of it in
which Napoleon is the principal figure. The general tendency
of recent French enquiries has been to some extent to redress
the balance in favour of the great conqueror. The historian
must, however, duly discount the brilliant romancings of
Marbot, the trustful confidences of Méneval, and the quaint
attempts of M. Lévy to depict his hero as a good-natured
bourgeois in private life. Fortunately, the other side of
the picture has been set forth in the sober and authentic
narratives of Chaptal, Macdonald and Pasquier. Besides
working through these and many other French Memoirs, I have
endeavoured to enter into the general spirit of the age by
studying the chief histories, memoirs and biographies relating
to other European lands, especially Germany. The perusal of
our Foreign Office records has also convinced me that much
more may be urged in defence of British policy than has
hitherto been conceded.

My best thanks are due to the Rev. Dr Marchand, of Angers,
and Signor Lumbroso, of Rome, for information respecting
French and Italian affairs respectively; also to Mr A. J.
Grant, and Mr J. W. Headlam, both of King's College,
Cambridge, for several valuable suggestions; but, most of
all, to the Editor of the series, Dr Prothero, for the care
which he has bestowed alike on multifarious details and on
questions involving a wide historical survey.

J. H. R.

August, 1894.

For the second edition the suggestions of critics have been
carefully considered and in some cases adopted.

J. H. R.

June, 1895.

PREFACE.

The dramatic intensity of many phases of the French Revolution has, until recently, so absorbed the attention of students as to obscure its relation to the European Revolution. It is the chief aim of this little work to show this inter-dependence, and to explain the influence of French ideas and policy on Europe. Though this plan somewhat restricts the arena of personal achievement and romance, it will, I trust, ensure a corresponding gain in historical interest; for the European nations were then first brought into close contact, not merely by dynastic interests, but by their own conscious aspirations or antipathies. My object has been to exhibit the influences in France and Europe tending to overthrow the old systems of government and society, to trace, even amidst the apparent chaos of the French Revolution, the growth of forces which tended towards a strongly centralised government and autocracy, to describe Napoleon's work of destruction and reconstruction, and finally to analyse the character of the new national impulses which overthrew his domination. Passing over unimportant details, I have everywhere endeavoured to concentrate attention on those events and crises which exercised most influence on the formation of the European system, and to show the connection, too often ignored, between the earlier and later phases of the French Revolution. To study the intricate strifes of French parties in 1789—1795, apart from the reorganisation effected by Bonaparte, appears to me as unprofitable as to master the enunciation and construction of a geometrical problem without proceeding to its solution.

The present time is singularly favourable to an attempt at reviewing the features of this momentous era. The researches

of MM. Sorel, Aulard, Vandal and others have added largely
to our knowledge of the epoch, especially that portion of it in
which Napoleon is the principal figure.   The general tendency
of recent French enquiries has been to some extent to redress
the balance in favour of the great conqueror.   The historian
must, however, duly discount the brilliant romancings of
Marbot, the trustful confidences of Ménéval, and the quaint
attempts of M. Lévy to depict his hero as a good-natured
bourgeois in private life.   Fortunately, the other side of
the picture has been set forth in the sober and authentic
narratives of Chaptal, Macdonald and Pasquier.   Besides
working through these and many other French Memoirs, I have
endeavoured to enter into the general spirit of the age by
studying the chief histories, memoirs and biographies relating
to other European lands, especially Germany.   The perusal of
our Foreign Office records has also convinced me that much
more may be urged in defence of British policy than has
hitherto been conceded.

My best thanks are due to the Rev. Dr Marchand, of Angers,
and Signor Lumbroso, of Rome, for information respecting
French and Italian affairs respectively; also to Mr A. J.
Grant, and Mr J. W. Headlam, both of King's College,
Cambridge, for several valuable suggestions; but, most of
all, to the Editor of the series, Dr Prothero, for the care
which he has bestowed alike on multifarious details and on
questions involving a wide historical survey.

J. H. R.

August, 1894.

For the second edition the suggestions of critics have been
carefully considered and in some cases adopted.

J. H. R.

June, 1895.

TABLE OF CONTENTS.

APPENDIX.

MAPS AND PLANS.

THE REVOLUTIONARY AND NAPOLEONIC ERA, OR, FRANCE AND EUROPE,

1789—1815.

CHAPTER I.

THE POLITICAL AND SOCIAL WEAKNESS OF EUROPE.

"The corruption of each form of government commences with that of its principles."—MONTESQUIEU.

THE French Revolution was a conquest in the spheres of thought, society, and politics, effected by a people over the old systems of authority, class privilege, and absolute rule. In its course it came almost inevitably into collision with governments founded on the old ideas and customs; and the shock of arms favoured the rise of a military dictatorship, which curbed the revolution in France while extending it over the Continent. The conflict with monarchical Europe is therefore the central fact of the revolution, determining not only the trend of events in France, but also the extension of French influence over Europe, and the formation of the chief Continental States.

What was the old Europe which the revolutionary ideas were to permeate and transform? How came it that the revolution organised itself in France so effectively as to over-throw States which had defied the power of Louis XIV? In

brief, what was the potential strength of the new ideas; whence
came the weakness inherent in the Continental States? A
survey of the chief tendencies in pre-revolutionary Europe will
serve as an answer to these questions and an introduction to
the momentous events of 1789.

The Holy Roman Empire is the nebulous material from
which most of the Continental States have been evolved. Central, Western, and Southern Europe with few exceptions acknowledged the sway of Karl the Great (Charlemagne) as "the
Emperor," crowned by the Pope, and wielding the temporal
power of Christendom, while the successor of Peter embodied
the spiritual authority of the Church. Though many peoples
never belonged to "The Empire," yet the underlying conception had been that of a central predominant State, not belonging to any one ruling house, or people. It was Catholic in a
political, as well as in a religious sense. The great religious
and political strife of the Thirty Years' War (1618—1648)
shook old Europe to its base. The cosmopolitan Empire was
divided by a perpetuation of the religious schism. North-
Germany became definitely Protestant; South-Germany remained Roman Catholic and under the influence of the House
of Hapsburg. By the Peace of Westphalia (1648) the Empire
not only lost the Dutch Netherlands and the Swiss Confederation, but also relinquished the control of the foreign policy of
the chief German States. The Thirty Years' War undermined
the power of the Emperor, just as the Reformation had impaired the authority of the Pope. The European system was
left without any dominant principle of government, and Central
Europe became an ever-shifting mosaic of States tending to
group themselves around Vienna or Berlin, around the House
of Hapsburg-Lorraine, or the House of Hohenzollern. Even if
Germany had not been open to the intervention of other
powers, as Sweden and France, her history would have been
ever distracted by this dualism of interests.

The House of Hapsburg had long made use of its tenure of the Imperial throne to aggrandise its hereditary States, Bohemia, Moravia, the Duchy of Austria, Styria, Carinthia, Tyrol, and scattered lands on the Upper Danube and Rhine; for though the Imperial crown was in theory elective, yet the reigning Hapsburg was nearly always chosen by the princely Electors to be 'Emperor.' Now, when the Imperial power decayed, the Hapsburgs redoubled their attempts to make Germany an appanage of Austria; but the diversity of peoples and constitutions of the Hapsburg States would have made this all but impossible, even if a vigorous purely German State had not opposed it.

The rise of Brandenburg-Prussia was due to the skill and foresight by which the early Electors of Brandenburg used their central position in North Germany to champion national interests against the Poles and the Swedes, or the encroachments of Hapsburgs and Bourbons. Prussia has always increased most in power and territory, when her policy has been truly German. She has fallen back, when, as in 1795—1806, or 1849—1851, her government has been subservient to France or Austria.

The policy of Frederick the Great had the result of making Prussia the first of purely German States, and one of the Great Powers of Europe. Frederick determined to unite his scattered dominions of Brandenburg-Prussia, and add to them whatever lands could be welded on to his realm.

Thus, when the Hapsburg possessions were weakened by the contested succession of Maria Theresa, Frederick seized the opportunity to invade and conquer Silesia (1740). The revival of some old claims on this province formed an insufficient excuse for so glaring a violation of dynastic rights; but, if the end can justify the means, the seizure of Silesia may be palliated. Community with the Protestant North in race, physical conditions and commercial interests, seemed to declare for a union of Silesia with Brandenburg, and its separation from the Slavonic and Roman Catholic states of the House of Austria; and Silesia has ever since remained Prussian. It was in Silesia and Prussia (proper) that the national rising of 1813 was most general and enthusiastic. The seizure of Silesia, however, was a signal instance of the spirit which since the Thirty Years' War had begun to undermine the European system. That respect for dynastic rights and treaty obligations which generally held sway when Christendom was more than a name, now gave place to a state policy which avowedly aimed at little else but gain of territory or markets.

The same incisive assertion of natural and national claims at the expense of governmental rights, is observable in Frederick's policy with regard to Poland. There seems to be an inherent antipathy between the Poles and Germans. For ages the two races have striven for supremacy on the banks of the Wartha, the Vistula, and the Niemen. In the 16th and 17th centuries, when the Polish nobles were public-spirited enough to prefer the public interest to personal gains, their martial spirit gained the victory; but while the Electors of Brandenburg were slowly consolidating the North-German power, the Polish and Lithuanian realms were disintegrated by faction. The Polish nobles succeeded in making the Crown elective, in curtailing the political rights of the towns, and in reducing the peasants to abject serfdom. While in Western Europe aristocracy was yielding ground to the Crown or to the people, the reverse had been the case in Poland. The absorption of the governing powers by the Polish nobles was as fatal to the effective action of the government as to the liberties of the lower orders; for in the General Diet, consisting of the nobles, the laws must be passed unanimously; the veto of a single noble could reduce the State to a deadlock. Montesquieu censured its government as being the worst of aristocracies, "where the part of the people which obeys is in civil slavery to that which holds sway." In Prussia the iron will of the great Frederick linked closely together the different provinces and distinct orders of his people; and, though the Prussian Government and society had little of the unity which the Revolution was to impart in 1807—1812, yet Frederick's ability and energy ensured a strength far greater than that of the more extensive Polish State.

In 1772 came the first of the three partitions of Poland, which by 1795 ended its existence as an independent Power. Frederick, in planning with the Czarina Catherine II and Maria Theresa the spoliation of Poland, could urge no legal claims. The restoration to Germans in West-Prussia and Erme-land of German rule, and their liberation from the rule of factious nobles who sought to impose the Roman Catholic creed, will now, however, be generally considered a valid excuse for Prussia's share in the first partition. By it Frederick gained West-Prussia (except Danzig and Thorn) and Ermeland, thus securing a continuous German territory from the Niemen to the Middle Elbe; and North Germans were now freed from the danger resulting from the increase of Russian influence over the Polish Government. Frederick was no revolutionist, by theory or design. His aim was to consolidate his monarchy by all the means in his power, relying on his own vast faculties of organisation to control his ministers and officials, on the devotion of his nobles to officer his army, and on the subservience of the peasant-serfs to furnish the sinews of war, and the rank and file of the army. His public works aimed at making Prussia rich in herself, and as far as possible self-sufficing. Frederick's foreign policy was, however, distinctly fatal to the old order of things in Central and Eastern Europe. The seizure of Silesia and the first partition of Poland showed how a State might grow in size and strength, which furthered natural and national claims against treaty obligations. It will be seen how largely the power of Prussia at the death of Frederick (1786) was due to his forceful will and intelligence. Her territories were still straggling; and parts, as Anspach, Baireuth, Clèves, and East-Friesland, were widely detached: her administration was cumbrous: her people were rigidly divided in the old orders: her power and prestige were due to an abnormally large army vigorously led.

In sharp contrast with the prudent boldness of Frederick stands the well-meaning but reckless policy of the reigning Hapsburg, Joseph II (1780—1790). He had noticed the power of Prussia, vigorously wielded by the able and ambitious Frederick, and determined to concentrate the government of his diverse territories at Vienna. His task was far more difficult than that of Frederick, for his States had their own constitutions, governments, and laws, which the House of Hapsburg-Lorraine had sworn to observe; and these differ-ences were by no means artificial, but represented deep-rooted national distinctions; in fact, the golden link of the Crown had been hitherto almost the only bond of union. He now issued edicts cancelling the most cherished laws, customs, and privileges of his kingdoms of Hungary and Bohemia, though these were kingdoms when Austria was not yet a duchy. So far did he push his innovations as to remove to Vienna the sacred crown, sent by the Pope in the year 1000 A.D. as a gift to the first Hungarian king, St Stephen. This was rank sacrilege in the eyes of all true Hungarians, who thenceforth looked on Joseph as the "hatted king," not duly crowned. It is possible that he might have succeeded if he had introduced his revolutionary policy piecemeal in time of profound peace, and with the support of the Roman Catholic Church. The national feelings were still well-nigh dormant. It was Joseph II who first aroused them to active hostility by seeking to centralise all power at Vienna, and to make German the official language for his Hungarian and Slavonic States. At the same time he irritated the Roman Catholic Church at home, and created troubles abroad by his meddlesome foreign policy. As long as the Hapsburgs supported the power and privileges of the Roman Catholic clergy, these had oiled the complex wheels of the Hapsburg Governments; but, when Joseph abolished the exceptional privileges of nobles and clergy alike, closed and confiscated the funds of most of the monasteries, and interfered with religious worship, he met with opposition everywhere, especially in his Austrian Netherlands.

As if it was not enough to provoke the privileged classes, as well as the religious and national sentiments, in his diverse States, Joseph II pursued an aggressive foreign policy which finally banded half Europe against him. Thus, he violated treaty engagements with the Dutch by declaring (1784) the navigation of the lower Scheldt completely open, even to his warships; and only the opposition of England and Holland, backed by the remonstrance of his ally France, led him to withdraw a claim which the French revolutionists were to revive in 1792. Despising the unreal glamour of his Imperial dignity, he sought the aggrandisement of his hereditary States, which then included numerous scattered lands along the upper Danube and Rhine. He desired to connect these with Austria by acquiring the Electorate of Bavaria, either by conquest or in exchange for his distant and troublesome Netherlands. This plan, which would have made Austria definitely the mistress of Southern and Central Germany, aroused the opposition of the German princes thus threatened; and one of the last acts of Frederick's policy was to form the Fürstenbund, or League of German Princes, joined by the spiritual Electors of Mainz and Trèves, against the encroachments of the Emperor himself.

The next Prussian King, Frederick William II (1786—1797) for the first few years of his reign maintained a strongly anti-Austrian and anti-Russian policy. The identity of English and Prussian interests in maintaining the authority of the

House of Orange in the Stadtholdership of the Dutch Netherlands and in checking the democratic party which was supported
by France, led to a Prussian invasion of Holland, and the
formation of the important Triple Alliance between England,
Prussia and Holland (1788). This aimed at maintaining the
balance of power in Europe against the attempts of France in
the Netherlands and the encroachments of Russia and Austria
on Poland and Turkey. Some of the most important results of
this conservative alliance must here be noticed. In the second
article of the Anglo-Dutch treaty of defensive alliance (April,
1788) the allies "guarantee each other mutually in the possession
of all their Dominions, Territories, Towns, Places, Franchises,
and Liberties." The two last designations of course included
the rights of the Dutch Government over the lower part of the
Scheldt, which, by the treaty of 1785 between the Emperor and
the States General of Holland, were to belong to the latter and
be "kept shut by them." The fact that the French Government gave a formal guarantee of the last-named treaty should
also be noticed; for the abolition of the Dutch rights over the
lower Scheldt by the French Convention in 1792, together with
other menaces to our Dutch allies, was the chief cause of the outbreak of war between England and France which had so lamentable an influence on the French revolution and determined
the general trend of European affairs throughout the whole era.

Though the influence of the Triple Alliance on the west of
Europe was distinctly conservative, yet in Eastern affairs its
interests were complicated by the need of checking or out-
witting those two restless and aggressive potentates, Catherine
II and Joseph II. Knowing that they were planning the partition of Turkey, and were striving to obtain the aid of Poland,
the Prussian Minister for Foreign Affairs, Herzberg, had already
endeavoured to stir up war between Sweden and Russia, to
encourage the Polish patriots to resist the Russophil policy of
their King Stanislaus, to paralyse the Hapsburg States by

fomenting the discontent everywhere prevalent, and to strengthen Turkey's power of resistance. He was for a time completely successful. Gustavus III of Sweden, after consolidating the royal power by a successful *coup d'état*, longed to recover parts of Finland from Russia, and marched his troops towards St. Petersburg (July 1788), which they would probably have taken but for the defection of some of their Finnish troops and an attack of the Danes on their western frontier. The troops of Catherine and Joseph encountered unexpectedly vigorous resistance from the Turks; and the Polish patriots seemed about to seize the opportunity to cast off the Czarina's influence, expel her troops from their land, and rehabilitate their distracted State. The Polish Diet, which met in Oct. 1788, proclaimed its intention of abolishing the *liberum veto* and of declaring the right of the majority to carry any measure; while Catherine as clearly showed her determination to perpetuate the anarchy of that unhappy land, by proclaiming that she would regard the least change in the Polish Constitution of 1775 as a violation of treaties. Prussia, feeling sure of the ultimate support of England, promised to help the Poles to recover their former Lithuanian lands, secretly stipulating for the cession of Thorn and Danzig as the price of her aid; and Frederick William in 1789 was only deterred from making war on the two Imperial Governments by the pacific advice of Pitt and the possibility of France and Spain joining them. But the projected Quadruple Alliance of Austria, Russia, France and Spain could not be formed owing to Louis XVI's dislike of Russian plans against Poland; besides which the impending troubles in France forbade the adoption of an energetic foreign policy. Even so, however, the prowess of Russian and Austrian troops later in the campaign gained some important victories over the Turks. Sweden was soon compelled to desist from her invasion of Russia by the invasion of the Danes and a conspiracy of the Swedish nobles against the Crown; and though

Gustavus III drove out the Danes, and in the Swedish States General succeeded in reducing his nobles to submission (Feb. —May 1789), yet Sweden was for the time reduced to the defensive. The influence of the Triple Alliance saved her from any severe pressure by Russia, and further prevented the two Imperial Powers from reaping the fruits of their victories over the Turks. The ferment in Poland still distracted the attention of Russia, while the discontent in Hungary and Belgium, which threatened to subvert the Hapsburg throne, was openly fomented by Prussia.

Joseph II's difficulties were vastly augmented, when the Belgian discontent against his sweeping reforms burst into open revolt (Dec. 1789). The student must, however, carefully distinguish between this Belgian or Brabant insurrection, headed by nobles and clergy, and the essentially democratic and social revolution which was swiftly transforming France into a modern State. In Hungary and in the Austrian Netherlands it was the ruler who was the revolutionist; and the discontent arose solely from his abolition of local privileges and charters, and his infraction of the historic rights and privileges of the nobles and clergy. In the Belgic provinces especially the revolt was strongly conservative and religious. Its leader, Van der Noot, appealed in his manifesto to the "primitive and imprescriptible rights" of the Belgian people and declared Joseph II deposed from the sovereignty for his violation of the fundamental charter of the land. On the overthrow of the Imperial troops by the patriots, Van der Noot entered Brussels in triumph, and with the nobles and "their mightinesses the Estates of Brabant," marched to the cathedral, where a Te Deum was sung to celebrate the restoration of the old religious and civic customs so heedlessly abolished by the Imperial innovator. In Jan. 1790 the Estates of the provinces assembled at Brussels and decreed the establishment of the United States of Belgium with a loose form of federal union similar to that connecting the provinces of the Dutch Netherlands. In its essential features this Belgian revolution resembles the revolts of the Vendéans in 1793 and the Tyrolese in 1809. The three risings were protests against the heedless application of a cast-iron Liberalism. The Brabant revolution, therefore, faintly foreshadows the beginnings of that national reaction which was finally to roll back the eastward rush of French democracy. Its immediate influence on the political situation in 1789—1790 was fatal to the sovereign who sought to reform and revolutionise by royal prerogative. Overwhelmed by this last of many bitter disappointments and failures, the well-meaning but unfortunate Hapsburg ruler came to an untimely end (Feb. 1790) ; and his policy was soon reversed by his cautious and diplomatic brother Leopold II.

Joseph II was the last and by far the most reckless of those great eighteenth century rulers who sought to remodel their realms according to the precepts of philosophy but who in effect only strengthened the central power at the expense of local liberties. So obviously was this the case that it is questionable whether even the most enlightened of these crowned reformers, Frederick the Great, Joseph II, and the statesmen Turgot in France and Pombal in Portugal, would in the least degree have sympathised with Rousseau's doctrine of the sovereignty of the general will. As for the reforms of Catherine II in Russia and the expulsion of the Jesuits from all the Bourbon realms, France, Spain, Naples and Parma, as well as from Portugal, they were certainly inspired mainly by the desire of strengthening the central power. However diverse were their motives, the crowned innovators of the latter half of the eighteenth century began that process of simplification and centralisation of governing powers which is so prominent a characteristic of the revolutionary and Napoleonic era. The sequel of this narrative will reveal the strange paradox that the revolutionary doctrines, and the dictatorship

which a warlike policy necessitated, were soon to end in a far
more sternly centralised rule than that for which Joseph II
had vainly striven.

Instead of leaving the Hapsburg States strong and united
from the upper Danube to its mouth, with Vienna as the political
centre of the Continent, Joseph II left them no larger than at
his accession, and eager to throw off his innovations. His
policy, foreign and domestic, was essentially revolutionary, and
bears some striking resemblances to that of Napoleon. Imbued
with the new ideas, both sought to level privileges and distinctions of rank, religion, and nationality: both sought to centralise their power by subordinating the Church to the State,
and the State to the ruler; while their rash or premature
attempt at a cosmopolitan sway, complicated by a grandiose
and ill-proportioned policy, was overthrown by a strongly
national reaction championed by the conservative Powers.
There is however this sharp distinction between the careers
of Joseph II and Napoleon, that whereas the latter, as "heir
to the Revolution," only completed the work of social reconstruction marked out by the French Convention, Joseph II
sought to force on his States a social revolution, for which there
had been little or no intellectual preparation. Consequently,
while the Hapsburg ruler had to lament the miscarriage of all
his schemes, Napoleon's measures of social reconstruction form
the basis of the France of to-day.

Even in many of the smaller European States there was a
division of interests and sympathy between the rulers and
ruled. Thus in the Bishopric of Liège the Prince-Bishop
endeavoured to encroach on the constitutional rights of his
subjects. In the neighbouring Republic of the Dutch Netherlands, the House of Orange, which had long held the Stadtholdership, had for some time attempted to change this
precarious dignity into an hereditary monarchy; and civil
strifes ensued, in which France supported the democrats or

"patriots." Finally England by diplomatic pressure on France, and Prussia by armed intervention in the Netherlands restored the Stadtholder to more than his old powers (1787). This victory of the two Northern Powers marked the recovery by England of her former place in Europe, and by revealing the financial and political weakness of France, dealt a fatal blow to the prestige of the Bourbons. In the Austrian Netherlands and Liège, however, Prussia helped the people to resist the innovations of Joseph II and the Bishop respectively. Indeed, there was nowhere any consistent support of political principles. Thus, Louis XVI, yielding to his courtiers and his army, supported the American colonists in their struggle against the English monarchy; but none the less did he help to crush the Swiss democrats.

The succession of Leopold to the Hapsburg dominions soon effected a change in the policy of those distracted States and in the general diplomatic situation. In order to hold Prussia in check and regain his power over the Austrian Netherlands, Leopold made friendly overtures to England with the hope of dissolving the Triple Alliance. They were well received; for Pitt now distrusted the ambitious designs of the Prussian Court which threatened to lead to a general conflagration. Moreover, it was a cardinal principle of English policy to keep the Belgic provinces in the hand of a strong friendly government as a barrier against French encroachments on the north. English influence was therefore used to aid in the restoration of Austria's power in her Netherlands, provided that she would guarantee to the patriots their ancient rights and customs. Thus began the breach between England and Prussia which was eventually to paralyse the First Coalition and lead to open hostility in 1800—1805. An Anglo-Austrian alliance now supplanted the *entente cordiale* between Paris and Vienna; and Pitt was able to take a high tone in the Nootka Sound dispute with Spain, in which Louis XVI by virtue of

the Bourbon Family Compact for a time seemed about to take
vigorous action against us.   In spite of the beginnings of an
Anglo-Austrian alliance, the Prussian Court persisted in its
warlike policy against that of Vienna, though the policy of the
latter had lost its aggressive character.   An alliance with the
Polish Government (March 1790) promised to strengthen
Frederick William's hands, and he massed a large army on the
Bohemian frontier.   At once the prudent Hapsburg ruler made
an armistice with the Turks (gaining Orsova), and turned to
face Prussia.   This Power suddenly found herself isolated;
for the Poles energetically refused to promise the cession of
Thorn and Danzig to Prussia as the price of her aid.   Frederick
William II, a *blasé* sentimentalist, was disgusted at suddenly
finding himself involved by Herzberg's ambitious policy in
a single-handed contest with Austria, at a time when the
principles of the French Revolution were beginning to sap the
foundations of the old governments.   Now that the prospect
of humbling Austria and of gaining two important fortresses
from Poland had completely vanished, the Prussian king
remembered that his duty as a German sovereign forbade an
almost fratricidal war.   He therefore favourably received overtures of peace which Leopold made at Reichenbach with a
view to an alliance based on monarchical principles and the
maintenance of the *status quo.*   The Austrian Government
deftly insinuated that the French Revolution was the foe to be
faced; and the Prussian envoy at Paris also hinted to his
master that one or two eastern districts of France might
become the prize of an Austro-Prussian war against the revolution.   The more pressing reason, however, for the peace
finally agreed on at Reichenbach (July 27, 1790) was that
both the Central Powers were in military or diplomatic difficulties.   Leopold desired to pacify the discontent in Hungary
and Brabant, and to secure his election as Emperor; while
Prussia was not loth to extricate herself from the false position

in which Herzberg's diplomacy had involved her. Indeed, while appearing to dictate the following terms of peace, she really accepted them. Austria was to negotiate peace with Turkey on the basis of the *status quo*. Prussia agreed not to intervene in Belgian affairs save with the accord of England and Holland, and would recognise the restoration of Austrian authority there if an amnesty were granted to the Belgian patriots.

The consequences of this peace were most important. Austria speedily regained her authority in the Netherlands and her prestige in Europe; while Prussia, which had appeared about to dictate terms to her, withdrew baffled and disconcerted. The Poles, annoyed at the insidious policy of Berlin, turned to Austria as a more trustworthy ally; and Sweden, left without support, had to conclude a disadvantageous peace at Werela with Russia (Aug. 1790). Catherine II was thus able to push on the war against Turkey; and until a definite settlement had been arrived at on the Danube it was impossible for the Eastern Powers to act vigorously elsewhere. The tardiness with which a definite peace was finally arranged between Austria and Turkey at Sistova (Aug. 5, 1791), proved the hollowness of the pretended European concert against revolutionary France. Austria, in fact, could not spare a great army to march on Paris while Catherine was still successfully pursuing the war against Turkey; and it was not till the Czarina signed (Aug. 11, 1791) the preliminaries of peace at Galatz and the definitive Treaty of Jassy five months later, whereby she gained the Turkish lands east of the Dniester, that there was any possibility of united and vigorous action by the other Continental Powers against the French Revolution.

After peace was restored on the Pruth and Danube, the Polish question threatened war on the Vistula. At the close of 1791 Catherine massed 130,000 men on the borders of Poland, intending to subject that land to her authority, and if

Austria and Prussia opposed her by force, to buy off their hostility by offering them a share in the partition, or "compensation" elsewhere.   In the hope of diverting all their energies westwards, the ambitious and unscrupulous Czarina affected great indignation against the French revolutionists and ostensibly prepared to take part in a monarchical crusade, the better to conceal her design of subjugating the whole of Poland.

I have judged it advisable to preface this little work by a brief sketch of the very complicated struggles in eastern and central Europe, in order to correct a prevalent misconception that the French Revolution was the only question then occupying the attention of statesmen.   On the contrary, the aggressive designs of Joseph II and the Czarina Catherine on Turkey and Poland riveted their gaze almost exclusively on the East; and the troubles in France were, down to the Midsummer of 1791, regarded as important, only because they reduced her to a passive rôle in the European embroglio, leaving the Eastern Powers free for their designs on the Danube and the Vistula and throwing on England the chief burden of maintaining the position of the States there threatened.   The democrats of Paris were therefore left free for fully two years to make or mar the destinies of France; while the Central and Eastern Powers, released from all fears of French intervention, proceeded with their designs, and reluctantly paused in their plans for the overthrow of the weaker States, only when it appeared necessary to save the cause of monarchy at Paris.   The tardiness with which in 1791—1792 they turned to uphold monarchical principles in the West, and yet ever cast backward glances on the plunder obtainable in the East, revealed the inner weakness of the European system, if that can be called a system which rested on no principle of action and set no limits to aggression on the weak except those dictated by the fears or jealousies of neighbours and rivals.

The whole spirit of European politics was such as to further the destructive aims of the French revolutionists. To strengthen and unite probable friends: to weaken and divide actual and possible foes, especially in neighbouring States—these were the marks of a successful ruler or statesman. Hence came the kaleidoscopic changes in continental diplomacy,—all finally ending in the general crash of the Revolution.

The Decay of the old Society.

In its best and truest form the old feudal relation between lord and vassal was a rough and ready means of organising local defence and government, of gaining some security from universal rapine. The lord gave protection. In return, the vassal owned his complete dependence on the lord for life and land, rendered him stated service in labour or in kind, paid dues for the use of his bridge, ferry, mill, wine-press, or oven, and was subject to the jurisdiction of the seigneurial law-court. As the feudal barons defended and governed their domains at their own charges, and brought their vassals to swell the royal army, they were free from king's taxes; for they gave what was in those troublous times more needed— military aid.

The security for property which the mail-clad baron won by prowess, the priest and the monk gained by their sanctity. Reverence felt by ambitious kings and lawless barons for mother Church, or the intrigues of clerics in the royal Council, dowered the clergy with rich and broad domains, which in France before the Revolution probably comprised nearly one-fifth of all the land; and the clergy formed a privileged Order, exempt from nearly all taxes.

The lack of any effective central power in Germany had allowed the bishops and feudal nobles to build up States which were almost independent of the Emperor. In France the ability and energy of the kings brought all the bishops and great nobles under the authority of the Crown, and by the time

F. R.

2

of Louis XIV, France was politically united; yet in both countries, and almost everywhere on the Continent, the nobles and clergy formed two powerful privileged Orders, distinct from the mass of the people. In Germany they retained their old governing functions; but in France the nobles now served merely as officers in the royal standing army. The old feudal forces, the *ban* and the *arrière ban*, were not called out after 1674: and Richelieu transferred to the *intendants*, or controllers of administrative districts, the remains of the old governing powers of the French nobles. Yet these remained almost exempt from taxes, as if they were still governing their fiefs, and helping in the defence of the realm, at their own expense. They formed no longer an aristocracy but a *noblesse*.

Even a supporter of the old social system, like Chateaubriand, could see whither this was tending:—"Aristocracy has three ages, first the age of force, from which it degenerates into the age of privilege, and is finally extinguished in the age of vanity." The age of privilege was then merging in the age of vanity, as was seen in the haughty disdain with which the old nobles regarded the relatively small, though increasing middle-class. Lawyers and jurists who distinguished themselves in the French provincial 'Parlements' often gained titles of nobility, whence they were called *noblesse de robe*: though they were looked down upon as *parvenus*, yet they gained exemption from taxation. So that by one means or another most of the wealthy classes escaped the burdens of the State taxes.

Consequently the King had to press hard on the lower orders for money to support the vast expenses of the new centralised State engaged in frequent and prolonged wars. Nearly all the costs of the wars, the magnificent palaces, and the gorgeous ceremonial of Louis XIV were borne by the middle and lower classes of France. These last were often reduced to piteous misery by the threefold burden of the feudal dues paid to the nobles, the tithes paid to the clergy, and the taxes paid to the State. The differences between the privileges of different provinces in the matter of taxation make a general computation difficult; but Taine has reckoned that a peasant, out of every 100 francs of income, would have to pay 53 in taxes to the State, 14 to his lord, 14 for tithes, and out of the remaining 19 to satisfy the exciseman and support life!

The French peasant was, however, far freer socially than the serfs of Germany, Italy, and Spain; and in Prussia, where the burdens of a vigorous and aggressive monarchy were added to those of feudalism, the peasants had to bear heavier loads even than those of central France. In Brandenburg it appears that for 30 acres of land yielding $9\frac{2}{4}$ crowns, the peasant often had to pay to the State 8 crowns, without counting what he owed to the lord and to the clergy. Prussia under Frederick the Great was, however, in a far healthier state than was France under Louis XV; the Prussian administration was as vigorous as that of France was corrupt. Frederick made his nobles work for the State not only as officers but as administrators of the law, and as governors of towns. He desired them to reside on their estates, and look after the interests of their peasants; and if the latter made any complaint against their lords, Frederick carefully investigated it. Thus the feudal system retained its vitality in Prussia longer than in France, where the old feudal privileges outlived the duties which had gone hand in hand with them. In the small states of Central and Southern Europe feudalism had not lost all its governing powers, and in the Hapsburg dominions the nobles had successfully resisted the hasty attempts of Joseph II to merge their governing functions in the central power. In all these countries feudalism was still a stern reality. The feudal government by the German, Italian, or Spanish nobles pressed harder on their dependents or serfs than was the case in

France, where serfdom still existed only in the provinces recently acquired from the Empire,—Alsace, Franche Comté, and Lorraine. The German or Italian peasant was still tied to the soil, and might be brought back by force if he escaped. Still, in Prussia feudalism involved a beneficial protection of the weak by the strong. There is much to be said, especially in a rigorous climate, for complete feudal dependence, or serfdom, if it be humanely exercised. But in France there was no such dependence on a present protector; only a number of complex dues survived, payable to a lord rarely seen on his estates. Absenteeism converted the tenure into the most irritating form of copyhold. From the time of Louis XIV onwards the feudal relation between lord and vassal was an anachronism, cramping the peasant at every turn. The feudal dues were irritating from their number and uncertainty, rather than burdensome from their weight. Corn, fowls, wine, etc. had to be paid when the farm changed hands, at stated seasons, or when the lord died, when his eldest son or daughter came of age, or was married. The peasant in many parts must bake his bread only in the lord's oven, press his grapes in the lord's wine-press and use only the seigneurial mill; and, worst of all, he must for a certain number of days give his labour gratuitously to mend the roads of the lord, or of the commune, and gather in the lord's harvest. Endless friction arose about other exclusive rights (*banalités*), the minute quit-rents (*cens*), and the damage caused by the lord's game. The game-laws were very oppressive. In most parts of Europe the farmer must not hoe or weed his crops, nor mow his hay and plough in his stubble before a certain time, lest the partridges should be disturbed; and the only legal way of protecting his crops from the deer or boars, was to sit up all night, and scare them away by shouting. These grievances, terrible everywhere, were at their worst in the *capitaineries*, or districts reserved for hunting to the princes of France.

In brief, while feudalism was socially or politically more oppressive elsewhere on the Continent, it was financially most burdensome in France, owing to absenteeism. Few French nobles resided among their dependents, save in the West and North-West of France; and it was in these very parts that the peasants rose in defence of their priests and nobles, when the patriarchal life was threatened by the innovations of the revolutionists. Even around Nantes, however, there were the same glaring contrasts between the splendour of the city and the misery of the country, which were so painfully evident in entering Versailles, Paris, Lyons, Bordeaux, and a few other chief provincial centres. "What a miracle (wrote Arthur Young at Nantes) that all this splendour and wealth of the cities of France should be so unconnected with the country. There are no gentle transitions from ease to comfort, from comfort to wealth: you pass at once from beggary to profusion.".......
"The country deserted, or if a gentleman in it, you find him in some wretched hole, to save that money which is lavished with profusion in the luxuries of a capital."

In no other part of Europe was there so perilous a concentration of wealth in a few centres. Elsewhere on the Continent, the feudal nobles as a rule still lived among their dependents; and wealth was not drawn away from the districts where it was produced. In France it was drained away from the country to a few of the chief centres of fashion; and to these pleasure resorts the toilers followed the spenders in any time of exceptional distress, as in the winter of 1789. The extremes of misery and luxury form an explosive combination. It was these contrasts which fired with indignation Voltaire, Diderot, and Rousseau.

The Intellectual Revolution.

The *élan* of French thought, its lucidity of expression, its concentration around a brilliant Court, an august Academy, or in *salons* where conversation became a fine art, conspired to make Paris at once the Athens as well as the Rome of the modern world.   The first of the French thinkers on politics and society whose works made any lasting impression was Montesquieu, whose *Esprit des Lois* (1748) aimed at discovering the laws which govern the action of men in political societies. There is nothing revolutionary in his spirit or conclusions. With philosophic impartiality he examines each form of government, pointing out its excellences and defects, the causes of its rise, duration, and decay.   As Aristotle considered virtue the mean between opposing extremes, so Montesquieu abhors all political extremes, especially an arbitrary despotism, and shows a bias in favour of the English constitution, as combining the excellences of monarchy, aristocracy, and democracy.   "It is sometimes necessary to change certain laws (he says) ; but the case is rare ; and when it comes, they ought to be touched only with a trembling hand."   His true greatness is that he first illustrated on a grand scale the relations of cause and effect in human affairs ; and his influence is traceable in the general and repeated efforts "to make war on absolutism."

Next there arose a school of thinkers, the Physiocrats, who sought to find the Natural Order which permeated the whole of society, and the economic conditions which formed the basis of its prosperity.   The most important writers and speculators of this school were Quesnay, author of *La Physiocratie, ou Constitution naturelle des Gouvernements* (1768), and Turgot, who was soon to apply his theories in the Limousin, and for two years to all France.   Looking around them at the actual state of France, where trade was shackled on all sides by privileges of classes, towns, districts, and trade gilds, while commerce was strangled by provincial customs' barriers, they proclaimed the famous maxim *laissez faire et laissez passer* as the cure for these economic evils.   They assumed that wages and profits were fixed by natural laws, and that the natural value of things was the result.   Though their reasoning was generally founded on theories rather than on observed facts, yet any inquiry was fatal to the old social and political order of things, which rested on nothing but custom.   Adam Smith, visiting Paris in 1763, was much stimulated by intercourse with these fathers of Political Economy; and his great work *The Wealth of Nations* (1776) paved the way in England, as did the Economists in France, for the commercial treaty between the two countries (1786—7) which was the first and premature approximation to Free Trade.

In the sphere of philosophy and speculation the revolt against authority and tradition had the most important influence on the trend of events.   It originated in England with the materialistic philosophy of Locke, who maintained that the human mind was in itself a blank, with no innate ideas: these were solely the result, either of external sensation falling on the *camera obscura* of the mind, or of internal reflection.   The materialist side of this theory was developed by Hume in Scotland, and by Condillac and others in France, viz. that ideas were solely due to external sensation and all knowledge was derived from experience : men were therefore perfect animals, and animals were imperfect men.   This materialism was pushed still further by Helvétius, who, in his treatise *de l'Esprit* (1758) asserted that self-love and self-interest are the source of all human action: morality must therefore be avowedly based on animal feeling, on pleasure and pain.

Following the leads thus given, a whole cohort of 'philosophers' began to assail existing beliefs and customs; and in that long reign of Louis XV, when the monarchy was at the lowest ebb of disaster and disgrace, when the king's mistress influenced foreign politics and jobbed appointments at Court and in the Church, there could be no sincere and successful defence of the threatened institutions and beliefs.   Never was a more brilliant attack made on a life so hollow and artificial; and if the peasantry had not been completely isolated by ignorance and unceasing toil, the revolution would probably have burst forth before the death of Louis XV (1774).

Prominent among the assailants was Voltaire, famous for his work as an historian, play-wright, versifier, man of science, and philosopher. Devoid of any decided originality, he yet possessed a marvellous faculty for adapting the results of research, and setting them forth in a limpid style sparkling with wit and sarcasm. For these reasons, and because he was the completest mirror of the French thought of his age, with its eager inquiries and lack of any fixed convictions, but winsome grace of style, his reputation far transcended the bounds of France. Frederick the Great's one weakness was Voltaire; he delighted to bandy verses with him, quarrel with him, scorn German men-of-letters—even the great Lessing—and declare that the German language must be reformed before it could be a fit vehicle for poetry! In his scientific, ethical, and historical work, Voltaire followed the general trend of thought, viz. to find the universal laws which underlie and govern all things. "All beings without exception are subject to invariable laws": it is the aim of the thinker to discover them, of the statesman and practical man to apply them; and only by obedience to these universal laws will the human race progress. He waged ceaseless war on ecclesiastical authority and tradition, and placed his hopes only on the discoveries of the human intellect. So far from being hostile to monarchy, Voltaire favoured reform by royal decrees as the simplest and most expeditious method. Thus, when Louis XV, on the advice of his minister Maupeou, suppressed the powers of the French Parlements (1771), Voltaire defended the act as a blow at provincialism and class privilege: "Have not these Parlements been often barbarous and persecuting?...Since one must obey, I had rather obey a lion of good family, whom nature has made much my superior, than 200 rats of my own species." Indeed, most of the 'philosophers' of

France would have consistently supported the monarchy if it had firmly suppressed all the social and economic abuses of the realm. It was against these that they declaimed, and only against the monarchy when allied with them. But though Voltaire did not attack the political forms of the *ancien régime*, he yet began to undermine its base, by bringing discredit on the ideas of authority, tradition, and custom, on which it rested.

If prudence kept Voltaire from scattering broadcast the new theories, because, as he once said, he did not wish to be murdered by his own valet, no such scruples or fears held back the two most outspoken champions of the intellectual revolution, Diderot and d'Alembert. Morality is only relative to the senses of the individual : " Pain and pleasure are the only springs of the moral universe." " Would you see man free and happy, do not meddle with his affairs." " Man is wicked, not because he is wicked, but because he has been made so."

Such are some of their assertions, implying that the individual is the supreme judge of his own conduct—a teaching which naturally led to moral, social, and political anarchy. All the old institutions and beliefs were vehemently assailed; and Diderot's destructive aims find their most ferocious expression in the wish that the last king might be strangled with the entrails of the last priest. These two men, aided by many other 'philosophers,' compiled the famous *Encyclopédie* (1766), a complete circle of education framed on the basis of the new scientific and philosophic research. It was designed to combat or tacitly exclude the older system of thought resting on authority or tradition. The Encyclopædists, as they were called, systematized the intellectual revolution,—the effort to emancipate and perfect mankind by means of human reason and knowledge.

This aim was not one which could speedily arouse the masses, sunk in ignorance or despair. Enthusiasm was aroused, not by the new philosophy, but by one who appealed to the heart rather than the head, who pointed to a blissful social past, and not to a future intellectual perfectibility. Jean Jacques Rousseau was the first to fire mankind with hopes of a social millennium easily to be attained. In his pages the return to a golden age of social equality, from which men had foolishly strayed, seemed so simple as to be within the reach of all. It was hope which made the Revolution, beckoning on those disciples of the new gospel, St Just and Robespierre, far into the Reign of Terror. It was despair which finally laid France at the feet of Bonaparte.

In his *Discourse on the Origin of Inequality* Rousseau fantastically traces social evil to its source, the growth of civilisation :—" From the time when one man needed the help of another, and it was seen to be useful for one man to have provisions for two, equality disappeared, property was introduced, toil became necessary, and the vast forests changed into smiling fields watered by the sweat of man, wherein slavery and misery soon took root and grew ripe with the crops." Agriculture and the working of metals helped on the fall of man, since completed by reason and reflection :—" It is philosophy which isolates man, and inspires the thought, at the sight of a sufferer, ' Die, if you will ; I am safe.' " How, then, is mankind to be regenerated? By going back—answers Rousseau in his *Social Contract* (1762)—as near as may be to the primitive compact which first brought men together free and equal. The problem is, " to find a form of association which defends and protects with all the common force the person and the goods of each member ; and by which each, uniting with all, yet only obeys himself, and remains as free as before." The solution of this difficult problem is reached with surprising ease :—" Each of us places in common his person and all his power under the supreme direction of the general will ; and we further receive each member as an indivisible part of the whole." As men enter the new social contract freely and on equal terms, there hence ensue the ideas of Liberty, Equality, and Fraternity—the watchwords of the French Revolution. Rousseau, however, proceeds to exalt equality at the expense of liberty, by asserting that the general will must be right, and must tend to the public advantage ; that the State, being the collective will of its members, "must have a universal and compulsory power to move and dispose each part in the way most suitable for the whole." Rousseau's return to nature therefore favoured the growth of a State despotism necessarily hostile to all institutions seeming to conflict with it ; and the fallacious ease and rigidity of his reasoning—due to its being based on theory, carried out by verbal proofs, and rarely checked by observance of facts,—impelled the French revolutionists to many of the outrageous acts which brought them into collision with the rest of Europe.

If Voltaire charmed by his wit and the lucidity of his reasoning, Rousseau was as widely read throughout Europe for his many tender appeals to the emotions. A wave of sentimentalism was then spreading over Europe, of which Richardson's novels in England, those of Rousseau in France, and Goethe's *Sorrows of Werther* in Germany, were the chief expression. Courtiers, affecting weariness of the artificial splendours of Versailles, discovered new charms in rustic life, even in the occupations of the field and dairy; and literary people, tired of pure reason, turned to the emotions as an undeveloped side of human nature.

In France the emotional school had no such lasting effect on literature as it had on politics ; but in Germany the revolt against the past was at the outset rather literary than political, as in the dramas of Lessing and Goethe. The separation of the national life in a mosaic of petty States limited the social and political horizon of Germans, and at first diverted their attention to individual achievement in literature or science; but the younger poet Schiller, coming under the spell of Rousseau's influence, revolted not only against the severely classical style, with its unities of time and place, but also against the narrow tyranny of nearly all the petty princes of Germany. In Schiller's youthful play *The Robbers* we have (to use his own words) "an example of the offspring which Genius in its unnatural union with Thraldom may give to the world." It is indeed the poetry of revolt, fiercer than any of Byron's. "Put me at the head of a troop of fellows like myself (exclaims his hero), and Germany shall become a republic, by the side of which Sparta and Rome shall seem like nunneries"; and he recommended the now famous prescription of "blood and iron" as the only cure for a corrupt world. For less daring utterances the Duke of Würtemberg had imprisoned the patriotic poet Schubart, and Schiller had to flee from Stuttgart. The influence of Rousseau's social teachings inspired many more of the younger German poets, e.g. the Göttingen Brotherhood, headed by Klopstock, which desired to enthrone naturalism in literature as in politics. These ideas were undermining the Germanic system of States—"a chaos upheld by Providence."

The German *savants* meanwhile were compiling an Encyclopædia with the same destructive aims as that of Diderot; and a secret club or order, the 'Illuminati,' founded in 1776 in Swabia, rapidly spread the revolutionary doctrines of the age all over Southern and Western Germany. Though suppressed in Bavaria and some other States, it had a powerful hold on educated people, especially in the important fortress and cathedral city of Mainz, where the Prince-bishop, though Chancellor of the Empire, patronised it. Priding himself on his enlightenment, he favoured the spread of an education inspired by Rousseau's *Émile*. His coadjutor and successor, Dalberg, was a member of the society; and the forms of religion and morality were barely respected in the Archbishop's Court. In the other lay and spiritual States of W. Germany there was no loyalty or respect for the effete goverments; and the learned Forster of Mainz wrote (1782)—"Europe seems to me on the brink of a terrible revolution : the mass is so corrupt that a bleeding seems necessary."

The same revolutionary ferment was beginning to spread in the Dutch and Austrian Netherlands, in oligarchical Switzerland and in oppressed and divided Italy. Everywhere thought con flicted with fact, the ideal with the real, the head with the body; and the events of 1789—1815 were to show that it is ideas which mould the destinies of nations.

CHAPTER II.

LOUIS XVI, THE PARLEMENTS, AND THE STATES GENERAL.

"The States General were like a bridge made for passing from the old to the new order of things."—(THIERRY.)

FOR generations thinking men had seen that France could not long endure the double strain of an ambitious monarchical policy and the cramping results of the old feudal social system. One or other must go. Few, however, expected that the conflict would lead up to a Revolution in which both would vanish.

The death of the vicious and despicable Louis XV (1774) brought to the French throne his amiable grandson, Louis XVI, who had lately espoused Marie Antoinette, the daughter of the great Empress Queen, Maria Theresa. Never has a heavier burden rested on shoulders so young and inexperienced. Louis XV had lost to England nearly all the French possessions in North America and India; and though he had added most of Lorraine to the French Crown, yet his reign was disgraced by failures abroad, distress at home, and his own cynical immorality. His successor had all the good qualities fitted to adorn a private station, but none of the foresight, determination, resource, and brilliance needed to retrieve the fortunes of the Bourbon House. His queen had more than all the attractive qualities, but none of the tact, prudence, and quiet tenacity of her mother. The jealousy of French statesmen and courtiers would not allow "the Austrian" to interfere with affairs of state. Hence she could not, save by fits and starts, bring her powers of exciting enthusiasm to supplement the kindly but phlegmatic temperament of her consort.

But in 1774 all seemed bright. Morality was no longer outraged at Court. Reforms were undertaken ; and the revolt of the American colonists soon gave France the opportunity of humbling her rival in the race for empire. The philosophers and economists now hoped that the golden age had come when society would be reformed by royal decrees; for Turgot, famed not only by his writings, but by his splendid achievements as 'intendant,' or royal administrator, of the Limousin, was appointed to the most important office in the Council of Ministers, the Control of the Finances. In the Limousin he had mitigated the hardships of compulsory enrolment in the militia, had freed trade from some of its many shackles, and had commuted the *corvée,* or forced labour of the peasants on the public roads, for a small tax, which, however, he could not exact from the privileged classes; and his enlightened policy had finally been as much resisted by the ignorant peasants as by the privileged orders. The same stupidity and selfishness was to foil his efforts to restore the prosperity of France by royal decrees. He said to the king, "Sire, you ought to govern by general laws, as God." Unfortunately the king and his diplomatic minister, Maurepas, had restored the powers of the old 'Parlements,' without any due restrictions to prevent their abuse. These 'Parlements' were the supreme judicial bodies at Paris and the twelve chief provincial capitals—Toulouse, Grenoble, Bordeaux, Dijon, Rouen, Aix, Rennes, Pau, Metz, Douai, Besançon, and Nancy. Their members were strictly mere jurists, who constituted an hereditary magistracy. The tenure of their offices had up to 1771 been, and now again was, saleable. Their functions were properly judicial; but they had long interfered in purely political matters, had even issued decrees in their several provinces, and severely punished any contravention of them. Their action as law courts was dilatory and venal; and, being composed mainly of the privileged orders, they now resisted reforms which assailed their privileges. The king could, however, overbear their opposition by bringing his personal authority into play, and, by holding what was called a *lit de justice*, compel them to register his edicts.

Turgot now freed the internal trade in corn and flour from all the old provincial customs dues, and abolished not only the exclusive right of many a seigneur to own a corn-mill on his domain, but also the privileges of bakers in towns. Riots caused by greed, or by fear that the corn would all leave the district, were promptly suppressed. The economies which he urged at Court and in the army aroused bitter hatred; and when in March 1776 he sent six edicts, suppressing various privileges, especially the old trade-gilds and *corvées* on the roads, for registration by the Paris Parlement, this body refused, until compelled to do so by a "bed of justice," which Voltaire hailed as a "bed of beneficence." It was now open war between the privileged orders and the reforming monarch and statesman. The Parlements objected above all to the substitution of a tax on all landed property for the *corvée* hitherto rendered by the peasants. In appearance the king and Turgot won their point; but cabals at Court and in the Ministry increased; and though the great minister liberated traders, especially vine-growers, from many shackles, freed the serfs on the royal domains, and curtailed the immunities of the nobles, yet he was unable to carry out his other beneficent plans. He tried in vain to consolidate the public debt, reform the collection of the *gabelle*, or salt-duties, and other taxes and

tolls (*octrois*), form a fund to aid peasants in the redemption of
the feudal services, and give local self-government not only to
the *commune* or parish, but also to the *arrondissement* (a larger
area), to the province, and to the whole realm. These reforms, which would have peacefully revolutionised France,
were never carried out. Turgot's somewhat rigid and arbitrary
methods of reform caused unnecessary friction; and the queen,
annoyed by an act which injured one of her favourites, persuaded Louis to dismiss him (1776). This victory of the
privileged orders over the monarchy made a democratic
revolution almost inevitable; but so unpractical were Frenchmen then, that they even rejoiced at this and subsequent
successes of the Parlements over the royal power, as if "to
make war on absolutism" were more important than to abolish
antiquated privileges. Turgot's reforms were soon nearly all
reversed.

His successor, Necker, a skilful banker rather than a far-
seeing statesman, did his best to promote economy, establish
the credit of the State, and postpone burning social questions.
He warned Louis that bankruptcy would follow an open
alliance with the American colonists against England. Yet
such was his financial skill and personal credit with bankers
that he was able to raise loans and tide over the financial
strain of that war; but success in borrowing enhances financial
difficulties in the future. Moreover, Lafayette and the French
soldiers returned from the United States inflamed with a love
of liberty and self-government. "The American revolution
(wrote Young) has laid the foundation of another in France, if
Government does not take care of itself." Yet at the time
when the proposed American Constitution was the general
topic of conversation in the *salons* of Paris, Louis was weak
enough to decree that only those whose families had been
noble for four generations could attain high offices in the
French army. Necker was brought by the financial needs of

F. R.

3

the State to demand that the privileged classes should be taxed. Feeling his fall to be near, he published (Jan. 1781) his "Account of the finances," laying bare for the first time the expenses of the Court, which were nearly one-third of the cost of maintaining the whole army.

Bankruptcy was soon brought nearer by the spendthrift policy of the frivolous Calonne—"Whoever wishes for credit must cultivate luxury"; and when in his much ridiculed Assembly of Notables he ventured to suggest the equalisation of taxation as the inevitable cure, he was dismissed (1787). His successor, Loménie de Brienne, the Archbishop of Toulouse, sought to carry out the aims of the Encyclopædists by the methods of Richelieu, to establish liberty and equality by royal decree. He extended to all the provinces the plan, conceived by Turgot, and commenced by Necker in Berri and Guienne, of provincial and parochial assemblies. He also permitted the redemption of the *corvée* by a money payment, abolished the provincial customs dues, and sought to impose a general land tax and a stamp tax. These last were resisted by the Paris Parlement, which declared itself incapable of registering a perpetual tax; but the king overbore their opposition by a *lit de justice* and for a time exiled them from Paris. Finally, Brienne in May 1788 suppressed nearly all the powers of the Parlements, and tried to substitute a Plenary Court, composed of dignitaries nominated for life by the king, as the sole authority for registering laws for all France. This *coup d'état* enraged all classes and interests—the privileged orders, who saw themselves thenceforth taxable at the will of the sovereign; the provincial patriots, menaced with a complete subjection to the capital; and the democrats, who longed for a complete representation of the nation. All rallied round the Parlements as the chief barriers against a central despotism: Mirabeau expressed the ideas of all friends of freedom when he wrote, "I will never make war on the Parlements save in presence of the nation." The people of Rennes and Grenoble rose in de-fence of their Parlements. Louis bowed before the storm, dismissed the Minister who had raised it, recalled Necker, and finally convoked for 1789 the States General of France, repre-senting the three orders—Nobles, Clergy, and Commons.

Lafayette, who had gained immense popularity in the American War, had already expressed the wishes of democrats that the States General should be called; and the Paris Parle-ment had also taken up this suggestion from a clerical coun-cillor, because it would benefit the commonwealth, embarrass the king, or add to its own popularity. After Brienne's utter failure there seemed to be no other course open, unless Louis took the prudently daring advice of his former minister, Malesherbes, and frankly substituted a National Assembly in place of the cumbrous States General which had not met since 1614. But Louis could not take occasion by the forelock. He desired to meet the deficit and remove some of the most glaring abuses; while most Frenchmen now wished to govern themselves and have social equality. A dignitary of the Paris Parlement, the Counsellor Pasquier, had truly said, "Sirs, this is not child's play: the first time that France sees the States General, she will see also a terrible revolution."

The States General formed three Chambers, consisting of deputies of the Nobles, Clergy, and Tiers État (Commons) of France, the last being chosen by 'secondary election'; that is, all the commoners of each town, bailiwick or *sénéchaussée*, could vote for 'electors,' who in their turn chose representatives of their Order in the States General. The *cahiers*, or instructions drawn up for each representative, evince no desire for a political revolution. They show the general wish that the sovereign should control the executive, but share the legislative powers with an Assembly meeting at stated times and representing the nation, to which the king's ministers should be re-sponsible. The *cahiers* of the Commons all demand that they

3—2

should have as many representatives as those of the nobles and clergy, and that the Orders should meet as one Chamber, not as three distinct Estates : those of the clergy and nobles vary on this point.   The recollection of the English parliamentary struggles against Charles I inspired the recommendation in some *cahiers* that no taxes should be voted until this constitutional question were settled.   All the *cahiers* of the Commons demand equal taxation, which some of those of the privileged Orders also admit, with the proviso, however, in several of the clerical *cahiers*, that in return the State should take over their special debt or liabilities.   There is a like approach to unanimity as to the redemption of the feudal dues, with infinite variety as to the means of effecting this complicated change.   Local privileges of towns, corporations, districts, and provinces are to be sacrificed, whether from conviction, generosity, or despair of keeping them.   Liberty of the press, personal liberty, inviolability of the deputies, abolition of *lettres de cachet* (sealed letters by which a minister could secretly order imprisonment), control of the finances by the States General, reduction of pensions and sinecures,—on all these points there is complete accord ; as well as on the question of improving the lot of the hard-worked *curés* by redistributing the revenues and rewards of the Church.   These *cahiers* refute the prevalent error that the privileged Orders would renounce nothing, and that the Tiers État alone was desirous of reform.   The king, quite half the clergy, and an influential minority of the deputies of the nobles, desired nearly all the reforms which would have placed France on a level with England as a constitutional State.

How came it then that the deputies who met at Versailles in May 1789 did not peacefully regenerate France, but set in motion the revolution ?   There was at the outset a great constitutional question, which also served as a test for a deep underlying principle,—Should the three Orders sit separately, or as one Chamber ; i.e. should they vote *par ordre*, or *par*

tête? If the former, then France was still divided in three
distinct Orders, and the Commons would be outvoted on any
question on which nobles and clergy were opposed to them; if
the latter, then equality was not a mere name, and the reformers would certainly carry the day in the Assembly. Great
blame must attach to Louis and still more to Necker, for first
raising the expectations of the Tiers État, and then leaving
this initial question to be fought out in wordy war by the
Orders. In the new provincial Assemblies the Orders sat
together. The principle of the 'double representation' of
the Third Estate in the Provincial Assemblies had been insisted on by the Notables two years before; and Necker had
lately conceded the same principle for the States General.
Why grant this, if they were to be kept distinct from the other
Orders? France was in a ferment of excitement. The commercial treaty with England (1786—7), allowing the import of
English goods at moderate duties, subjected French manufactures to sharp competition from our more advanced industrial system, and was causing much distress in the north of
France. A protracted drought in the summer of 1788, closing
with a terrible hail-storm, had ruined the crops in northern and
central France; and the winter of 1788—9 was one of the
severest ever known. Crowds of starving wretches flocked to
the relief works foolishly opened in Paris and the large towns.
The distress embittered the whole course of the elections in
the early spring of 1789; and while philosophers and senti-
mentalists were dreaming of human perfectibility, universal
brotherhood and the abolition of armies, the fortunes of
France were more and more at the mercy of the Paris mob,
now swelled by thousands of ignorant and desperate peasants.
The revolution prepared by the *savants* was to be carried out
by the men of the slums. The social and political danger was
seen in the Réveillon riot at Paris; while the determination of
the nobles and titled clergy of Brittany to adhere to the

ancient constitution of their provincial estates and sit separately from the lower clergy and commoners, provoked bloodshed at Rennes.   Everything showed that it was on this social and constitutional question that discord would break out.

Nevertheless on the meeting of the States General the 600 deputies of the Commons were kept rigidly distinct from the 300 deputies of the clergy, and the 300 of the nobles; and at the opening ceremony (May 5) their enthusiasm was quenched by a long dissertation from Necker on the deficit.   The Tiers État when left alone, following the instructions of many of its *cahiers*, refused to do anything to recognise the separate existence of the other two Orders.   This policy lasted six weeks, during which time Necker's suggestion, that the nobles and titled clergy should form an Upper Chamber, was shelved.   On the repeated refusals of the two other Orders to join them, the Tiers État finally declared itself (June 17) to be the *National Assembly* of France—a bold declaration of sovereign power by the very body which Louis had looked forward to as an ally in his contest with the privileged Orders.   The Assembly at once asserted its new claim by declaring the present taxes legal only during its existence, by taking under its protection the creditors of the State, and by naming a committee on food-supply.

The king, puzzled at these events, was now persuaded by his queen and his youngest brother the Comte d'Artois to reject these bold innovations, as inroads on his prerogatives. Three courses were open to Louis, (1) to surrender to the Tiers État: (2) to expel them by force, which would bring on a civil war: (3) to forestall their actions by royal reforms. Louis resolved to try the last, and have troops at hand to overawe the people.   Necker had drawn up a list of royal reforms : these were to be read out at a "royal session" before the three Orders; but owing to the influence of his queen and youngest brother, the reforms were so reduced that Necker would have no more to do with this policy. The hall at Versailles where the Tiers État met was closed to prepare for the royal session; but the deputies at once flocked to the Tennis Court, and, electing Bailly the astronomer as their first President, they swore the famous oath—that they would in no case separate, but would meet in all places, under all circumstances, till they had made the Constitution (June 20). Fortified by the adhesion of 149 deputies of the clergy and 2 nobles, they were ready for the royal session (June 23). Louis annulled their decrees, and imposed reforms in 35 articles: if the three Orders (voting as such) cannot agree on these reforms, " I alone will effect the welfare of my people."

To impose political reforms, while reviving the old system of three distinct Orders, showed a complete disregard of those passionate longings for social equality and self-government which were fusing provinces and Orders into a united nation. Louis' unfortunate attempt to solve the difficulty aroused more opposition than ever. At the end of the session the Orders were bidden to retire. The Tiers État and their new adherents did not stir. When the master of ceremonies repeated the king's command, the national consciousness flashed forth in a withering retort from Mirabeau, " We are assembled by the national will: force alone shall disperse us."

The royal session has been as much misunderstood as Mirabeau's actual words have been improved upon. It was not a mere exhibition of arbitrary power, but a spasmodic attempt to recur, when too late, to the policy of imposing reforms by royal decrees, always till then followed by continental rulers and statesmen. It was the policy of Frederick the Great, of Pombal in Portugal, of Maria Theresa, of Joseph II, and of Turgot. The Tennis Court oath, the retort of Mirabeau, and the collapse of Joseph II's reforms, mark the end of that era, and the commencement of a new age, inaugurated by Rousseau and the American patriots, when the people insist that reforms shall be effected not only for them, but by them.

If the king's unskilful policy had for the time confused the cause of royal reform with that of the privileged orders, yet on the other hand the attitude of the Tiers État in resisting all compromise must be held partly responsible for the first rupture. Jefferson, the American patriot, had strongly urged them to accept the reforms which Louis would at once have granted, viz. a representative legislature meeting every year with the right of originating laws and the control of taxation, responsibility of the king's ministers to the Legislature, trial by jury, freedom of conscience and of the press: "with these powers they could obtain in the future whatever else was necessary to perfect their Constitution. They thought otherwise, and events have proved their lamentable error; for after 30 years of foreign and domestic war, and the loss of millions of lives, they have in the end obtained no more, nor even that securely." The defiant attitude of the National Assembly and the adhesion of forty-seven reforming nobles with the Duke of Orleans at their head, disconcerted the Court; and the king, after the "timid violence,"—as Malouet phrased it—of the royal session, now desired the rest of the noble and clerical deputies to join the Assembly (June 27), and requested Necker not to resign.

The Court retired only to take a better spring. Disorders in Paris in the privileged regiment of the Gardes Françaises served as a pretext for massing between Versailles and the capital a large force of troops, among whom were several mercenary German and Swiss regiments. Everything was thought to be ready for the *coup d'état*. Necker was dismissed, and quietly withdrew to Brussels. On July 12 this news was brought to the excitable crowd always thronging the gardens of the Palais Royal, by the ardent young journalist Camille Desmoulins; and all Paris rushed to arms and demonstrations. After a brush with the 'Royal Germans' in the Champs Elysées, the crowd, always helped by the Gardes Françaises, plundered the 'Invalides' of 28,000 muskets, and then rushed to the famous Bastille (July 14). This fortress, built three centuries before to command the St Antoine gate and suburb, had been often used as a prison for political offenders; but under the milder rule of Louis XVI it now held only seven prisoners, and these not for political offences. Yet its eight lofty towers still seemed to threaten Paris; and an excited crowd, on Delaunay's firm refusal to surrender, rushed at the outer drawbridge, which soon fell under the blows of two old soldiers. The arrival of the Gardes Françaises with their cannon finally dispirited the little garrison of 114 men, and they compelled Delaunay to surrender. The mob massacred four of the soldiers and five officers, including Delaunay; and de Flesselles, Provost of the Merchants of Paris, soon after fell a victim to their suspicions of his treachery at the Hôtel de Ville. Sensation-mongers have added almost a cycle of legends to the so-called 'Storming of the Bastille.' The prosaic truth is thus declared by an eye-witness, the Counsellor Pasquier:—"What has been called the fight was not serious : resistance there was none. In the Bastille there were neither provisions, nor munitions of war : there was no need to invest it. ......It did not for a moment terrify the many spectators who flocked to see the result. Among these were several elegant ladies, who, to approach nearer, had left their carriages at some distance."

Paris could now defy the royal troops. As disaffection was rife among them (for reasons stated in the last chapter), they were withdrawn to Versailles; and the Comte d'Artois, with many reactionary nobles, quitted France, in what was called the 'joyous emigration.' The surrender of the Bastille marks the commencement of outbreaks of violence, which culminated in 1793. The news aroused wide-spread Jacqueries, or risings of the peasants, especially in the east of France, from Dauphiné to Alsace. The sky was red with the flare of burning castles; but in many parts the peasants only burned the hated feudal deeds enumerating their services and dues. There were riots in the autumn of 1789 at Strassburg, Troyes, Rouen, Caen, and other towns, generally arising from the dearness of bread or the poverty of the *ouvriers*. In nearly every case order was ultimately restored by the National Guard, mainly composed of *bourgeois*. Power was everywhere passing from the royal *intendants* to the new citizen force; and it was soon seen that the revolution advanced as quickly in the provinces as at the capital. In the manufacturing districts of the north, where the recent commercial treaty with England had ruined many manufacturers, the outbreaks were directed against the machinery which would have helped them in the competition with English goods. The industrial revolution, then peacefully proceeding in England, was soon to be checked in France, by the internal disorders and by a desire to completely exclude English goods. In Paris the trades which depended on the luxury of the few were at once paralysed by the flight of the wealthy. "I saw (says Bailly in his memoirs) mercers, jewellers, and other tradesmen implore the favour of being employed at 20 sous the day"—on public relief works.

But even amid these disorders, social and political reconstruction was vigorously begun. The king, in a memorable visit to Paris (July 17), donned the new tricolour cockade; and on the balcony of the Hôtel de Ville recognised two new creations of the popular will, the Paris Municipality with Bailly as first Mayor, and the National Guard commanded by Lafayette. These institutions spread through France. Popular municipalities everywhere replaced the old corporations of royal nominees, as the National Guard replaced the militia. Every citizen was expected to serve as a National Guard—the commencement of the great citizen armies of our day.

CHAPTER III.

THE CONSTITUENT ASSEMBLY.

"A people so badly prepared to act by itself, could not set about reforming everything at once, without destroying everything."—DE TOCQUEVILLE.

MEANWHILE at Versailles the National Assembly (which on July 9 had taken the special title of 'Constituent,' as having to frame the Constitution) was beginning to organise itself and France. Not till after its removal to Paris did its members sit in a semi-circle, facing the fortnightly President; but the names Right, Left, &c. were beginning to be used to denote its political groups. Those close by the President's right were the ultra royalists, reactionary nobles, titled clergy led by the clever Abbé Maury, or factious defenders of the privileged Orders in the Parlements—as d'Espréménil. In the Right Centre were the reforming nobles and other partisans of a Constitution like that of England, as Mounier and Lally Tollendal, who soon found themselves left high and dry by the rush of events. The Left Centre included more pronounced reformers, such as Mirabeau, destroyer of a worn-out social order, but champion of monarchy in its hour of need; Rabaut de St Étienne, leader of the Protestants; the Jansenist Camus; Grégoire, the leader of the country priests in their onset on clerical abuses;

the versatile Talleyrand, soon to become the chief diplomatist of the age; and the Abbé Siéyès, with his clear-cut face and incisive phrases, whose constitution-mongering was finally to help Bonaparte to power and himself to inglorious ease. Farther round the Chamber to the President's left sat the professed revolutionists, organised by Duport, Barnave, and Lameth, who desired at the outset a reconstruction of the State on demo-cratic principles; while on the extreme left was a party, called the 'trente voix,' desirous of a complete social revolution, as sketched by Rousseau. This small group, led by Pétion, Buzot, and Robespierre, was to swallow the fat kine of the Assembly and of France.

For the present these groups were only beginning to crystal-lize into parties, and generally voted on the sentiment of the moment. There was no more sequence in the speeches read from the *tribune* than there was order in the procedure. When Mirabeau laid on the table a translation of Romilly's little work on English parliamentary procedure, it was rejected; for "we are not English, and we want nothing English." The lack of political experience, the interference of the public in the galleries, and the weakness of the fortnightly Presidents, often reduced the Assembly to a mere Bedlam; yet, when emotion stilled its strifes, it could act with spasmodic energy. Thus, when the report on the Jacqueries thrilled the deputies, there arose a generous rivalry in self-sacrifice (Aug. 4). The mem-bers of the privileged Orders kept thronging to the table to give up their immunities. Nobles, clergy, towns, districts, and corporations, alike gave up all their immunities from taxation: serfs were liberated, and all degrading forms of servitude were swept away without compensation: slaves in the colonies were declared to be free, though the slave-owners disputed the validity of this decree: nobles consented to modify the harsher provisions of the game laws, as well as to give up their right of administering justice in their own seigneurial law-courts:

the clergy saw their tithes abolished without definite compensation, on a motion of the sceptical Bishop Talleyrand : the suppression of plurality of benefices, the abolition of the old exclusive trade-gilds, the sacrifice of the *droit de colombier*, or sole right of keeping a dove-cote, and the admissibility of all classes to all civil and military appointments, completed the fusion of the Orders in one nation ; and the Assembly broke up at dawn with fervent cries of "Vive le roi."

In a single sitting it had carried what the royal authority had been unable to gain from the Parlements in fifteen years ; but, in spite of this feverish haste, the concessions now came too late to calm the people. They seemed like a jettison of cargo to lighten the ship in the storm now raging around. The peasants and liberated serfs, realising their power, acted as though the Assembly had swept away all the game laws and all the feudal dues. In all parts, but especially in the east, they killed the game, and, instead of redeeming the ordinary feudal dues, refused to pay them one and all. It was in vain for the Assembly to proclaim the law on these points. The royal intendants had no power to enforce order, or even payment of taxes. Necker was ever bewailing the increase of the deficit ; and when the Assembly jealously refused to strengthen the executive for the collection of taxes, he proposed (Sept.) that a "patriotic contribution" should be made by every citizen of one fourth of his income to rescue the State from bankruptcy. The Assembly was wavering, when Mirabeau's eloquent support carried the measure : "Bankruptcy, hideous bankruptcy is there : it threatens to consume you, your honour, your fortunes —and you deliberate!" Even after this appeal, the patriotic contribution was a dismal failure ; and the first year of the revolution was to close with a deficit of over £7,000,000. Both the Assembly and the populace were less concerned about the payment of taxes than the correct phrasing of the Rights of Man. After long deliberation these were accepted ; but a proposal that the duties of the citizen should also be defined was lost by a small majority. To insist on rights, and shirk disagreeable duties, was the radical defect of the new civic life, fatal to the solvency, order, and stability of the State.

Still longer and more animated were the debates on the bases of the new Constitution; and it was soon apparent that the theories of Rousseau, as to the complete sovereignty and indivisibility of the nation, would triumph over results of experience gained in English and American parliamentary life. Siéyès showed most logically that logic forbade the existence of a Senate, or of the royal veto; and the Assembly decided that the legislative power should remain with one Assembly, having the sole right of initiating laws, and controlling all the legislative functions of the State. Though the three National Assemblies successively proclaimed the need of a "distinction of powers," i.e. between the legislative and executive functions of government, they were brought by a curious irony of events to encroach more and more on the latter. Distrust of the king's ministers and officials, rumours of plots against the Assembly and the nation, finally the strain and stress of civil strifes and war against the combined States of Europe, gradually led to an almost complete absorption of the executive by the legislative. The beginnings of this process were at once observable. Distracted by its many difficulties, the Assembly even at the close of July 1789 empowered a Committee of its members, renewable every month, to procure information leading to the conviction of persons suspected of plotting the overthrow of the Assembly. This Committee of Inquiry was finally to become the terrible Committee of General Security of 1793.

Passion rose high in the debates on the royal veto, i.e. the right of the king to stop the passing of a law; and when Mirabeau defended the veto, people in Paris begged him to desist: "If the king has the veto, there will be no occasion for a National Assembly. We shall all be slaves again." Threats were uttered against the Assembly if it should admit the veto; but it was strong enough then to despise them, while the Paris municipality for a time suppressed seditious gatherings in the Palais Royal. In the Assembly the democrats all followed Siéyès' argument that the "division of powers" required the king's authority to be solely executive :—"The Assembly is the head, the king is the arm; and the head never admits the arm to deliberate with it." Mirabeau defended the veto by showing the need of some check on the acts of a single Assembly, and proved that the division of powers, if rigorously followed out, would place the legislative and executive as rivals with no links of connection. Necker's ministry ended these disputes by declaring in favour of a compromise called the suspensive veto, by which the king's refusal to pass any measure was to hold good only throughout two sessions, but must lapse if the measure was passed in a third session. The new Constitution was, however, not to be subject to any exercise of the veto.

The balance of political power was finally upset by the events of Oct. 5. The loss of trade caused by the disorders, and the dearth caused by a poor harvest, increased popular excitement. No tale in the new journals or pamphlets was too wild for belief. "The aristocrats destroyed corn before it was ripe, paid the bakers not to work, suspended trade, and threw flour into the rivers." The arrival of a new regiment at Versailles, and the effervescence of its loyalty to the king and queen in a banquet held there on Oct. 1, appeared a real cause for alarm; and the report that the national tricolour had been insulted seemed to foreshadow a new Court conspiracy. Seeing that the men had lately been strictly controlled by the Paris authorities, the women assembled, pillaged the Hôtel de Ville, and began their weird march to the Assembly and Palace at Versailles. After invading the Assembly "to hear our little mother Mirabeau speak," and to get the Rights of Man finally accepted, and the price of bread fixed, they and the riff-raff following them encamped opposite the great Château, which Lafayette undertook to protect with the Paris National Guard. At dawn of Oct. 6 a few of the mob burst in by an unguarded side-door, and the royal family barely escaped massacre by the devotion of a *garde du corps* and the arrival of Lafayette's men; but, to make sure that bread would be cheap, the mob clamoured in the courtyard for the king to go to Paris. Thither the royal family of France had to go, amidst a crowd of National Guards, repentant body-guards, and fish-wives dancing around cart-loads of corn,—the funeral march of the old monarchy.

The Assembly soon followed, though 56 members were afraid to trust themselves in Paris. It had prevailed over the privileged Orders and clipped the wings of monarchy; but Oct. 6 was the victory of the Paris mob, which henceforth exercised a predominant and fatal influence on the National Assembly and its successors. Camille Desmoulins thought the revolution was now finished; but the events of Oct. 5—6 really inaugurated an era of mob rule, culminating in the supremacy of the Clubs and the Paris Commune.

It is thought that the factious Duke of Orleans had insti-gated the march on Versailles. Mirabeau, who then had some secret connection with him, said of that event, "Instead of a glass of brandy, a bottle was given"; and he seems to have desired that a sharp lesson should be given to the Court, to make reaction impossible. Lafayette, who was now for a time almost dictator, insisted that the Duke should leave France; and, if a close understanding had been formed between Necker, representing the Ministry, Mirabeau, whose eloquence nearly always carried the Assembly with him, and Lafayette at the head of the Paris National Guards, a party of order might still have rallied around this triumvirate, strong enough to prevent the political clubs from becoming supreme; but the vanity or folly of Lafayette and Necker hindered any co-operation with a man of so doubtful a character as Mirabeau. The cause of order was weakened by the withdrawal from the Assembly of Mounier and some other supporters of a monarchy like that of England. Parties began to separate more clearly, the gain being decidedly to the democratic Left; and the Assembly soon showed its jealousy of the executive, which Mirabeau now desired to strengthen, by decreeing (Nov. 7) that none of its members could join the king's Ministry, nor for six months after resignation. By this rigid division of powers the Assembly weakened the executive, which alone could legally put into force its decrees. So the cause of order was weakened, while what was most dreaded by Mirabeau came to pass—"Anarchy organised itself" in the political clubs.

The most famous of these was the Jacobins, so called from the disused monastery where it met. At first it comprised men of all parties; but revolutionary ardour disowned first the moderates, then Mirabeau, and, after the flight to Varennes, Duport, Barnave, and the Lameths, until Robespierre, the inflexible exponent of Rousseau's ideas, was there omnipotent. The power of the club lay in its network of branches spreading over all France, so that a motion carried by the Jacobins was soon better executed than any decrees of the National Assembly. An early offshoot from the Jacobins was the Cordeliers' Club, representing the extremists of Paris, such as the witty Desmoulins, the obscene Hébert, the brazen-lunged Danton, half demagogue, half statesman; and that queer compound, part man of science, part social martyr, part homicidal lunatic, Marat. These men by their newspapers or mob-oratory had great hold on Paris; and in the dynamics of the revolution they may be named the prime motors, influencing the Jacobins, who then pulled the strings all over France.

The intense interest in the debates of the Assembly and the Clubs may be measured by the mushroom growth of

F. R.

4

pamphlets and newspapers, the names of some of which still survive—as the *Journal des Débats* and *Moniteur*; and French journalism still retains the strongly individual tone which marked its beginnings; for in 1789 every prominent politician, or group of deputies, strove to carry on a journal; Desmoulins, Marat, and, in 1793, Hébert, gained more power by the pen than by their speeches. Posters (*affiches*) and cheap pamphlets spread the revolutionary notions far and wide, carrying along France in the wake of Paris.

Mounier and some other seceders were trying to stir up against the Assembly the old provincial spirit, so fatal to Louis XVI's reforming efforts; but the change of political power was seen in the ease with which the Assembly overthrew the Parlements and the provincial system. Lameth's proposal (Nov. 3), that the Parlements should be left in vacation, was carried, and scarcely an arm was raised in their defence. The provinces with their immunities and, in some cases, their separate constitutions, were swept away; as well as the administrative areas of the intendants, or royal controllers. By the early spring of 1790 all France was politically unified, as it had been socially unified by the decrees of Aug. 4. Siéyès desired to see France divided into eighty squares designated by numbers! But as her boundaries conflicted with a chessboard pattern, the remodelling took the form of 83 Departments named after natural features. The provincial system had represented the differences derived from the great fiefs of old France: the new system symbolized the natural unity of the French people, first united by the monarchy and now indivisibly welded together by the Revolution. Each Department was divided into districts or arrondissements, each of these into cantons; while the smallest unit was the rural municipality or commune, which through its mayor and council had at the outset very wide powers of self-government. The canton was the electoral district, where the 'electors' were chosen by the 'active' citizens, i.e. by those who paid in direct taxes a sum equal to three days' earnings: the 'electoral colleges' were then to choose the representatives for each Department in the National Assembly. The new Departmental System thus sought the expression of the nation's will from each commune or parish, by secondary election, through the medium of the canton and Department. It not only secured self-government to the communes and Departments, but also local defence; for each 'active citizen' was to serve as a National Guard. Moreover, as the jury system and election of magistrates and judges subjected the law courts to the control of the Department and of the nation, the Departmental System quietly took the place of the feudal and monarchical governing powers in the spheres of local government, defence, and justice. This system, admirable in the symmetry of its outlines, yet had the great defect of subjecting all the functions of government to oft-recurring elections by men who had no experience of public duties; and power fell more and more into the hands of the local Jacobin clubs.

In its policy towards the Church of France the Assembly had the double aim of asserting the sovereignty of the nation over every institution, and of re-establishing the finances. Despite the protest of Siéyès—"They would be free, and know not how to be just"—it had already abolished all tithes, thereby transferring about £3,000,000 a year from the clergy to the landowners. Talleyrand in Oct. 1789 had proposed that the nation should take over all the Church property, assuring to the clergy two-thirds of its rentals; but Mirabeau brought forward a much more extreme motion, that the nation should hold this property, bear the costs of public worship, and should pay to every curé not less than £48 a year, exclusive of lodging. The desire to redress the scandalous inequalities of income, and to reduce the clergy to salaried officers of the State, secured the success of this motion (Nov.

1789). The Church lands were forthwith used as security for an issue of paper notes, or *assignats*, for small amounts. The design of Clavière and Mirabeau, who proposed this scheme, was that only 400,000,000 francs' worth should at first be issued; though in Sept. 1790 they were compelled to a second issue of double this amount, with the proviso—also soon disregarded—that there should never be more than 1,200,000,000 francs' worth in circulation. Assignats alone were to be received in payment for the purchase of the new national domains sold by the municipalities; but the fatal facility with which the credit of the State seemed to be thus restored, soon lured the financiers who succeeded Necker deeper and deeper into debt. The Church lands were wastefully sold, and little financial benefit resulted from the confiscation, though it somewhat increased the number of peasant proprietors.

The Assembly, after decreeing complete liberty for all religious beliefs, and suppressing and confiscating the property of religious orders, completed the subjection of the Church to the State by its 'Civil Constitution of the Clergy' (June 1790), by which the Jansenists, Camus, Grégoire, and Lanjuinais, hoped to restore the simplicity of the early Christian Church. By this important measure bishop and priests were to be chosen by the electors of the Department and the district respectively, and were not to apply to the Pope for confirmation of their election nor for canonical investiture, but must take an oath of obedience to the civil authorities and to the new constitution. The fairer apportionment of stipends which accompanied this decree does not redeem it from the charge of persecution. Orthodox Roman Catholics could not recognise the supremacy of the State in place of that of the Pope; and though Bishop Talleyrand and others began to institute the new 'constitutional' priests, yet about two-thirds of the clergy of France (called orthodox or 'non-jurors') refused to obey the decree. This was the beginning of a schism in the Church of France, which embittered the whole course of events and was only healed by Bonaparte's 'Concordat' in 1801. Ultimately it was seen that the State, in subjecting the clergy, only bound them the more closely to the Papal See.

All through the spring of 1790 the general rejoicings at the new civic life inaugurated by the Departmental System took the form of 'federations' of towns and districts that they would keep the law and see it respected by aristocrats, forestallers of corn, and all other traitors. After a great federation at Lyons of the centre and south of France, a federation of the entire nation was held in the Champ de Mars at Paris (July 14, 1790), when King, Queen, National Assembly, representatives of every Department, and a vast concourse of people, took an oath to obey the laws and the Constitution. In the words of an eye-witness, M. Ferrières—"The soul felt oppressed beneath the weight of a delicious intoxication, at sight of a people actuated by the gentle emotions of a primitive fraternity."

This imposing demonstration of national unity could not heal the disorders. There had been many a riot to seize corn or prevent it leaving the district: the anti-clerical policy of the Assembly fanned the slumbering embers of the old religious feuds into fierce flame at Montauban and Nîmes: troops at Nancy, enraged at arrears of pay, mutinied, and were crushed only after a fearful fight (Aug. 31, 1790): tolls and taxes were generally left unpaid, and Necker in despair fled to Geneva.

There was only one man who seemed able to breast the revolutionary torrent—Mirabeau; and he was losing his control over the people. This had been seen in the debates on the right of the king to declare war (May, 1790). The question might have been all-important, if England and Spain had gone to war over a dispute about Nootka Sound in California; for by the Bourbon Family compact of 1761 France and Spain would have made common cause; and as Austria was annoyed at our preventing the partition of Turkey between her and Russia, it seemed for a time that a war of France, Austria, and Spain against England and Holland might alter the whole aspect of Europe. Lafayette with the French moderates strove for this, that he might become dictator, and stay the course of the revolution. But this was just what the Jacobins feared; and it needed all Mirabeau's passionate eloquence to convince the Assembly that the king, as head of the executive, should have, conjointly with the Legislature, the right of declaring war. The first article of the law ran thus—"The right of peace and war belongs to the nation. War can be decided only by a decree of the National Assembly, which shall be passed on the formal and necessary proposal of the king, and which shall be sanctioned by him"—a Pyrrhic victory for the monarchy, and for Mirabeau. The foreign complications were somewhat lessened by the treaty of Reichenbach which, as previously explained on page 14, brought Prussia and Austria to accord, and tended to the maintenance of the *status quo* (July, 1790); but the danger of a war against England over the Spanish difficulty did not vanish until the mutiny at Nancy and the general insubordination in army and navy convinced even the French royalists that war was impossible.

Not only was Mirabeau by conviction a monarchist, as seeing no stability in one almost irresponsible Assembly, but he had been brought into close communications with the king and queen by means of Lamarck and the Austrian ambassador. He urged the passive king to play a vigorous part, to denounce the emigrant nobles, and control the revolution by putting himself at its head. He accepted a large sum from the king to pay his debts, and £240 a month besides. His childish love of display revealed the secret; and during the war debates he was denounced by the Jacobins as "the traitor." On the other side the Court utterly distrusted the man who had done so much in 1789 to overthrow the king's old powers; and it regarded him merely as the arch-demagogue, now at last bought over. Both charges were equally beside the mark; for Mirabeau's conduct and policy was from first to last an attempt to found a democratic monarchy, strong enough in the support of the people to act as a check on the Assembly; but his policy of statesmanlike compromise was impossible, with an inert king, a jealous Assembly torn by conflicting extremes, and a populace leavened by Rousseau's doctrines. Not till political experiments had been tried and had failed, was a compromise between authority and democracy likely to succeed. Mirabeau's efforts may be regarded as Titanic struggles for the impossible. In 1791 even Buonaparte must have failed. No one could have made Louis XVI a leader, or endowed Assembly and people with the spirit of reasonable compromise. "It is clear that we are perishing, royalty, authority, the whole nation. The Assembly is killing itself and us with it." Such are his words in one of his last notes to the king; but even so, his fertility of resource kept weaving plans of propping up the monarchy by discrediting the Assembly, buying over deputies or demagogues, luring it into unpopular acts (especially against the clergy, in which he himself took the lead), and setting the Departments against Paris. Mirabeau's Machiavellian policy cut both ways. The king could not understand him: the Court feared and hated the Tribune of the people: the democrats distrusted or despised him as the bribed ally of the monarchy. Not even Mirabeau's energy and eloquence could overcome the mutual distrust of Court and people; and, worn out by ceaseless toil and frequent debaucheries, he ended his many-sided career with the prophecy —"I carry in my heart the death dirge of the monarchy: the dead remains of it will now be the spoil of the factions" (April 2, 1791).

Mirabeau had often advised the king to retire to Rouen or

Compiègne.   The events of the spring of 1791—especially his forcible detention at the Tuileries at and after Easter—decided Louis to fly to Metz or Montmédy, where Bouillé still held together some faithful regulars to guard the frontiers.   The flight was on the point of success, when at Sainte Menehould the village postmaster Drouet recognised Louis beneath his disguise, and, galloping on, secured the bridge at Varennes; while Bouillé's troopers, wearied at the delay of the royal coach (caused by a breakdown), were not at hand in time for a rescue (June 21, 1791).

Gloomy silence greeted the king on his return to Paris. It is surprising that the Assembly did not dethrone him at once; for he had left behind a declaration revoking his assent to every decree passed by the Assembly since the royal session of June 23, 1789; but the prospect of a civil war appalled the Assembly, which was also desirous of ending its constitutional labours.   It even sanctioned the rigorous dispersion by Mayor Bailly of the 'clubbists' who were petitioning on the Champ de Mars for the dethronement (July 17); and a show of energy on the part of the Feuillants, or Constitutionalists (now joined by Barnave and the Lameths), temporarily checked the anarchic forces at work in Paris and the Departments.

The acceptance by Louis of the new Constitution for a time seemed to still foreign and domestic complications (Sept. 1791).   Reared on the bases described above (see pages 46 —51), it transferred the chief power from the sovereign to a National Assembly elected every two years, which alone was to initiate laws, and could not be dissolved by the king.

Under the ancient régime there had been a perfect chaos of intersecting governing powers, seigneurial, provincial, and royal, the latter having gradually absorbed most of the two former in the King's Council and in the administration by royal 'intendants.'   The revolution, ever tending towards Rousseau's sovereignty and indivisibility of the national will,

at once simplified and unified the functions of government;
and many a loyal courtier reflected with secret joy that when
the king recovered his authority, he would not be hampered
by factious Parlements. The work of the Constituent Assembly
cleared the way for Buonaparte, and the modern centralised
State. The radical defect of the Constitution was the jealous
isolation in which it placed the king's Ministry, nominally entrusted with the execution of the laws, but practically powerless.
So, only those laws were observed which were approved by the
people, especially by the political clubs; and France when
face to face with invaders, and groping for a vigorous executive,
was to find it in secret and finally irresponsible committees.
The first encroachment of the legislative on the executive
functions in July, 1789, has been already noticed. The king's
flight to Varennes enabled the Assembly to seize still more of
the executive power. Its decrees, though unsigned by Louis,
had for a time the force of laws, and it sent commissioners to
secure the public safety and maintain order in the frontier
Departments. These steps were provisional and temporary;
but, in general, the effective work and influence of the Assembly
was mostly due to the vigorous action of its twenty committees,
which supervised or sought to control, not only the preparation
of laws and of the Constitution, but even purely executive
business, such as diplomacy, war, the navy, food supply, and
plots against its own authority. In these committees, most
of which were permanent, lay the germ of that tyranny under
which France was to groan in 1793—4; and the sequel will
show that this same dominant aim of controlling the executive
by a permanent commission selected from the Legislature, led
to the installation of the Directory in 1795, and inspired Siéyès
with his scheme of that perfect Constitution of 1799, which
helped Buonaparte to power.

In sharp contrast to the imprudence of the Constituent
Assembly in constitutional efforts, is its swift, unerring, and

permanent work of Constitution Assembly

irreversible action in social questions.   The fusion of the three
Orders, the abolition of Feudalism, and the recognition of
individual liberty and civic equality, laid the foundations broad
and deep, not only of the French State, but of every country
directly influenced by the revolution.

CHAPTER IV.

THE GIRONDINS AND EUROPE.

The causes of the outbreak of war with Austria & Prussia.

"Divided into a number of different governments, Europe has no bases for a general resistance; and the first great continental nation which changes the face of society, has only disunited members to fear."

MALLET DU PAN, 1792.

THE flight to Varennes, and the ludicrous spectacle of a king held on his throne lest he should run away, seemed to call for the intervention of absolute monarchs. They had hitherto politely ignored the clamorous requests of French emigrant nobles, once headed by the Comte d'Artois, and now by the Comte de Provence; but after Varennes the Emperor Leopold II, alarmed for the safety of his sister Marie Antoinette, drew closer to Prussia, in order to assert the cause of monarchy against the Paris Jacobins.

Another influence was secretly urging the two central Powers to a rupture with France. The ambitious Czarina, Catherine II, was anxious to keep them busy in the west, so that she might have a free hand to intervene in the Polish crisis. The Polish patriots, fired by the success of the French Assembly in sweeping away old abuses, desired to regenerate their unhappy realm. Having gained the support of their king, Stanislaus, they carried through their Diet decrees which transformed their aristocratic government into a constitutional monarchy (May, 1791). The *liberum veto* was suppressed, the

Diet was divided into two Chambers, in which the balance of power lay with the Chamber of Nuncios or Deputies, and the monarchy, instead of being elective, was to be hereditary in the line of the Electors of Saxony. This admirable Constitution, which followed the aims of Voltaire and Turgot rather than those of Rousseau's "Gouvernement de Pologne," would have founded a strong executive on a democratic basis. Art. V declared : "All power in civil society should be derived from the will of the people, its end and object being the preservation and integrity of the State, the civil liberty, and the good order of society, on an equal scale, and on a lasting foundation." As this Constitution closed the door to Russian intrigues, which had used the election of the Polish king and the *liberum veto* to foment disorders, Catherine II plotted its overthrow. Relieved from the pressure of wars with Sweden and Turkey, she strove to gain a free hand in Poland, by encouraging Austria and Prussia to intervene in French affairs, and we shall see that the outbreak of war with France in 1792, and still more its expansion in 1793, were to be fatal to the nascent liberties of Poland.

These hidden reasons smoothed the way for the Austrian and Prussian sovereigns, and enabled them to come to a close understanding ; while Gustavus III, the chivalrous ruler of Sweden, tried to form a league of kings against the French Revolution. Austria and Prussia, improving on the policy of Reichenbach, now guaranteed to each other the possession of their States. But though they affected great concern at the position of Louis XVI, they had only temporarily laid aside their mutual jealousy, their designs on Poland, and their dread of Russia's aggression in that quarter ; and they were above all disgusted at the presumption of the Comte d'Artois in asking that they should invade France to re-establish the ancient régime and place the Comte de Provence (Louis XVIII) on the throne. The conferences at Pillnitz, near Dresden (Aug. 1791), led to their declaration that they considered the re-establishment of order and monarchy in France an object of interest to all the sovereigns of Europe; "they will not refuse to employ con-jointly with them the most efficacious means" to strengthen the French monarchy. "Then and in that case" they "are re-solved to act promptly." As all well-informed persons knew that England would remain neutral, the words which required the action of all the sovereigns showed that the Declaration of Pillnitz was only meant to intimidate the French revolutionists. It had the opposite effect.

A conflict between the disciples of Rousseau and the upholders in old Europe of the complicated feudal and dynastic claims was perhaps inevitable. The eager enthusiasm of the French reformers had brought them into collision with the German princes, when on Aug. 4, 1789, the abolition of all feudal dues and services swept away some of their claims on parts of Alsace. The princes had declined the money compen-sation offered as inadequate; so this question opened a dispute with the Empire, which was intensified when the Constituent Assembly decreed the annexation of the Papal County of Avignon, though by the new constitution France was to renounce all conquest or aggrandisement. French patriots, on their side, were enraged at the gatherings of bands of the French emigrant nobles near the frontier; and now the Declaration of Pillnitz aroused a martial feeling among the inexperienced members of the Second National Assembly—known as the 'Legislative'—which met in Paris on Oct. 1, 1791.

Members of the Constituent Assembly were by its own act excluded from the Legislative, which was much more hasty and revolutionary than its predecessor. More than half of its members were under thirty years of age. The ardent monarch-ists numbered scarcely 100; the supporters of the Constitution —generally known as Feuillants from the name of the Consti-tutionalist club—could muster 164 votes, while the professed foes of the Constitution were about 236—including Girondins and Jacobins. The balance of power at first rested with a 'Centre' of some 245 members, as yet pledged to no definite programme, but soon destined to join the extreme party. Yet the partisans of the Constitution might have held their ground if they had been as determined and as well organised as the Jacobins; but their right hand, Lafayette, resigned his command of the Paris National Guard, which was thenceforth commanded for a month by each colonel in turn: so power fell more and more into the hands of the *sansculottes.* The troubles of the time also fomented discontent; thus serving to discredit the Constitution of 1791 at the outset. A terrible massacre at Avignon, a revolt of the slaves in the French West Indies in assertion of their equality, and continued Jacqueries through France—all these events in the autumn of 1791 and winter of 1791—2 increased the financial embarrassment; and yet *assignats* were being issued with reckless rapidity to meet the ever-increasing deficit. The consequent distress and stoppage of trade appeared to the excited imagination of Frenchmen as the work of aristocrats, and the completion of the revolution as the only hope for France. The whole state of affairs, therefore, vastly increased the difficulties of the quickly changing Feuillant Ministries in their attempts to govern by a Constitution which was designed to hamper the executive power. Augustus Miles, writing from Paris in the last days of 1791, gives the following description, and ventures on a remarkable conjecture about the future.—"The *assignats* have fallen to above 40 per cent. discount, and the explosion—temporary bankruptcy, and all the evils attendant on the guilt and folly of these sorry legislators in Paris—cannot long be deferred. Yet, mark my words, France will recover from her present delirium: the fulness of her crimes will be the measure of her debility and weakness, and, acquiring a wise and free Government, she will overawe the imperial eagle and threaten the liberties of Europe."

Foremost in the Legislative Assembly was a group of ardent young orators, known as the Girondins, because three of their prominent members—Vergniaud, Gensonné, and Guadet— came from the Department of the Gironde. Other members of this interesting group were Pétion, now Mayor of Paris in place of the more moderate Bailly; the philosophic Condorcet, timid in action, yet gifted with so lofty a spirit as to complete his work on "The Human Mind" while he was being hounded to death; the ambitious journalist and wire-puller Brissot, eager for war with feudal Europe; the handsome young advocate Barbaroux, once leader of the Marseilles rabble; the novelist Louvet, bold in attack; the impetuous Isnard, of hot southern blood; the stoical, methodical Roland; and the conscientious and talented Buzot, secretly loving and beloved by Madame Roland, whose beauty and enthusiasm marked her out as the inspiring genius of the party. Her keen instinct detected the weak points of each and all: she admired the orations of Vergniaud, "strong in logic, burning with passion, sparkling with beauties, sustained by a noble elocution":—"and yet I do not like Vergniaud: what a pity that genius such as his is not animated by love of the commonwealth, and by tenacity of purpose." This last defect she saw to be the defect of the party, and with masculine force of will she strove to push them on from words to sustained action.

At the outset the political views of the Girondins were as advanced as those of the 'Mountain' (so called because they filled the highest benches of the Assembly); but, as the Girondins were men of culture, antique Romans in the loftiness of their views, the distinction soon came to be one of methods and morality. As Sainte Beuve finely says—"The Girondins drew back with a cry of horror from the river of blood." This did not stop the men of the Paris clubs, and of the 'Mountain.'

Girondins and Jacobins alike desired to absorb the few

functions left to the king and his ministry, and finally to over-
turn the monarchy. A committee of deputies sat to control
even the Minister for Foreign Affairs; he and other ministers
were often threatened with impeachment, and the Assembly
soon reduced them to the position of chief clerks. It determined to override even the suspensive veto granted to the king,
when he vetoed their decrees declaring non-juring priests to be
suspects, and confiscating the lands of emigrant nobles who did
not return.

    After the efforts of the Feuillants (or Constitutionalists) to
bolster up their ever-shifting ministries had failed, Louis had to
accept a Girondin ministry (March, 1792). It desired war, so
as to complete the revolution—as Brissot afterwards said, "to
set traps for the king, to expose his bad faith, and his relations
with the emigrant nobles"; while many of the Constitutionalists,
especially Lafayette, thought that war would strengthen the
Constitution by diverting men's minds from home troubles!
Crusading zeal for liberty carried all before it, even though the
clear-sighted Robespierre foretold the danger of a war managed
by "aristocrats who could not be trusted"; but Robespierre,
Danton, and some others of the extreme Left were unable, even
at the Jacobins' Club, to restrain the war party, headed by
Brissot. The war craze was kept at fever heat by armed bands
of the emigrant nobles at Coblentz and Trèves, threatening to
reimpose the hated ancient régime on France; and one of the
few imprudences of the Emperor Leopold II was to send a
despatch (Feb. 17), urging the French people to deliver themselves from the war party. His sudden death (March 1)
placed over the Hapsburg dominions, and on the Imperial
throne, the young Francis II, who was not averse from war;
and when the new French Minister of Foreign Affairs, Dumouriez,
demanded that the Austrian alliance with Prussia should be
suspended, he replied that this should be done when France
compensated the German princes for the loss of their rights in

Alsace, and the Pope for the loss of Avignon. On April 20, 1792, the Girondin ministers brought Louis to propose a declaration of war against the King of Bohemia and Hungary, which the Assembly passed almost unanimously; as also, a month later, against the kingdom of Sardinia. Thus inconsiderately was begun the most tremendous series of wars known to civilised nations—wars which, though propagating the revolution throughout Central and Southern Europe, were to bring back France to a military despotism wielded first by a secret Committee, then by the Directory, and finally by the great soldier of the revolution, Buonaparte.

The French Minister of Foreign Affairs, Dumouriez, sprung like Mirabeau from the new noblesse of Provence, resembled him also in his wide range of talents, his quick perception, and his secret desire to found a strong monarchy on a democratic basis. Foreseeing that this war would be one against old Europe, his plan was a defensive campaign where France had definite or defensible frontiers—as the Pyrenees, and upper Rhine,—but a vigorous offensive where—as in the Austrian Netherlands and Savoy—no natural obstacles opposed her advance. Thus grew up the idea of the 'natural frontiers,'—ocean, Pyrenees, Alps, and Rhine—which has played so great a part in French politics.

Though the Belgians welcomed the French invaders, yet these were so undisciplined that two columns fled at the first skirmish, scarcely firing a shot. At Paris also difficulties thickened. The State had to meet its expenses by partly repudiating its debts, and by issuing more *assignats*; but the Girondin Ministry (except Dumouriez) plotted to turn these disorders against the monarchy. It deprived the king of his royal guard, and proposed that a camp of 'federates' from the Departments should be formed outside Paris; but Louis firmly forbade this. He also vetoed a bill for banishing non-juring priests, and dismissed the Girondin Ministry (June 13).

F. R.

5

The revolutionists of the Paris faubourgs, seeing their chance, organised a demonstration against the king. A vast crowd burst into the Tuileries, and vainly demanded the withdrawal of his veto. Louis remained calm and inflexible, when conscience was at stake; and Pétion finally persuaded the mob to withdraw (June 20). Lafayette, realising too late the fatal trend of events, came from his army to crush anarchy at its source, the Jacobins' and Cordeliers' clubs; but the Court disowned his effort, orderly citizens kept timidly in their homes, the National Guard was now full of *sansculottes*; and the last chance of maintaining order was lost.

A month later came the Prussian declaration of war, followed by a foolish manifesto issued on July 27, against his better judgment, by the commander of the Prussian forces, the Duke of Brunswick, that Paris should suffer condign vengeance if it injured its king and queen. These unhappy sovereigns were now distracted between hope of Prussian succour, and despair at the menaces of the Paris revolutionists; but while Brunswick set about a methodical plan of campaign, the revolutionists rushed on their prey. They were reinforced by 500 men of Marseilles, who, at the call of Barbaroux, marched through France chanting the 'Marseillaise,' to strike down the "tyrant"; and in Paris a new revolutionary power— the Paris Commune—was formed by members from the 48 'sections,' which began to usurp the powers of the legal municipality.

At dawn on Aug. 10, vast crowds, headed by the Marseillais, the men of Brest, and other 'federates,' closed around the Tuileries palace, defended by about 1000 Swiss Guards, and a larger number of National Guards. Many of these were disaffected, and when their commander Mandat, a Constitutionalist, was ensnared and slain by the new Commune, resistance seemed hopeless. Urgently pressed to seek refuge with the National Assembly, Louis at last consented, hoping, as ever, to avoid bloodshed by surrender; but his hope that violence would be avoided was vain. He had left no orders for his gallant Swiss. They patiently held their ground under many provocations. Two shots fired by the mob at last drew from them a volley and a successful charge: but in the midst of a splendid resistance they received an order from the luckless king to retire to their barracks. Breaking up under the hot fusillade, they were relentlessly pursued, and all who stood their ground at the Tuileries were cut down by the infuriated mob, which then sacked the palace, killing every man found there. Meanwhile the Assembly (or rather the 284 members who dared to show themselves) provisionally dethroned the king, and restored three Girondins to office, with Danton as Minister of Justice. Another National Assembly—the "Convention"—was to be elected by all men of over 25 years of age, to decide on the form of government for the future. The royal family was soon lodged in the 'Temple' and guarded by the all-powerful Paris Commune.

That the 10th of August was the victory, not of the Girondin idealists, but of the desperadoes of the Commune, was soon shown by the terrible September massacres. The new revolutionary Commune seized the control over the police of Paris, over its prisons, and its barriers: it dictated its will to the moribund Assembly, and sent commissioners to the armies. These were in dire disorder; for Lafayette, after failing in an attempt to turn his army and the north-eastern districts against Paris, now fled over the frontier, with Lameth and many other officers. The Prussians, accompanied by a force of French emigrant nobles, took Longwy, and on Sept. 2 the fortress of Verdun surrendered to them; while in the west the peasants of La Vendée began to rise in arms for their king and their faith. It seemed that France, without any real government or well organised armies, must fall beneath the invasion, and that too though crowds of volunteers enlisted to die for the country. This distracting news was the excuse for, though not the cause of, the September massacres in Paris.

The records of the Commune show a careful preparation for this event. Its executive committee established a tribunal to decree summary justice, ordered suspects to be kept in its prisons as "hostages," hired a band of desperadoes, ordered the barriers of Paris to be closed, made a house to house search for suspects; while everywhere the rumour ran that, after the patriots had departed to fight the invaders, the aristocrats with their bands of brigands would hold another St Bartholomew. All was now ready. On Sept. 2—6 the paid agents of the Commune methodically "purged" the prisons" of all who were thought to be aristocrats, though a few suspects were released by order of the tribunal. The National Guard and the police "had no orders" to stop these orgies; the National Assembly and one or two of the Ministers (*not* Danton, Minister of Justice) feebly protested. France shuddered, but turned to face her invaders.

"Oil and vinegar, fire and water, Prussians and Austrians, are united to carry war among 26 millions of men": so wrote Young in 1792. The Duke of Brunswick was equally apprehensive: he thought it unsafe to attempt in 1792 anything more than the reduction of the fortresses on the Meuse; but the Prussian king, Frederick William II, ardent in the cause of monarchy, desired to press on to Paris, though he knew that his troops might soon be needed for more profitable work in Poland. This division of opinion at Prussian headquarters gave time for a genius to infuse a new spirit into the ill-organised French troops. Dumouriez, rallying the fragments of the armies on the Belgian frontier, marched, as ordered by the War Minister, Servan, to seize the position of the Argonne, a low range of clay hills then clad with forests. The invaders seized one of the five forest defiles, and Brunswick, by disregarding the raw levies in his rear, and pressing on for Paris, might have drawn them into the open. He shrank from such a departure from rules, faced round, and attacked the greater part of the French forces on the hill of Valmy. These, animated by their leader, Kellermann, firmly kept their ground, and Brunswick, afraid of losing too many men, called off his troops. It was a cannonade rather than a battle : the troops never came to close quarters, but the moral effect was immense. Goethe, who was with the Prussian army, truly said "From this day and this hour dates a new epoch in the history of the world."

The results of Valmy would not have been so decisive, if the action of Russia in Polish affairs had not called for Prussian intervention there : so Brunswick soon led his troops, enfeebled by dysentery, back towards the Rhine, after coming to a secret understanding with Dumouriez to suspend hostilities. The French general was also anxious to keep his army intact, so as to carry out his pet scheme of invading the Austrian Netherlands. The Austrians, always weakened by the dis-affection of their subjects there, had been foiled by the obstinate resistance of Lille and Thionville; and now, on Dumouriez' advance with superior forces, they fell back on the villages of Jemmappes and Cuesmes, in front of Mons. After desperate charges on both sides, the French troops, advancing to the strains of the Marseillaise, drove the Austrians out (Nov. 6). This great victory laid the Austrian Netherlands and Liège at their feet,—the inhabitants everywhere welcoming them, until fraternity was found to be a mask for spoliation by the French commissioners.

Nice and Savoy were in that autumn overrun by the French almost without striking a blow. The Savoyards were almost entirely French : their land is cut off from the rest of the kingdom of Sardinia by the huge barrier of the Alps. The kings of the House of Savoy rarely visited the cradle of their race. The writings of Rousseau, the sight of Liberty, Equality and Fraternity in France, the hatred of the old feudal

dues, the gabelles, the corvées, in a word, of Piedmontese
supremacy—these had made Savoy French, before Montes-
quiou's troops occupied it (Nov., 1792). At that same time
the Italians in the county of Nice made no resistance. Italian
nationality still slumbered.

German patriotism seemed equally dead, when the dashing
French general Custine, pressing on to the Rhine, seized the
strong fortress of Mainz (Oct. 21), and for a time occupied the
free city of Frankfurt. The Illuminati everywhere welcomed
them; and it seemed that the policy "peace to peoples: war
to governments" would easily overthrow the old Empire.
Dumouriez' statesmanlike plan of seizing the "natural frontiers,"
and surrounding France by friendly democratic republics,
might possibly have prevented the extension of the war; but
unfortunately power at Paris was passing into the hands of
the extreme party, to whom all compromise was treachery.

The National Convention which met at Paris (Sept. 21,
1792) at once proclaimed the Republic, and from that autumnal
equinox a new revolutionary calendar was soon to be dated, in
which the decade replaced the week, while terms conceived in
a naturalistic spirit dethroned the old Roman names of the
months. Everywhere we see the influence of Rousseau in the
abolition of the chaotic social arrangements based on custom,
and the foundation of simple uniform methods on a natural
basis: thus, in place of the old weights and measures, varying
in many districts, came the metric system based on the *mètre*,
with ten as the sole multiple. Amidst all the strifes of its
parties, committees of the Convention quietly laid the basis of
the new social order by a splendid scheme of National Education (drawn up by Condorcet on Rousseau's ideas) in primary
schools, central schools, and a normal school for the instruction
of teachers. Another committee worked at the Civil Code
(afterwards methodized, under Napoleon's orders), which aimed
at founding the whole social life on the principle of equality:

thus, it decreed compulsory equality of inheritance by all the children of a family, a law which—though since slightly modified—has diffused wealth but restricted population in France.

The general aims of the Convention may indeed be summed up in Camille Desmoulins' fine phrase—"to make the people"; but in their application of Rousseau's theories by methods fully as rigid, and almost as faulty, as his reasoning, the revolutionists aroused strife at home and abroad which wrecked their hopes, and led France back, not to a social millennium, but to a military despotism. The Girondins, who at first generally had a majority in the Convention, soon showed their powerlessness in face of the more determined Mountain and the Clubs. They failed to drag the September murderers to justice, and to carry out the enrolment of a Departmental Guard for the Convention. Useless attacks on Robespierre and Danton only brought back the charge that they were plotting to divide the republic "one and indivisible," a charge which was to be their ruin. Even their culture and talents made them suspected by *sansculottes*, to whom Marat's sordid rags and Hébert's obscenity seemed the signs of a true patriot. Every incident was skilfully used against their ministers: thus, when Roland neglected to verify in presence of witnesses the papers found in Louis' "iron chest," he was charged with tampering with them.

These documents fatally compromised Louis XVI, and the Mountain saw that his trial would further embarrass the Girondins, who had some regard for justice and mercy. An enthusiastic follower of Robespierre, the young St Just, thus expressed the views of the extreme Left: "The death of the tyrant is necessary to reassure those who fear that one day they will be punished for their daring, and also to terrify those who have not yet renounced the monarchy. A people cannot found liberty when it respects the memory of its chains." Robespierre, as usual, spoke in the spirit of Rousseau—"When a nation has been forced into insurrection, it returns to a state of nature with regard to the tyrant. There is no longer any law but the safety of the people." The Convention nevertheless decided that Louis should be tried before it. The Jacobins packed the galleries, to intimidate those deputies who leaned towards mercy. In vain Thomas Paine asked that Louis should be banished to America. In vain did several Girondins propose to refer sentence to the primary assemblies of voters. Their party was too disunited to maintain this motion. Though it was once carried, it was soon rescinded, as likely to spread discord in France. The Jacobins, small in numbers, but clear in their views and unscrupulous in their methods, pressed for the king's death with the double aim of discrediting the undecided Girondin party and hurrying on the revolution to further extremes. They succeeded. The last of the Girondin attempts to save the life of Louis, viz. to postpone the execution, fell through, owing to the divisions of their party; and Danton's whispered comment—"Your party is ruined"—reflected the opinion of all France. Finally the Convention voted openly, member by member; and most of the Girondins, from fear of the galleries, voted for death. Even so it was carried only by a majority of one. The silence of horror which speedily followed the execution (Jan. 21, 1793) showed that it outraged the feelings even of Paris. Men knew that the mutterings of La Vendée presaged a civil war. "We have burnt our ships behind us" exultantly cried Marat after the deed; and Danton defied the Powers of Europe to fight—"Let us fling down to the kings the head of a king as gage of battle."

It is a mistake as serious as it is wide-spread to suppose that the war proclaimed by France against England (Feb. 1) was solely a war of principles between a republic and a monarchy. To a large extent it was a question affecting material interests—whether French influence should or should not be paramount in the whole of the Netherlands, Dutch as well as Austrian. It is true that general provocations had a considerable effect in embittering the controversy. Thus, in the exultation caused by the conquest of Savoy, Nice, and the Austrian Netherlands, the Convention abandoned the proclamation of the Constituent Assembly, which forbade wars of aggrandisement. It further passed a decree (Nov. 1792) offering assistance to peoples who rose against their governments; and a month later declared that: " Wherever French armies shall come, all taxes, tithes, and privileges of rank are to be abolished, all existing authorities annulled, and provisional administrators elected by universal suffrage. The property of the fallen government, of the privileged classes and their adherents, is to be placed under French protection...." But a special challenge was also given to England by a decree (Nov. 16) throwing open the navigation of the Scheldt to all nations. By the Triple Alliance of 1788 we had guaranteed to the House of Orange the Dutch Netherlands with all their rights; among these was the control of the lower Scheldt in Dutch territory. This was not a mere abstract question of natural *versus* treaty rights; but the French, then besieging Antwerp citadel, wished to make that port a station for their navy; and French warships sailed up the Scheldt to bombard the citadel.

Hitherto, every principle of sound policy, domestic and foreign, had prescribed to England a pacific policy; and Pitt had maintained a strict neutrality, unmoved by all the diatribes of Burke against the revolution. In the spring of 1792 he had reduced our army and navy; and his great desire was to reduce our national debt, foster trade with France, and uphold Turkey and Poland by diplomatic means against the attempts of Russia, Austria and Prussia. Armed with a secret understanding with Prussia, Catherine II, in the autumn of 1792, was arranging a second partition of Poland. As for the Emperor Francis II, he might, as a set-off to his neighbours' gains, acquire Bavaria instead of his Netherlands—if he could now recover these, so as to offer them in exchange to the Elector of Bavaria. Now, both the partition and the exchange were strongly objected to by Great Britain, it being a cardinal principle of English foreign policy to support a weak State like Poland against powerful and aggressive neighbours, and also to keep the Netherlands in the hands of a generally friendly Power such as Austria, as a firm barrier against French encroachments.

Pitt therefore desired peace, so as to leave England free to resist these revolutionary schemes of the monarchs. At the end of November, he was still desirous of recognising the young French Republic if it would desist from opening the Scheldt; but Chauvelin, the French agent in London, in order to enhance his reputation as an ardent republican, irritated our government by intriguing with the clubs of English malcontents, by striving to stir up revolt in Ireland, and by the assertion that we could not trust our militia. It was in answer to this that our government speedily enrolled the militia and increased the regular forces to 27,000 sailors and 17,000 soldiers. Efforts were made by some persons on both sides, however, to arrive at a pacific settlement. Miles, who had consistently striven to form an Anglo-French alliance, warned an assistant agent who had just been sent from Paris, Maret, that "if the Executive Power in Paris thinks of meddling with our internal affairs or seeks to sow dissension in England, this alliance, so much desired by all sensible people, will never be realised"; but Maret sorrowfully informed him that though orders were sent to Dumouriez not to invade Holland, yet war with England was inevitable not for any reason of external politics, but "in order to get rid of 300,000 armed brigands, who ought not to be allowed to re-enter France." Other evidence points in the same direction, viz. that Pitt desired to bring about a general peace, and, if possible, an Anglo-French alliance, while the French Convention and people, flushed with the brilliant victories of Dumouriez and Custine, saw less danger in war than in the return of their armies. A member of the French Convention wrote to Miles Dec. 9, 1792 in this sense.—"I tell you again that war is inevitable, and that if we had no cause of complaint against the Cabinet of St James, it would be necessary from policy and for our internal security to break with it, rather than consent to a general peace, which, I conceive, is the principal object of your minister. I am not insensible to the difficulties and dangers of a general war, and that whenever England declares against us, we shall have to contend with all Europe; but you seem to have a very imperfect idea of our resources, and of the wonderful enthusiasm which prevails throughout France....It is Mdme Roland's opinion, as well as mine, that we cannot make peace with the Emperor without danger to the Republic, and that it would be hazardous to recall an army, flushed with victory and impatient to gather fresh laurels, into the heart of a country whose commerce and manufactures have lost their activity, and which would leave the disbanded multitude without resources or employment."

We notice here the extension of that policy which was to turn Europe into a gigantic battle-field and blast the efforts of the friends of liberty. Seeing that past dangers had only goaded on the revolutionists to fiercer energy at Paris and on the frontiers, and believing that the British Government was as ripe for overthrow as that of the Hapsburgs, both Girondins and Jacobins drifted into a policy which promised further conquests abroad and temporary respite from internal strife. Thus, long before the advent of Buonaparte, the revolution took that bias towards militarism which was to propagate its principles abroad even while they were being curbed or abrogated in France itself.

On the last day of 1792, the French Minister for the Navy sent a letter to the French sea-ports, urging a descent on England to help their brother republicans: "We will hurl thither

50,000 caps of liberty, we will plant there the sacred tree of liberty." The menacing attitude of the French Convention led to a dignified protest from the British Government. "If France really desires peace and friendship (wrote Grenville to Chauvelin, Dec. 31) she must show herself disposed to renounce her views of aggression and aggrandizement, and confine herself within her own territory, without insulting other governments, without disturbing their tranquillity, and violating their rights." The Executive Council of the Convention held to its point, and by the middle of Jan. 1793 was bent on war.   The execution

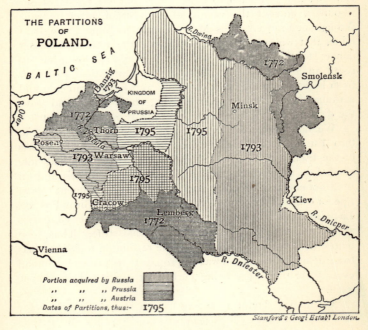

PLAN OF "PARTITIONS OF POLAND."

of Louis made it certain. Chauvelin was ordered to leave England; and the irrevocable step was taken when the Convention unanimously declared war on England and Holland (Feb. 1, 1793).

These events were to react fatally on Poland. England, instead of resisting the further partition of that unhappy State, had thenceforth to support the central Powers against France: to defend the Dutch Netherlands was now her first thought. In May, 1792, a Russian army under Suvóroff had entered Poland. Overpowered by superior force, the Diet abrogated the Constitution of 1791, and soon afterwards the second Partition was carried out. Austria took no part, but Prussian troops co-operated with the Russians, and these two Powers divided the spoils, Prussia receiving Posen, Thorn, and the districts along the Wartha, while Catharine II seized nearly all the land between the upper Dwina and Moldavia. The overthrow of the Polish Constitution of 1791 dealt as fatal a blow to ordered liberty, as the downfall of the sister Constitution of France. Regenerated Poland might have been a solid barrier between Prussia, Russia and Austria. The European system, strengthened by the events of 1791, now fast crumbled away beneath the unscrupulous intrigues of autocrats in the East, and revolutionary violence in the West.

CHAPTER V.

The Jacobins and the First Coalition.

"Solon's weak confidence threw Athens into fresh slavery, while the severity of Lycurgus founded the republic of Sparta on an immovable basis."—(*Decree of the Committee of Public Safety*).

"Without war the republic would not have existed": such were Louvet's words in his attack on Robespierre. The republic was now to be strengthened by a war against kings. When Spain and the Empire joined the Coalition in March, 1793, France was at war with more than half Europe.

The connection between panic on the frontiers and excesses at Paris had been shown in the preceding summer: it is even more closely traceable in 1793. The Austrians, now making a great effort to regain their Netherlands, decisively defeated Dumouriez at Neerwinden (March 18), and drove out the French as quickly as these had overrun the land. There was, in truth, little similarity between the Belgian revolution of 1789—90 and that of France. The former was a strongly national and conservative reaction against the philosophic innovations of Joseph II; and the Belgians soon evinced as little desire for the fraternal embraces of Danton and other French Commissioners as for confiscation of Church lands, and imposition of worthless assignats as payment. The change from the rule of Francis II to that of their 'liberators' was speedily found

to yield no immediate benefits. The statesmanlike Dumouriez
had not only protested against the mad decrees of the Convention and the spoliation of the Belgians, but he had vainly
attempted to save Louis. The War Minister, Pache, now sent
him bitter recriminations and no supplies. Determined to
overthrow the regicides, and if possible to place the young
Louis Philippe on the throne, he entered into secret negotiations with the enemy, imprisoned the Commissioners sent from
Paris to arrest him, and failing to gain over his troops, fled
to the Austrians with Louis Philippe and some 800 men
(April 3).

Had space permitted, the connection between an increase
of national danger and the need of a stronger control over the
executive powers might have been fully detailed. Suffice it to
say that the Legislative Assembly had composed from its 20
committees a Commission to supervise the Feuillant Ministries,
and aid in overthrowing the monarchy. The Convention also,
at the close of 1792, had formed a central Committee of
General Defence of 25 members; but after Neerwinden a small
secret body was needed for vigorous action. "Secrecy is the
soul of government," said Barère. "We must establish the
despotism of liberty" cried Marat "to crush the despotism of
kings." Appalled by the news from Belgium, the Convention
now established (April 6) a secret Committee, at first of nine
members, to control the acts of the Girondin Ministry. This
Committee, known as the Committee of Public Safety, was
also to keep a tight hold on each army by sending one
or more Commissioners to stimulate the devotion of the
soldiers to the republic, to examine and report on the conduct
of the commander, and thereby to secure the dependence of
the military on the civil power. St Just once expressed to the
Committee his fear that some ambitious general would be fatal
to the republic; whereupon Barère replied that this would be
impossible while the Committee existed. The apparatus of

despotism was now nearly perfected, and on the collapse of the Committee it would pass into the hands of any future government.

For the present these powers, and the disposal of a secret fund, enabled the Committee of Public Safety to absorb the functions of the twenty special committees. A weekly report to the Convention placed it under nominal control; but the later Committees, consisting of ten or twelve members, were able to carry out their policy when acting in concert; and the Convention soon became the slave of the Committee. As for the Ministry, it was left with a mere shadow of authority.

There was also a secret Committee of General Security, dating from Aug. 1789, which now enjoyed greatly increased powers. It controlled the police, received the reports of informers, ordered the arrest of conspirators or 'suspects,' and drew up the lists of those who were to be tried by the Revolutionary Tribunal. As its powers threatened to conflict with those of the sister Committee, Danton proposed and carried a decree (Sept. 13, 1793) that its members, as well as those of all the committees, should be named by the Committee of Public Safety, which thus ultimately controlled all the executive functions of the State. For all serious cases the two Committees met together; and they soon found plenty of work for the new Revolutionary Tribunal and its engine. According to a *mot* of the day—The French became republican "*à coups de guillotine.*"

The breach between the Girondins and the Mountain yawned wider every day. The former had lost ground during the trial of the king. Dumouriez' treason was their death-blow; for he had been one of them. In vain did they charge Danton with Orleanism and complicity with the traitor. It added one more powerful voice to their enemies; for Danton and his friends formed the majority in the first Committee of Public Safety. Again, when the extraordinary 'maximum' law aimed at rigorously limiting the price of provisions, the opposition of the Girondists (who knew some political economy) roused the fury of the hungry mob.   After a last vain attempt to quell the disorders, the Convention was surrounded by the Paris National Guards, and was compelled to give up the 22 Girondin leaders. Madame Roland was also arrested.   Some of them escaped to arouse the Departments against the mob-rule in Paris; but the national instinct, except in the royalist west and north, forbade a rising against the new vigorous central power.   Unity alone could save France from the invaders.   A Girondin and royalist rising at Caen was a sorry failure; and the only result of this last flicker of Girondin idealism was that it inspired a beautiful Norman girl, Charlotte Corday, to go to Paris and stab Marat to the heart.   This deed, again, reacted fatally on the Girondins and Moderates.   Guadet, Barbaroux, Pétion, and Buzot were hunted down as traitors in the Gironde Department.   The Girondin party fell because it strove after revolutionary aims while rejecting any resort to mob violence.   It could not cope with the storm which its war policy and overthrow of the monarchy had raised the year before.

In revolutions things tend to extremes.   This same month of July 1793, so fatal to the cause of the ideal republic, saw the Dantonists or ' *indulgents* ' lose their hold on the Committee of Public Safety, the majority of which now became Robespierrist; but, while at Paris power was being seized by the extreme faction, the royalist reaction was gaining strength in the south and west.   At Marseilles and Lyons the citizens, indignant at the violence of the Jacobins who had just seized power, rose in arms, and after sharp fights restored order.   Lyons became the centre of resistance to the Paris committees; but a decree, offering it as plunder to its captors, drew a great revolutionary force, which reduced it (Oct.), decimated its inhabitants, and renamed it "Commune affranchie."   By the autumn the Jacobin triumph, checked in the spring, was complete, except in the west of France. There the simple peasants of La Vendée, attached to the monarchy, the Church, and to the nobles who lived among them, rose in arms (March, 1793) against the regicide republic, which was banishing the orthodox priests, and striving to enrol their own sons in its armies. If they had to fight, they would fight against it, not for it. Luring column after column of the blue National Guards into the depths of the Bocage forest south of Nantes, they defeated them with immense loss. They took Saumur, attacked Nantes and Angers, and tried unsuccessfully to spread the revolt into Brittany and Maine. Even so, it was not till the autumn that they were checked by Kléber with his brave troops, who had had to surrender Mainz to the allies. The want of a thorough and intelligent organisation ever paralysed the royalist efforts. It was not till after decisive defeats of the Vendéan royalists that Brittany and Maine began to rise against the republic in isolated revolts, which soon degenerated into mere brigandage or *chouannerie.*

Checks in the spring and summer, followed by triumphs in the autumn and winter, also marked the course of the war on the frontiers. If the troops of the fifteen States then at war with France had been vigorously led, they might have achieved as much as the half-armed Vendéan peasants; but Poland still interested the Eastern Powers more than France; and after Neerwinden the only important successes of the allies were the capture of Condé, Valenciennes and Mainz. Corsica, under the patriot Paoli, had thrown off the French yoke, Piedmontese and Spaniards were passing the Alps and Pyrenees, and the royalists of Toulon admitted Admiral Hood and an English fleet to hold that great arsenal for Louis XVII (Aug.). These reverses only incited the Jacobins to fiercer energy. Arms, organisation, commanders, ammunition—everything was wanting, except zeal. "Better that 25,000,000 beings should perish, than the republic one and indivisible": such were the words of one of the commissioners of the Convention, whose "powers had no limit save that of the public activity." Arms were forged. Saltpetre works were organised by the chemist, Chaptal. Military camps were formed by the great Carnot, who had signalised his entry into the Committee of Public Safety (Aug.) by calling for a *levée en masse*; and soon 13 armies, of 750,000 men in all, began to press back the disunited allies. The French, having the advantage of a central position, first forced the English and Hanoverians to raise the siege of Dunkirk: in October the Austrians were defeated at Wattignies by General Jourdan; and, at the close of the year 1793, the young St Just, breathing his own fanaticism into the half-clad levies of the republic, headed the charges which drove the Austrians from Weissenburg in the north of Alsace. In the south fortune also favoured the revolutionists, who recaptured Toulon from the English and royalist forces (Dec. 17). There the young Napoleon Buonaparte was virtually in command of the besiegers' artillery, and gave proof of that skill and deter-mination which changed the face of the world; and yet in the official report his name appears only side by side with officers of small note. The close of 1793 saw France freed from foreign foes—an astonishing change which foreshadowed the triumphs of French revolutionary fanaticism, wielded by a vigorous dictatorship, over the disunited governments of Europe.

Meanwhile at Paris the Terror had been ever increasing. Along with the collapse of public credit the *assignats* fell in actual value, and prices of goods rose in proportion. It was in vain for the Convention to order a more stringent tariff of maximum prices. Specie was hidden, or steadily flowed out of the country; for forced loans on the wealthy and progressive taxation scared it away. Speculators and forestallers were denounced, and often guillotined, for causing a scarcity of ready money and dearness of food; but owing to the collapse of public credit and the persistent fall in the exchange, money continued to leave the country; and the economic situation was not improved when the Convention made the French tariff more and more stringent, and finally adopted the heroic remedy of prohibiting all foreign commerce (Oct.—Dec. 1793).

The appalling dangers from domestic treason and the triumphs of the invaders in August had but served to rekindle Jacobin fanaticism and reinforce its despotic power. When, in the early days of September, the Committee of Public Safety was blamed for its want of vigour, the accusers, Billaud-Varenne and Collot d'Herbois, were promptly added to its number. The entry of these sombre blood-thirsty fanatics conciliated the Paris Commune and redoubled the Terror. Chaumette, another man of this faction now predominant in the Commune, proposed and carried through the Convention the infamous Law of Suspects (Sept. 17), subjecting to arrest all courtiers and members of the old privileged classes or the Parlements, all speculators in corn or in *assignats*, and (later on) those who spoke of the misfortunes of the republic and the shortcomings of its authorities. Finally, on the motion of St Just (Oct. 10), the government of France was declared to be "revolutionary" until the general peace. The Revolutionary Tribunal was divided into two sections, to double its speed; and as the property of victims was confiscated to the State, the deficit was partly met—for a time. As Barère, the versatile reporter to the Committee, remarked—"We coin money by the guillotine." Its first notable victim was the widowed Marie Antoinette, her hair blanched ever since the agonies of the flight to Varennes. She nobly repelled the insults of Hébert at the trial, and died calmly, leaving the charge to her son never to revenge the wrongs of his parents. The boy was slowly done to death by the brutalities of his keepers at the Temple. The remaining Girondin chiefs were next put on their trial, and when Vergniaud's noble oratory made the issue doubtful, the trial was closed, and they were condemned, Oct. 29. Philippe Égalité, Madame Roland, Bailly, Lavoisier, Barnave, the generals Custine and Houchard, Manuel, Jourdan *coupe-tête*, the du Barry, mistress of Louis XV, and Madame Elisabeth, sister of Louis XVI, these names of victims will suffice to show the impartiality of Jacobin vengeance on royalists, Feuillants and republicans alike, on vice and virtue, on men of thought and men of blood. To have done something worthy of death if the royalists ever regained power,—this was the only sure pass-port to safety before the Tribunal. On the news of the capture of Toulon, all citizens were held to be suspects who did not show decided joy. And yet a royalist who passed through many dangers noted that as they increased, so did the faculty of disregarding them. Certain it is, that throughout the Reign of Terror the theatres of Paris were full.

Amidst these horrors, the Committee of Public Safety had profited by its victories to definitely constitute the new govern-ment, which its emissaries, the omnipotent 'representatives on mission,' had already enforced in all parts of France. In Nov. 1793, the Convention, on its recommendation, had sternly re-pressed the almost unlimited powers of local self-government which the Constituent Assembly had given to the Communes and Departments. That excessive devolution of power having led to widespread anarchy, there was now a sharp rebound towards centralisation. Henceforth the communes or municipalities were on every tenth day to report to a larger area, the district, how they had executed the revolutionary laws or measures enacted at Paris by the Convention or the two secret Com-mittees; and in place of the elected procureurs-syndics of each district, executive authority was to be wielded by a national agent, appointed by the central power at Paris. Except the apportioning of taxes, no important duty was left to the larger areas, the Departments. In a word, local self-government was succeeded by an almost complete centralisation of power at

Paris; and the publication of a decree in the new official '*Bulletin des Lois*' sufficed to render its execution valid. France was, in fact, ruled by the two secret Committees sitting at the Tuileries.

But while the government was fast becoming an almost irresponsible despotism, France seemed on the verge of moral dissolution.

The revolution passed to its lowest circle of horrors when Hébert and Chaumette—all-powerful in the Paris Commune—installed atheism by dances and the hymn of Reason in Notre Dame. Their followers outraged the tombs of the kings at St Denis, and steeples were ordered to be demolished as an insult to equality! Robespierre, seeking to save the revolution from disgrace, with Danton's aid finally sent these men to the guillotine (March 24).

Danton himself fell next. He was not in the secret Committees, and had for a time retired in disgust. The astute Robespierre now carried with him the Committees and the Jacobins, and, on an insidious charge of complicity with the Orleanists and Dumouriez, crushed his burly rival who had breasted his way to the front by sheer strength, and was now desirous of retiring to rest on his laurels. With Danton fell the witty Desmoulins, and several other '*indulgents*,' guilty of pity or remorse (April 5).

The unwearied labours of M. Robinet and M. Aulard have recently proved that the charges of peculation showered on Danton by Mdme Roland and others are devoid of foundation and that his property did not increase during the revolution. M. Aulard has also discovered the copies of his accounts submitted to the Executive Council, which seem clear and satisfactory. The secret funds which he administered to stimulate the national resistance seem to have been so effectively used as to leave little room for malversation. The efforts to clear Danton of complicity with the September massacres are less successful; but it may be freely granted that he was a straight-forward zealot who knew that the ardent revolutionists were in a minority, and believed it necessary to strike terror into the royalists. With his fall France lost a statesman who could possibly have dominated the course of events. To the very end he protested against needless severity in France and the reckless policy which banded Europe against her. It was he who inspired the decree of April 13, 1793, by which the Convention declared that it would not interfere with the affairs of other peoples.

Robespierre and his Committee were now supreme. The Council of Ministers was replaced by twelve Commissions dependent on the all-powerful Committee of Public Safety, in which Robespierre, Couthon, and St Just formed the dominant 'triumvirate.' Never had there been seen so complete a concentration of power in modern Europe. An order from the Committee sufficed to stop the brutal orgies at Nantes and Lyons; but it was only so as to methodize the Terror at Paris. Rousseau had declared that atheists ought to be banished, as devoid of virtue and the social instincts; so now, his high priest caused the Convention to decree that the idea of a Supreme Being and of the immortality of the soul was a continual appeal to justice. This return to deism was celebrated in a festival, at which Robespierre appeared in ecstasy as the saviour of humanity. The social millennium was surely now at hand !

Murmurs arose at his dictatorial pretensions. To allay them, he redoubled the Terror by the Law of Prairial (June, 1794), framed by him and Couthon alone to render justice more expeditious by suppressing witnesses, and giving to the Committee of Public Safety the right of sending suspects before the Tribunal. The Mountain and most of the members of the Committees felt themselves threatened. Many of the Terrorists, led by Tallien, finally combined to oppose Robespierre, roused the 'sections,' and, victorious in a street fight, sent him and his followers, St Just, Couthon, and many others, to the guillotine (July 28, or 10th Thermidor, 1794). From the law of Prairial up to this Thermidorian reaction, i.e. from June 10 to July 28, as many as 2085 victims fell at Paris.

Robespierre's career exhibits a singular mixture of philosophic fervour with mean intrigue. Puny in person, and uninspiring in speech, he yet had the power which an honest and intense conviction gives to a small nature, even over abler men like Danton, who had less definite principles. Efforts have been made, and with some success, to show that he was at last helplessly pushed along by violent men, who wrenched from his hands the law of Prairial, the weapon which he aimed at them; but a comparison of his rise to power with the number of victims seems to show that his inflexible fanaticism was the mainspring of the Terror. Though his general aim to found a republic of the virtues resembled that of the Girondins, yet his methods were diametrically opposed. If their fall was due to reliance on moral suasion and inability to cope with facts, Robespierre's overthrow resulted as naturally from the very nature of his attempt, to secure liberty by terrorism. "In peace" (he wrote) "the strength of popular government is Virtue. Amidst revolution it is both Virtue and Terror— virtue, without which terror is fatal, terror, without which virtue is powerless." Hence his policy was to methodize the Terror by crushing the factions whose clemency might ruin, or whose excesses might degrade, the republic. It is, moreover, certain that the last excesses of the Terror at Paris were regarded by all as the work of Robespierre. Though his disposition and his methods showed more of feline than of human nature, yet his sincerity of conviction and incorruptibility in the midst of bribers and bribed, must ever raise him above the mere wolves of the clubs and the hyenas of the Commune. The young St Just, even more than Robespierre and Couthon, is a striking instance of fanaticism steeling an estimable nature. Firmly believing that the immorality of the old régime could only be stamped out in blood, he shared with them the hope that the youth of France would be regenerated by a severely Spartan training in the schools of the nation, and by the extirpation of all luxury. Unfortunately for these men, their social experiment broke down towards the end of the guillotine stage, and at the time when they were trying to muzzle the bloodhounds whom they had urged on. Hence their supremacy remains a frightful example of the tyranny of tyrannicides, and the despotism of fanatics in the cause of liberty and equality.

There is one other character in the Committee of Public Safety who merits attention—the great Carnot. Though M. Aulard's researches have recently established Carnot's direct responsibility for its sanguinary deeds, yet it is true that his special task was to organise victory, by drilling and equipping the vast masses of men who rushed to arms. The successes of 1793 were repeated. In June, 1794, the French forced the Austrians to retire from the field of Fleurus; and as the English and Prussians gave little help to their allies, they had even before the defeat determined to evacuate their Netherlands; for Thugut, the Austrian Chancellor, looked to Poland as a near and easy prize. Jourdan's troops soon entered Coblentz, and occupied the whole left bank of the Rhine, where two years before the emigrant nobles had gaily prepared to reduce France. " Eight pitched battles gained, 116 towns and 230 forts taken, 90,000 prisoners and 3,800 cannons captured "—such were the results of the campaigns of 1794, as stated in the Convention (Oct. 21). At the close of the year the French, under Pichegru and Macdonald, easily overran the whole of Holland, a severe frost now rendering untenable fortresses which had defied the might of Louis XIV. In Jan. 1795, Pichegru occupied Amsterdam.

The Dutch patriots everywhere welcomed the French; and the new government of the Batavian Republic at once surrendered its ships to the French, without the intervention of the legendary squadron of French cavalry on the ice. The flight of the Stadtholder to England, and the pursuit of the Prussians by Macdonald as far as the Ems (April), dissolved Pitt's Triple Alliance between England, Prussia, and Holland, and secured French supremacy in Holland—a brilliant contrast to the collapse of Louis XVI's Dutch policy in 1787 before Prussian arms and English menaces. Almost equally decisive were the French successes in the south, where the revolutionists now drove Spaniards and Piedmontese back across the Pyrenees and Alps.

The sequel will show how fatal was the contrast between the patriotism and devotion of the French armies, and the cruelties of the civilians who disgraced the revolution at Paris, Lyons, and Nantes. France was to be found in her armies rather than in the factions struggling for power at Paris. The great commanders—Hoche, Jourdan, Marceau, Kléber, Macdonald, Murat, Davoust, Bernadotte, Masséna, Moreau, and Buonaparte,—began to rise from the ranks. "Victory or the guillotine": such was the alternative which brought the best men to the front, though it sent to the block some good generals, as Houchard and Custine. In the first three years of the war as many as 373 French generals resigned, or were cashiered. In striking contrast to this revolutionary rigour, was the favouritism which placed the fortunes of the allies in the hands of the incompetent Duke of York, or of pedants like Brunswick and Clerfait. Energy, enthusiasm, the weight of numbers, absolute unity of plan, promptness to take the offensive, the advantage of a central position,—these were the main causes of the French triumphs over foes disunited alike in methods and in general policy.

Poland was now, as ever, the ulcer which ate into the

vitals of the First Coalition. In May, 1794, the Poles, inspired by the patriot Kosciusko, rose against the Russian garrison, and soon drove the Prussian forces almost out of the lands which remained to Poland; but the terrible Suvóroff was now at hand with Russian troops whom he had always led to conquest. Kosciusko was badly wounded: the Russians stormed Praga, a suburb opposite Warsaw, with fearful slaughter; and the surrender of the capital was the end of Poland (Nov. 1794). Early in the next year the last partition of this unhappy land was arranged. Catherine II seized all the land between the lower Dwina and Galicia[1]. Austria gained a large tract to the east and south of Warsaw, while Prussia had to be content with Warsaw and the land between the Bug and Niemen. This favour shown to Francis II, who had not fought, was due to his complaisance towards Russian schemes on Turkey, which Prussia had resisted.

The latter Power showed her resentment by deserting the First Coalition and coming to terms with France in the Treaty of Basel (April 5, 1795). The republic evacuated some Prussian land which it had conquered on the right bank (i.e. east) of the Rhine, but retained Clèves and Obergeldern, on its left bank: it accorded peace to those States of the Empire for which Prussia interceded, viz. Saxony, Mainz, the Bavarian Palatinate and the two Hesses. In secret articles of the treaty, France promised, if she gained the Rhine frontier, to help Prussia to compensation on its right bank; while French troops were not to operate north of a demarcation line separating the neutral States of Germany from those which, following the lead of Austria, remained at war with France.

This peace was a terrible blow to the First Coalition. The monarchical crusade broke down owing to the scramble

---

[1] See Plan of the Partitions of Poland, page 76.

for the remains of Poland, and the ceaseless rivalry of Austria and Prussia in German affairs. Prussia now enticed away most of the north and central German States to follow her jackal policy of subservience to France, which finally met with due chastisement in 1806. Catherine II, now near the end of her intrigues and aggrandisements, had not moved a soldier in the crusade which she had ostensibly favoured. Gustavus III had been assassinated by an agent of his turbulent nobles. Spain made peace with France, yielding up her part of Hayti (July, 1795). England, Austria, and Sardinia alone actively persevered with the war. These diplomatic triumphs were the last work of the Committee of Public Safety in its first phase. After crushing foreign and domestic foes, it had virtually gained for France the boundaries desired by Richelieu and Louis XIV—the Rhine, the Alps, the Pyrenees and the Ocean. Its organising energy, aided by Jacobin patriotism, had revealed to the astonished world the weakness inherent in the imposing fabric of the First Coalition.

CHAPTER VI.

The Directory and Buonaparte.

"Despotism is there, watching for the moment of our exhaustion to offer us peace and bread, along with chains!"—BUZOT.

EVENTS in France had shown how short could be the steps from anarchy to despotism. Indeed, if Robespierre had been a less sincere republican and a man of greater powers, he could probably have seized the dictatorship which St Just proposed for him. By his fall the tendencies towards despotism were temporarily checked: but France had learnt that only a strongly centralised power could save the republic in time of danger, and the attempts at a royalist reaction were now to favour the rise of a far abler man than the pedant of Arras.

We have seen that the Thermidorian reaction was begun by a few terrorists from personal fear. Its main strength, however, was in the support of the many, who were weary of bloodshed. The long terrorised Convention now regained its powers from the two secret committees, which for a time sank to the level of the other 14 committees of the Convention supervising the special executive departments. It further abolished the payment of citizens who attended the meetings of the 'sections' of Paris,—a premium on sedition: it closed the Jacobins' Club for a time, and the Paris Commune entirely, and recalled to its midst the wrecks of the Girondin party;

while nearly all the most prominent terrorists—except Carnot, Tallien, and Fouché—were guillotined or banished. The suppression of forced loans, of the ridiculous 'maximum' law, of the persecuting decrees against priests and emigrant nobles, as well as the abolition of revolutionary names, marked a still further return to ordinary government. In vain were two attempts made by the mob to overawe the Convention. The National Guards freed the deputies, though not till one had lost his life (May 20). The disarming of the revolutionary suburb, St Antoine, and the presence of regular troops, at last ensured some rest to Paris.

The Convention was equally determined to prevent a recoil towards monarchy, and three events in 1795 dashed the royalist hopes. The little Louis XVII, as he was called, at last succumbed in June to the brutal attempts of his keepers to wear out his frail life; so now the succession passed to the Comte de Provence (Louis XVIII), hated by Frenchmen as being at the head of the emigrant nobles. An equal misfortune was the disastrous failure of these *émigrés* to make a descent at Quiberon in Brittany and rekindle the embers of revolt. Though supported by an English fleet, they were shut in by the able young General Hoche ; and by the orders of Tallien, who wished to clear himself of charges of royalism, some 700 nobles were shot in cold blood. Hoche succeeded in pacifying the north-west of France, where the genuine royalism of the peasants had proved to be as serious a danger to the republic as all the armies of the coalition. Still the royalist reaction gathered strength in other parts of France; and the Convention, afraid of trusting to the voice of the nation at the forthcoming elections, decreed, as an appendix to its new Constitution (Aug. 1795), that two-thirds of the next Legislature must be chosen from the members of the Convention itself. This unheard of violation of electoral freedom exasperated all malcontents, whether royalists or constitutionalists; and 40,000 National

Guards of Paris, mainly royalist after the purging of pikemen and *sans-culottes* from their ranks, openly menaced the Convention. Barras, entrusted with its defence, bethought him of the young artillery officer Buonaparte, then in Paris. He, who had helped to regain Toulon, was now to defend the republic at its very heart. Murat seized cannons from the Sablons camp. These Buonaparte planted so as to sweep the approaches to the Tuileries, where the Convention sat. For the first time in the revolution was seen the effect of cannon in a street fight. The royalists were swept from the riverside quays ; and Buonaparte brought his guns to bear on the church of St Roch, and then along the Rue Honoré (Oct. 5). The republic was saved —by the man who was to overthrow it, and by the means which have always been fatal to constitutional liberty.

The importance of Buonaparte's service at Paris can hardly be over-estimated. It enabled the Convention to impose on France a republican Legislature, and its new Constitution. That of 1793 having been set aside at Thermidor, France was subjected to a new experiment, which, avoiding the defects of that of 1791 and the despotism of the Committees, was yet strongly republican. Every citizen who had lived a year in one place and paid a tax could vote for 'electors,' who in their turn voted for the 750 deputies. These were to form two Chambers : the 500 younger members (none under 30 years were eligible) were, in three 'readings,' to propose decrees, which then came before the 250 older members in the Council of Ancients,—a democratic form of Senate. The executive powers were to be controlled by a Directory of five, who supervised the execution of decrees by Ministers named by them and individually responsible to them. The Directory therefore inherited the chief functions of the Committee of Public Safety: both derived their powers from the Legislature, deliberated secretly, controlled the action of the Ministers, and, in fact, aimed at securing unity of action in the legislative and executive powers. The two fatal defects in the present ingenious arrangement were that the Directors had no legal means of opposing a law passed by the two Councils ; and that, as one Director in five was to retire each year, while one third of the Councils was submitted to annual re-election, the latter would change their political complexion more quickly than the former. Hence, in any time of reaction or disaffection, conflicts were sure to break out between Directory and Councils, which would wreck the Constitution and leave the ground clear for any skilful intriguer.

The Convention, quietly finishing the most stormy career known to any representative Assembly, now handed on its powers to the Councils and the Directors named by them : these were Barras, Carnot, La Réveillère, Letourneur, and Rewbell (Oct. 1795). For the first two years all worked well. A firm national government began to quell the brigandage rife in many parts of the west. To quote Mdme de Staël : " The old landlords lived quietly side by side with buyers of land confiscated by the nation : the roads in the country became safe : the armies were only too victorious : liberty of the press was restored ; and one could have called France a free country, if the two classes of nobles and priests had enjoyed the same guarantees as other citizens." In brief, the government was Girondin in spirit, but Jacobin in energy ; and in May 1796 it promptly suppressed a communistic plot, headed by Babeuf and some members of the old Hébertist faction, who desired to overthrow the Directory and abolish property, " the greatest scourge of society, a veritable public crime." Events, how-ever, were tending not towards Communism, but were even now favouring the rise of the greatest autocrat of modern times.

The young Napoleon Buonaparte, born at Ajaccio in 1769, united the Florentine skill and suppleness of his father's family with the Corsican pride and stubbornness of his mother's race ; and his early life, spent amidst family feuds and civil strifes, inured him to habits of intrigue and violence. Sent by his father to the military schools at Brienne and Paris, he there evinced a versatility of genius and a masterful temper, which startled his comrades. The first year of the Revolution found him with poor health and prospects, working hard in his spare time at a *History of Corsica*, and sympathising with the abolition of privileges; but the mob violence in June 1792 aroused his disgust. "One must confess (he wrote) when one sees all this close at hand, that the people are little worth the trouble that one takes to deserve their favour." A little later, on returning to Corsica, he even for a time thought of offering his services to the British East India Company, for they "made more account of a good artillery officer than the French did." And yet, though admiring Paoli's Corsican patriotism as much as he probably detested the Jacobinical terrorists then devastating France, he would not hear of the separation of Corsica from France; and when the islanders, led by Paoli, definitely threw off the foreign yoke (April, 1793), the Buonapartes took the side of the French, and were forced to flee to Marseilles.

There they espoused the cause of the dominant Jacobin faction; and Napoleon talked and wrote the revolutionary jargon with such success as to be called the "little Robespierre." His services at Toulon availed to save his head after the fall of the Robespierrists, and procured his liberty. After varying fortunes, he entered the topographical bureau of the Committee of Public Safety, taking Carnot's place for a time (Aug. 1795). The strange whirl of events drew from him these strange reflections in a letter—"Everything makes me brave death and destiny. My reason is sometimes startled at this; but it is the effect which the moral spectacle of France, and the custom of running risks, have produced in me." He even applied for leave to go to Constantinople to organise the Sultan's artillery; but, fortunately for himself, was refused leave, owing to the critical state of France; and at the same time, after resigning his post in the topographical committee, he was cashiered by an order of the Committee of Public Safety for not having proceeded to a post assigned him in the army campaigning in La Vendée. In September all careers seemed closed to the thin yellow-cheeked ex-officer. In October he was hailed as the saviour of the Republic for dispersing the Paris malcontents; and the grateful Barras now smoothed the way for his marriage with a charming widow, Josephine de Beauharnais. The story that Barras also gave him the command of the army of Italy as a dowry for Josephine is disproved by the evidence of two other Directors, Carnot and La Réveillère. It was Carnot's discernment of Buonaparte's great abilities which most availed to gain him this command; for the " organizer of victory" desired to replace the incompetent General Schérer by one who had shown his powers of energetic action, and had also sent in a remarkable plan of campaign for the war in Italy. Buonaparte owed little or nothing to favour: he forced his way to the front by sheer power and ability. " I am terrified" (wrote Josephine) "at the empire which he seems to exercise on all who come near him. His keen gaze has something uncanny and inexplicable in it which imposes even on the Directors....'My brothers in arms will all be only too happy some day to have my protection (he said to me): my sword is at my side, and with it I will go far.'" Such were the influences which moulded a character naturally proud, ambitious, profoundly able and far-seeing. The Italian blood of his father is seen in his appreciation of the arts and his far-reaching powers of intrigue and civil organisation. As a Corsican chieftain ('caporal') he ever at heart despised the Jacobin rabble, and sought the aggrandizement of his family; and his masterful personality was completely to dominate a generation enervated by the sentimentalism of Rousseau and well-nigh paralysed by the fever of revolution. Events brought him to the front when France was saddled with a third impracticable Constitution, when the energy of her armies had all but broken the First Coalition; and fortune sent him against that part of Europe which offered the most splendid field for conquest.

The revolutionists, after beating back all the attempts of the Austrians and Piedmontese to regain Nice and Savoy, had already conquered the Italian Riviera as far as Savona. North of this seaport there is a depression which marks off the Maritime Alps from the Apennines. There the Piedmontese and Austrian forces were posted—in all about 52,000 men. Bonaparte (so he spelt his name from this time) inspired his 40,000 men, badly equipped, but inured to war, by his trenchant words—"Soldiers, I am to lead you into the most fertile plains in the world. There you will find honour, glory, and riches." He at once put in force his four maxims— "Divide for finding provisions: concentrate to fight: unity of command is necessary for success : time is everything."

His first aim was to strike at the joint connecting the allied armies; and by five successful battles in and beyond the pass (April 12—25, 1796) he forced them back on divergent lines of retreat, the aim of the Austrians being to protect Milan, that of the Piedmontese to cover their capital Turin. Seeing his exhausted little State open to the incursions of a powerful foe, the King of Sardinia at Cherasco concluded an armistice, consenting to cede to France Savoy and Nice, and allowing Bonaparte to occupy the fortresses of Coni, Tortona, and Alessandria (April 28). In 16 days he had detached Sardinia from the Coalition.

It now remained to drive the Austrians out of their Milanese province, of which the only great stronghold was Mantua. The Austrian general Beaulieu had lined the banks of the swiftly flowing Ticino; but Bonaparte outflanked this strong position by a secret and speedy march along the south bank of the Po, and by the seizure of Piacenza. Crossing the Po at this city, he was now almost in the rear of the Austrians : these

. hastily fell back on the Adda, another northern affluent of the Po, trusting to 10,000 men and 20 cannon to render the long narrow bridge of Lodi impregnable. Bonaparte sent forward a column of 6000 picked men to charge over the bridge: a storm of shot tore through its ranks. Again the young general with Lannes, Berthier, and Masséna cheered on his men; while French cavalry, fording the river higher up, turned the scale in favour of the French. Bonaparte's daring won him the title of "le petit caporal" from his soldiers. "It was a strange sight (says Bourrienne) to see him on the bridge of Lodi: mixed up with his tall grenadiers he looked a mere boy." Lodi cleared Lombardy of the Austrians: and the French, amidst popular rejoicings, entered Milan fifteen days after the second part of the campaign began.

Twenty-nine days sufficed to hurl back the remains of the Austrian forces beyond the Mincio into Mantua, or up the valley of the Adige; also to make a rapid incursion into the northern part of the Papal States (the Legations) and to confiscate English merchandize at Leghorn (June).

The next events bear even more strongly the impress of a master mind. The French were besieging Mantua, when they learnt that a new Austrian army of some 47,000 men, under General Würmser, was marching to its relief in two parts, one west, the other east, of L. Garda. There was only one hope of safety for Bonaparte's 42,000 men—to raise the siege of Mantua, and fall on the two parts before they re-united. He crushed the western army at Lonato (Aug. 3), and by skilful manœuvres at Castiglione cut in half Würmser's main force, pressed it back into Tyrol, again defeating it at Bassano. The gallant old Austrian finally reached Mantua; but in a fortnight he had lost 27,000 men to a force less than his own. The effect of concentrated vigorous action against superior, but disunited forces, has never been more strikingly shown[1].

[1] The figures given above are from official sources and therefore differ from the estimates given by Thiers. See my articles on Col. Graham's Reports on the Italian Campaign in the *Eng. Hist. Rev.* of 1899.

Another Austrian army under Alvintzy descended the Adige, and checked the French at Caldiero; but Bonaparte's skill and persistence at Arcola compelled the foe to retire outflanked after three days of desperate fight (Nov.). The crowning victories of Rivoli and La Favorita (Jan. 1797) reduced the Austrians to despair, and Mantua to surrender (Feb. 2).

A fortnight's campaign against the Papal States next showed the utter weakness of the Pope's temporal power. The Papal troops hardly awaited the onset of the French; and by the Treaty of Tolentino (Feb. 1797) the Pope gave up all claims to Avignon, paid a war indemnity and yielded up many precious manuscripts, pictures and statues, beside ceding the Legations of Bologna and Ferrara, and the Romagna. These districts soon formed, with Austrian Lombardy and Modena (whose Duke had been deposed by Bonaparte), a compact State called the Cisalpine Republic,—the nucleus of the future Kingdom of Italy. From the outset the new State was completely under French control. As Bonaparte frankly said to Melzi—"Italy contains still fewer elements of republicanism than France: but we must temporize with the fever of the moment, and we are going to have one or two republics here of our own particular kind." The kind was to be that which would admit of changes responsive to changes in France. For the present, however, the summoning of a representative Assembly, the abolition of feudal dues, and a decree of civic equality, seemed the dawn of a new political and social life for Italy.

In the spring of 1797, Bonaparte resumed hostilities against the Austrians, drove them across the Carnic and Noric Alps, and dictated preliminaries of peace at Leoben, within two days' march of Vienna. He thus snatched the laurels of victory from the French forces on the Rhine. These under the command of Jourdan and Moreau had been about to effect a junction near the upper Danube, when the Austrian Archduke Charles completely defeated the former near Würzburg. Jourdan's retreat behind the Rhine was fatal to Moreau's plans; and the latter only by great skill and determination withdrew his troops into Alsace (Oct. 1796). The Directory had, therefore, to support these beaten troops; while Bonaparte's forces were living on Italy and were even sending to Paris contributions levied on the liberated people, to fill up the yawning gulf of the French exchequer. In the spring of 1797, Hoche, replacing Jourdan, crossed the Rhine and gained a success; yet Moreau could not cross that river for want of pontoons, before the news came of the armistice with Austria. The army of the Rhine seemed doomed to misfortune. In September following, the death of its able commander, the sincere republican Hoche, removed a possible rival from Bonaparte's path.

Another motive, connected with new and far vaster political schemes, urged Bonaparte to arrange matters with Austria. The Venetians had been enraged at the exactions of the French and at the protracted violation of their neutral territory. At Eastertide, 1797, the people of Verona rose and massacred several of the French wounded left in hospital; and elsewhere risings against the 'liberators' provoked severe reprisals. Other excuses for disputes with the Venetian Republic led to menaces from Bonaparte which frightened the timid oligarchs into resignation; and under pretence of coming to terms with their democratic successors, he gained control of Venice, its fleet, and even its Ionian Isles. While on May 26, 1797, he assured the new municipality of Venice that "its people alone were worthy of liberty," on the very next day he wrote to the Directory:—"Venice, which has been decaying ever since the discovery of the Cape of Good Hope, and the rise of Trieste and Ancona, can hardly survive the blows we have just struck. With a cowardly and helpless population, in no way fit for liberty, without territory and without rivers, it seems natural that she should be left to those to whom we give the mainland territory." As for her Ionian Isles, he wrote later on, France must take them; for "the time is not far distant when we shall feel that, to destroy England, we must make Egypt ours."

This explains the favourable terms of peace finally granted by him to Austria in the Treaty of Campo Formio (Oct. 17, 1797). Francis II, though ready to give up all claim to his Netherlands, firmly demanded all Venetia as far as the R. Oglio; and Bonaparte, desirous of isolating England, finally acceded (sorely against the wishes of the Directory) to his acquisition of Venetia east of the Adige, and all the possessions of Venice along the Adriatic, viz. Istria and Dalmatia. France was to acquire the Austrian Netherlands, the Ionian Isles and the Venetian fleet. Austria recognized the Cisalpine Republic, which was to include Lombardy, the western part of Venetia, the Legations, Romagna, and Modena; and she was to give the Breisgau to the deposed Duke of Modena. In secret articles she promised to recognize the extension of the French frontier as far east as the Rhine. As a set-off to her losses she received most of the Venetian lands, and she soon gained Salzburg for one of her Arch-Dukes. (See Map opposite page 126.)

It remains to sum up the results of this brilliant campaign on the combatants, on Italy, and on the relations of Bonaparte to the Directory.

The Treaty of Campo Formio shattered the remains of the once great First Coalition. England alone was left to struggle against the ever increasing power of France; for the Directors had curtly repulsed attempts made by Pitt to come to an understanding. France now definitively gained what Louis XIV had vainly striven for, the Rhine frontier down to the border of the Batavian Republic, which was virtually subject to her. She had gained her "natural frontiers" on the south-east by the definitive acquisition of Savoy and Nice; and now by the formation of her dependent Cisalpine Republic, she held the balance of power in Italy; while her Ionian Isles were so many stepping stones towards Egypt. On the other hand, Austria, after terrible disasters in Italy, still held a commanding position there, and by the acquisition of Venice and Dalmatia became a sea-power. If she had lost her outlying possessions such as the Netherlands, Breisgau, and Milan, she had consolidated her territory; and had the prospect of doing so still more in the disputes for German lands soon to begin at Rastadt.

Italy had just received a shock comparable to that dealt by the French King Charles VIII in 1494, so fatal to the older order of things in Italy as in Europe. The once vigorous kingdom of Sardinia had lost its transalpine provinces; and in 1798 the king fled to Sardinia when his capital was menaced by French troops. The Republic of Venice, on the most frivolous pretext, was made a victim to Bonaparte's policy, and partitioned with Austria, even against the protests of the Directory. Its sister Republic of Genoa was encouraged to overthrow its oligarchs, and under the new name of the Ligurian Republic, became nominally democratic, but really French. The most important State of the peninsula, the Cisalpine Republic, accepted a French form of government, was occupied by French troops, and sent frequent subsidies to Paris. Lucca, Tuscany, and Naples were left alone for a time. The Pope's temporal power, already crumbling away, was early in the next year replaced by a Roman Republic proclaimed by a French general.

The Directors had hoped to be free from Bonaparte's dictation during the Italian campaign; but when they proposed to send him Kellermann as his equal in command, his retort "one bad commander is better than two good commanders" showed not only his sounder judgment but his

complete independence. Throughout the campaign he accustomed his officers and soldiers alike to look to him alone
for advancement and wealth; and while conducting the
negotiations with Austria, in defiance of the Directors' orders,
he had an opportunity of rendering them also subservient to
him. The royalist reaction in France brought to a crisis the
inevitable conflict between the Directory and the Councils.
As has been pointed out, the Councils were renewed by one-
third every year; while only one of the five Directors was subject
to annual re-election by the Councils. Thus, by the middle
of 1797, while four of the five Directors were Jacobins, there
was a royalist majority in the Councils and the country. At
Marseilles, Lyons and elsewhere the old Jacobin party had
met with its deserts from royalist vengeance in the "white
terror"; and the royalist club at Clichy on the outskirts of the
capital aimed at overthrowing the Directory. Two reasons
impelled Bonaparte to crush this reaction. Not only would
the return of Louis XVIII be fatal to his hopes, but also
the French armies still retained much of their revolutionary
fervour. They were fighting against feudal Europe and
knew little of Jacobin cruelty and the meanness of the new
despotism at Paris. " The soldiers are asking (wrote Bonaparte) whether they are to be rewarded by assassination on
their return home:...I see that the Clichy Club means to
pass over my corpse to the destruction of the Republic."
He therefore sent his General Augereau, a blustering Jacobin,
with a strong body of troops to Paris. These in the early
morning of 18th Fructidor (Sept. 4, 1797) surrounded the
Tuileries, where the Councils were sitting, and arrested 53
deputies; while three Directors caused their royalist colleague
Barthélémy to be arrested; even the great Carnot, who now
desired peace and moderation, only saved himself by flight.
As a sequel to this Pride's Purge, liberty of the press was
suspended, the elections in forty-nine of the Departments

were annulled, many deputies, including the now royalist General Pichegru, were banished to Cayenne, and the old persecuting laws against non-juring priests and nobles were re-enacted. In fact, there was a recrudescence of the Terror, "into which (as the Duc de Broglie wrote) France plunged without consolation and without hope."

This *coup d'état* of Fructidor 1797 was followed by a national bankruptcy. The Directory had in vain replaced the worthless *assignats* by *mandats territoriaux*, directly exchangeable for the national lands. The expedient only enriched stock-jobbers and swelled the vulgar ostentation of the *nouveaux riches* at Paris, which showed itself in *fêtes* resplendent with Greek costumes, and in a life depraved by worse than Greek immorality. In fact, now that the old bonds of society were broken, there remained no other ideal of conduct than the Rights of Man, and a fantastic Deism, into which La Réveillère tried hard to breathe some life. It was in vain. The feverish gaiety was only a proof of the despair and utter unrest of the times. Men shut their eyes to the future; for the past five years had seen the revolution reverse most of the aims of 1789. Instead of liberty and equality there was an equality in servitude to a vulgar despotism propped up by bayonets; and the crusade to liberate Humanity had ended in wars of conquest and plunder. A careful study of the inner significance of events shows that the fundamental cause of this degradation was the absence of any inspiring principle of social and political duty. What wonder then, that in the cruel disenchantment which followed on the roseate hopes of 1789, France, weary of being tossed from one extreme to another, turned her gaze more and more away from the moral and political chaos at Paris, to the discipline, devotion, brilliance and glory of the army of Italy and its young leader?

The victor of eighteen pitched battles, who in a year had changed the face of Italy and Europe, was received with boundless enthusiasm at Paris; and Barras, clasping the conqueror to his breast, exclaimed—"Go, capture the giant corsair that infests the seas: go, punish in London outrages that have been too long unpunished." Under the guise of admiration for his genius, the Directors nourished a secret fear of his domination, and desired above all his absence from Paris; and for other reasons of State, the time seemed favourable for the reduction of England's power. Our economic troubles were scarcely less than those of France; for in the spring of 1797 the Bank of England stopped cash payments, and for 22 years we subsisted on what was virtually a paper currency. In 1795—6 the price of wheat was for some time over £5 the quarter; and there had been bread riots in London. If the naval victories of St Vincent and Camperdown (1797) restored to us the supremacy of the high seas, yet the mutinies at the Nore and Spithead in that very year had threatened our ruin. The alliance between France, Holland, and Spain gave the Directory a fleet numerically stronger than ours. The Mediterranean was fast becoming a French lake; for we had lost our hold on Corsica, and then held only Gibraltar, while France was now mistress of Northern Italy and the Ionian Isles, and secretly bought over the Commander of the Knights of St John at Malta. In India, Tippoo Sahib, helped by the French, was contesting our supremacy. Cape Colony, it is true, had in 1795 been acquired by a British force from the Dutch. But if France seized Egypt, could she not cut off our Eastern commerce, and so compel us to surrender? "Let us concentrate all our activity on our fleet (wrote Bonaparte to Talleyrand, Minister for Foreign Affairs) and destroy England. That done, Europe is at our feet." The Directors were equally anxious to send away their imperious deliverer on a distant enterprise; and Bonaparte, though it realised a dream of his youth, fostered the impression that he was being banished by the jealous Government.

Two other events in the early part of 1798 increased the responsibilities of the Directory, when they were losing their best support. The murder of a French general at Rome gave the excuse for French troops to march in and proclaim the Roman Republic (Feb. 1798). The Pope was removed in honourable captivity, which he survived for only a year; and the Eternal City furnished rich plunder in jewels and still more precious objects of art. The latter were sent to adorn the Paris museums: the former went towards the expenses of the Toulon armada.

The invasion of Switzerland had a similar result. There had been risings in Valais and in the subject district of Vaud, against the oligarchic rule of the old governing cantons or towns. The unionists, who desired a closer union of the 13 cantons on the basis of complete political equality, received the help of the French. The forces of oligarchic Berne and of the democratic 'forest cantons' were overpowered by the invaders; and though the mountain districts bravely held out, yet by 1799 they were reduced. Cantonal and municipal privileges and exceptional governing powers were at once abolished. Vaud was freed from the rule of Berne, and the vale of the upper Ticino from the control of Uri. What had previously been a league of cantons with sovereign powers, now became, at the order of the Paris Directory (April, 1798), "the one, indivisible, democratic and representative Helvetic Republic," the cantons being subdivided so as to form mere administrative Departments. Fortunately this new centralised Government, imposed from Paris, did not permanently replace the primæval democracy of the forest cantons, where the citizens had hitherto always met in a *Champ de Mai* for the adoption of laws and the election of their magistrates. The old federal system was partly restored by Bonaparte in his Act of Mediation of 1803; and Switzerland ultimately gained by the abolition of municipal bureaucracy and cantonal inequalities.

The immediate results of the French invasion were the annexation of Geneva, Biel and Mühlhausen by France, and the plunder of the treasuries at Berne, Zurich, Lucerne, Fribourg, &c., for the benefit of Bonaparte's expedition. The ex-Director Carnot thus vigorously characterised the whole affair: "The Directory has sought where it could find most free men to immolate, and so has flung itself on Switzerland."

In May, 1798, the French armada was ready to sail. Bonaparte was ordered to seize Malta and Egypt, with which France was at peace, to cut through the isthmus of Suez, and to drive the English from India. The first detail was easily accomplished. The Grand Master of the Knights of St John had been bought over by the French; only a pretence of resistance was made; and Valetta passed into the hands of the French. After remaining there a week to organize his new conquest, and showing his splendid powers of administration, Bonaparte sailed for Alexandria. Fortunately for him, Nelson, in his eager search for the French, had left that port the day before. The French hurriedly disembarked and captured the city by a rush. Then ensued a weary march across the desert to the Nile and Cairo. Loud were the complaints of his men— this then was the land where they were to gain enough money to buy six arpents of land apiece on their return! A brilliant victory near the Pyramids, over the splendid Mameluke cavalry, and the plunder of this governing caste, reconciled the French to Egypt. Bonaparte occupied Cairo, and was organizing his new colony, when news of a disaster came.

Nelson, after twice narrowly missing Bonaparte's armada, had at last found the French men-of-war drawn up near the shoals of Aboukir Bay. "Where there is room for ships to swing, there is room for my ships to run alongside between them and the shoal," was Nelson's reasoning; and, near sunset though it was, he placed the French line, as it lay at anchor, between two fires. After three hours' desperate conflict, the French flagship, l'Orient, caught fire and blew up; and by morning, out of the French squadron of 16 ships only four had escaped (Aug. 1—2).

"We are condemned to do something great" was the resolve of the indomitable Bonaparte, on hearing of this disaster. He laboured to assure his position by developing the resources of Egypt, and by a public profession of Mohammedanism. "Do you not think that the Empire of the East was worth a turban and a pair of loose trousers?" was his subsequent comment on this burlesque. After crushing a revolt at Cairo, and inspecting the traces of the old canal cut across the isthmus, he resolved to strike at Turkey by an invasion of Syria. After defeating the Turks at Jaffa and massacring some 2,500 prisoners who encumbered his march, he attacked Acre; but his siege artillery had been captured by Sir Sidney Smith, while on its way from Alexandria, and was now used against the French. Assault after assault was beaten back with heavy loss; and though the French routed near Mt Tabor a Turkish relieving force, yet all Bonaparte's efforts (March—May, 1799) failed against Acre—"that miserable hole which came between me and my destiny." With some 8,000 men, many afflicted by the plague, he retreated to Egypt, to show his and their prowess by driving a Turkish force into the sea at Aboukir. During the exchange of prisoners which followed, Sidney Smith sent him a packet of French newspapers. In them Bonaparte eagerly read news of France threatened by the Second Coalition, of Italy lost to her, of the Directory once again threatened by the royalist reaction. If ever he was to seize power, it must be now. Casting aside his dreams of an Eastern Empire stretching from the Ganges to the Danube, he bequeathed his "exhausted enterprise" to Kléber; and taking with him Berthier, Lannes, Marmont, Murat, and a few other generals, he secretly sailed for France, which by marvellous good fortune he reached in time to be rapturously received as the conqueror of the East (Oct. 1799).

His expectations with regard to the failures of the Directory had been more than realised. Its foreign and domestic policy was at once exasperating and weak. Only a firm conciliatory government could have made its new conquests a source of strength. Instead of that, the Germans of its Rhineland were irritated by the appointment of Frenchmen to every paid post; and even the Illuminati lost their enthusiasm for France when the four new Rhenish Departments were seen to be mere *pashalics* for the favourites of the Directory. It is true that many changes, such as social equality, trial by jury, and the abolition of tithes and feudal dues, were generally welcomed; but the laws which abolished the old German education, from the school to the University, in favour of the new French system, and other decrees which compelled the observance of the *decadi* in place of Sunday, and handed over all monastic and Church property to the administration of French officials, soon provoked a return of German feeling.

This reaction of sentiment encouraged Austria and the dis-possessed German princes; and French demands met with increasing resistance at the Congress of Rastadt, which from Sept. 1797 to April 1799 was settling the affairs of Germany. The weakness of the Germanic system was glaringly shown at this Congress, State quarrelling with State, while the German princes, dispossessed of their domains west of the Rhine, clamoured for "compensation" at the expense of the ecclesi-astical lands. A great ruler might even then have banded most of Germany together against France; but when the dissolute and hapless Frederick William II of Prussia died in 1797, his successor, of the same name, continued the spiritless policy of alliance with France, which long cleft Germany in twain. Austria, however, felt herself threatened by the French occupation of Switzerland and by the dictatorial treatment of the Cisalpine Republic by the Directory and its generals. The excitable Czar Paul, who had succeeded Catherine in 1796, imagined himself insulted by the seizure of Malta, of which he desired to be the protector; and the Bourbons of Naples, alarmed at the creation of the new Roman Republic and the spread of French principles, were openly meditating war. Nelson on his return from Egypt was rapturously welcomed by the Neapolitan Court, and developed a plan for the restoration of Italy to its old rulers.

The Directory, after passing the first law of universal conscription (Sept. 1798), sent armies to occupy Naples and Turin, whence the kings fled to their insular possessions, Sicily and Sardinia respectively, and the south of Italy was now reorganized by the French as the Parthenopaean Republic; while the occupation of Lucca and Tuscany completed their domination in Italy.

A slight acquaintance with facts suffices to dispel the error that the Coalitions were "built up by Pitt's gold." To the French this has seemed a sufficient cause for events which really resulted quite naturally from their own aggressions. This Second Coalition was an attempt made by Russia, which took the initiative, England, Austria, Naples, Portugal and Turkey, to set some limits to French domination, which had now spread from the mouth of the Adige to that of the Rhine. At first the allies gained some signal successes. The young French conscripts were not ready to take the field; and only about 180,000 trained troops were ready to defend this immense line. Bonaparte and many of the best generals and troops were in the sands of Syria. Jourdan was badly beaten at Stockach, near Lake Constance (March, 1799); and even the brilliant and tenacious Masséna could make no headway against the superior numbers of the Austrians, who began to invade the central bastion of the French line—Switzerland. The struggle entered on a new phase when two of the French envoys to the Congress of Rastadt were after its close (April) assassinated by Austrian hussars, who carried off their papers.

In Italy the arrival of a great Russo-Austrian force under Suvóroff and Mélas drove back the French from the Adige and even from Milan, which the Russians entered in triumph. Moreau withdrew his shattered forces behind the strongholds of Alessandria and Genoa, there to await the arrival of Macdonald from the south. This able general had long held southern Italy against vastly greater forces of insurgents. Brushing these aside, he now tried by a skilful march across the Apennines and along the River Po to join hands with Moreau. After some successes he was overwhelmed by the Russians at the Trebbia (June); and the two French armies in Italy, passing the Apennines, had much difficulty in uniting near Genoa (June). Except the Genoese coast line, Italy was lost to the French; and, as they retired, the artificial character of their rule was shown by wide-spread insurrections. A defeat at Novi (Aug.) completed their disasters in the very land which Bonaparte had associated with victory.

In September the folly of the allies and the genius of Masséna somewhat turned the scale. Owing to the complaints of Austrian generals at Suvóroff's arrogance, he was finally required to cross the Alps, join the Russian forces under Korsakoff, and drive the French out of Switzerland. The power of jealousy to wreck a whole campaign has rarely been more signally shown. After toiling for five days over the St. Gothard pass, against a skilful resistance, he arrived at the southern end of the Lake of Lucerne (Sept. 26) to find no help from Russians or Austrians; for Masséna on that very day seized the opportunity offered by the withdrawal of the Archduke Charles northwards, to crush Korsakoff's Russians at Zürich, capturing all their cannons, stores, treasure, and nearly one-fourth of their men. Korsakoff led the wreck of his forces towards the Rhine, while Suvóroff's weary men had to traverse

F. R.   8

frightful mountains and defiles, harassed by the foe, until with the loss of half their men, and all their horses and stores, they reached the Upper Rhine valley. In Holland the Anglo-Russian forces were scarcely more fortunate; and the Duke of York, by the capitulation of Alkmaar (Oct. 18), withdrew his troops, sore stricken with marsh-fever.

Thus, before Bonaparte's arrival in France, Masséna in Switzerland and Brune in Holland had restored victory to the French arms, and cleared these dependent republics of the allied forces. There was now little danger of an invasion, except from the Austrians, who threatened Nice and Alsace. The Czar Paul, indignant at the treatment of his brave troops by the allies, soon came to terms with France.

And yet the Directory was in great danger. If victory had finally returned to the tricolour flag everywhere except in Italy, the policy of violent repression had brought France to the verge of revolt and royalism. Far from putting an end to the civil strifes, the *coup d'état* of Fructidor was repeated on a small scale in May 1798, when the Directory annulled the elections of sixty members, on the plea of excluding from the Councils those who had declared against the Constitution. General Jourdan and other Jacobins protested against the new tyranny as reducing the Councils to a mere registration court; and the defeats of the spring and summer raised a storm of execrations at these civilian Directors ("lawyers" they were dubbed) whose temerity was jeopardising France. In the elections of the spring of 1799 the Jacobins gained ground against the directorial party. Siéyès was chosen Director in place of the unpopular Rewbell, and a change of constitution was therefore imminent. The Councils repealed the exceptional laws passed at Fructidor, compelled three Directors to resign, and declared the national representation to be inviolable (June 1799). This *coup d'état* of the Councils was a reversal of that of the Directors and the troops in Fructidor 1797; but forced loans, progressive taxation, and the exaction of hostages from Breton villages where royalism lurked under the guise of brigandage, showed that the new Councils and Directory were as little royalist as the men of Fructidor. Siéyès determined to prevent any revival of the Terror, by closing the Jacobin Club, which had for a time re-assembled, and by making over 500 arrests at Paris; but even his reputation and skill could hardly bear up against Jacobins in Paris and royalists in the country.

Such, then, was the political situation on Bonaparte's arrival from Egypt—the executive and legislative powers at open variance, the Directory hated for its tyranny and despised for its failures, a general desire for any government which would secure the safety and order of the State. Siéyès had said that France only needed a head and a sword. He himself of course was the head; but would the trenchant sword now returned from Egypt be an obedient tool in his hands? Bonaparte cautiously looked around. He was too young to be chosen as a Director; and he hated the Jacobins as much as the royalists; but he skilfully made use of all parties who were dissatisfied with the Directory or with the Constitution of 1795; and among the latter class were three Directors, Siéyès, Ducos, and Barras. After combining these diverse elements of opposition for the work of overthrow, they could be left to fall asunder afterwards. At the outset Bonaparte declared that he would save France from the red as well as from the white terror. An understanding with Siéyès assured him the support of the moderates who desired a firm rule undisturbed by yearly revolutions; and Siéyès, after making a ladder for Bonaparte to seize power, was a man who could easily be shelved. A committee was secretly formed by Siéyès, Bonaparte and his brother Lucien, Talleyrand, and a few others, to arrange the *coup d'état.* The threats of the Jacobins furnished an excuse for removing the Councils to St. Cloud. Bonaparte commanded the armed

8—2

forces, and had the support of the generals, except Jourdan and Bernadotte. The Directors, Siéyès, Ducos, and Barras, connived at the *coup d'état*, and the two others, Gohier and Moulins, who refused to recognise the dissolution of the Directory, were guarded by troops at the Luxemburg Palace. It remained to coerce the Councils. Of these the Council of Ancients desired a change in the constitution of 1795 while the Council of Five Hundred began its memorable sitting at St. Cloud (19th Brumaire, or Nov. 10) with an oath of obedience to that Constitution, in which even Lucien and other conspirators joined. So strong was the Jacobin enthusiasm which swayed the Five Hundred, that when Bonaparte entered their Chamber he could gain no hearing and was hurried out half fainting by his friends. Their cause seemed lost; but Lucien, then President of this chamber, refused to put the vote of outlawry against his brother, and leaving the hall harangued the soldiers against the deputies in the pay of England, armed with daggers which they had lifted against the general. The lies took effect. The charge was sounded; and the representatives of France fled before the levelled bayonets. Representative government, which had survived the Reign of Terror, succumbed to the attacks of a victorious general; and the power of the Jacobins, who desired to perpetuate the policy of the Convention, was now decisively overthrown by the very means to which they had appealed in 1795 and 1797 —military force.

A Commission consisting of members of the Council of Ancients now decreed the creation of a provisional executive committee of three; and Lucien, re-assembling a handful of his adherents of the Council of Five Hundred, proposed that these three should be Siéyès, Ducos, and Bonaparte, with the title of Consuls; further, a Commission representing the Five Hundred was to help the Consuls in modifying the Constitution of 1795, and in preparing a new Civil Code.

Thus ended that Constitution:—"turn by turn invoked by all the factions, incessantly violated by all, it had ceased to be a means of safety for the Republic. It was necessary to prevent the principles on which it rested perishing with it." So ran the official justification of the events of Brumaire. Its defects had led to constant friction between the executive and legislative powers, and in 1797—1799 to a revival of the Terror. France longed for peace and quietness wherein the civil and social conquests of the Revolution might be consolidated. The strifes between the Directors and the Councils had rendered imminent a relapse into the Jacobin tyranny of 1793 or the royalism of the old *régime.* It was the aim of the 'men of Brumaire' to combine order with liberty by a new constitution which Siéyès was known to have long been perfecting. Even in 1789 he had said—"The science of politics is one in which I think I am perfect." The fortunes of France in 1799 rested apparently on Siéyès and Bonaparte—its brain and its sword!

The interest of this epoch of the Directory centres in Bonaparte's achievements and those of the French armies. In France the work of pacification and consolidation, begun in 1795—1797, had been largely undone in the two troublous years which followed; and the only great constructive effort of this period was the famous law of conscription (Sept. 5, 1798) which rendered permanent the great *levées en masse* of the earlier years of the Revolution. The battalions of volunteers had in 1794 been amalgamated with the regular forces; and the work which Carnot had begun was then completed by another great organising genius, the former terrorist Dubois-Crancé, to whom is due the formation of armies in divisions, brigades and half-brigades. The whole war organisation was now carried out under three heads—*personnel, matériel,* and *secrétariat.* Thus the vast masses of men raised by the conscription soon became parts of a powerful and smoothly working machine destined to overthrow the disjointed forces of the Coalition.

Conscious of its potential military strength, the Directory had adopted a policy of provocation and aggrandisement against all neighbouring States. Its conduct towards Switzerland and the Pope has already been described, as also the recklessly revolutionary and Gallicising policy of its commissioner Rudler towards its new subjects in the Rhineland. In Holland the Directory had aided the democratic party, or "patriots," in over-throwing the Stadtholder's or federal party and had in March 1798 imposed a constitution closely resembling that of France. After the Duke of York had in Oct. 1799 evacuated Holland, that unhappy land fell a prey to the exactions of the victorious French general Brune. The Cisalpine Republic in northern Italy had in the previous year felt the weight of Brune's hand, and a constitution like that of the French Directory had been imposed. Dumouriez' design of surrounding France with a ring of friendly republics had ended in a policy of imperious dicta-tion and pillage by the French in the Batavian, Helvetian and Cisalpine Republics; and the same militarism which repressed these vassal States, was even now building up a despotism at Paris.

CHAPTER VII.

THE CONSULATE.

"France did not hesitate to sacrifice political liberty, of which she as yet knew only the abuse, in order to preserve the civil conquests of the Revolution." (*Lebon*.)

THE three provisional consuls thus described their aims— "to organise order in all parts of the administration, re-establish tranquillity at home, and procure an honourable and solid peace." They thus gained the support of all who had been oppressed and harassed by the Directory. Political prisoners —especially the non-juring priests—were released. Forced loans and progressive taxation were discontinued; and 37 terrorists and prominent Jacobins were exiled (Nov. 1799). The appointment of Talleyrand to the Ministry of Foreign Affairs (he held it from Nov. 1799 to Aug. 1807) ensured the conduct of negotiations with more skill and suavity than had been shown during the last years of the Directory.

Siéyès soon had to yield to a more commanding will. He had gained his chief reputation in 1789 and again in 1798—9 —years when there was no one of commanding powers, prestige and experience. The theorist was now at once outdistanced in the race for power, by a nature profoundly able, far-seeing, and determined, endowed with a subtlety in intrigue more than Italian, and with the elemental strength of a race unexhausted by sentimentalism and anarchy. Full of scorn for the 'ideologues' who by their theories had brought France to her present desperate straits, he, the descendant of Corsican chieftains, resolved to bring her back to order and prosperity by what he regarded as the sole effective means of rule, personal authority. France, he declared, had had but one real government since 1789, the Committee of Public Safety. He was now to improve on its methods, even while discarding the passionate beliefs which alone had made its tyranny excusable. Against theories he pitted facts. Instead of the perfectibility of the human race by means of watchwords and constitutions, he recognised only the weakness and credulity of the average man. A Jacobin when Robespierre was supreme, and the saviour of the Directory in 1795, he had now overthrown the latter, and exiled the chief Jacobins. His opportunism is as conspicuous in his actions as in his political professions. In reality he consistently opposed only those who hindered his advancement or menaced his security. His wide-sweeping ambition only served to stimulate that scrupulous care about details which ensures a brilliant triumph. —"If (he wrote to Talleyrand in 1797) we take as the basis for all operations true policy, which is nothing else than the calculation of combinations and chances, we shall long remain *la grande nation*, the arbiter of Europe. I say more. If destiny decrees it, I do not see why we should not attain in a few years, those splendid results, of which the heated and enthusiastic imagination catches a glimpse, but which the extremely cool, persevering, and positive man alone can grasp."

The first question in which Siéyès, the man of words and phrases, was worsted by the man of keen insight and practical sense, was that of the new constitution, devised by the former on two chief principles—"confidence coming from below: power coming from above." Its basis was universal suffrage,

carefully filtered by three decimal divisions. The five millions
of French voters were to choose one-tenth of their number;
and from these 500,000—called notabilities of the communes—the central executive at Paris was to *select* the
authorities for the communes or parishes. The 500,000 in
their turn chose one-tenth of their number, from whom the
authorities for the Department were to be *selected* by the
central executive power. The 50,000 also were to choose
one-tenth of their number; and from these 5,000 the Consuls
or Senate were to *select* members of the Council of State,
Tribunate, *Corps Législatif*, Judges of the Supreme Court,
and Ministers of State. Of these bodies the right of initiating
legislation lay with the Council of State; that of criticism
of the proposed measures lay with the Tribunate named by
the Senate; while the *Corps Législatif*, chosen by the Senate,
after listening to the arguments for and against the measure,
silently accepted or rejected it. Not content with safeguarding
his constitution by these elaborate checks and balances, Siéyès
placed above them an august Senate of 80 members, chosen
partly by the Consuls, partly by co-optation, to veto any
unconstitutional proposal or action. At the apex of his
pyramid were to be two Consuls, subordinate to a Grand
Elector; and the Senate was to safeguard liberty against any
coup d'état by having power to *absorb* into its ranks any
functionary—even the Grand Elector himself. It was against
this last part of the scheme that Bonaparte furiously and
successfully protested in the sub-commission which at the
close of 1799 was secretly disposing of the destinies of France.
The Grand Elector, he said, would be a "fatted hog, or the
chained-up ghost of a *roi fainéant*." Siéyès had to yield.
The Senate lost its powers of deposition and 'absorption';
and, for the name 'Grand Elector,' was to be substituted that
of First Consul, who wielded considerably greater powers than
Siéyès had intended. As finally amended at Bonaparte's

instance, the new Constitution gave to the First Consul the rights of nominating the members of the Council of State (and hence of initiating legislation), all the chief military, naval, diplomatic, and judicial officials and functionaries, of deciding the questions of war or peace, foreign policy and the conduct of military and naval affairs. He named his own Ministers, who were individually responsible to him for their own departments of affairs, but not collectively responsible. The two subordinate Consuls were mere ciphers who might be consulted or not, as the First Consul chose. In fact, he wielded more than all the powers enjoyed by the Directors; and through them he became the lineal descendant of the Committee of Public Safety, nearly all of whose functions were now concentrated in him alone.

This new Constitution, promulgated Dec. 15, 1799, was offered to the French people for acceptance or rejection with the famous phrase—"Citizens, the revolution is fixed to the principles which commenced it. It is finished." The fear of renewed disorder, and the magic of Bonaparte's name as a pledge of glory and order, led to more than three million affirmative votes being given in the *plébiscite*, against a minority of 1567 negatives. Thus France passed rapidly and almost unwittingly from a distinctly republican constitution to one which was more autocratic than she had ever known. The power of Louis XIV had been limited by the provincial laws and customs. The Revolution had swept these away; and Garat truly said of the new rule—"The limits of the executive power would henceforth be not in a charter, but in the heart and in the very passions of a great man." The provisional Consuls now made way for three Consuls—Bonaparte, Cambacérès, and Lebrun. Siéyès was thus shelved. The empty honour of presiding over the Senate marked his retirement from active public life and his "absorption" by his own creation; while his acceptance from the First Consul of a fine

estate at Crosne served as a token of the services which his
constitution had rendered to Bonaparte, and as a pledge for
his own nullity in the future.   In the words of a contemporary
epigram :

> " Siéyès à Bonaparte a fait présent du trône
> Sous un pompeux débris croyant l'ensevelir.
> Bonaparte à Siéyès a fait présent de Crosne
> Pour le payer et l'avilir ! "

The Consuls, or rather the First Consul, used their extensive
powers of selection to name men of moderate opinions to the
Legislature and capable men as Ministers to carry out the
laws.   He proclaimed an amnesty for most political offenders,
especially for the victims of the Jacobin triumph of Fructidor,
1797 : he allowed all but the most obnoxious emigrant nobles
to return to France, if they would ; and, reversing the policy
of Fructidor, he permitted religious worship to be publicly
celebrated by all priests who took a formula of obedience to
the government.   These acts tended to reassure the royalists,
who with their *Chouan* followers had kept Normandy, Brittany
and la Vendée in a ferment of revolt ; and the withdrawal of
the cruel law of hostages, latterly imposed by the Directory,
together with the promise of liberty of public worship, pacified
(Jan. 1800) these districts, which had enjoyed barely a year
of peace since 1792.   Bonaparte began to build up his power
by healing the internal discords and conciliating the important
interests, which the zeal or folly of the revolutionists had
provoked in 1792—1795, and again in 1797—1799.   His rule
was at once a pledge for order, and a guarantee against a
return of the social and financial abuses of the old *régime*,
though he at once aimed at restoring all, and more than all,
its absolutism in government.

The local self-government which the Constitution of 1791
had so fully extended to the Departments, districts, cantons,
and communes, had at once fallen into disrepute owing to the

total inexperience of those who worked it. Centralisation was therefore the tendency under the rule of the secret Committees, and the Directory (see page 85). Bonaparte emphasized this reaction towards the old governmental system of 'intendants,' by a law (1800) which imposed a Prefect and Sub-Prefects on every Department. These officials, appointed by the central executive power at Paris, were to control all the local affairs of their several Departments, and act as "little First Consuls"; while the mayors of the communes, also appointed from Paris, were to regulate the affairs of the parishes. The elective rural municipalities, and Directories of Departments, which had played so important a part in 1790—1793, now became mere consultative bodies. The principle of election by the people was now completely subordinated to that of selection by the Paris Executive, i.e. by Bonaparte.

It is very doubtful whether Bonaparte was sincere in the informal requests for peace which he sent to George III and the Emperor Francis II. The forces of Austria and Southern Germany had held their own on the Rhine, and had driven the French from all Italy except Genoa and its coast-line; while British squadrons had taken Minorca, were on the point of re-ducing Malta by blockade, and kept a French army imprisoned in the sands of Egypt. Peace under such conditions could only have been damaging to the *prestige* of Bonaparte's new rule; but the sending of these overtures for peace—and again to Francis II after Marengo,—enabled him to pose as the would-be pacifier of a world weary of strife, while their rejection speedily rallied around him the warlike enthusiasm of France.

The Austrians opened the campaign of 1800 by cutting in twain the French forces which sought to hold the Italian Riviera. Masséna with 18,000 French was shut up in the fortress of Genoa, which he held with splendid tenacity (April—June). The victorious Austrian general Melas began to press back the other French forces on Nice and the line of the R. Var. These losses were partly balanced by the victories of Moreau and Lecourbe over the Austrian and South German forces on the Rhine and Upper Danube. The military situation in Italy there-fore called for all Bonaparte's energies. Echeloning his troops between Dijon and Geneva so as to leave it doubtful whether he intended to march to the Upper Danube, or against Melas, he secretly made his plans for leading his forces over the Great St Bernard Pass, so as to cut the communications both of the troops of Melas and of the Austrians besieging Genoa. With the help of Carnot, now again Minister of War, Bonaparte organised his army for this dramatic enterprise, which bears the impress of a spirit at once daring in conception and patient in the execution of myriads of details. He overcame the gigantic difficulties of transporting 35,000 men with artillery and baggage across the Alps, and at the end of May 1800 the French army, reinforced by 15,000 men who crossed the St. Gothard, were in the rear of the Austrians. These reduced Masséna to surrender Genoa (June 4) ; but their main body now had to fight to keep open their communications with Mantua and Tyrol. Concentrating his available forces at and around Alessandria, Melas began the Battle of Marengo (June 14) by pushing aside the scattered French divisions which barred his way. The battle seemed lost to Bonaparte, when Desaix, coming up with 6,000 men, renewed the fight, and a brilliant cavalry charge by Kellermann cut in pieces an Austrian column, which then laid down its arms. A panic seized the other Austrian forces, and they rushed wildly for the bridges in their rear. Melas, with perhaps needless despair, on the next day ceded to Bonaparte all Italy west of the Mincio, on condi-tion that the Austrian troops should go free to Mantua. Marengo thus reversed all the successes gained in Italy by Austria in the war of the Second Coalition, and reduced her to the limits imposed by the Treaty of Campo Formio in 1797.

Bonaparte re-established the Cisalpine Republic, and garrisoned Piedmont with French troops.

The French arms were equally successful north of the Alps. Five days after Marengo, Moreau turned the strong defensive positions held by the Austrians in and around Ulm, and by the far more important victory of Hohenlinden (Dec. 3) he finally compelled the Emperor to sue for peace. The Treaty of Lunéville (Feb. 1801), which dissolved the Second Coalition, was in its main outlines a repetition of that of Campio Formio; but the independence of the Helvetian, Cisalpine, and Ligurian Republics was guaranteed; and, by secret arrangements with the Courts of Spain and Vienna, the Hapsburg Grand Duke of Tuscany was to receive the Archbishopric of Salzburg, while Tuscany, re-named the Kingdom of Etruria, was to be transferred to the young Duke of Parma. As this young duke was a scion of the Spanish Bourbon House, Bonaparte received a secret promise from Madrid that on the completion of this exchange France should regain from Spain the vast district of Louisiana, comprising most of the basin of the Mississippi. By these politic schemes Bonaparte hoped to regain part of the colonial empire lost by Louis XV. The loss in these exchanges fell ultimately on Austria and Germany. Central Europe was again distracted by the question of indemnities for the German princes, who now lost all hope of their old domains west of the Rhine. The Duke of Modena was to receive the Breisgau from the House of Hapsburg. The King of Naples and Pope Pius VII were left by Bonaparte in the possession of their States, on condition that they closed them against English goods.

If Bonaparte had failed in the Marengo campaign, his power in France would probably have been overthrown by malcontent Jacobins or royalists. Even as it was, a desperate attempt was made to take his life by an infernal machine, as he was driving to the Opera in Paris (Dec. 24 or 3rd Nivose, 1800). Profiting

by the general indignation against the Jacobins, who were
hastily supposed to be the authors of this outrage, Bonaparte
demanded a law which should " purge France and also reassure
her." When the police inquiry was beginning to make it clear
that the Jacobins had no hand in the outrage, the servile
Senate, in its capacity of guardian of the constitution, passed a
" *senatus-consultum*," conferring on Bonaparte summary powers,
by which he at once exiled 130 of the Jacobin leaders to
Cayenne or to the Isle of Oléron; nor were they released
when it was absolutely proved that the attempt on the First
Consul's life was the work of some Breton *Chouans*, six of
whom were caught and executed.

Not only did Bonaparte disregard the protests of some
members of the Senate, Corps Législatif and Tribunate against
this gross illegality, but in the early months of 1801 he began
to restrict the already limited powers of the two latter bodies.
Thus, on the pretext of reasons of State, he withheld from them
the details of the national expenditure; and from this time on
to 1814 Bonaparte and his Ministers alone regulated the public
expenditure. The peace with Austria, however, gave him an
opportunity of re-establishing the credit of France, which had
fallen very low since the State bankruptcy of 1797. The duty
of levying the national taxes was now taken from local bodies,
which had little interest in careful collection, and was given to
840 controllers of taxation appointed by the Executive at Paris.
After Lunéville new stocks could be issued on favourable terms
on the security of confiscated lands which were as yet unsold;
and these stocks were used to indemnify the State creditors for
what they had lost in the "bankruptcy of the two-thirds" of
1797. The money gain was to the many an ample compensation for the loss of political liberty; and while the *bourgeoisie*
regarded Bonaparte's rule as a pledge of order and prosperity,
the peasants hailed it as the only security against the return of
feudalism, and the restoration of confiscated lands to their

former owners. In no sphere of action was Bonaparte so emphatically the "heir of the revolution" as in that of material interests; and his keen sense of the share which hunger had had in the Revolution is shown by his efforts in time of dearth to keep the price of bread in Paris artificially cheap, at the expense of the bakers.

It is an unquestionable though humiliating fact that the ideal aims of the early revolutionists had never permeated more than a small minority of the people; and though the fiery zeal of Mdme. Roland, Condorcet, and Robespierre had for a time dominated the inert mass, yet, when the enthusiasts fell a prey to their own dissensions, the less pronounced zealots were gradually re-absorbed by the apathetic multitude; and the revolution, which to the many had always been merely a struggle for individual rights and a higher standard of comfort, entered on its second chief phase—the endeavour to retain and consolidate the newly-won privileges and possessions against the real or fancied hostility of monarchical Europe.

While Bonaparte was consolidating his power in France, Great Britain had to face a new and formidable maritime league, at the time when she was losing the support of her chief ally, and the guidance of her one great statesman, William Pitt. The same month of Feb. 1801 which saw Austria sign the Treaty of Lunéville with France, was marked by the resignation of Pitt, owing to George III's vehement opposition to Catholic Emancipation, and by our preparations for war against the Armed Neutrality League. This League was formed by Russia, Sweden, Denmark, and was reluctantly joined by Prussia, to maintain the rights of neutrals as asserted in the previous Armed Neutrality League of 1780. Great Britain now again contended that (1) an enemy's goods might be seized on neutral merchantmen, (2) that these might be seized when sailing for a port the blockade of which was merely nominal, (3) that iron, hemp, timber, pitch, and corn were contraband of war, and might be seized on a neutral ship under any circumstances, (4) that a neutral ship might be searched even when convoyed by a man-of-war. The neutral powers denied these claims, one and all.

Personal disputes with the Czar Paul tended to embitter these questions; for while we had relaxed the stringency of our claims in 1794 and 1798, so far as to allow neutral ships to trade direct between their country and French colonies, yet we had given great offence to the Czar Paul by our capture of Malta (Sept. 1800) which Bonaparte, shortly before its expected surrender, had presented to him. The Czar had at once seized some British ships in Russian ports, and almost compelled Prussia to join the Armed Neutrality League (Dec. 1800). Our Government, treating its declarations as equivalent to war, determined to overpower the Danes before their allies could come up, and so close the entrance to the Baltic. Admirals Parker and Nelson set sail from Yarmouth Roads, and, aided by the severe frost which held the northern fleets ice-bound in their harbours and prevented the construction of batteries on the Swedish side of the Sound, arrived before Copenhagen without opposition. Nelson, with twelve sail of the line and a few frigates, determined, on April 2, 1801, to repeat the tactics which had been so effective at Aboukir Bay, viz. to crush in detail the line of 20 heavily-armed anchored hulks which protected the Danish capital. The swift current carried three of his large ships aground; but, undaunted by this and by " the most terrible fire of all the battles in which he had been present," Nelson's ships silenced most of the hulks, though the forts defied all their efforts. Persisting in his attack, in spite of Parker's signal to desist, Nelson, by a generous appeal to the Danes for an armistice, finally put an end to the carnage. The Danish regent had received private news of the assassination of the Czar Paul, and gladly accepted an armistice for fourteen weeks.

F. R.

The caprice, fury, and almost proved insanity of this Czar had led to the formation of a palace plot for his deposition in favour of his son Alexander. The conspirators on the night of March 23, 1801, strove in vain to extort his abdication; and, fearing the arrival of his guards, they strangled him. Alexander I, though full of remorse at an end to the plot never contemplated by him, did not hesitate to reverse the anti-English policy of his father; and when our Government yielded its claims (2), (3), (4) given above, the famous League of the Neutrals was dissolved (June, 1801). Alexander also surrendered his father's claim to Malta, accepting, however, the title of Protector of the Knights of St John.

Our maritime supremacy also gained us a signal success in the Mediterranean. A British force, landing at Aboukir, drove the French from their entrenchments, though with the loss of the gallant Abercrombie's life. Aided by Turkish forces, and by the landing of some sepoys at Suez, our forces compelled the French to surrender at Alexandria (Aug. 1801), on condition that they should be taken back to France on British ships. The collections of Egyptian antiquities, made by the French *savants* for their government, went to enrich the British Museum. Another practical result of Bonaparte's Egyptian Expedition was that our efforts to thwart it had secured our supremacy in India by the storming of Seringapatam (1799) and in the Mediterranean by the capture of Malta (1800). The failure of Nelson's attack on the (first) flotilla at Boulogne (Aug. 1801), and the pressure successfully put by France and Spain on our ally Portugal to close her ports to us, showed that the land power of France was as invulnerable as was our maritime supremacy. To prolong such a struggle was futile. Negotiations for peace were opened at London with the peace-loving Addington Cabinet; the preliminaries were signed Oct. 1, 1801, but five months passed before the Treaty of Amiens was signed.

Shortly before, or during, this interval several events showed that Bonaparte intended to respect the terms of the Treaty of Lunéville no further than it suited him. Though that Treaty stipulated for the independence of the Batavian, Helvetic, Ligurian, and Cisalpine Republics, yet Bonaparte imposed a new Constitution on the Dutch or Batavian Republic (Sept. 1801) and kept 10,000 French troops in its chief fortresses at the expense of the Dutch.

Shortly after the assassination of the Czar Paul, who had championed the interests of the King of Sardinia, Bonaparte virtually annexed Piedmont. He also prepared for the Cisalpine Republic a Constitution, which, like that of France, should unite the form of democracy with an almost unbridled autocracy; and 452 notables of that Republic, invited by Bonaparte to meet him at Lyons, not only accepted the Constitution, but, adopting the suggestion given by Talleyrand, offered to Bonaparte the Presidency of their State, now renamed the Italian Republic (Jan. 25, 1802). Similar changes were soon brought about in the Ligurian Republic, of which Bonaparte became the *doge;* so that he was now master of North Italy.

The Addington Ministry, in its supreme desire for the conclusion of the definitive treaty of peace, did not offer any firm protest against these interventions of Bonaparte; and the Treaty of Amiens was signed March 27, 1802, by which (1) Great Britain retained Ceylon, taken from the Dutch, and Trinidad, taken from Spain, but restored her other conquests, the Cape, &c.: (2) France evacuated Naples, and the Roman territory, and restored Egypt to Turkey: (3) the independence of the Ionian Isles was acknowledged: (4) Portugal surrendered a strip of Guiana to France: (5) Great Britain was to restore Malta and Gozo to the Knights of St John, subject to thirteen conditions, the chief of which were that the Order should be reconstituted so as to be independent and for ever neutral under the guarantee of all the Great Powers, that the British forces should leave the island within three months, and that it should be garrisoned for one year at least by 2000 troops of Southern Italy.

These terms were evidently favourable to France; for, in spite of her losses at sea and in Egypt, she regained all her old colonies, with a slight addition, while her dependent allies, Spain and Holland, were made to suffer for her maritime reverses. The Treaty contained no reference to the state of the Continent, except that the House of Nassau should receive adequate compensation for its losses in Holland. This added one more dispossessed prince as a competitor for German lands, with the Dukes of Tuscany and Modena and the host of German nobles driven by the French over the Rhine.

These complicated interests were to be re-adjusted in a special deputation from the States of the Empire, which from Aug. 1802 to Feb. 1803 largely altered the map of Central Europe. The Germanic system, resting on a perfect network of traditional rights, was revolutionised by the law of the survival of the fittest and strongest. The example set by the Eastern Powers with regard to Poland, and improved upon by Bonaparte at Campo Formio, was now followed in Central Europe, where the small weak States began to be transformed or absorbed. The ecclesiastical States, the less important Free Cities, and even some of the small domains of the Imperial Free Knights now furnished the 'indemnities' for the losses sustained by the larger States in the wars against France. As the extensive territories of the Church in Germany were now transferred to secular princes, these spoliations were known by the euphemistic term 'secularisations.' Thus, (1) Austria consolidated Tyrol by gaining the bishoprics of Trient and Brixen, while the scions of the Hapsburg House, ousted from Tuscany and Modena, received respectively the Electorate of Salzburg with other smaller territories, and the Breisgau. (2) Prussia, by the acquisition of the sees of Paderborn and Hildesheim, parts of Münster and Mainz, &c., in place of

Geldern, part of Clèves, and other smaller districts, gained nearly 400,000 inhabitants in lands nearly contiguous. (3) Bavaria was more than compensated for her heavy losses of the Rhenish Palatinate, Jülich and other Rhine lands, by gaining the bishoprics of Würzburg, Bamberg, Augsburg, and several Free Cities. (4) Würtemberg, Baden, and Hesse-Cassel extended and consolidated their domains at the expense of their neighbours, and became Electorates of the Empire. (5) The Princes of Nassau received various ecclesiastical lands opposite Coblenz and Mainz instead of their once important domains— the head of the Nassau-Orange branch receiving Fulda and other church lands in place of his rights in the Netherlands. The lesser potentates received scant satisfaction, the general tendency being to strengthen the strong at the expense of the weak. The Illuminati further gained a striking victory in the decision of this 'Reichs-deputation' that the property of all sees, abbeys, and convents was at the full and free disposal of the secular power for defraying the expenses of public worship, education, useful institutions, as well as for the relief of the finances! Nowhere was this policy carried out so fully and ruthlessly as in that abode of clericalism, Jacobinism, and bankruptcy, the Electorate of Bavaria, where the 'Illuminat' Minister Montgelas in 1802—1810 effected almost as complete a revolution as that of the French National Assemblies. The new Germanic system of States thus began to rise on the ruins of free municipal rule and of the temporal power of the Church in Central and South Germany; and the Emperor shared in spoliations which tended to strengthen the States of moderate size, and to emphasize their independence of the Empire and of Austria. The result was to be seen in the campaign of Austerlitz and in Napoleon's Confederation of the Rhine.

While in Germany the dissolution of the old Imperial power was accelerated by these revolutionary methods of the rulers, Bonaparte consolidated his power in France by reducing anarchy to order in nearly every department of the national life. In gratitude to him for having given peace to the world, the Senate was desirous of prolonging his Consulate for a second term of ten years after the first term of ten years should have transpired; but when Bonaparte showed his displeasure at this paltry gift, Cambacérès suggested to the subservient Council of State that it should propose to the people by *plébiscite*, whether Bonaparte should be Consul for life. Some three and a half million votes in the affirmative, against about 8000 negatives, showed that France was indifferent to the form of her government, provided that she gained order at home and glory abroad (May, 1802); and the Senate—the guardian of the Republican Constitution—proclaimed him Consul for life and shortly after gave him power to name his successor. He thenceforth used his Christian name Napoleon, and began to restrict those governmental powers which Siéyès had intended to be safeguards for liberty. Thus, in place of the decimal system of the 'lists of notabilities' (see page 121) there were now to be 'electoral colleges' consisting of electors appointed for life. The Senate was now (June—Aug. 1802) to have power to dissolve the Corps Législatif and the Tribunate; and the new Senators were to be chosen by Napoleon and not by co-optation. The Tribunate, which had occasionally ventured to criticise the government, was now reduced to fifty members, deliberating secretly and in five separate sections; while Napoleon withheld from these so-called representative bodies the yearly budgets and treaties with foreign powers.

A comparison of the Constitutions of 1791, 1793, 1795, 1799, and 1802 will show how rapidly France passed from rule by one all-powerful Assembly to a monarchy absolute in all but name—from a complete control of the Executive by the Legislature to as absolute a supremacy of the former. The thoughtful student will observe the fundamental and irre-sistible force in this extraordinary reaction to be the supreme need for a strong Executive in any great military State. In fact, the means, which in 1799 and 1802 ensured the supremacy of the Executive over the Legislature, may be summed up in the phrase '*divide et impera.*'

It will be convenient to consider here the civil institutions of the years 1801—1804, which form the most solid and lasting tribute to Napoleon's genius. The means by which he curbed local government and restored the national finances have been noted above. It was equally important to heal the religious schism which had been caused by the iconoclastic zeal of the revolutionists, and by their desire to completely subject the Church to the State. Bonaparte had annulled the persecuting policy revived in Fructidor (1797); but public worship was as yet only tolerated, not recognised; the 'constitutional' clergy were looked upon by the orthodox or 'non-juring' clergy as renegades from the Roman Catholic Church; and the schism rent French society in twain. Bonaparte felt the need of religious peace, and foresaw the prestige which he would gain as 'restorer of the altars' and nominator of the bishops. After long discussions with the Papal See and its envoy, the famous compromise called the Concordat was finally signed (July, 1801). By it the Papacy resigned all claims to the Church lands confiscated during the revolution, even to those few which were still unsold. In return the Government of the Republic recognised that "the Catholic Apostolic and Roman faith is the religion of the great majority of French citizens"—as well as of the Consuls: all the French bishops were to resign, or to be deposed if they refused; and Bonaparte, as Chief of the State, was to nominate the bishops fairly from both parties; the 'constitutionals' were to be received back into the Church by canonic rites, those who had married having first put away their wives: the new bishops were then similarly to re-instate the *curés* or parish priests. Church discipline was to be regulated by the State, which promised to pay bishops and *curés* nearly the same stipends as those proposed by Mirabeau in 1789. These promises were not strictly kept by Bonaparte; but, by healing the schism, he soon made the clergy his interested and docile supporters; and many of the clerics prominent during the revolution had to give their countenance to the new Imperial catechism which taught children that "to honour our Emperor and to serve him is therefore to honour and serve God Himself." At Easter, 1802, Bonaparte and the chief officials attended mass at Notre Dame, and a Te Deum was sung to celebrate the return of religious peace and order—"the most brilliant victory which could possibly be gained over the revolutionary spirit."

An equally politic and more generous measure was that which cancelled (April, 1802) all decrees and laws which kept very many suspects out of France as *émigrés*. Most of these were of noble or wealthy families; and with some few exceptions they were now, in spite of some qualms of conscience in the Senate, to be allowed to return to France, though their estates were not restored. As Mdme de Staël said, the "priests and nobles were to be the caryatides of Napoleon's future throne." These two measures cut the ground from under the Bourbon princes, who now began to despair of ever reigning in France. Bonaparte's success equally enraged the older revolutionary generals, twelve of whom (so he said to Chaptal) made a secret treaty "to divide France into twelve provinces, generously leaving me Paris and its vicinity. Masséna was named to bring it to me. He refused, saying that he would in that case come out from the Tuileries, only to be shot by my guard. He knew me well!" Whether this be true or false, it is certain that Bonaparte ever distrusted his chief generals except Berthier, Duroc, and Junot.

The keen mind of the First Consul discerned in education a potent means for attaching the youth of France to his rule.

The splendid scheme of national education, drawn up by the Convention during the Reign of Terror, had never taken deep hold on France. The primary or elementary schools were now very few in number: there were only 102 *écoles centrales*, where more advanced instruction was given; and the *écoles supérieures*, for higher education, were doing little work. Grand as had been the aims of Condorcet and his co-workers, they had really effected little more than the destruction of the old clerical education. Bonaparte had, therefore, a vast field for his energies in re-organising (1802) the education of France. The expense of elementary instruction was now made the reason for delegating it to the local authorities, who had also to super-vise and control all the private schools in their districts. Prac-tically, very little was done for elementary education; but secondary education received a very characteristic development. The 29 most successful *écoles centrales* were now re-organised as *lycées*, where the pupils were to be drilled and trained in semi-military fashion, the lessons beginning and ending with the roll of drums; and, to bind these new schools as closely as possible to the State, 6400 pupils, called "pupils of the nation," were to receive their education free, most of these being sons of deserving soldiers and officials selected by Bonaparte him-self. Technical and special schools were also soon founded; and we may notice here that later on Bonaparte completed his autocratic system of education by founding (1806—8) the University of France, organised in 17 Academies—one at Paris, the others at large provincial centres—to control all the public education of France in accord with his own will. Education, which had been up to 1790 in the hands of the clergy, became a powerful tool of the new State.

Another creation of the year 1802 revealed Bonaparte's ulterior aims. By the Legion of Honour he began to construct a new aristocracy as a reward for services rendered to the State, classed in various grades of merit, and comprising in all some

6800 members named for life. The sharp opposition to this departure from social equality, offered by the Tribunate, led to the curtailment of its functions, as above described.

The most lasting work of this period was the Civil Code (1800—1804), which reduced to order and harmony the best of the laws and social customs established by the revolution. In place of the complex tangle of Frankish or Roman, royal, provincial, and seigneurial laws and customs, a committee of the Convention had begun to construct one legal system for all France, based on principles of personal liberty and social equality, as far as these could be harmonised. A perfect mania for legislation had characterised the first three National Assemblies. Bonaparte, after stilling the clamorous and often useless debates, now, with his usual stern common sense, summed up their chief results by means of a small committee of experts. In 1800 he commissioned four jurists to complete the gigantic work, and often brought his own powers of incisive thought and trenchant expression to emphasize or simplify their phraseology. With a few subsequent additions in 1807, it was then renamed the *Code Napoléon*, and forms the basis of present French law. In 2281 articles it regulated French life in its legal aspect—civil rights and duties, marriage, divorce (wherein it restricted the facilities granted by revolutionary customs), the mutual duties and rights of parents and children, guardians and wards, &c.: it somewhat modified the law of compulsory equal division of property among the children of a family, which has tended to equalise wealth but check the growth of population in France. Other codes of civil procedure, commerce, criminal instruction, and penal laws, soon followed ; and very many of these laws extended to the whole of Italy, southern and central Germany, and the Grand Duchy of Warsaw. It is in the domain of law that the principles of the revolution—as modified by these codes—have gained their most lasting conquests over the chaotic systems of nearly half of the Continent ; for Switzerland,

Prussia, Spain, Holland and the Illyrian Provinces followed the lead of France. (See Chap. IX.)

Napoleon's name will always be associated with many great public works in France. The construction of canals joining her chief river systems, and of good roads on the left bank of the Rhine, along the Riviera, and over the Simplon and other Alpine passes, served to promote commerce and to protect the new boundaries of France; while the commencement of the great breakwater at Cherbourg, planned by Vauban, served as a menace to England. The previous abolition of the monasteries and convents had made it possible almost to rebuild many parts of Paris and other large towns. The Rue de Rivoli, the conversion of the old palace of the Louvre into a great museum and art-gallery, and (later on) the construction of several bridges over the Seine, and of the Arc de Triomphe, gave a new splendour to the French capital. After the sordid misery of 1793—1795 and 1797—1799, the new policy of *panem et circenses* was completely successful.

Bonaparte determined to revive the French colonial Empire not only by the acquisition of Louisiana from Spain, but also by the re-conquest of Hayti or San Domingo, which a French expedition effected in May 1802. The gifted negro ruler, Toussaint l'Ouverture, was sent to perish in a cold dungeon in France; but in Dec. 1803 the negroes regained their independence. The First Consul also sent out men-of-war to survey the south coast of Australia for a settlement; and a French map (1807) gives to that land and its chief inlet the names '*Terre Napoléon*' and '*Golfe Joséphine.*'

Such was Napoleon's success in healing the wounds left by the revolution, and in stilling the strifes of the factions, that the year 1793 seemed (wrote Chaptal) to have faded into the past as completely as the events of Greece and Rome. In all this many-sided activity, only one parallel to which can be found in all history, the First Consul figured not only as the "heir to the revolution," but the restorer of autocracy. Though the social basis of France remained revolutionary, yet the new centralisation of rule, the restriction of political liberty, the vigorous impulse given to useful and splendid public works, and the restoration of the colonial empire lost by Louis XV, all marked a return to the methods of Louis XIV and Colbert. Nay more! France, after having thrown off the feudalism imposed by the Franks, was now ripe for a far vaster experiment—a return to the Romano-Gallic ideal of equal citizenship in one great State controlled and safeguarded by an enlightened Cæsarism. To the duties of Rousseau's ideal dictator Napoleon was now adding the functions of a Cæsar restrained by no scruples from assuming the crown.

As there is a wide-spread belief that Napoleon was entirely occupied by these pacific undertakings, and was only forced into war by 'perfidious Albion,' it will be well to examine carefully the causes of the renewal of war in 1803. It has been noted above (pages 130—131) that the Peace of Amiens was due chiefly to the facts that both combatants were wearied by the long fight, that neither could now materially injure the other, and that the pacific Addington Cabinet was disposed to overlook the interventions of the First Consul in the affairs of Holland and northern Italy. But when, after the signature of the Peace of Amiens, Napoleon kept his troops in Holland and in the Cisalpine and Ligurian Republics, in violation of the Treaty of Lunéville, the British Government in Nov. 1802 charged its ambassador at Paris, Lord Whitworth, to protest against these acts, as also against the definitive incorporation of Piedmont in France (Sept. 1802) and the renunciation of the Duchy of Parma in favour of France, which last had been kept secret at the time of signing the Peace of Amiens. Moreover, Napoleon's refusal to make any treaty of commerce with England kept English goods out of every land subject to his will, such as Holland and North and Central Italy; and British manufactures and commerce suffered as much as during the war from a policy which fore-shadowed the Continental System[1].

Civil strifes in Switzerland, perhaps fomented by French influence, gave Bonaparte an excuse for sending an army there and imposing his will as 'Mediator.' In a speech which startled the Swiss deputies by its vigour of thought and intimate knowledge of their affairs, Bonaparte proved that the associations of the past and the physical conditions traced by nature herself, declared against the rigorous centralisation decreed by the French Directory in 1798 and called for a return to the old government by the cantons. The Act of Mediation (March, 1803) restored to the cantons, now 19 in number, most of their old powers; but Napoleon as 'Mediator' was careful to gain the upper hand in the central government; and the seigniories and suzerainties of the old governing families were not revived. Here again, then, we find the principle of *divide et impera* successfully applied; and the cantons had to furnish levies of troops to their 'Mediator' for his wars. A short time previously, canton Valais had been detached from the federation, ostensibly to form an 'independent republic,' but really to secure a completer control to France of the Simplon road into Northern Italy. Austria and Germany were too much engaged in the scramble for the 'ecclesiastical lands' to join England in her protest against this perpetuation of French influence in Switzerland; and Napoleon proudly said, "It is recognised in Europe that Italy, Holland, and Switzerland, are at the disposal of France."

When angry newspaper articles were appearing on both sides of the Channel on these and other questions, the French *Moniteur* published (Jan. 30, 1803) the official report

---

[1] I have discussed the importance of commercial affairs at that time and Bonaparte's plan for the invasion of England in an article entitled "Napoleon and British Commerce" in my *Napoleonic Studies,* pp. 166—203 (2nd edition).

of Colonel Sebastiani's 'commercial mission' to the East. It stated that the Ionian Isles would willingly receive the French again, and that 6000 French troops could easily reconquer Egypt. By the beginning of March, British troops had evacuated the Cape and also Egypt; but, as war seemed imminent, they were retained at Malta. The technical excuse for this was that the guarantee for the neutrality of Malta had not as yet been given by Prussia and Russia; but the real reason for our clinging to Malta was that, after evacuating the Cape and Egypt, we should have no hold on either route to India, if the threatening war-cloud burst; and the British Government declared that it could not entertain the idea of abandoning Malta unless it received a satisfactory explanation about the threats contained in Sebastiani's report. That Sebastiani's mission and report were regarded in well-informed circles in Paris as the chief cause of war, is clear from a vehement expression of Joseph Bonaparte to Miot de Melito: —"Let him (Napoleon) once more drench Europe with blood in a war which he could have avoided, and which, but for the outrageous mission on which he sent his Sebastiani, would never have occurred." After our army and navy had been strengthened by votes in Parliament (March 8—9), Napoleon had a 'scene' with Lord Whitworth, the importance of which has been much exaggerated. Insults to ambassadors are very rarely the *sole* cause of war. The *casus belli* arose out of the need of safeguarding one of our routes to the East. The Addington Cabinet, on April 23, demanded as a set-off to French interventions and annexations (*a*) the occupation of Malta by our troops for ten years: (*b*) the evacuation of Holland and Switzerland by the French troops: (*c*) an indemnity to the king of Sardinia for the loss of Piedmont: (*d*) our acquisition of the Isle of Lampedusa; whereupon (*e*) England would recognise the Kingdom of Etruria and the new Italian Republic, &c. Though these claims may appear excessive, yet they were really small compared with the gains effected by Napoleon since the peace, and he had recently admitted the right of our government to some 'compensation.' Besides this, the Addington Ministry had seen its previous mistake in being too pliable, and was now determined not to yield all the stepping-stones to the East. The Cape and nearly all Italy were virtually in the hands of the French; and there was no doubt that the policy of 1798 would be renewed if England gave up Malta, the key of the Mediterranean. A review of all the evidence shows that, while after April 1803 we were technically guilty of violating the Treaty of Amiens by holding Malta, yet the policy of Napoleon compelled us to do so, if we were not to see both routes to India fall into his hands. Both sides were inexorable on the chief points at issue; and Lord Whitworth left Calais May 17, 1803, at the same time that the French ambassador left England. Napoleon showed his rancour by ordering some 8000 or 10,000 English travellers in France to be kept prisoners; and most of them were detained until 1814.

Thus began the mighty struggle which was to extend to all the Continent, revolutionise its social systems, and, after arraying the land power against the sea power, finally end in the victory of Great Britain and the rising nationalities of Europe. On the renewal of war, England was in a far worse position relatively to Napoleon than in 1801. We had restored all our maritime conquests except Ceylon, Trinidad and Malta; while Napoleon now had control over the French and Dutch colonies restored by us at the peace, as also over Holland, Switzerland, Elba, and most of Italy. The sale of Louisiana to the United States for 60,000,000 francs, the annual revenue from North Italy, and subsidies which Spain and even Portugal were secretly compelled to pay, relieved Napoleon from entire dependence on French taxation; and two French armies were at once sent to seize and occupy the chief positions in Naples and Hanover, at the expense of those territories.   Prussia was too much occupied in profitable exchanges of German land forcibly to resent this violation of North German neutrality, which closed the Elbe and the Weser to British trade; and Napoleon ere long made skilful use of his seizure of Hanover to separate Prussia from England.   Russia and Austria were deeply incensed at the French violation of the neutrality of northern Germany and southern Italy; but for the present they awaited an opportunity for effective intervention.   The payment of a subsidy by Spain to France having become known to our Government, it ordered Spanish treasure ships to be seized on their way to Spain; and this high-handed action on our part led to the active hostility of Spain from Dec. 1804 on to the middle of 1808.   Thus skilfully did Napoleon use his supremacy on land, not only to save his own revenue, but to separate us from our old allies in the previous wars against France.   By these beginnings of the Continental System, our goods were soon shut out from nearly all central and southern Europe; and the doom of the 'nation of shop-keepers' seemed assured.

This commercial war could not by itself satisfy the ardent nature of the First Consul.   He must, if possible, strike at England's heart.   In a progress, made with regal pomp, in Belgium and the north of France he ordered the construction of a great port and arsenal at Antwerp, the assembly of a host of some 120,000 men near the north coast of France, and the building of more than 1200 large flat-bottomed boats, to transport his men from Boulogne and neighbouring ports to the coast of Kent.   But though the resources of Holland, Belgium and North France were pressed into his service, yet the progress was slow; for the type of boat and the size of the cannon had to be altered to secure stability in a sea way.   Indeed, in spite of constant practice, it was found that the embarkation of the troops could not be managed in one tide; and the currents

of the Strait drove the heavy boats far out of their direct
course. The American inventor, Fulton, whose steamboat
was three years later to be a practical success, came to
Boulogne to offer his as yet untried invention for the flotilla,
but was "peremptorily repulsed." How different might have
been the course of history if the invention had come a few
years earlier and had been used by Napoleon!

Even as it was, the menace of invasion served to put
England to ruinous expense in preparing a national defence;
but our people, not trusting alone to the increase of the regular
forces, thronged to join the volunteer regiments, everywhere
being raised as in the years 1794—1798.

> "No parleying now! In Britain is one breath:
> We all are with you now from shore to shore.
> Ye men of Kent, 'tis victory or death."

These lines of Wordsworth written in Oct. 1803 expressed the
growth of a larger British feeling, in which Whigs and Tories,
Scots and English, all joined. It was felt that the Addington
Ministry was unequal to the strain of responsibility. Pitt
returned to power (May, 1804), and only George III's prejudice
against Fox prevented his inclusion in what would then have
been a broadly national and non-partisan Ministry. Even so,
the British Ministries up to 1807 were coalition rather than
party Ministries.

On the other side of the Channel this same month of May,
1804, showed the influence of a great war in stilling party
strifes and in raising to supreme power the one necessary man.
Napoleon had already gained immense *prestige* as the champion
of injured French honour and virtue against 'perfidious Albion';
and a further incident enabled him now to don the imperial
purple. That evil genius of the Bourbon House, the Comte
d'Artois, had, with other reactionary French nobles in London,
concocted a plot by which Georges Cadoudal, the Breton leader,
and the royalist General Pichegru were to proceed secretly to

Paris and take the life of the First Consul. But too many were in the secret. One of the Chouan suspects, when arrested and threatened with execution, revealed the details of the plot. Pichegru, Cadoudal, and others were seized; and on the information of some of these that Moreau had had several interviews with Pichegru and one at least with Cadoudal, he too was arrested. At the beginning of the trial Pichegru was found strangled in prison, probably by his own hand. The complete frustration of the plot was far from satisfying Napoleon. Unable to catch the Comte d'Artois, he now resolved to strike terror into all his foes by an exhibition of the Corsican vendetta against some Bourbon prince. French horsemen, crossing the Rhine by night, kidnapped the young Duc d'Enghien, then residing in Baden, and hurried him to Vincennes, there to be tried by a commission of French colonels. On their request that the duke's prayer for an interview with the First Consul should be granted, Savary, who was in Napoleon's confidence and had received special orders through Murat, forced on the execution; and the last scion of the great Condé was shot four hours before any sentence was officially passed by the commission (March 21). The indignation which this brutal murder aroused throughout Europe, found little open expression in France. Indeed, the old revolutionists welcomed the deed as for ever cutting off Napoleon from the royalist party, and the holders of confiscated lands felt his rule to be more than ever a guarantee against retrocession to their former owners. It must be distinctly noticed that the hereditary principle was most strongly supported by the old revolutionists as well as by all who dreaded the return of Louis XVIII as likely to endanger their lives or their property. The recent danger to the First Consul's life was used by prefects and servile officials as a pretext for sending up addresses and petitions that he would establish a dynasty, and so "guarantee France for the future." The Senate—the guardian of the Republican Constitution—accordingly passed a *Senatus-consultum* decreeing to Napoleon the title of Emperor of the French (May 18, 1804).

The two other Consuls now became arch-chancellor and arch-treasurer; all Napoleon's relatives became grand dignitaries of the Empire, the succession devolving upon Joseph in default of a direct heir; the term hitherto used in address, 'citizen,' was discontinued, as harmonising ill with the new imperial pomp, and the revolutionary calendar was quietly dropped on Jan. 1, 1806. The most serviceable or pliable generals were rewarded with the title of marshals, though brusque or ardently republican soldiers, as Macdonald and St Cyr, did not as yet share this honour. There was another contrast still more glaring. In spite of the want of any definite proof, Moreau was soon found guilty of conniving at the royalist plot; but by Napoleon's imperial clemency he was allowed to retire to America. The careers of Moreau and Napoleon illustrate the superiority in revolutionary crises of keen foresight and Macchiavellian intrigue over military genius alone.

In accordance with the policy of the 'Concordat,' the Pope, Pius VII, was invited to assist at Napoleon's coronation at Notre Dame, Dec. 2, 1804; but when he was about to crown the Emperor, the latter, gently repelling him, placed the crown on his own head, and then on that of Josephine. Incidents like this and the murder of the Duc d'Enghien enabled many of his subjects to believe that they were still 'revolutionary,' but only one prominent Frenchman, Carnot, accepted voluntary exile rather than recognise the Empire.

CHAPTER VIII.

NAPOLEON AND THE OLD GOVERNMENTS.

"It was chiefly in the dilatoriness and blunders of the other Governments
that Napoleon found his greatest strength."—FOUCHÉ.

THE history of Napoleon now becomes, for twelve momentous years, the history of mankind. His arms, directly or indirectly, revolutionise the political and social systems of central
and southern Europe. By consummate military genius and
organising power, he seeks to weld the Continent into one vast
State and humble the mistress of the seas; but he is finally
baffled by British persistence and industrial skill, by Spanish
pride, and by Russian immobility. In the struggle the States and
social systems of modern Europe are evolved. Across the seas
the English race is left free to extend westward across the
Mississippi, to occupy the best parts of Australia, and to consolidate its supremacy in India; while the immunity of Great
Britain from internal war and revolution enables her to carry
on the new mechanical inventions of Watt, Arkwright, Cart-
wright, and others, to become the workshop of the world, and
the only cheap source of supply for the devastated Continent.

Napoleon's violation of the neutrality of Baden in order to
wreak his vengeance on the duc d'Enghien had an effect on
the European situation similar to that which the execution of
Louis XVI had exercised in 1793. Both events hastened the
formation of coalitions which would otherwise have been

formed more tardily to resist the encroachments of France. Both coalitions suffered in their inception and finally fell to pieces mainly owing to the aggrandising schemes of some of their chief members. In 1804 the fear of Napoleon so paralysed the rulers of Central and Southern Europe, that there was some disposition to condone his late outrage and to overlook his military occupation of Switzerland, Northern Italy, Holland and Hanover. Events soon showed that only distant Powers, Russia and Sweden, dared to stand forth as the champions of the law of nations. Russian and Swedish notes to the old Imperial Diet at Ratisbon, protesting against the violation of German territory, met with the most timid response from that effete body. Prussia soon recognised Napoleon's Imperial title; and diplomatic pressure from Paris drew from Francis II a similar recognition, subject to the condition that an Imperial title should be for ever held by the House of Hapsburg in its hereditary States. The House of Hapsburg, still the possessor of the elective Imperial dignity, which it felt to be little more than honorary, now showed its desire to consolidate its motley States in one hereditary Empire, the name of which should indicate the connection of the House of Hapsburg with the old Holy Roman Empire, and with the Archduchy of Austria. Francis therefore took (Aug. 1804) the title of Francis I, Hereditary Emperor of Austria, an innovation fatal to the traditions of the old Empire, which had been undermined in the previous year by the revolutionary policy of the Hapsburgs and Hohenzollerns. The Courts of Vienna and Berlin were, indeed, far more desirous of consolidating their newly-won States, than of risking them in conflicts with the prodigious power of Napoleon. The cause of European independence therefore passed to a worthier champion, the young Czar.

Alexander I, suddenly raised at the age of twenty-four to the throne by the plot which ended with the murder of his father Paul I (March, 1801), was desirous of carrying out the reforming ideas imparted by his Swiss tutor, Laharpe. Ardent, impressionable, and full of enthusiasm for the principles of the French Revolution, he had hailed with joy the advent of Bonaparte to power, as consolidating the new French State; and, while making peace with England in 1801, he had sought the alliance of France and the personal friendship of the First Consul. The events of 1802—3, however, soon showed him that Bonaparte was no sincere friend of liberty. The persistent maintenance of French influence in Holland and Switzerland, the annexation of Parma and Piedmont, and the assumption by Bonaparte of the Consulate for life, severed their friendship; and a slight to the Russian ambassador at Paris nearly led to an open rupture in the autumn of 1803. The seizure and murder of the duc d'Enghien drew from the Russian Embassy a spirited protest against this "gratuitous and manifest violation of the rights of nations," and the Court of St Petersburg went into mourning to mark the Czar's indignation at the outrage.

Laharpe, and another loved and trusty friend, the Polish Prince Czartoryski, now the Russian Minister for Foreign Affairs (1803—1806), concurred in urging on Alexander the duty and the wisdom of championing the principles of 1789 against Napoleon. Alexander's chief aims were set forth in the instructions (Sept. 11, 1804) to the Russian envoy sent to London for a preliminary understanding with our Government. The coalescing States, "in order to restrain the French power within just limits," must snatch from France her most effective weapon—"the idea that her cause is that of liberty and the prosperity of the peoples." The first object of the league should be "to deliver from Napoleon's yoke the peoples whom he oppressed"; the next "to free France from the despotism under which she groaned, to leave her the free choice of the government which she would choose." All European Governments should aim at nothing but "the greatest welfare of their

subjects"; and after the war, a Congress should arrange the basis
for a new European Federation.   In these ideas of the young
Czar, the Swiss idealist, and the Polish nationalist we see the
chief aims of Alexander's policy in the Third and Fourth Coalitions and in his unfortunate Holy Alliance formed in 1815. It
is needless to remark that the practical statesmen at Vienna
and London never shared the Czar's generous enthusiasm for
constitutional principles, while they secretly distrusted him for
the fickleness and love of *finesse* which marred an otherwise
noble character.   Furthermore, Czartoryski's secret intention
of crowning Alexander king of a constitutional Polish State
became known to Prussia, which then held all the Polish lands
between Silesia and the R. Niemen. Indeed, the Russian
State papers reveal his design of extending the Russo-Polish
frontier to the Vistula, with compensations for Austria and
Prussia in West and North-west Germany respectively, even
Holland being named for the latter Power !   Moreover, Russian forces were holding the Ionian Isles and some positions
on the Albanian coast; and in the distracted state of the
Turkish Empire it would be easy to gain the support of the
Greek Christians and commence a partition of Turkey with
Austrian aid, which was soon offered by the Court of Vienna.
It was thus a strange mixture of generous and ambitious motives
which impelled Alexander to take the initiative in forming a
new Coalition.

As there is a prevalent misconception that the Third Coalition
was "built up by Pitt's gold," attention must be called to the
fact that definite overtures for an Anglo-Russian alliance were
handed in at London on June 26, 1804, when the English
Ministry was framing its proposals for a league with Russia
and Sweden. Indeed, the Swedish King, Gustavus IV, in a
prolonged tour through Germany, so openly endeavoured to
form a league of the old Governments, that a plot, which nearly
succeeded, was laid by the French police to carry him off from

Munich. The negotiations between the three northern Powers progressed very slowly. Russia desired us to waive our claims respecting neutral commerce, and to give up Malta, both of which we refused. The Swedish king wished the restoration of the Bourbons to be the avowed aim of the Coalition, to which Russia and England equally demurred. The rumour of an Austro-Russian scheme for partitioning Turkey aroused English suspicions; and before satisfying the exorbitant claims of our future allies for British subsidies, we desired to know full details of Russo-Austrian policy. A preliminary agreement between those Powers (Nov. 1804) merely offered the Czar's help if Austria should be attacked by Napoleon, but did not commit that timid Government to any definite alliance. The Anglo-Swedish and the Russo-Swedish Conventions remained a dead-letter until the autumn of 1805, owing to Gustavus' desire for a crusade on behalf of the Bourbons, and his extravagant claim for an English subsidy. The Anglo-Russian negotiations were interrupted by the Czar's indignation at our treatment of Spain (see p. 144), while Pitt objected to some of the Russian plans for the future of Europe. Finally, without the knowledge of Austria, an Anglo-Russian Convention was signed at St Petersburg (April 11, 1805), aiming at the formation of a general league of the European States to compel Napoleon to withdraw his troops from Italy, North Germany, Holland and Switzerland, restore full liberty of action to the two last-named republics, and reinstate the king of Sardinia in his continental possessions. 'Barrier States' were to be formed between France and her weaker neighbours; but France was not to be compelled to change her form of government. Any towns or districts occupied by the allies were to be held in the name of the country to which they rightfully belonged; and at the end of the war a Congress of the Powers was to endeavour to form a European Federal System based on the rights of nations. As to means, it was hoped that Russia and Austria would raise at least

400,000 men; and England engaged to support the continental struggle by yearly subsidies of £1,250,000 for every 100,000 troops actively engaged. Differences of opinion between England and Russia as to the reconstruction of Europe, and still more the Czar's demand that we should restore Malta to the Knights of St John and mitigate our maritime code, delayed for three months the ratification of this agreement as a definite treaty, Alexander finally waiving these claims, with a formal protest.

The chief obstacle, however, to the formation of the Coalition was the ambiguous policy of the Berlin Court. Distracted between annoyance at the French occupation of Hanover, and the alluring offers from Paris of its cession to Prussia, Frederick William III finally decided on a policy of neutrality in the impending strife. He and his Gallophil Ministers foresaw a balance of profit to Prussia from that policy of friendly neutrality towards France which had brought so many gains since 1795. Moreover, English treatment of neutral ships caused constant friction between London and Berlin; and the Prussian Court rightly distrusted the Polish schemes of the Russian Minister, Czartoryski. From Paris came the friendliest overtures; for Napoleon then desired a Franco-Prussian alliance as a set-off to the impending Coalition. The French party would probably have prevailed in the councils of Berlin had not Prussian supremacy in Northern Germany been insulted by the seizure of the British envoy, Sir G. Rumbold, in Hamburg by French gensdarmes (Oct. 1804). Frederick William at once wrote to Napoleon asking for his release as a proof of the French Emperor's "friendship and high consideration...a seal on the past, and a pledge for the future." Though Napoleon grudgingly released Sir G. Rumbold and renewed the offer of Hanover, yet Frederick William now remained neutral.—" He will declare for the side which offers the most chances of safety with the least exertion "—was the comment of Metternich, then

Austrian ambassador at Berlin; and all the efforts and menaces of the Czar failed to draw Prussia from a neutrality fatal first to the allies, and a year later to herself.

It remained to draw Austria into the Anglo-Russian alliance. Though her ablest general, the Archduke Charles, declared it madness to undertake a war before the spring of 1806, yet pressure from Russia, and the offer of four months' preliminary subsidy from England, caused her to hurry on her military reorganisation under the incompetent and self-satisfied General Mack. Finally the provocations which she received from Napoleon in Italy decided Austria to join the Anglo-Russian alliance.

It is indisputable that the French Emperor took no step to avert the war of the Third Coalition, and many steps to provoke it. In March, 1805, he made the constitution of the Batavian Republic more autocratic; and while Alexander's envoy was journeying to Paris with the final demands of the allies for the independence of Holland and Italy, Napoleon crowned himself King of Italy in Milan Cathedral with the iron crown of the old Lombard kings (May 26, 1805), and annexed the Genoese Republic to his Empire (June). French memoirs agree with the records of diplomacy in attributing to Napoleon's aggressions the tremendous wars which followed. At a meeting of the Council of State (Jan. 1805), at which the memoir-writer Miot de Melito was present, Napoleon justified the expense of the Boulogne forces as giving him "fully twenty days' start over all enemies."—"A pretext had to be found for raising them and bringing them together without alarming the Continental Powers; and that pretext was afforded me by the intended descent on England." Fouché, Minister of Police, also states that on the Council protesting against his projected title of King of Italy, Napoleon replied— "I must have battles and triumphs…I shall be able to strike the blow before the old coalition machines are ready." Indeed, the French Emperor desired a diversion from the struggle against England 'nullos habitura triumphos.' Sure of the support of Baden, Würtemberg and Bavaria, and of the neutrality of Prussia, he could also rely on troops accustomed to victory, and fully equal in number to the allied forces. France was throbbing with the vigour of life renewed, while Central Europe had but just passed through a political revolution. No time was better for a conflict which he professed to regard as inevitable; for "old dynasties put up with new ones only as long as they fear them."

This brief recital will suffice to show that the tremendous war begun in 1805 cannot be called a war of political principles. Indeed, the cant about a crusade for liberty, which had figured largely even in the later revolutionary wars, was now dropped at Paris. On the other hand, the aims of Alexander and Czartoryski were far from being disinterested; yet the success of the allies might perhaps have led to a reconstruction of Europe more favourable to popular desires than that of 1815, when compensation for the fearful losses of warfare overrode more generous considerations. A study of the formation of the Third Coalition also reveals the hollowness of the agreement: eight years of disunion and disaster were needed to bring the allies to any practicable compromise of their interests. The possible alternatives before Europe in 1805 were a federation of the old Governments, with some approach to constitutional principles, or the overthrow of those Governments by Napoleon applying abroad the revolutionary methods which he had suppressed in France. The victory of the Coalition could have led to little more than a political readjustment of Europe carried out in the spirit of Frederick the Great; whereas Napoleon's triumphs at Austerlitz and Jena were destined, not merely to change the map of Central Europe, but also to revolutionise the structure of its society.

The plan of campaign drawn up at St Petersburg aimed at

attacking Napoleon with "at least 400,000 men," mainly through Bavaria. A Russo-Swedish force acting from Stralsund with "at least 10,000 British troops," was to drive the French from northern Germany; while an Anglo-Russian force was to free southern and central Italy. These schemes were marred by the obstinate neutrality of Prussia, by the inability of the English War Office to send troops until the need for them was past, and most of all by the nervous precipitation with which Austria rushed alone into the fray. The war began with the invasion of Bavaria by 80,000 Austrians under General Mack (Sept. 8, 1805). The Court of Vienna, ever desirous of uniting its scattered Swabian lands by that annexation of Bavaria which the combined Powers secretly contemplated, now hoped to overpower the Elector's army—since Aug. 24 allied to the French—before the latter could come to its succour. Mack therefore hastily led his troops up the Danube valley, but failed to surround the Bavarians, who retreated north to join the French columns marching southward from Hanover. Foiled in his first attempt, Mack encamped most of his troops around Ulm, from which fortress as his base of operations he proposed to set about the invasion of France, as soon as Napoleon should have crossed the Straits of Dover. The French Emperor, however, was not concerned only with his schemes against England. Without relying too much on his later assertion to Metternich—"the army at Boulogne was always an army against Austria"—it is obvious that persistence in a scheme for the invasion of England, when half Europe was arming in his rear, would have been to court a disaster far worse than that which threatened France when his army was imprisoned in the sands of Egypt. It is quite probable that Napoleon never seriously intended to "jump the ditch," unless (as he said) "a revolution broke out in England"; and that he aimed rather at ruining our commerce by the extension of his 'coast system.' Many of the best informed men in London and Paris believed that the Boulogne flotilla was an empty threat; and it is certain that French funds fell sharply on every report of an intended embarkation at Boulogne. Napoleon's plan of a grand naval combination, by which French squadrons from Toulon and Rochefort, and Spanish ships from Cadiz, should assemble at a *rendezvous* in the West Indies, probably aimed at the destruction of our commerce there quite as much as the assembly of a considerable naval force. If the latter only had been desired, the Azores would have served equally well as a *rendezvous*.

After cruising off Toulon for 21 months to blockade the French squadron there, Nelson had been driven away by storms ; but now, learning that the French and Spanish fleets were making for the West Indies, he gave chase to them across the Atlantic. He was in time not only to save our commerce from serious damage, but also to divine their second aim —a speedy return to liberate the French squadrons blockaded at Rochefort and Brest, so as to sweep the English Channel and convoy the Boulogne flotilla across to Kent. As Villeneuve, the French admiral, had some days' start in the return race for the Channel, Nelson sent one of his swiftest ships to warn our Admiralty. Fortunately, Sir Robert Calder's squadrons off the Bay of Biscay were strengthened in time to oppose a stout resistance off Cape Finisterre to Villeneuve's return (July 22); and the French admiral, worsted in the fight and discouraged by the bad working of his ships, put back to Ferrol, and later on retired to Cadiz. It is thought by naval writers that Villeneuve ought to have pushed on from Ferrol to Brest, even against a fleet superior in efficiency, so as to liberate the French ships blockaded there. Certainly, his prudence did not save his fleet from destruction; for Nelson, after a brief rest, soon took command of the English fleet blockading Cadiz; and when Villeneuve put out to sea, his 33 ships of the line were met off Cape Trafalgar by 27 British ships. Nelson's two attacking columns, in spite of a terrible raking fire on his leading ships, broke and completely disordered the enemy's crescent-like formation ; but the capture of 18 French and Spanish ships was poor consolation to the British people for the loss of their great naval hero, who survived a mortal wound just long enough to know that England would thenceforth be undisputed mistress of the seas (Oct. 21).

On the day before Nelson's last and greatest achievement, Napoleon had still more signally asserted his supremacy on land.   Furious at Villeneuve's retreat to Cadiz, he had at once determined on carrying out his alternative plan, namely to turn his splendid Boulogne army against the Austrians on the Upper Danube; and the precision of his orders shows that he had been carefully preparing to deal his foes a blow as terrible and as well prepared as Marengo. The position was somewhat similar to that of 1800. As Mélas had then advanced far from his base of supplies in his invasion of the French *riviera*, so now Mack had ventured into the heart of Bavaria, with the plan of invading France while Napoleon was attempting the invasion of England. The Austrian success in the occupation of the Upper Danube valley blinded them to the danger of being far away from their Russian allies, who, unable to advance in force while Prussia maintained a suspicious neutrality, were vainly endeavouring to compel her to join the Coalition by an armed demonstration on her frontiers. The temerity of General Mack's advance gave Napoleon the long-wished-for opportunity. Marching his troops at the average rate of 15 miles a day from Boulogne and the Low Countries towards the valleys of the Main and Neckar, he thus turned the Black Forest, on which Mack relied as his screen of defence from a front attack. Bernadotte was ordered to march southward from Hanover with the French troops quartered there, though he violated Prussia's neutrality by passing across her Principality of Anspach. The French columns began to converge on Mack's rear, while that presumptuous commander persisted in regarding their march merely as a menace to the Bohemian frontier. Awaking when too late to their real danger, two divisions of the Austrians strove in vain to break through to Bohemia and Tyrol. Only a few hundred men finally succeeded; while the main body, weakened by these spasmodic efforts, had to surrender to the French at Ulm (Oct. 18—20).

As Marengo had strengthened Bonaparte's position in France as First Consul, so his even more important victory at Ulm consolidated his prestige as Emperor. The wearisome and inglorious sea war against England had aroused much discontent in France, which was aggravated by a financial crisis; but now, discontent gave way to admiration for a genius who could decide a campaign by rapid marching. "Our Emperor (said the soldiers) has found a new way of making war: he makes it not with our arms, but with our legs."

The loss of a great army with all its cannons and stores paralysed Austria for the rest of the campaign; and the victorious French pressed on to Vienna, which they occupied. The Austrian Archduke Charles, though successful in Venetia, had hastily retreated north to protect the capital. Arriving too late for this, he retired into Hungary. Napoleon's pursuit of the Russians, who fell back into Moravia, was facilitated by a perfidious *ruse* whereby Marshals Murat and Lannes gained possession of the bridge over the Danube north of Vienna without the loss of a single man. Four years later this passage of the Danube was to cost the French more than 30,000 men.

Even now, if Prussian policy had been as clear and decisive as it was confused and vacillating, the French forces might have been placed in great danger by an onset of the splendid Prussian army on their communications. Frederick William III had ample cause for such action; for while he was successfully maintaining against the Czar the neutrality of Prussian territory in the east, Napoleon's troops were marching through

his Principality of Anspach on the Upper Main. This insult
for a time decided the Prussian monarch to offer his armed
mediation on behalf of the allies against Napoleon; and a conditional treaty of alliance between Austria, Russia and Prussia,
was signed at Potsdam (Nov. 3). In case France did not
accede to the demands of the three Powers,—almost similar to
those of the Anglo-Russian treaty,—Prussia was to declare war,
four weeks after the departure of the envoy charged with these
terms to Napoleon. England was to be invited to join this
compact, paying the Prussian and North-German forces at the
yearly rate of £12. 10s. per man; but Alexander, on the insistence of the Berlin Court, promised, in a secret article, to
use his good offices with the British Government for the cession
of Hanover to Prussia at the end of the war. Pitt indignantly
refused even to mention these insulting terms to his aged
sovereign, lest they should occasion a return of his mental
disease; and the English refusal enabled Haugwitz and the
French party at Berlin to nullify the effect of the Potsdam
Convention, and seal the doom of old Europe. He himself
was to be the envoy to Napoleon, with the message that
Prussia would unite her forces with those of the two Imperial
Courts, if the French did not stay their victorious career.
Purposely delaying his journey as long as possible, Haugwitz
found that Napoleon had set out from Vienna, and followed
him to Brunn in Moravia—only to be referred back by the
French Emperor to his astute Minister Talleyrand at Vienna.
During these delays the powerful Prussian and North-German
forces, which were marching to threaten the French flank and
communications, did nothing while the fate of Europe was
trembling in the balance.

Knowing that the Czar was desirous of changing the inglorious but successful policy of retreat for a bold offensive,
Napoleon fell back on an admirable position between Austerlitz
and Brünn. By concealing his own forces and by affecting

discouragement at the dangers gathering around, he encouraged the impatient Alexander to attempt to cut off the French communications with Vienna. Such an attack had to be delivered in front of frozen marshes and a small lake; and when the Russian left was lured into this position by a feigned withdrawal of Napoleon's right wing, it was by a vigorous offensive move of the dense masses of French hurled back on the lake, the ice of which gave way under a plunging fire from French cannons. "We saw"—says General de Marbot in his memoirs —"thousands of Russians, with their horses, guns, and waggons, slowly settle down into the depths. It was a horribly majestic spectacle which I shall never forget." The loss to the allies of 15,000 killed and wounded, 18,000 prisoners, and 150 cannon, ended not only the campaign, but the war. With ordinary prudence and skill, the forces of Russia and Austria, if aided by those of Prussia, should have overpowered the French army. If the old Governments could have acted in concert, the Battle of Leipzig would have been ante-dated by six years: but concerted action was impossible in 1805. Just as Prussia's armed neutrality had ruined the early part of the campaign by detaining the Russians on her frontiers, so too her delays after joining the Coalition wrecked its chances in December. Dismayed by the disaster of Austerlitz, and disgusted at the self-seeking policy of his allies, the Czar withdrew his shattered forces under cover of a truce.

It remained to dispose of Austria and Prussia. The latter had (as we have seen) made an offensive and defensive alliance with the Powers; but Alexander's signature of the truce with Napoleon furnished Haugwitz with an excuse for evading obligations, from which he had, even before Austerlitz, striven to escape; but how should he now face the conqueror? To his surprise and joy, Napoleon again offered Hanover as the price of Prussia's alliance, though she was to cede Anspach to Bavaria, and Clèves and Neufchâtel to France. The magnitude of the gain decided Haugwitz to sign at once the conditional Treaty of Schönbrunn (Dec. 15); and the Prussian monarch, preferring a profitable though ignominious peace to a struggle with the victors of Austerlitz, gave his general assent to its terms, in spite of the entreaties of his spirited queen and the indignation of his soldiers. By skilfully working on the fear and cupidity of the allies, Napoleon was thus able to deal singly with Austria, and, ten months later, with Prussia.

Austria was forthwith constrained by the Treaty of Presburg (Dec. 26, 1805) to surrender Venetia, Istria and Dalmatia— her spoils of the old Republic of Venice—to the kingdom of Italy: to cede Tyrol to Bavaria, and her Swabian domains to the new kingdoms of Bavaria and Würtemberg, and the Grand-Duchy of Baden. As a slight set-off to these losses she acquired Salzburg, for the loss of which the Archduke Ferdinand received Würzburg as compensation.

The campaign of 1805 will ever be memorable not only for the inconsiderate rashness of the allied leaders, the imbecility of Prussian policy, and the skill with which Napoleon shattered their armies and dissolved their alliances, but also for its abiding results on the social and political systems of Central Europe. Before Napoleon began to march his legions towards the Upper Danube, it seemed possible that the helpless rule of the elective 'Emperor' of the Holy Roman Empire might give way to the supremacy in Southern Germany of the hereditary Emperor of Austria, and that Central and Southern Europe might be reconstructed according to the chivalrous aims of the young Czar. After Ulm and Austerlitz the impulse, which was temporarily to transform Central Europe, could come only from Paris, not from St Petersburg or Vienna. It was to be no mere merging of Bavaria in the Austrian Empire, no mere readjustment of frontiers according to 'natural equilibrium,' but a social and political revolution welding Germans into a great federation under the supremacy of Napoleon. Though warmly attached to liberty, Alexander could never have imposed his will on Central Europe with the power which the French Emperor wielded by right of conquest.

The throne of France had never been the ultimate aim of the young Corsican's ambition. To found an Empire in the East and then "take Europe in the rear," was his mental post-script to the instructions of the Directory before the Egyptian expedition; but Ulm and Austerlitz had shown that Europe might be easily overthrown by a front attack; and, just as the Italian campaign was but a prelude to his rise to power in France, so now his triumphs over Austria and Russia heralded the far vaster aim—to found the United States of Europe under his supremacy. The time was ripe for some such attempt. When the old order of things was being sapped by the intellectual revolution, the rulers of Central and Eastern Europe weakened its political structure by their rapacious designs on Bavaria and Poland; and these two weak places in the European system were now to be effectively used by Napoleon against the old Governments. Furthermore, the ease with which in 1803 scores of petty German States had been absorbed by their more vigorous neighbours, showed the possibility of some yet wider union. Nowhere had feudalism brought itself to so complete a *reductio ad absurdum*; nowhere was there more yearning for a fraternity based on liberty and equality. But the Germans, separated for centuries from each other and from public life, needed a man of action to destroy the old barriers and complete the work of fusion. "Our journalists" (wrote the German patriot Perthes in Aug. 1805) "take up the cause of the tyrant and the *grande nation*, either from meanness, stupidity, fear, or for gold....but has not every people, until consolidated by unity, been ready to receive a leader, a deliverer? There is here a universal panting, longing, grasping after some *point d'appui*."

What firm nucleus could be found on which these chaotic

States could build up a new Federation adapted to the needs of the times? Napoleon seemed marked out by destiny for this vast work; for an old prophecy foretold that when everything was falling to ruin, a second Frankish ruler should arise to heal and renovate. Amidst all their divisions and discords, Germans looked back to the dim past when the Frank, Karl the Great (Charlemagne), had ruled over Teutons and Italians, levying his tribute from the Ebro to the Elbe.

Rarely, indeed, have fact and fiction so favoured the designs of a conqueror. Germany presented to Napoleon as vast a sphere for beneficent re-organisation as France in 1799. Both lands were passing through a political and social revolution, which seemed likely to end in mere chaos, unless some able man, by retaining the essential and rejecting the chimerical, could found law and order on the half-formed desires of the many. Napoleon's skill in satisfying the need of France for social equality and political stability, seemed to mark him out as the new Charlemagne, the re-organiser, not of Germany alone, but also of Southern Europe. Napoleon did all in his power to complete the parallel with the mediæval Frankish hero. The insignia of Charlemagne had been brought from Aix-la-Chapelle to Paris for Napoleon's coronation; and a little later the Emperor remarked to Bourrienne—"I have succeeded, not to the throne of Louis XIV but to that of Charlemagne." Even in April, 1805, before his triumphs, he said—"I have formed some projects about Germany. It is there I will give a mortal blow to England. I will deprive her of the Continent: besides I have some ideas, not yet matured, which extend much further. European society must be regenerated—a superior Power must control the other Powers, and compel them to live at peace with each other; and France is well situated for that purpose."

We here approach the second mighty effort of Napoleon's career. His first great sphere of activity, the reconstruction of

France, had been in many respects an extraordinary, and in in the main a beneficent, success. We must now recount the salient features of the second and vaster enterprise, with its startling though temporary success, and its momentous failure.

The exclusion of Austria from Germany and Italy by the Peace of Presburg gave Napoleon a free hand in the affairs of those countries; and the day after the signature of the peace, the victor declared, in a proclamation to his soldiers at Vienna, that the King of Naples had ceased to reign. His crime was that after promising in Sept. 1805 strict neutrality, he had two months later joined the Coalition and admitted Russian and English forces. For this 'perfidy' he was to yield up his throne to Napoleon's brother Joseph. French troops under Masséna and St Cyr overthrew the Bourbon dynasty at Naples, the Russian and English forces retiring to Corfu and Sicily respectively.

The utter failure of the Coalition at all points, added to troubles in his Ministry, sapped Pitt's vital force. "The pilot who weathered the storm" sank under the blow of Austerlitz, and bequeathed to his rival Fox the helm of State; but the generous Whig statesman, on making overtures for peace to Napoleon, found himself duped, and he also was soon to succumb to the cruel disappointment of his long cherished hopes. No twelve months in our annals have been more fatal than those which took from us Nelson, Pitt, and Fox.

Master of all the mainland of Italy except the Papal States, Napoleon now disregarded the protests of Pius VII against the occupation of Ancona by French troops. "Tell him (he wrote to his uncle, Cardinal Fesch) that I am Charlemagne, the Emperor, and must be treated as such"; and the Papal States continued to be occupied by French troops.

The Emperor of the French also imposed his will on France and Europe by reviving titles of nobility, generally at the expense of the lands lately ceded or appropriated. Thus

Talleyrand became Prince of Benevento and Bernadotte Prince of Ponte Corvo, Papal fiefs in South-Italy; Marshal Berthier became Prince de Neufchâtel; Murat, Grand Duke of Clèves and Berg, &c.[1]; and to mark his supremacy in the Netherlands, Napoleon made his brother Louis King of Holland (June, 1806). In place of that early aim of the French revolutionists —a ring of friendly republics around the borders of France— Napoleon had begun to encircle her with vassal States, held by his relatives or paladins, which were to buttress the Empire as Vauban's fortresses had girdled the realm of Louis XIV. Such were the aims of the conqueror of Austerlitz. In place of Rousseau's vision of a federation of small republics, Europe was fast being merged in a vast military Empire.

Equally high-handed was Napoleon's policy in Germany, especially towards Prussia. The statesmen at Berlin, endeavouring to get more favourable terms than those of the conditional treaty with France, had the inconceivable folly to demobilise their forces before the definite settlement of the treaty. At once the French demands rose: Prussia was to close all her coast line, including that of Hanover, to English commerce, make common cause with France in every war, and hand over three small domains to Murat, Grand Duke of Berg (Feb. 1806). Helpless under French threats of immediate war, Prussia agreed to these much severer terms, the first of which, together with the occupation of Hanover by Prussia, led to a commercial and maritime war with England. "All that is contemptible in slavery"—said Fox of Prussia's action —"is now united with all that is hateful in robbery"; and more than 300 Prussian ships were forthwith seized and confiscated in English harbours (April, 1806). Not satisfied with his successful use of the bait of Hanover, first to separate Prussia from her allies, and next to embroil her with England, Napoleon allowed it to bring about a rupture with that unfor-

---

[1] For a list of these dignities, see Appendix II., at the end.

tunate Power. In the course of negotiations for peace, which
the Fox-Grenville Ministry opened in the spring of 1806,
Napoleon let it be known that the restoration of Hanover by
Prussia to George III would make no difficulty:—"Hanover
for the honour of the British crown, Malta for that of the
navy, and the Cape of Good Hope for that of British commerce" (June 19). The fact that the first of these terms
became known in diplomatic circles, and that the whole negotiations soon broke down owing to a change of front of
the French Government as to Sicily and our recent colonial
conquests, shows that Napoleon did little to avoid a rupture
with Prussia in her then isolated and discredited position.
The treaty of peace, which the Russian *chargé d'affaires* had
been induced to sign at Paris (July 20), was soon disavowed
by the Czar, who even now did not despair of arraying Europe
against Napoleon; and with this chief aim Alexander signed
with Prussia a secret treaty (July 1) binding the two Powers in
a defensive league against the French Emperor. Their compact was soon to be tested; for Napoleon, believing himself
sure of a definite peace with Russia, and of the dependence of
Prussia, perhaps even hoping for a cessation of hostilities on
the part of the Fox-Grenville Ministry, ventured on the final
overthrow of the old Germanic system.

In this month of July, 1806, so fruitful in negotiations and
treaties, the French Government signed a compact with sixteen
princes of Southern and Western Germany, who, renouncing
their allegiance to the Holy Roman Empire, formed under
Napoleon's Protectorate the CONFEDERATION OF THE RHINE.
This new Germanic federation, consisting of Bavaria, Würtemberg, Baden, Hesse-Darmstadt, Nassau, and several smaller
States, bound itself to entire union with Napoleon in foreign
policy, thus placing 63,000 German troops under his orders.
In return for this surrender of foreign policy the federated
princes were to enjoy full sovereign rights in their own

States, their disputes being adjusted before a Federal Diet, which was to sit at Frankfurt. All the smaller princes, barons, and Imperial Knights, within the limits of the Confederation, were mediatised, i.e. they were deprived of their governing rights by the State within which their domains lay. Similarly, the old Free City of Nuremberg was acquired by Bavaria, while Frankfurt went to the Archchancellor Dalberg. The same policy was to be extended to all States which might in future join the Confederation. We notice here the same tendency towards consolidation of powers as had recently occurred in France, Italy, and elsewhere; for the mediatised princes were deprived of governmental rights by their more powerful neighbours, who in their turn acknowledged the supremacy of the new Charlemagne in military affairs and foreign policy; while the fact that the proposed Frankfurt Diet never assembled, shows that the capital of the new Confederation was really Paris. The resources of all lands from the North Sea to the Adriatic, from the Pyrenees to the Böhmer Wald, were now at the disposal of Napoleon. A brief message from the envoys of the newly federated princes to the Diet of the Holy Roman Empire at Ratisbon, announced that its authority was now at an end ; and Francis II, recognising accomplished facts, resigned his title as Emperor of the Holy Roman Empire, and thenceforth used only the title Francis I, Emperor of Austria.

As to Prussia, equally threatened by the creation of this powerful Confederation, she was ostensibly encouraged to form a North German Confederation with Hesse-Cassel, Saxony, &c.; while her indignation at the proposed restoration of Hanover to George III (a proposal which Talleyrand dangled before the British Ministry up to the end of Sept. 1806) was met by the insidious suggestion that Prussia should receive or take some neighbouring territory with 400,000 inhabitants as 'compensation.' The Berlin Government also found French intrigues at work in Saxony and Hesse-Cassel, to prevent those States joining any North-German Confederation. These repeated insults cut Frederick William to the quick. Even Haugwitz advised him to place his army on a war footing; and the rejection by Alexander of the treaty which his Minister had signed at Paris, showed to Europe the Third Coalition of the Powers in its second phase, viz. Russia, Prussia, England and Sweden.

The execution by Napoleon's orders of the Nuremberg bookseller Palm for selling patriotic German pamphlets, gave to the opening war something of the appearance of a national crusade. The philosopher Fichte, hitherto the devotee of a cosmopolitan creed which contemplated the rise and fall of States with indifference, now felt that Prussia was the champion of all that was dear. In his "Speeches to the German war-riors" he wrote:—"This war is to decide whether all that Humanity has from the first by a thousand sacrifices gained for order and skill, morality, art, science, and pious entreaties to Heaven, shall continue and grow according to the laws of human development—or whether all that poets have sung, wise men have thought, and heroes have accomplished, is to sink in the bottomless abyss of one arbitrary will." Un-fortunately this academic address could have no effect on the uneducated serfs who formed the great mass of the Prussian army. There was less community of interest between the soldiers and their officers, nearly all nobles, than in the old royal army of France; for the social chasm was widened by the harsh Prussian discipline which enacted corporal punish-ment for the slightest fault. According to the common saying, "they reckoned one cane to every seven men." In many cases the company, or troop, was the property of its captain; and, as promotion generally went by seniority, most of the officers were old and worn out. The Prussian General Gneisenau later on thus reviewed the causes of Prussia's disasters: "The inability of the Duke of Brunswick to form a sound plan of campaign, his bad fortune in 1792, the army's distrust of him, and its want of practice in war; ... the bad quality of our weapons, the incapacity of most of our generals, and, to sum up, our conceit, which did not allow us to advance with the times."

Relying on the *prestige* of Frederick the Great's time, Prussia now rushed into war, as if desirous of effacing the memory of her late halting diplomacy. The inconsiderate strategy of Brunswick was now to complete the ruin begun by the delays of the pacific king. The Prussian and North-German forces, by advancing to occupy the valley which the R. Saale has worn through the Thuringian mountains, committed a strategic blunder similar to that of General Mack eleven months before. Their troops were far away from their Russian allies, and exposed to a sudden attack from a more powerful foe. Napoleon, with 170,000 French and Rhenish Confederation troops, was about to cut the communications of the 128,000 Prussians and Saxons, when Brunswick evaded Mack's fate by a retreat down the Saale valley. The campaign was decided by two great battles fought simultaneously at Jena and Auerstädt (Oct. 14). At Jena 50,000 Prussians under Prince Hohenlohe faced double their number of French, who, guided by a Saxon clergyman, had secretly made their way up a height dominating the Prussian position. Hopelessly outnumbered and out-manœuvred, Hohenlohe's troops were broken after a brave resistance. This was a disaster. Near Auerstädt there was disaster and disgrace; for there Brunswick's greatly superior force failed to cut their way through Davoust's 30,000 French who several times repulsed the main Prussian and Saxon army. Brunswick was mortally wounded. The Prussian charges were made piecemeal against strong positions obstinately held; 18,000 men of their reserves never joined in the fight; and, finally outflanked, the main Prussian army retreated, to join the wreck of Hohenlohe's forces. Relentlessly chased by Murat's squadrons, Hohenlohe surrendered near Stettin, and the gallant Blücher was overpowered at Lübeck. Fortress after fortress tamely capitulated to the French. Never in modern times was there so complete a collapse of a great military Power. A fortnight after Jena, Napoleon made his triumphal entry into Berlin, most of the Prussian 'Guard of Nobles' marching as prisoners past the French Embassy, on the steps of which they had ostentatiously sharpened their swords two months before !

We have already seen that Napoleon had determined to strike a mortal blow at England in Germany. "England is everywhere" (he remarked to Bourrienne) "and the struggle is between her and me. The whole of Europe will be our instruments, sometimes serving one, sometimes the other." However exaggerated his estimate of England's power to 'build up' Coalitions, he now had the means of excluding her from nearly all the Continent; and on Nov. 21, 1806, appeared his Berlin Decree. This declared the British Isles in a state of blockade, enjoined the seizure of all English subjects, goods and letters in any land held by French or allied troops, and excluded from the ports of France and her allies all ships coming from Great Britain or her colonies. Half of the confiscated British goods were to serve as indemnity to French or allied merchants for their losses in the maritime war.

The British Government took up the gauntlet. Two months later appeared the first of our Orders in Council, which, "in order to retort upon our foes the evils of their own injustice," forbade neutral ships, under pain of seizure, to trade between ports from which British vessels and merchandise were excluded. To Napoleon's empty threat of blockading the British Isles, the English Ministry replied by measures which soon excluded colonial produce from the Napoleonic States.

Napoleon's decrees, as applied to French and allied lands,

formed the Continental System, which aimed at compelling England to surrender, by cutting off her commerce. Our war with France thus became more and more a gigantic mercantile struggle which soon embraced the whole world. To Napoleon's Continental System we retorted by a blockade of the Continent; and our policy became more and more commercial, leading to expeditions against French, Dutch, and Spanish colonies, and the occupation of vantage posts such as Sicily, Heligoland, &c., whence our goods could be smuggled into the Napoleonic States. Except for trifling subsidies to our few allies, and our participation in the Peninsular War, the struggle between France and England was, up to 1814, one of Land-Power against Sea-Power.

Every extension of Napoleon's dominion on land widened the application of his commercial policy, until by 1808 it embraced all the Continental States except Turkey and Sweden. We must now consider first the events which enabled Napoleon to impose this system on Russia, and, later on, how it involved him in his Spanish policy, in the Russian expedition, and the Wars of Liberation of 1813.

The Czar's troops had no more share in the disasters of Jena-Auerstädt than in Mack's catastrophe at Ulm in the previous autumn. In both cases they were many days' march behind their too venturesome allies. Amidst the break-up of the Prussian military system and the surrender of the Oder fortresses to the French, Frederick William and his gallant queen still hoped to retain all their Prussian and Polish lands east of the Vistula, which then formed quite one-fourth of their possessions. At first Napoleon's troops gained some decisive successes over the Russian troops in Poland; and the news of a rising in Warsaw led to the defection of the Polish troops from the Prussian colours, leaving only 13,000 for field-service. But the campaign entered on a new phase with the desperate and successful resistance of the Russians and Prussians at

Eylau (Feb. 8, 1807). " What a massacre, and without result ! "
was Ney's description of the square league of carnage. Reduced for a time almost to inactivity, Napoleon vainly tried to
detach Frederick William from the Russian alliance. The
Prusso-Russian compact was strengthened by a treaty of offensive and defensive alliance at Bartenstein (April), which
England and Sweden soon joined, and to which Austria was
urged to adhere; but that unfortunate Power, courted also by
France, could not be induced to move; and the English
Ministry—on Prussia's renunciation of Hanover to George III
—sent money and arms, only when it was too late. The
neglect of the English Government to send sufficient money,
or to despatch at once an army to Stralsund for the help
of the hard-pressed Swedish forces, was Alexander's chief
excuse for the change of front which soon astonished the
world.

The campaign was ended by a fatal blunder of the Russian
General Bennigsen. In order to save Königsberg from the
French, who were marching northwards nearly parallel with his
army, he crossed the R. Alle at Friedland, believing that only
Lannes' division of 10,000 men would resist his advance; but
Napoleon, probably expecting this step, had a large force near
at hand. A daring charge of Marshal Ney drove the Russians
back on the bridges of Friedland, which were broken by the
fire of the French cannons; and, swinging round his left wing,
Napoleon captured or drove into the river nearly all the
Russian centre and right (June 14). The loss of nearly
25,000 men killed, wounded, or prisoners, and 80 cannons
decided Alexander to ask for a truce. Both in its military and
political aspects, Friedland corresponds to Austerlitz. Before
both battles Napoleon could have been overpowered by
prompt and united action of all the States threatened by his
domination; but their mutual jealousies, the tardy action of
their Governments, and the culpable rashness of the Russian

commanders, gave the victory to the one Power, whose diplomatic and military tactics were unerring.

Disgusted at the continued neutrality of Austria and at the dilatoriness of England, which sent arms only to be captured by the French at Königsberg, the Czar now met his great foe at Tilsit with the words :—"I hate the English as much as you do." "In that case"—replied Napoleon—"peace is made." Yielding to the charm of the French Emperor's conversation, and captivated by the prospect of sharing as an equal in his Continental domination, Alexander gladly accepted a peace which promised gains of territory at the expense of Turkey. It is true that Napoleon had recently encouraged the Sultan to declare war on Russia and had helped him to withstand the menaces of an English fleet at the Dardanelles; but the deposition of this Sultan by a palace revolution (May, 1807) helped Napoleon to the excuse that his friendship had been merely personal, and did not extend to his successor. Never did tidings come more opportunely; and never have they been more astutely used. "It is a decree of Providence"—exclaimed Napoleon to the Czar—"which tells me that the Turkish Empire can no longer exist." Dazzled by the prospect of the lion's share in an approaching partition of Turkey, Alexander abandoned as quixotic his earlier schemes for the liberation of Europe, and fell back on Russia's traditional policy, the southward march towards Constantinople. Such was the policy underlying the Treaties of Tilsit. On his side of the bargain, Napoleon was to extend his influence at the expense of Prussia, by cutting her off from western Germany, and by forming her Polish provinces into a State dependent on France, called the Grand-Duchy of Warsaw. Sure of the alliance of Saxony —thenceforth to be a kingdom—Napoleon would thus control a line of States from the Rhine to the Niemen, save for the narrow neck of Lower Silesia. On her seabord Prussia was to be crippled by Danzig becoming a 'free town,' under a

French commander.   In fact, the fourth clause of the Treaty affirmed that only out of consideration for the Czar, did Napoleon restore to the King of Prussia any of his States.   It was in vain that the lovely Queen Louisa came twice to beg that at least Napoleon would give her Magdeburg.   After some empty compliments, he bade Talleyrand get the treaties signed as soon as possible.

The Treaties of Tilsit (July 7, 1807) may be thus summarised :—Prussia lost nearly all the lands gained in the three partitions of Poland.   These territories, except the district of Bialystok, were to form the Grand Duchy of Warsaw under the sovereignty of the King of Saxony.   A military road across Lower Silesia was to keep open the communications between Saxony and the Duchy, while complete freedom of navigation on the Vistula served to connect Warsaw with the new 'free town' of Danzig.   Prussia also surrendered all her lands west of the Elbe, parts going to swell Murat's Duchy of Berg, other territories, with Hesse-Cassel, forming the new kingdom of Westphalia for Napoleon's brother Jerome; while his brother Louis received from Prussia East Frisia as an addition to Holland.   France gained three fortresses and one district on the right bank of the Rhine, and the fortress of Erfurt as a stronghold in the midst of the Confederation of the Rhine. Hanover, Baireuth, and a few other German States were also to be occupied 'provisionally' by the French.   The Czar reluctantly received (on Napoleon's insistence) the frontier district of Bialystok from the hapless Prussian monarch whose lands he had two months before solemnly promised to defend. The Russian troops were to evacuate Moldavia and Wallachia, but these provinces were not to be re-occupied by Turkish troops until the conclusion of peace between Russia and Turkey under the mediation of France.   Similarly, Napoleon accepted the mediation of the Czar to bring about peace between France and England, if the latter accepted it within a month. Russia also recognised the Napoleonic States in Germany and Italy.

In a separate and secret Treaty of Alliance of the same date (the full details of which have only quite recently become known), the Czar agreed to join Napoleon against England, if she did not before Nov. 1, 1807, abate her maritime claims, and consent to restore the conquests made since 1805 to France and her allies. If England did not by Dec. 1 assent to these terms, the two Emperors would "summon the three Courts of Copenhagen, Stockholm, and Lisbon to close their ports to the English, and declare war on England. That one of the three Courts which refuses shall be treated as an enemy ; and in the case of Sweden refusing, Denmark shall be compelled to declare war on her." Similar compulsion was to be used to compel Austria to join the Continental System. If, however, England agreed to the French terms, she was to receive Hanover as compensation for the French, Spanish, and Dutch colonies restored by her. Similarly, if Turkey refused the French mediation or the Russian terms, then the Emperors would make war on her " to withdraw from the burdensome yoke of the Turks all the provinces of the Ottoman Empire in Europe, the city of Constantinople and the province of Roumelia only excepted." Other secret articles provided for the cession to the French of the Cattaro district of Dalmatia as also of the Ionian Isles, both of which had been occupied by Russian troops ; also that if, at the future peace with England, Hanover should be added to Jerome's Kingdom of Westphalia, Prussia should then recover some of her lands west of the Elbe with about 400,000 inhabitants.

The Treaty with Prussia to a similar effect was signed two days later, Napoleon declaring that his words to Queen Louisa were merely "amiable words which bound him to nothing," and that but for the intercession of the Czar, the whole of Prussia would have been given to Jerome Bonaparte.

Talleyrand inwardly revolted at "the barbarity with which Napoleon treated Prussia at Tilsit"; but worse was to follow. The Convention of Königsberg provided that the lands left to Prussia should be evacuated by French troops only in proportion as the war indemnity (as yet not specified), or securities to its amount, should be forthcoming; and Prussian taxes were to be set apart for the satisfaction of French claims. Much of Napoleon's popularity in France was due to his policy that "war must support war," whereby France gained the glory of victory without any exceptional financial burdens. Prussia was now to support the Grand Army; and the financial exactions were so prolonged that Berlin was not completely freed from the French till the War of Liberation in 1813. As if the loss of half her subjects and all her foreign commerce, the incubus of a huge debt and a rapacious army of occupation, had not sufficiently humbled Prussia, she was ordered a year later to limit her army to 42,000 men.

Never has the European system sustained such a shock as at Tilsit. The Czar, who at Bartenstein had solemnly pledged his word to preserve the "natural equilibrium" of Europe, now at Tilsit made a profitable alliance with its destroyer, and Russian policy reverted to the aims of Peter the Great and Catherine,—conquests over Sweden and Turkey. Finland and the Danubian Provinces were to be the ultimate prizes gained by alliance with France; while Alexander joined hands with Napoleon to hold down the centre of Europe. Nay more! The Land Power was to form an irresistible league for the ruin of the Sea Power. Our sole remaining ally, Sweden, could not resist the onset of 40,000 French who, marching into her province of Pomerania, compelled the surrender of Stralsund (Aug.). Russia and Prussia not only excluded English commerce, but the former Power joined Napoleon in trying to force on us a ruinous peace.

Was the English Ministry justified in rejecting the mediation projected by the Czar, but ultimately proposed by the Austrian Emperor? In the first place, it must be remembered that alone of all the allies, England had suffered no disasters, but had made considerable conquests. Nearly all the French, Dutch, and Spanish colonies had fallen, or were likely to fall, into our hands. Our position in India was securer than ever before. Napoleon's Berlin decree had as yet only served to exhibit his impotence at sea; for while his blockade of the British Isles remained a mere threat, our blockade of the Napoleonic States was so far effective that the neutral commerce of the world was passing into our hands. There was therefore no urgent reason for making peace. Secondly, the British Government knew from the terms of the (published) Treaty of Tilsit with what severity Napoleon pressed on a vanquished foe; and it further had heard that a secret treaty had been signed between Napoleon and Alexander. When, therefore, the Czar proposed to offer his mediation between England and France, the British Government requested (Aug. 29) to be informed what were "the just and equitable principles on which France intended to negotiate," as also what were the terms of the secret Treaty of Tilsit. No answer came; but our Government had some knowledge—Fouché's memoirs hint that Talleyrand was the informer—of the policy secretly arranged at Tilsit to compel Denmark, Sweden, and Portugal to join the continental league against England; and that Denmark would be occupied by the French troops already on the borders of Holstein. Canning, English Secretary for Foreign Affairs in the new Portland Ministry, at once decided "to do by Napoleon what he has so long been doing by others." A great fleet under Admiral Gambier sailed for the Sound, there to be joined by a British force already sent to aid the Swedes in Pomerania. Our envoy offered to the Prince Royal an Anglo-Danish alliance, or strict neutrality in the impending struggle. In either case the Danish fleet was to join ours as 'deposit,' partly for our own protection, partly to remove the reason for French demands of an alliance with Denmark. Not even the display of an imposing force of more than 80 British ships could overcome the indignation of the Danish Prince at this high-handed policy. The British land-forces under Lord Cathcart accordingly disembarked near Copenhagen; and after the investment of its walls, a last offer was made of receiving the Danish fleet in deposit. On its rejection the works and the city were bombarded for the greater part of four days until (Sept. 5) it agreed to surrender the fleet unconditionally; six weeks' armistice were allowed to equip the 16 ships of the line, 13 frigates and 30 smaller vessels, which formed the sole prize of this expedition. The archives of our Foreign Office show that Canning desired far more, viz. an Anglo-Scandinavian league which might preserve the North of Europe from Napoleon's grasp. But the Danish Prince refused all overtures for an alliance which would have drawn on him the armies of Napoleon; while a French alliance promised a share in the spoils of the Swedish monarchy. The result of the Copenhagen expedition was, in some ways, disastrous for Great Britain. Denmark became the most trusty of all Napoleon's allies; and the Czar, casting aside his first scruples, soon declared war on England (Nov. 7, 1807). Our ally Sweden, menaced by the Danes on the side of Norway (then under the Danish crown), and threatened with the loss of Finland by an invasion of the Russians, maintained the unequal struggle for two years; but after the deposition of her quixotic monarch Gustavus IV, by his uncle, who succeeded as Charles XIII, she ceded Finland and the Aland Isles to Russia (Sept. 1809) and four months later agreed to exclude all British goods.

At the opposite end of Europe the results of the secret compact between Napoleon and Alexander were seen far more immediately. Exasperated by our conduct at Copenhagen, Napoleon, at a meeting of the diplomatic circle, thus addressed the Portuguese ambassador : "I will no longer tolerate an English ambassador in Europe. I will declare war against ·any Power that receives one, after two months from this time. ...The English no longer respect neutrals at sea. I will no longer recognise neutrals on the land." The Court of Lisbon, summoned to close its ports to us and seize English goods, refused to confiscate the property of a Power so closely allied for a century past; but even before the refusal of the Portuguese Regent had reached Napoleon, the latter had signed with his Spanish allies the secret treaty of Fontainebleau (Oct. 1807) for the partition of Portugal and its colonies between France and Spain. In pursuance of this scheme, French troops under Junot marched through Spain to overthrow the rule of the House of Braganza. The Portuguese Regent, unable to offer any resistance, set sail (Nov. 30) from Lisbon for Brazil, thus fulfilling a boast in the Paris *Moniteur*—" The fall of the House of Braganza will be a new proof how inevitable is the ruin of all who attach themselves to the English."

Rendered desperate by these extensions of Napoleon's system to all Europe—for after Austria joined the Continental System, Oct. 1807, only Sweden and Turkey remained friendly to us, or neutral—the British Ministry issued its second series of Orders in Council (Nov. 1807). These declared that every neutral ship trading between ports, from which our vessels were excluded, was "good prize of war"; but neutrals were invited to avail themselves of facilities for discharging their goods in British harbours, such merchandise being bonded and under certain conditions re-exported.

Annoyed at these efforts to attract neutrals to British ports, Napoleon retorted by his Milan Decrees (Nov. and Dec.):— that all neutral ships submitting to the British maritime code were thereby denationalised, and became good and lawful prize. Between belligerents so exasperated, neutrality on sea was almost as impossible as on land ; and the disastrous year 1807 closed with the imposition by the United States of a general embargo on European vessels. Cut off from direct trade with the Continent and the United States, our position seemed gloomy indeed. Our policy had apparently resulted in a victory for Napoleon all along the line. The help to our allies had always been sent too late; while our high-handed actions against Spain and Denmark had driven these Powers into his arms. Our great enemy, on the other hand, had shown all the qualities which ensure success in diplomacy and war. The bait of Hanover adroitly used to secure Prussia's neutrality until her allies were crushed, specious generosity to the Czar after Austerlitz and Friedland, crushing terms to Austria and Prussia when isolated and helpless, the skilful diversion of Alexander's ambition from the West towards the East—these main features of the Napoleonic policy secured as brilliant a success in state-craft as his swift and hitherto un-erring strategy had won on the field. "An union which the world never before saw, of irresistible force with the most con-summate art (wrote Mr A. Baring, M.P., in Feb. 1808), is employed to rear his gigantic fabric; while the total lack of energy and genius on the other side appears to exhibit the hand of Providence in this extraordinary revolution."

Every brilliant military and diplomatic triumph of Napoleon was marked by the increase of his power in France itself. Rivoli and Campo Formio had raised him far above all French generals. Marengo and Lunéville consolidated his power as First Consul. The Peace of Amiens gained him the Con-sulate for life with almost unbounded power. The over-throw of the Third Coalition now enabled him to suppress the one public body in France which occasionally ventured to timidly criticise his acts. The Tribunate, designed by Siéyès as the criticising organ of the body politic, had been already shorn of some of its powers, and divided into sections which debated secretly (see p. 134). The Emperor now announced that he was about to "simplify and perfect French institu-

tions": the Tribunate had preserved something of "the dis-
quieted and democratic spirit which had long agitated
France." This reason sufficed for its total suppression (Aug.
1807) and the transference of its few remaining functions to
the more submissive *Corps Législatif.* Commissioners in this
body were now to draw up drafts for laws; but in reality most
laws emanated from Napoleon or his obsequious Ministers, the
thin disguise of calling them *Senatus Consulta* being often
dispensed with.

Never, perhaps, have all the activities of government been
so concentrated in one all-absorbing personality. Amidst the
dearth of really able men in the later years of the French
Revolution, Napoleon's genius had shone forth with dazzling
splendour; and the contrast was even more marked when he
measured his strength with the rulers, diplomatists, and generals
of Europe. Nothing, indeed, is more surprising in his career
than the swift expansion of his faculties and ambition along
with extended power. After his most brilliant successes his
behaviour ever denoted that he had done nothing as yet.
Keen foresight in developing the resources of democratic
France and diverting them into the path of military glory,
Macchiavellian skill in dividing his foes and attacking them
when severed and disheartened, political tact in welding the
shattered fragments of old Europe into his own system of
States—these were powers which paralysed or fascinated a
Mack, a Haugwitz, or an Alexander. Add to this the fear
caused by his terrifying personality, his invincible strength of
mind and body, his long and furious rides which wore out
all his suite, his machine-like power of endurance in long
conferences which left his Ministers prostrate with fatigue, his
correspondence, often ranging far into the night, on all matters
from the conduct of a campaign to the repair of a road or the
chit-chat of the royalist *salons* in the Faubourg St Germain—
and the almost superstitious awe with which he inspired

idéologues and men of action alike, may perhaps be imagined. " The gigantic (wrote one of his Councillors of State) entered into our very habits of thought."

But the student who has realised the social and political weakness of the old European system, will find nothing super-natural even in the extraordinary career of the young Corsican who now swayed the destinies of the Continent. He himself, in words remarkable for their candour and perspicacity, once revealed the causes of his success—" Nothing has been simpler than my elevation. It was owing to the peculiarity of the times....I have always marched with the opinion of great masses and with events."

CHAPTER IX.

THE NATIONALIST REACTION.

"At first the great man had enlisted his high intelligence and powerful will in the service of the general sentiments and desires. He now seeks to employ the public force in the service of his individual ideas and desires. He attempts things which he alone wishes or understands. Hence general disquietude and uneasiness."—GUIZOT.

THE latter part of 1807 may be regarded in many respects as the zenith of Napoleon's career. In ten months he had humbled Prussia to the dust. His will reigned supreme from Lisbon to Warsaw, from Copenhagen to Naples. There was as yet no discord in his relations with the Czar. Sweden was struggling hopelessly against her foes; and England seemed to be slowly succumbing to the commercial strangulation of the Continental System. Everywhere he had encountered a half-hearted or ill-organised resistance from armies and Governments weakened by mutual jealousies or by want of hearty support from the nations which they claimed to represent. But after 1807 the struggle enters on a new phase. The resistance to Napoleon slowly deepens, as defeated rulers and statesmen begin to enlist on their side the forces which France had so triumphantly wielded.

The State which suffered the most disastrous overthrow was the first to profit by the lessons of adversity. Two months after the loss of half his dominions at Tilsit, Frederick William

III entrusted the regeneration of Prussia to that able and determined reformer, Baron vom Stein. This great man, whose influence on Prussia is comparable to that of Napoleon on France, was by birth an Imperial Knight of the old Holy Roman Empire; but, attracted by the reforming zeal of Frederick the Great, he had in 1780 entered the Prussian service, with the ultimate hope of furthering the unification of Germany. In all his early organising work,—whether road-making, canalisation of the R. Ruhr, or the incorporation of Münster in the Prussian dominions—there appeared a passion for thoroughness, and for vigorous government in the interests of the people. An earnest student of Turgot and Adam Smith, he strove to carry out in Clèves and Münster what the great French reformer had planned for the Limousin; for he saw clearly the defects in the social and political life of Germany. Arthur Young's description of the solitudes around the mansion of a French seigneur is not more vigorous than Stein's comment on the results of feudalism in N. Germany:—"The abode of the Mecklenburg noble, who, instead of helping his peasants, hunts them, seems to me like the lair of some beast of prey which devastates all around and encircles itself with the stillness of the grave." Equally spirited, after he entered the Finance Ministry at Berlin, was his protest against the Cabal, or secret irresponsible Cabinet, which intervened so disastrously between the king and his Ministers; and in Jan. 1807 Frederick William dismissed him as a "scornful, obstinate and disobedient official." But after Tilsit, all was changed. The Prussia of Frederick the Great had utterly collapsed. The unhappy land lay under the heel of a conqueror whose exactions had no limit except the inability of his victim to pay any more. Indeed, nothing but fear of arousing the Czar's jealousy kept Napoleon from annexing the whole land, which his army continued to occupy. In a crisis so desperate a complete break with the past was inevitable. The king accordingly urged Stein to take office with almost unlimited powers; and he as frankly accepted (Oct. 4, 1807) the Herculean task of reforming the social and political systems of Prussia by royal decrees. His successful inauguration of this policy not only saved Prussia from the social convulsions which followed the fall of feudalism in France, but indissolubly connected the fortunes of the Hohenzollern House with the cause of social equality. Alone of the old reigning families it found the great man, "the demi-god, who," according to Rousseau, "was fit to give new laws to men." Whereas the failure of Louis XVI and his Ministers to overcome the resistance of the Parlements had sealed the doom of the Bourbons, the legislation of Stein and Hardenberg secured the continuity of monarchy in Central Europe. The contrast is reflected in the national characteristics of to-day. While Paris represents the cause of militant democracy, Berlin is as distinctly the symbol of an enlightened and vigorous personal rule.

If the French, after nine years of revolution, had needed a master mind to consolidate its results, how much more necessary was "reform from above" in Prussia, where the people at large had no share in public life? Stein's predecessors, Hardenberg and others, had recommended that the nobles should surrender their exclusive rights and their immunities from taxation, also that the serfs must be freed in Prussia Proper. Five days after Stein received his great powers, the Edict (Oct. 9, 1807) for the emancipation of the serfs throughout the whole Prussian monarchy appeared at Memel. It was to take effect from Martinmas, 1810. The same edict swept away the ancient restrictions on the possession of land, whereby only 'noble land' could be owned by nobles, only land belonging to towns could be held by men of the citizen class, and only 'peasant land' by peasants. Henceforth there was to be free trade in land, while nobles might follow 'citizen occupations'; the sharp lines marking off the callings of the citizen from those of the peasant were also obliterated. Precautions were, however, taken to prevent unlimited competition for land leading to the extinction of the peasant proprietors and land-holders who had formed, and were still to form, the backbone of the Prussian army.

The edict of emancipation was an almost despairing effort of the Prussian monarchy to retrieve the fortunes of its over-burdened States by allowing for the first time free play to all faculties and callings. The watchword of the revolution, "*la carrière ouverte aux talents*," was now proclaimed in Prussia, yet with a characteristic difference in the method of enunciation. Quietly and from the remotest corner of Prussia came the royal edict which reformed the basis of her society almost as completely as the spasmodic decrees of Aug. 4, 1789, had revolutionised the life of France. Another contrast must also be noticed, namely that in the Prussian edict the methods of confiscation were avoided,—except in the extinction of the status of serfdom or villainage. The former serfs were declared to be still "subject to all the obligations which bind them as free persons by virtue of the possession of an estate or by a special contract"; and it was not till Hardenberg's agrarian law of 1811 that the peasants became freeholders of two-thirds of their holdings, ceding one-third to their former lords in lieu of the feudal services which then were abolished. The two Prussian edicts, therefore, by transforming the serf into the peasant proprietor, quietly effected no less a change than that of the French copy-holder into the freeholder brought about partly by the decrees of the Constituent Assembly and partly by force. About the same time serfdom was abolished in Swedish Pomerania, the Grand-Duchy of Warsaw, and the States forming the Con-federation of the Rhine.

These new rights were to be closely associated with a vast extension of the sphere of civic duties, especially in connection with national defence. In the Prussian army the officers and the rank and file had been drawn almost exclusively from the two extremes of society, nobles and serfs respectively. That system had achieved wonders when worked by Frederick the Great against armies similarly composed; but even at Valmy it was seen that the Prussian army was a lifeless mechanism, and at the shock of Jena it collapsed helplessly before Napoleon's forces. If enfeebled Prussia was now to renew her strength, she must evidently have recourse to that system of universal conscription by which France had vanquished the Second and Third Coalitions. Frederick William himself urged on a great scheme of army reform; and the military commission suggested that whereas the army "had been hated and in some degree despised by the other classes, it ought to be the union of all the moral and physical energies of the nation." As the citizen class was now to be called to arms, there must be an end of the degrading punishments so prejudicial to the spirit of the men, though it had been often necessary in the past when foreign adventurers formed no small portion of the army. Further, as Prussia was overwhelmed by the increasing French demands for a war indemnity, and could not keep up a large force on active service, the famous organiser Scharnhorst proposed (1807) to drill men, and, after service in the standing army, to pass them into a provincial militia, "an internal supplementary police." This unambitious project would save the Prussian exchequer and perhaps allay Napoleon's jealous suspicions. In Sept. 1808, however, came a demand from Paris that the Prussian army should not exceed 42,000 men. Compliance was inevitable. Thus the conditions of the time almost compelled Scharnhorst, Gneisenau and other army reformers to form a secret reserve which in three years gave Prussia 150,000 trained troops; but it was not till 1813 that the Landwehr and Landsturm were actually formed as second and third lines of reserve. In the meantime officers received a new and skilful training, arms and uniforms were adapted to the swifter movements required in the Napoleonic wars, and new cannon were cast for the eight fortresses which remained free from the French army of occupation.

We saw that in the early days of the French Departmental System the terms citizen and National Guard were almost co-extensive, though the municipalities had to surrender nearly all their liberties to the central government after Nov. 1793. While a similar travesty of local self-government was being extended by the French in the Confederation of the Rhine, a desire was expressed by a few Prussian towns for some such self-government as had flourished in the mediæval Free Cities of Germany. Accordingly, with the help of his colleagues and the entire approval of the king, Stein promulgated his famous Municipal Reform of Nov. 19, 1808, which freed Prussian towns from their irksome control by the central government or the lord of the manor, and from government by half-pay officers. All towns, even those subject to manorial lords, were placed in the same relation to the State and were divided only according to population into great towns (those above 10,000), middle towns (above 3500) and small towns (above 800 souls). The old distinctions between 'great' and 'small' citizens now ceased, and all Prussian civilians who owned land in the town or followed town occupations were henceforth during good conduct to enjoy the rights and fulfil the duties of citizenship; all others were merely 'residents,' who must pay rates but were without the franchise. The citizens were to elect an executive magistrate and a representative council, exercising a general supervision of all town affairs: only those councillors and other officials were to be paid who gave their whole time to public duties; and nearly all citizens were when elected bound to serve even in unpaid offices. The frequent appeals to civic spirit, and the use of German terms (e.g. 'Gemeinde' instead of 'Commune'), mark the desire of the Government to foster local patriotism as the first approach to a future national patriotism. The success of the measure may be seen in the superhuman efforts made by all parts of Prussia in 1813; while the practical nature of its details is shown by its continuing unchanged down to 1831—a striking contrast to the hasty and unfortunate French scheme of 1789—90.

Stein unquestionably designed this measure as a stepping-stone towards a national Parliament; but he barely had time before his resignation to draft a measure (which, in a modified form, became law in Dec. 1808) for unifying and strengthening the cumbrous administration of the State. In Prussia the responsible Ministers had formed no collective Cabinet but had consulted individually with the king, whose decisions were often warped by the secret advice of irresponsible 'cabinet secretaries' forming a sort of 'cabal.' Another cause of weakness and confusion was the local division of the departments of government, viz. that according to the separate and very diverse States or provinces of the monarchy. Indeed, nothing but Frederick the Great's genius and energy could have imparted clearness and energy to this 'cross division'—to use a logical term—of powers and functions called the Prussian Government. To put an end to this confusion, a Ministry of State, comprising only the responsible Ministers, was now to form the supreme legislative and executive Council presided over by the king or one of the Ministers. The local division of ministerial functions was abolished. The provinces were subdivided for administrative purposes into districts (*Bezirke*); and judicial tribunals were completely separated from the old governmental Chambers.

Stein was also able to abolish various trade monopolies of the old gilds, along with the exclusive rights of erecting mills in East Prussia. In fine, his thirteen months of office effected well-nigh as much for Prussia as the Constituent Assembly had done for France, that is, it transformed an almost mediæval social and political structure into a modern State. The parallel would have been still more complete if he had been able to crown his work by founding self-governing institutions for the parish and the circle (*Kreis*), and parliamentary representation for the nation. That he had prepared the way for this last innovation was clear by the king's ready assent to the convocation of the Provisional Parliaments which met in 1811 and again in 1812—1815; but this was to be the work of his scarcely less able successor, Hardenberg. The reforms actually promulgated by Stein had aroused a storm of opposition from the Prussian nobles and from what was known as the French party at Berlin; but the immediate cause of his dismissal was the seizure by the French (Aug. 1808) of an indiscreet letter in which the patriot Minister described the rapid growth of exasperation against Napoleon, the sensation caused by the Spanish rising, and the imminence of a Franco-Austrian war. This discovery gave Napoleon a pretext for pressing heavier terms on Prussia (Sept. 1808) and led to Stein's resignation of office. After the French had occupied Madrid the Emperor launched a decree of proscription against Stein (Dec. 1808), who fled for his life to Austria.

A change in laws and institutions writes itself but tardily in the national life, unless the nation itself has been quickened to a new and vitalising receptivity. If the work of the legislator is to yield plenteous fruit, the impulses which come from the poet and the thinker, or which spring unconsciously from the people itself, must first have played their part. The enthusiasm for Rousseau's teachings and the Rights of Man had aroused through Central Europe a wide-spread desire for some connection with democratic France; but the invasions of the revolutionary and Napoleonic armies began to dispel the dreams even of German Jacobins. Instead of forming a federation of free States, Germany was becoming the parade-ground and commissariat department of French armies, and groaned under the ever-increasing pressure of the Continental System. The most phlegmatic temperament was moved by the French domination to think more kindly of the cumbrous old empire; while an ardent nature like that of the historian and poet Arndt revolted at the sight of "the old German splendour overthrown and trodden underfoot by these insolent French....When Austria and Prussia had fallen, then first I began to love Germany truly, and to hate the foreigner with an utter hatred." Schiller's last drama, *Wilhelm Tell* (1804), describing the rising of the Swiss mountaineers against Hapsburg usurpations, seems designed to unite Germans by the claims of brotherhood, patriotism and love of freedom to repel all French aggressions on the Fatherland. Unfortunately, the greatest of German poets, Goethe, after his *Hermann und Dorothea* (1797), remained deaf to the new patriotic movement and belittled himself by accepting from Napoleon the Cross of the Legion of Honour (Oct. 1808). But a school of young patriotic poets was rising, which shook off the indifference of the 18th century poets to the claims of country, and soon gave forth many a patriotic song to inspire their brethren on the battle-field.

The new spirit of the age invaded the domains of philosophy and education. The first man on the Continent to utter a public protest against the Napoleonic domination was the great thinker Fichte, who up to 1805 had professed complete indifference about the rise and fall of States; but in the days of Prussia's humiliation, patriotism dethroned his cosmopolitan philosophy, and in the early part of 1808 inspired those glowing appeals to national sentiment, the *Addresses to the German Nation.* As Germany had perished owing to the selfishness of its members, so now it could be restored only by a new ideal, the self-surrender of the individual for the good of the community. Every noble nature, he insists, will value life not for its own sake, but for the work which it can accomplish; and the perpetuity of that work can be assured only by the survival of the nation which values and protects it. Seeing that the old education had done nothing to curb individual

selfishness, there must be a new national education which may
"fashion the German people to a unity throbbing through all
its limbs." Fortifying his idealist appeals by a reference to the
days of Arminius, he shows that a nation which "fastens its
gaze on that vision from the spiritual world, Liberty, will
certainly prevail over a people which is used only as a tool for
lust of foreign sway." These inspiriting calls, uttered at the
risk of his life while the French garrisoned Berlin, sank deep into
the consciousness of the people, and helped on the formation
(1808) of a non-political association, the "Tugendbund," for the
"revival of morality, religion, serious taste and public spirit."
Fichte's influence also powerfully aided the impulse towards
national education. William von Humboldt, the great classical
scholar, was in April, 1809, appointed Minister of Education;
and in a year he extended and reformed the system of public
training in the public schools (Gymnasia). To compensate
for the loss of the University of Halle, and to bring culture and
practical life into close contact, two new Universities were
founded, at Berlin and Breslau, for the former of which the king
gave a royal palace. Just as Napoleon had desired by his
lycées and the University of France to enlist an army of
teachers in his service, so now Prussia in a wiser and less
autocratic spirit relied on the strength which a State gains from
the support of enlightened and devoted citizens. The result
was to be seen in the ardour with which professors and
students rushed to arms in the War of Liberation of
1813

"The Spaniards were the refrain to everything, and we
always returned to them": such is Varnhagen von Ense's summary of an interview with that humorous genius, Jean Paul
Richter, in Oct. 1808. The momentous influence of the
Spanish rising on German and European affairs now claims
our attention.

We have already seen that in pursuance of the policy of

Tilsit, Portugal had been occupied by French troops, while by
the secret Treaty of Fontainebleau (Oct. 1807) her lands were
to be divided between Napoleon and the Court of Madrid.
Accordingly Spanish troops helped General Junot in the occupation of Portugal. Spain was thus almost denuded of regular
troops; for after a foolish proclamation of the Spanish Court on
Oct. 4, 1806, calling the people to arms, Napoleon had required
that 4000 Spanish horse and 10,000 foot should be sent to
assist him in defending the mouth of the Elbe against England.
Even more favourable for his plans against Spain was the open
discord between Ferdinand, heir to the Spanish throne, and
his parents. The queen's favourite, Godoy, was bent on ruining Ferdinand and excluding him from the succession; and
when the prince attempted to overthrow Godoy on a hasty
charge of treason, he himself was placed under arrest by his
father Charles IV and was pardoned (Nov. 5) only on Napoleon's demands. It is generally assumed by historians hostile
to the French Emperor, that he all along intended to have the
crown of Spain at his disposal, in revenge for the ambiguous
and threatening call to arms issued by Godoy and Charles IV
just before Jena. There is, however, not much evidence for
this view except that the French ambassador at Madrid had
intrigued with Prince Ferdinand against the king. Mollien
even asserts that Napoleon's first intention in attacking Portugal
was merely to lure the English on to the mainland and
so decisively defeat them. But the unguarded state of Spain,
the apparent lethargy of its people, and the discords in the
royal palace, seem to have tempted him on to the perfidious
policy which culminated at Bayonne. The first sign of this
was his confidential order to Junot to send him a description
of the roads and resources of Spain, and drawings of its fortresses carefully made by his engineers. At first no suspicions
were aroused. Indeed, the march of 49,000 French troops
towards Valladolid caused no less joy to Ferdinand and the

great mass of the people than alarm to Godoy and Charles IV. They were at first welcomed as deliverers from the yoke of the insolent favourite who was seizing the chief emoluments of the State; but this feeling changed to alarm and indignation when all the chief strongholds of north Spain were by ruse or force occupied by the French (Feb.—March, 1808). Threatened by the French invaders, and hated by their people, the despicable king and queen prepared for flight to the New World, the very step to which Napoleon wished to drive them. The news of this cowardly intention aroused a storm of indignation; and a popular outbreak against Godoy brought about not only his resignation but the voluntary abdication of Charles IV in favour of "his very dear son Ferdinand" (March 19). Enraged at her ignominious fall, the queen besought the aid of Murat, commanding the French troops, to restore Charles IV to the position of which mob violence had deprived him.

The ambitious marshal, hoping that the crown of Spain would be his own, secretly promised to forward to Napoleon a protest against Ferdinand VII's accession; while the young king, hoping for Napoleon's continued support, facilitated the entry of Murat's troops into Madrid. Everything seemed to favour Napoleon's plans; and his clever agent Savary was now sent to induce Ferdinand to meet the Emperor in the north of Spain, with the assurance that his title as king would be recognised and his promised marriage with Napoleon's niece would be arranged. On this understanding the young king set out for Vittoria, where secret preparations were made by Savary to carry him off by force, if he refused to go further. Surrounded by French troops, he departed for Bayonne. The arrival there of his parents and Godoy increased his difficulties; for Charles IV demanded his abdication and yet disclaimed any intention of ruling again himself or even of returning to Spain. The news of a fierce popular rising in Madrid against the French and its ruthless repression by Murat (May 2) enabled the parents to heap on Ferdinand their bitterest taunts and Napoleon to threaten him with execution as a rebel. The young king's spirit at last was broken. On May 5th he resigned the crown to Charles IV, who in his ignoble desire for revenge on his people surrendered all his claims to Napoleon. Pensions and estates in France sufficed for these degraded descendants of a long line of kings; and Napoleon boasted to Talleyrand that he was "master of the situation in Spain as in the rest of Europe."

In reality he had compassed his own destruction both in Spain and throughout Europe. Instead of securing complete possession of Spain, this infamous treachery at Bayonne aroused a passion for vengeance in the Spanish people, nerving them to desperate struggles which even Napoleon's power could not crush. It was in vain that the dethroned princes and some official bodies counselled submission to overwhelming force, in vain that Napoleon promised to become "the regenerator of Spain." Without waiting to count the odds, the Spaniards rushed to arms, formed popular Juntas in their chief cities and a central one at Seville; and Europe saw the rise of a new and potent influence when the little province of Asturias with sublime audacity declared war against Napoleon and sent a request for English aid. Putting aside the consideration that we were nominally at war with Spain, Canning at once declared (June 15) that any nation opposing Napoleon "became instantly our essential ally"; and soon an English force was sent to assist in freeing the Peninsula. Meanwhile, though the patriots were in many places routed, they achieved two important successes, beating back the French from the streets of Saragossa and compelling the surrender of General Dupont's 20,000 troops at Baylen in Andalusia (July 21),—events which broke the spell of French invincibility. Joseph Bonaparte, named King of Spain by his brother—Murat had to accept with disgust the throne of Naples vacated by Joseph—after a nine days' sojourn at Madrid had to retreat with the French forces to the line of the Ebro. The fortunes of the patriots were advanced still further by the landing in Mondego Bay of 18,000 British troops under Sir Arthur Wellesley, and their victory over Junot's forces at Vimiero (Aug. 21); but the arrival of the senior commanding officers Burrard and Dalrymple led to the much censured Convention of Cintra, by which the French troops in Portugal were to be conveyed on British ships to France. The commencement of the Peninsular War was thus marked by two considerable successes, one gained by the numbers and enthusiasm of the Spanish levies, the other by the tenacity of British regulars and the skill of a military genius, Sir Arthur Wellesley, whose patience, powers of organisation, and unerring judgment supplied just those qualities in which our allies were most deficient. A further gain to Spain was the escape on British ships of the Spanish troops compelled in 1806 to serve Napoleon in Denmark. The annexation to Napoleon's dominions of the east of the Papal States in April 1808, and of Rome in May 1809, gave the Spanish Rising the aspect of a crusade against infidels; and every able-bodied man who did not serve against the French was looked upon as a traitor to his country and his faith.

This explosion of popular fury, from what had long been considered an extinct volcano, thrilled Europe with astonishment and Napoleon's foes with hope. The French funds which after Tilsit rose to 94 now sank to 70; and the Emperor, after ante-dating the conscription of 1809 so as to replenish his armies, turned to assure himself of the Czar's support before crushing the Spanish patriots. The change in policy was significant. Before Tilsit Napoleon had posed as the champion of democracy against the old Governments. Henceforth he relied on dynastic alliances, while his foes could for the first time appeal to a potent principle, that of nationality. The moral force, which he himself measured even in warfare as three times the effect of the physical force, now began to pass over to the side of his enemies.

Outwardly, however, the fabric of his power was more imposing than ever. The meeting of the Emperors of the West and East at Erfurt was graced by an assemblage of German kings and princes, who were clearly made to perceive their dependence on the conqueror. But there was another object more pressing than that of parading the humiliation of Germany, namely to renew the Franco-Russian alliance. The policy of Tilsit had aroused, but not satisfied, Alexander's ambition for conquests on the lower Danube. The conquest of Finland from Sweden, agreed upon between the Emperors at Tilsit, had been virtually accomplished; but Alexander desired above all to revive the Eastern Empire by extending his Empire to the Bosphorus. He had accordingly heard with great chagrin (Jan. 1808) that Napoleon disapproved of any partition of Turkey and demanded Silesia for France if Russia kept Moldavia and Wallachia. The Spanish question, however, led to Napoleon's renunciation of this claim, and to the revival of the partition scheme; for Alexander insisted that the expulsion of the Turks from Europe was required by the enlightenment of the age even more than by sound policy. But for the Spanish rising, it is certain that the interest of the world would have turned to the East; for Napoleon in the early part of 1808 often said that Constantinople was the centre of his policy. Indeed, his correspondence of May, 1808, shows that after settling Joseph in Spain, he desired to ruin English commerce by a Franco-Russian expedition overland to Egypt, Persia, and India, while French and Spanish squadrons despatched to the Cape and other parts were to distract and humble the mistress of the seas.

The Spanish rising changed all that. An immediate breach with Turkey was now most undesirable. Alexander's support was also more than ever necessary to hold in check Central

Europe, now aroused by French reverses beyond the Pyrenees; for the Hapsburgs feared that after the fall of the last Bourbons their turn would come next. Austria accordingly began to arm. From his dreams of eastern conquests, the French Emperor was thus suddenly brought to the need of renewing that agreement with the Czar, on which rested his domination in Central Europe. Relying, however, on his ascendancy over Alexander, he determined to win a diplomatic triumph such as he had gained at Tilsit. He thus summed up his desires to Talleyrand, whom he charged with the negotiations at the Erfurt interview:—"I want to come back from Erfurt free to do what I like in Spain: I want to be sure that Austria's uneasiness will be held in check; and I don't want to be definitely engaged with Russia in eastern affairs." This was virtually the result of the famous interview. The Czar agreed to postpone the joint expedition against Turkey and the East; but he firmly refused to join in a demand for Austrian disarmament. Vainly did Napoleon resort by turn to blandishments and exhibitions of temper. "From me"—retorted Alexander —"anger gains nothing. Let us reason, or I depart." Sumptuous festivities, appropriate dramas acted by the *Comédie Française*, interviews with Goethe and other German *savants*, hid from the world these inner dissensions; and at the end of a fortnight of unexampled splendour, Napoleon gained the substance of his demands in a secret Convention (Oct. 12, 1808). It renewed the Franco-Russian alliance formed at Tilsit, and offered peace to England, with the retention of conquests by each belligerent, if she would recognise Joseph Bonaparte as King of Spain, and the cession of Finland, Moldavia and Wallachia to Russia. Napoleon also, under the strictest secrecy, consented to the Czar's acquisition of the Danubian Provinces. If Turkey renewed the war with Russia, France was to remain neutral, unless Austria helped the Sultan. In that case Austria was to be attacked by France; and if she made war on Napoleon, the Czar promised to give active aid to his ally. Finally, Denmark was to receive an indemnity for the losses sustained in 1807. The diplomatic victory here rested with Napoleon as decisively as at Tilsit. His new engagements to the Czar involved him in no immediate breach with Turkey; and in secretly assenting to the Russian acquisition of the Danubian Provinces and Finland, he only acknowledged what then seemed definite conquests. Alexander, on the other hand, promised to keep Austria quiet while Napoleon finished with Spain. An envoy sent by the Emperor Francis to Erfurt failed, notwithstanding Talleyrand's private assistance, to avert this understanding, though Talleyrand's secret preliminary advice to the Czar, that Austria was necessary to the equilibrium of Europe, led to his rejection of the joint proposal for her instant disarmament. Furthermore, a hint dropped by Napoleon to Alexander, and developed by Talleyrand, that the interests of France required Josephine's divorce and that one of the Czar's sisters was of a suitable age, met with an evasive though not unfriendly reply. Thus opened that rift within the lute, which somewhat marred the majestic harmonies of Erfurt.

Without waiting for the "diplomatic mummery"—as Fouché termed it—of proposing peace to England on condition that she would desert the cause of the Spanish patriots, Napoleon set out for the Ebro to end "this war of peasants and monks," scattered their ill-organised forces and on Dec. 2 received the capitulation of Madrid. There he at once ordered the abolition of the Inquisition and sequestration of its property, the reduction of monasteries and convents by two-thirds (the property of the suppressed houses being also confiscated), the abolition of all feudal rights over rivers &c., the *banalités* of mills, all seigneurial courts of justice, and provincial Customs' barriers; but these sweeping social reforms made little impression on a people whose feeling he had so deeply outraged.

For the present Napoleon turned to crush Sir John Moore's

army, which, relying on the promises of the Spaniards, had marched from Portugal towards Burgos in the vain hope of rallying the Spaniards, or at least of diverting the French march from Madrid. The English force of about 24,000 men was now exposed to Napoleon's victorious armies, which when united numbered over 80,000; but Moore by a skilful retreat amidst terrible hardships withdrew his troops to Corunna. There, armed with new muskets, his men beat back Soult's superior forces (Jan. 16, 1809) and embarked for England, leaving their gallant leader buried in the citadel of the fortress. This ill-fated expedition did not alter the current of English public opinion; for two days before the Battle of Corunna a treaty of alliance had been signed at London between Great Britain, 'Ferdinand VII,' and the Central Junta of Seville, binding the contracting parties to a close alliance against France. The return of Napoleon to Paris, to extirpate the germs of discontent and confront Austria, scarcely lessened the pressure on the Spanish patriots. Everywhere they were defeated. The determined men of Aragon, after the most desperate defence of modern times, were compelled to surrender to Marshal Lannes the ruins of their capital, Saragossa (Feb. 21). Yet, though all parts of Spain except the most mountainous districts were in a military sense conquered, the peasantry still flocked to arms with a dogged perseverance which defied the efforts of over 300,000 French; and when some 40,000 of Napoleon's troops were withdrawn to confront the war preparations of Austria, and Sir Arthur Wellesley landed at Lisbon, the Peninsular War entered on another phase.

In Prussia, as we have seen, Stein had striven to excite a war *à outrance* against Napoleon; but Frederick William refused to stir without the aid of the Czar, which was not to be obtained. The war party in Austria had however gained the upper hand in the autumn of 1808, seeing in the Spanish rising as powerful a help as that offered by the regular armies of Russia and

Prussia before Friedland.   In truth, the position of Austria since the Treaties of Presburg and Tilsit had become insupportable.   Shut out from her traditional influence in Germany and Italy, threatened by Napoleon's troops in Prussia, Saxony, Bavaria, and Venetia, she saw her foreign commerce decaying under the influence of the Continental System, and heard with anguish the groans of her faithful Tyrolese under the cast-iron liberalism of Franco-Bavarian policy.   Five centuries of Hapsburg rule in accord with Tyrolese traditions had been cut short by the cession of Tyrol to Bavaria in Dec. 1805, but with a promise from the newly-styled King of Bavaria that the rights of that ancient county would be respected.   No sooner, however, was Tyrol fully occupied by his troops than he and his Minister Montgelas began to force on innovations like those recently introduced at Munich.   The property of Tyrolese bishoprics was confiscated, religious rites and customs were interfered with, in May 1808 the Estates were dissolved, and the name of South Bavaria was imposed.   As this happened at the time of Napoleon's usurpation in Spain, the annexation of half the Papal States to the kingdom of Italy, and the proposed Franco-Russian scheme for a partition of Turkey, it seemed part of a project for assuring universal dominion to Napoleon and his allies.   The result of the Erfurt Conference was by no means reassuring to the Emperor Francis, except to show that Alexander desired to maintain Austria as a bulwark between Russia and the Napoleonic States.   The belief that the Czar was secretly jealous of French domination, that England would help her by an expedition to the Low Countries, the certainty that the Tyrolese would revolt against the Bavarian rule, and that Napoleon must keep fully 250,000 men in Spain, decided Austria to prefer the risks of war to an intolerable peace.   So far from her action being an aristocratic plot for the overthrow of French democracy, Austria's conduct in the spring of 1809 showed a greater reliance on popular sentiment and support than ever before. In June, 1808, Francis had ordered the enrolment of a defensive militia, to act also as a reserve for the regular army; and the Archduke Charles, by improving not only the military organisation but also the condition of the soldiery, greatly increased the efficiency and tenacity of his forces. The Chancellor, Count Stadion, talked of inaugurating reforms like those of Stein in Prussia; and Austria stood forth as the champion of German nationality. "Soldiers"—so ran the proclamation of the Archduke Charles, April 6, 1809—"the freedom of Europe has sought refuge under your colours. Your triumphs will loose her fetters, and your German brethren still in the enemy's ranks await deliverance from you[1]." The last wish was to be falsified. Fear of Austrian conquest or of Napoleon's vengeance kept on his side the troops of the Rhenish Confederation, but as soon as an Austrian corps entered Tyrol, the whole country arose: 6000 Franco-Bavarian troops were compelled to surrender, and in five days Tyrol was freed by these brave peasants under the lead of Hofer and Hormayer.

Space will admit only the briefest account of the chief campaign—that on the Danube. The Archduke Charles, leading a force of about 120,000 men up to Ratisbon, for a time placed the French and confederate troops in great danger; but Napoleon, hurrying from Paris, at once massed his forces and by vigorous blows at Haussen, Abensberg, Landshut, Eckmühl, and Ratisbon (April 19—23) defeated the Austrian forces and drove them down the opposite sides of the Danube. By the side of these terrible reverses, temporary Austrian successes in

[1] Some writers call this the war of the Fifth Coalition, reckoning the Fourth as being inaugurated by the Treaties in the spring of 1807. It is preferable, I think, to reckon the struggle of April—June, 1807, as the Third Coalition in its second phase. That of 1809 was not a Coalition, there being no treaty between Austria and England, or between Austria and the Spanish patriots.

Venetia, Tyrol and at Warsaw were of little avail; for the defeats on the upper Danube precluded the hope of that general rising of Germany, for which Stein and all patriots had hoped and worked. A hopeless attempt was indeed made near Cassel; and the brave Colonel Schill, leading his cavalry regiment out of Berlin, strove to excite a national war against the French; but, meeting with little support, he marched northwards to Stralsund, there to be overpowered and slain by Dutch troops in Napoleon's service (May 31). The young Duke of Brunswick also began a daring raid from Bohemia into Saxony, gaining some signal successes over Jerome Bonaparte's troops; but the issue of this and other isolated efforts, even of the far more important and sustained Tyrolese rising, depended on the main campaign on the Danube.

Meanwhile Napoleon had entered Vienna; but in his attempt to drive the Austrian army from the north bank of the Danube, he met with his first great repulse at Aspern-Essling (May 21—22), finally having to draw back his shattered troops into the great island of Lobau, with a total loss of about 20,000 men. A thrill of expectation ran through Europe at this unexpected change of fortune. "In Prussia" (wrote Varnhagen von Ense) "the enthusiasm is general. The spell is broken. Napoleon is no longer invincible....His downfall may well be expected." If Schill's and Brunswick's attempts had been made conjointly after the news of Aspern, and England had made her projected diversion on the North Sea coast in time, it is probable that Germany would have been aroused, and Napoleon's overthrow assured; but again he was to be saved by the maladroitness of his foes and his own surprising energy. Marmont, Marbot, and other French commanders, admit that a vigorous attack on their rear immediately after Aspern would have placed their army in the greatest danger; but the Archduke Charles, dismayed by his own heavy losses, remained strictly on the defensive, and allowed Eugène's army from Italy to strengthen the French communications. After six weeks of quiet preparation and concentration of all available forces, about 170,000 French crossed the Danube at night, far below the Austrian batteries, thus compelling the enemy to fall back on another strong position at Wagram. There a long and most obstinate conflict (July 6) was finally lost by the 140,000 defenders, mainly owing to the non-arrival of the Archduke John, who was to support their left wing, and by the skill and persistence of Macdonald's attack on their centre; but this Marshal —he received the title on the field of battle—himself wondered why the Austrians, after an orderly retreat, should have sought an armistice (July 15) from victors who were in almost equally great straits owing to want of ammunition. The despondency of the Austrian Government was deepened by Wellesley's retreat on Portugal after Talavera and by the failure of England to make any timely and effective diversion on the North Sea coast.

The surrender of the Hapsburgs was fatal to the daring attempt of the Duke of Brunswick, as well as to the Tyrolese patriots. After defeating Jerome's troops and occupying Brunswick, the brave leader had to retreat to the North Sea coast, where he was saved by an English squadron (Aug. 10). The Tyrolese resistance was harder to break. After the first defeats of the Archduke Charles on the upper Danube, the Franco-Bavarian forces again occupied Innsbruck (May 19), only to be driven out of Tyrol at the close of that month so disastrous for Napoleon's arms; and after Aspern the Emperor Francis promised that he would sign no peace which would sunder Tyrol and Vorarlberg from his Empire. The men of the latter province made successful raids into Baden, and even captured Constance; and Tyrol enjoyed two months' rest under Hofer. Once an inn-keeper near Meran, Hofer now resided at the castle of Innsbruck with the title of Imperial Commander-in-chief, levied taxes, issued a coinage, organised

a militia, and restored the old system of government. After
Wagram, Lefebvre led 25,000 troops up the Inn valley and
occupied Innsbruck; but at Hofer's summons the brave Tyrolese
again rose. In a deep valley near Oberau their sharp-shooters
harassed another invading column. The mountaineers crushed
the Saxons with rocks and trees, and the invaders were rolled
back on the capital, where another reverse decided the French
marshal to evacuate the county (Aug. 14). All the devotion of
the Tyrolese, however, was futile, if unaided by some show of
energy on the part of the British Government and by determination in the councils of the Emperor Francis. He and his
new Minister of Foreign Affairs, Metternich, foreseeing no
effective help from any quarter against Napoleon's superior
forces, finally agreed to conditions of peace. These the French
Emperor, by a discreditable *ruse*, considerably aggravated, and
hurried on to the final stage of the Treaty of Schönbrunn
(Vienna), Oct. 14,—"a treaty (Metternich declares) full of un-
worthy artifices, having no foundation in international rights."
By it Austria recognised the Bavarian rule over Tyrol and
Vorarlberg, besides ceding to Bavaria Salzburg and a strip of
Upper Austria as far as the R. Inn. To the French Empire
she yielded up Croatia, Carniola, with Trieste and the greater
part of Carinthia—all of which were reorganised by Napoleon
as the Illyrian Provinces. The Grand Duchy of Warsaw
received from the Hapsburgs all West and New Galicia (their
share of the spoils of 1795) together with a district around
Cracow; while the Czar received a strip of land from East
Galicia. Beside these losses of 4,500,000 subjects and of her
maritime provinces, Austria agreed to pay a war indemnity of
£3,400,000, bound herself closely to the Continental System,
and secretly agreed to limit her army to 150,000 men, as well
as to dismantle some of her fortresses, including Vienna. After
the least disastrous of her four wars against Napoleon she now
suffered the severest losses ever sustained by the Hapsburgs;

and worse than their cessions of territory was the abandonment of the reforming policy which had recently promised to yield to them the moral as well as political hegemony of Germany. Even so, the patriotism of the Viennese, clinging ever more firmly to the Hapsburgs amid the storms of adversity, gave to the return of their Emperor Francis the appearance of a triumphal entry. Indeed, it is significant that the most stubborn and successful resistance to Napoleon in 1809 was offered by the rank and file or by armed peasants, while timidity still paralysed the councils of commanders and diplomatists. A keen eye could discern, even amidst disasters, that the reaction against Napoleon was deepening in intensity.

After having by their own gallantry three times freed their land from foreign troops, the Tyrolese refused to accept as final the terms of the Treaty of Schönbrunn which abandoned them to Bavaria. Towards the end of October 50,000 invaders began to press up the three chief Tyrolese valleys, the Pusterthal and those of the Inn and Adige. On the advice of the Archduke John, even Hofer leaned towards surrender until the fiery zeal of a few fanatics rekindled the embers of revolt. But the enemy held the main valleys, and the snows of winter gradually drove the Tyrolese from their fastnesses. Hofer, betrayed by an acquaintance, was taken to Mantua and there shot as a rebel (Feb. 20, 1810). To stamp out Tyrolese feeling the famous county was divided, part of the south-eastern districts going to the Illyrian Provinces, and most of the Adige valley being annexed to Eugène's kingdom of Italy; but readjustments of boundaries were powerless to efface the memory of the Tyrolese exploits against the might of Napoleon.

The student will probably have noticed that in many of the revolutionary and Napoleonic wars (especially in the campaigns of 1792—4, 1799—1800, 1803—1807) fortune favoured the allies in the spring and early summer, only to return more decisively to the tricolour standards in the latter part of the year. It was so in 1809 both in Central Europe and in the Spanish Peninsula. The withdrawal of 40,000 French from the Tagus to the Danube gave little relief to the Spanish patriots, until the advent of a military genius altered the whole character of the struggle. The French, numbering about 270,000 men under the lead of Soult, Ney, Victor, and St Cyr, were pressing back the Portuguese and Spanish levies, when Sir Arthur Wellesley took command of some 25,000 allied troops at Lisbon. Marching swiftly northwards, by a skilful and daring move he crossed the Douro above Oporto and compelled Soult with the loss of 58 cannon to evacuate Portugal. The rapidity with which the English commander organised the defence of Lisbon, marched 200 miles through rugged country, and, striking at the communications of a powerful foe, forced him to retreat with the loss of all his cannon and stores, may well challenge comparison with those masterly moves of Napoleon a month earlier, which, changing a weak defensive into a crushing offensive, drove the Archduke Charles from Bavaria. Could Wellesley have changed commands with the Austrian prince, the liberation of Europe might have occurred in 1809. The English general further showed his powers of quick insight and rapid action in a campaign against Victor on the Tagus. Deprived of necessary reinforcements by the British Ministry, neglected and almost starved by their Spanish allies, his troops yet penetrated to Talavera, where King Joseph and Victor assailed them. The English infantry stood firm, and though the centre was at one time broken, an opportune infantry charge of the 48th regiment gained the day (July 28); but the southward march of Soult's army compelled Wellesley to beat a speedy retreat on Portugal, indignant at the conduct of the Spanish forces. "We are here worse off than in a hostile country (he wrote to the English Government): never was an army so ill-used. The common dictates of humanity have been disregarded by them." He determined henceforth to dispense with Spanish aid and to act for the present on the frontier of Portugal, where he soon was able effectively to control the military organization. The complete rout of 52,000 Spaniards at Ocaña (Nov. 1809) by about half the number of French, with the loss of 26,000 prisoners, seemed to promise the speedy subjection of Spain. But the Central Junta of the patriots at Seville still breathed defiance to the French, and Miot de Melito, Joseph's adviser at Madrid, after all the French triumphs in Catalonia, Aragon and Castile, wrote despondingly—"We have conquered but not convinced."

This expression aptly characterises the whole European situation at the close of 1809. The new national impulses in Germany and Spain were as yet ill-organized, and had produced only one leader worthy of entering the lists against Napoleon; and Wellesley was at the head of only 20,000 British troops, while double that number were being sacrificed at Walcheren by the incapacity of Chatham. This splendid expedition, which might have aroused North-Germany and effected a most important relief for Austria, did not set sail till a month after she had been crushed at Wagram. It was then aimed against Antwerp; but time was wasted in reducing Flushing until the former could no longer be carried by a *coup de main.* Our forces retired into Walcheren, whence after the loss of nearly half their number by disease they were withdrawn before Christmas, 1809. In this year of disjointed efforts the Walcheren failure was by far the most disgraceful; yet the Danube campaign shattered a reputation which had hitherto been second only to that of Napoleon. The Archduke Charles, skilful tactician though he was, so lost his power of initiative when opposed to the French Emperor as to paralyse the arm of Austria in April and July; while born leaders of men like Schill and the Duke of Brunswick were condemned to a merely guerrilla warfare in the level plains of Germany where such methods were hopeless. Nevertheless this disastrous year had shown that Napoleon's domination rested only on force, fear, and the incapacity of the governments opposed to him. That he recognised the merely personal character of his supremacy was shown by a remarkable event at its close.

As soon as Napoleon gained the Consulate for life some members of his family had urged him to divorce Josephine, who had borne him no child. Amidst the glories of Tilsit and Erfurt the need of an heir to consolidate his dynasty was more patent than ever. So persistent were the rumours of a divorce after Erfurt, that Fouché undertook to plead with Josephine to promote the interests of France by agreeing to a separation from Napoleon, as "the most sublime and also the most inevitable of sacrifices." An affecting interview between Napoleon and Josephine led to a disavowal of Fouché's act. It was certainly premature, for at that time a bride was still to be found. The elder of Alexander's surviving sisters had been engaged to the Duke of Oldenburg, immediately after the Erfurt interview; and the present tension in Franco-Russian relations promised no better success to a request for the hand of the younger sister. The extreme reluctance with which the Czar drew the sword against Austria (May, 1809), as he was bound to do by the Erfurt Convention, and the ostentatious inactivity of his troops, exposed him to the charge of perfidy; but after the somewhat doubtful issue of the Danube campaign, and amidst the discontent of all Roman Catholics at the imprisonment of the Pope (July, 1809), the French Emperor could not break with the autocrat of the East. The Czar's annoyance at the Treaty of Schönbrunn was, however, partly appeased by a promise from Napoleon that Poland should not be re-established. This act of complaisance was accompanied closely by a formal request (Dec.

1809) for a matrimonial alliance. A few days previously
the Emperor had announced his intentions to Josephine, who
flung herself down in a transport of grief with the words "No:
I will never survive it." He tenderly aided one of his chamber-
lains to carry her to her apartments; and the agitation which
shook his frame should prove to all but his bitterest enemies
that he had retained much of his early devotion for her; while
the friendship which in her retirement at Malmaison she to
the end of her days preserved for him, may well prove the
sincerity of his alleged reasons for the divorce.

This sinister event took place (Dec. 15); but the proposal
for a marriage with the Czar's younger sister met (Jan. 1810)
with the same reply as the Erfurt proposal, namely that these
matters were entirely in the hands of the Czar's mother, who
was known to be bitterly opposed to the French. Foreseeing
the possibility of such a reply, and keenly impressed with the
need of gaining as soon as possible a direct heir to his throne,
Napoleon had already caused his envoy at Vienna to meet
half-way some cautious advances which Metternich, the new
Austrian Foreign Minister, had made (Nov. 30, 1809) on the
subject of an Austrian princess. It was in pursuance of the
policy which this skilful statesman had recommended to his
master on his assumption of the heavy cares of office:—"We
must confine our system to tacking, and turning, and flattering.
—There remains but one expedient, to increase our strength
for better days, and to work out our preservation by gentle
means." At Paris it is certain that Josephine herself, her son
Eugène, Talleyrand, and many others urged on the Austrian
marriage alliance as having a more lasting effect, as tending to
preserve the equilibrium of Europe in favour of France, and as
"absolving France from a crime not her own, but only the
work of a faction." The skilful pleading of Talleyrand at the
Privy Council meetings at Paris (Jan. 29 and Feb. 6) would
perhaps have availed little but for Napoleon's knowledge of

the first evasive answers from St Petersburg. The Council meetings gave him the appearance of choosing between a Russian and an Austrian bride; and, before the final refusal of the Czar's mother was made known, a courier set out from Paris for Vienna, asking for the hand of the Archduchess Marie Louise. Napoleon's *amour propre* was thus saved from a public slight, but only at the expense of Alexander's feelings; and the mutual annoyance at the whole proceeding was evinced and accentuated by the French Emperor's immediate refusal to ratify in treaty form his promise that he would never re-establish Poland. Alexander on his side took this as a thinly-veiled threat that the French Emperor meant to use the Poles in a war against Russia, and soon remarked to his friend and former minister, Czartoryski, that he expected war in 1811.

The marriage of Napoleon (April 1, 1810) with the niece of the ill-fated Marie Antoinette was something more than a visible sign of the repentance of France for the crime of 1793. It effected far more than the admission of the Corsican *caporal* and heir to the revolution, into the proudest of reigning families. It was an event of far-reaching importance. Napoleon had long ago remarked that his position could only be secured by an alliance with Russia or Austria. After Wagram he had reduced the latter almost to a second-rate Power, and seemed to desire a partition of the world between the Empires of the West and the East. The policy of Tilsit and Erfurt was now undermined by the Austrian marriage. Henceforth he began to support the Hapsburg Empire, to isolate Russia, and while holding her fast to his commercial system, to push her out of Europe in matters political and military. The marriage with Marie Louise further marks a recurrence to the Charlemagne ideal, somewhat discarded in 1807—1809 for what may be called the Romano-Byzantine policy of Tilsit and Erfurt. As the old Frankish hero's failure to gain the hand of the Eastern Empress Irene had limited his aims to central and southern Europe, so too Napoleon after 1809 reverted to a more Frankish or Germanic policy. His correspondence and his conduct to Goethe and Wieland at Erfurt show his desire of propitiating the nascent sentiment of German nationality which so nearly caused his overthrow in May—June 1809. The alliance with the Hapsburgs now marks the final effort of Napoleon to reconcile Central Europe to the increasing hardships which his Continental System imposed. Outwardly the Austrian marriage consolidated the Napoleonic supremacy in Central Europe; and the birth of a son, the 'King of Rome,' seemed to place the keystone on the arch whereby he sought to span the gulf hitherto separating the old dynasties from the French Revolution. One other result of this momentous event must be observed. It emphasized the abandonment by Austria of her reforming projects and of her championship of German nationality from which Stein had hoped so much; and the tortuous time-serving policy necessitated by this ignoble alliance was to yield to Prussia, in the decisive struggle of 1813, the moral and political leadership of Germany.

Long diverted from his efforts against England by the Spanish Rising and the Austrian War, Napoleon now desired to end the Peninsular War and complete the ruin of England by hermetically sealing the Continent against her goods. This cause or pretext for the annexation of maritime districts to his Empire—e.g. that of Etruria in 1808 and the Papal States in 1809—now began to operate with renewed vigour. Sweden was compelled (January, 1810) to adhere rigidly to his Continental System, and renounce the exceptions in favour of salt and colonial produce which she had for nine months striven to maintain. Louis Napoleon was overwhelmed with reproaches from Paris for his neglect to apply that system with full rigour to his kingdom of Holland, which lived by its foreign and carrying trades. When, after numerous quarrels, Louis saw himself menaced by Napoleon's troops, he abdicated in favour of his son (July 1); but this act was promptly set aside, and Holland was annexed to the French Empire (July 9).

Hitherto the Continental System had been more or less evaded in Holland and even in the French Empire; for while both the English and French Governments nominally forbade all intercourse, they secretly issued licences to merchants for trading even with a prohibited State in goods which were greatly needed. Indeed, the chief aim of our Orders in Council, the control of the ocean commerce of the world, had been so far attained that Europe had to procure colonial produce directly or indirectly through our shippers, or submit to the privation of coffee, sugar, cotton, indigo, and the many products required in manufacture. Even where the license system failed, smuggling effected much the same result. From our ports of vantage in Malta and Sicily, from many ports of the Spanish Peninsula, the Channel Islands, and Heligoland, our goods secretly found their way into Europe, or even by way of Salonica and the Balkan passes into Austria and Germany.

A French decree of October 1809, forbidding the importation of all colonial produce into Hamburg, proves that Napoleon even at that time regarded all such wares as being of British origin. It also states incidentally that about six hundred women had been engaged in smuggling coffee and other colonial produce into that city, though it was then garrisoned by French troops. In this connection we may quote the testimony of Bourrienne, who was then the French agent at Hamburg. "Smuggling on a small scale was punished with death, whilst the French Government carried it on extensively....Licences for the sale of English goods were procured at a high price by anyone who was rich enough to pay for them. The speculation in licences was carried to a scandalous extent only to enrich a few, and to satisfy the short-sighted views of the contrivers of the system. I informed Napoleon that, notwithstanding his precautions, every prohibited article was smuggled in, because the profits on the sale in Germany, Poland, Italy, and even in France, were too considerable to deter persons from running any risks whatsoever to obtain them....This profound ignorance of the maxims of political economy caused general privation and misery, which in their turn occasioned general hostility. The system could only succeed in the impossible event of all the Powers of Europe honestly endeavouring to carry it into effect. A single free port would have destroyed it. In order to ensure its complete success, it was necessary to conquer and occupy all countries, and never to evacuate them....It is necessary to have witnessed, as I have, the numberless vexations and miseries occasioned by this baneful system, in order to understand the mischief which it effected in Europe, and how much that mischief contributed to Napoleon's fall."—This interesting extract will serve to justify a statement which I shall often have to emphasize, that Napoleon's wars after 1807 had a vital connection with his Continental System ; and it incidentally refutes the prevalent belief that his later wars were solely the result of an unbridled ambition. On the contrary, they sprang almost necessarily from the adoption of a system which aimed at hermetically sealing the Continent against England, at securing a lasting peace and the undisputed supremacy of France. We must now return to consider the underlying causes of his failure and ultimate overthrow.

The Continent, oppressed by conscription or devastated by war, was never so dependent on England for cheap and good manufactures as at this time. Napoleon's system and the English Orders in Council ruined neutral commerce, thereby compelling Europe to exist on its own resources, or buy through English merchants at prices enormously enhanced by the risks encountered or the devious routes adopted. Knowing that practically all colonial produce was bought through English traders, Napoleon now endeavoured by the decrees of

Aug. and Oct. 1810 to raise a large revenue on colonial wares and yet destroy English goods. By the former he imposed duties averaging 40 or 50 per cent. on the value of colonial produce, because that was assumed to be the profit made by the merchant or smuggler. By the latter decree he ordered that all British manufactured goods should be seized and publicly burnt not only in his Empire, but in dependent States as Switzerland, the Rhenish Confederation, and the Hanse Towns. By these tyrannical orders the Emperor hoped finally to assure England's surrender; but the means adopted pressed more heavily on his own States than on his foes.

The confiscation and destruction of English goods brought present ruin on multitudes of his subjects in order to exclude those products in the future; while the 50 per cent. tax was of course paid by the consumer in the enhanced prices of all colonial wares. The result of Napoleon's determination to "make commerce manœuvre like a regiment"—to use Chaptal's phrase—was seen in the enormous increase of prices. Dyes, cotton, and other necessaries for manufactures now rose to twice, and sugar and coffee to five times, their natural values; and while the English manufacturer gained his raw materials as cheaply as before and economised in production by the use of the power-loom, his continental rivals enjoyed scarcely any of the new inventions, and were further handicapped by the very system which claimed to protect them from English competition. "When stripped of all political prestige (wrote Mollien) this system was seen to be the most mistaken and disastrous of fiscal inventions." It is, indeed, a remarkable fact that, when the economic blunders of the earlier revolutionists had so aggravated the miseries of France in 1793—5, the heir to the revolution should have assured his own overthrow by persisting in a policy, the results of which his own Finance Minister clearly foresaw. A few industries, it is true, were thereby started in his Empire;

and interested monopolists were loud in the praise of his
system as the "perfection of the prohibitive system" adopted
by the Mountain in 1793. Beetroot sugar began to be made;
the growth of cotton was attempted in Italy; and a few callings—especially that of the smuggler—received an artificial
stimulus from the high prices; but that France gained little
real benefit was proved by the growing discontent and by the
use of State credit to stave off a severe crisis in 1811.

That year was the crisis of the commercial struggle
between England and France. Our commerce, relieved in
1808—9 by its admission into the Spanish colonies, suffered
severely in 1810—1811 from the collapse of rash speculation
there, as also from the civil strife following their conflicts with
Spain; while the interruption of intercourse with the United
States, the increasing stringency of Napoleon's decrees, and the
failure of our harvest in 1810, threatened our industrial classes
with ruin and starvation. Trade was at a standstill in the
manufacturing districts; and the Luddite riots of 1811 threatened
a social revolution, had not relief come at the end of that
terrible year through the Czar's secession from the Continental
System. The depreciation of our paper currency, then almost
the only medium for our internal trade, and the alarming fall
in the exchange value with other lands, seemed to presage the
speedy collapse of our credit; but this very fall in the exchange tempted Continental traders to deal secretly with the
land where their money would go furthest. For these and
other reasons English trade survived the strain which was so
terrible to Continental industries.

In Germany the distress was felt more keenly than any-
where. The necessity of complete control of the North Sea coast
brought Napoleon to decree the annexation (Dec. 13, 1810) to
his Empire of all the lands between the Lower Rhine and the
Free City of Lübeck, including the Duchy of Oldenburg, ruled
by a relative of the Czar; and a fortnight later Canton Valais

was incorporated into the Empire so as to gain complete control over the great Simplon road into Italy. The results of complete subjection to the Continental System were thus described by F. Perthes, then dwelling at Hamburg.—"Of the 422 sugar-boiling houses at Hamburg, few now stood open: the printing of cottons had ceased entirely: the tobacco-dressers were driven away by the government. The imposition of innumerable taxes, door and window, capitation and land taxes, drove the inhabitants to despair."—The extension of the conscription to these new Departments of the Empire filled to the brim the measure of hatred against the tyrant of the Continent. It was indeed the height of folly for the new Charlemagne to nullify the undeniable benefits of his rule by measures which emptied every purse and every larder. To sweep away all relics of feudalism, to abolish serfdom throughout his Empire and dependent States, to decree religious liberty and civic equality, was futile when prosperous cities were ruined by his military exactions and commercial decrees. It was indeed the strangest contradiction to his earlier policy of healing the wounds and satisfying the material interests of France. In trusting to the proclamation of social equality to keep ruined communities in a state of idyllic content, the Emperor was now committing the very blunder of the revolutionary *idéalogues* whom he despised.

Whether Napoleon was sincere in the offers of peace which he made to the British Government after Marengo, to Fox in 1806, again just after Erfurt, or in 1809 before the annexation of Holland, is too large and complex a question to be discussed here. Those who believe in his desire for peace have to explain how it was that during the Peace of Amiens he proceeded with annexations as if in time of war, how far his designs in Jan.—March 1808 for the partition of Turkey and the East were consonant with a pacific policy, and whether his tentative proposal (March, 1810) of evacuating Holland and the

Hanse Towns if England would withdraw the Orders in Council, had any other aim than that of weakening our alliance with the Spanish patriots. Further official advances (apart from those made by Louis Napoleon and Fouché, for which the latter was disgraced) had been met by the reply from London that Napoleon must give up all claim to Spain, Sicily and Malta. The crushing terms imposed by him on Prussia and Austria were an ominous warning that peace might be worse than open war; and the British Government decided to remain true to its treaty of Jan. 1809 with the Spanish Central Junta.

It is more within our limits to point out that the weight of his government, the fearful drain in men and money, had long been producing discontent in France itself. The extension of his power, as a guarantee against a Bourbon restoration with the retrocession of the confiscated lands to their former owners (for therein lay the strength of Napoleon's position), was felt to be purchased at too high a cost when French blood was poured forth every year in quarrels which concerned French interests hardly at all. Farseeing Frenchmen—according to the testimony of Mollien—had long been dreading that his severity to the conquered States would "nationalise the resentment" against France; but after the disgrace of Talleyrand and Fouché his Ministers were little more than passive tools, as completely subject to his will as were the Ministries of 1793—4 to that Committee of Public Safety whose functions he inherited and developed. Remonstrances only served to bring disgrace on the very few who were so indiscreet as to offer them; while, by the strange irony characteristic of the years 1794—1814, those who at the earlier date had been the most ardent republicans were now foremost among the servile officials who desired to strengthen Napoleon's rule and to robe the new Empire with all the trappings of an ancient monarchy.

The ceremonial of Louis XIV's Court was revived with all its splendour, and with far more *ennui* to the courtiers than was possible in that age of wit and intellectual brilliance; for though Napoleon in private possessed great charm of manner, and generally unbent in a *tête-à-tête* with a Minister, his conduct in public always inspired a certain uneasiness or dread. Brilliant *causeur* though he was, the incisiveness of his questions, the sharp military ring of his sentences, generally recalled the associations of the parade ground. The effect of the smile which played about his cheeks and lips was marred by the ever fixed aquiline gaze of the eyes; and the general impression left on the beholder was one of ill-defined fear. "After the Emperor's departure"—wrote a foreign *attaché*—"we all breathed freely again as if a heavy weight had been taken off. The conversation became loud and general as before his entry; and the loudest of all were the hangers-on of the French court, who made amends for their previous silent dread by loud hilarity." Napoleon's dislike of "political women"—witness his exile of Mme. de Staël—allowed none of those witticisms at the expense of government which had often tempered its rigour under Louis XIV. Even in the royalist *salons* of the Faubourg St Germain criticisms on the imperial rule were uttered with bated breath, lest they should find a place in the weekly or daily letters sent to him by informers who reported the state of public opinion. As for the Emperor's Court, it is succinctly characterised by his Minister, Chaptal, as "a slave-galley where each courtier pulled the oar to the word of command."

Far more oppressive was the strain on the material resources of France. Vastly as these had been developed by the splendid activity of the First Consul, they were soon unequal to the demands of an aggressive Imperialism. Though Mollien had succeeded in balancing revenue and expenditure for 1808, yet the Budget was hopelessly deranged by the Spanish War, and the year 1811 closed with a deficit of 47,000,000 francs. For the first time Napoleon's adage that "war must support war" was completely falsified. The pay of Joseph Bonaparte's armies was generally a year in arrears, and the most pressing needs of his government could not be met from the scanty taxes of a land where revolt was general. Though Napoleon sent to Madrid part of the sums which he wrung from helpless Prussia, yet Spain continued to be so heavy a drain on French finance that he threatened to annex the land between the Pyrenees and the Ebro as a recompense. Talleyrand's quiet but firm disapproval of Napoleon's Spanish policy reflected the general sentiment of France. That whole struggle, envenomed by the perfidy which commenced it, disgusted France, and wearied troops accustomed to the short and dramatic campaigns in Italy or Germany. "It was the war in Spain (wrote Marbot) which brought about Napoleon's fall."

There were many reasons for the military failure in Spain. The Emperor, intent on supervising the myriad details of his administration and on maintaining his domination in Germany, could not control in person all the operations beyond the Pyrenees, and so ensure that unity of action which the jealousies of his generals compromised at many critical junctures. The hatred of the Spaniards for a government thrust upon them by treachery, nerved them to struggle on, even when in a military sense they were vanquished, as at the close of 1808 and 1809. Further, all the skill of the French commissariat, and the experience of their troops in foraging and plundering, failed sometimes to solve the problem expressed in Henri IV's phrase—"In Spain large armies will starve, and small armies will be beaten." Finally the vast extent of the peninsula, divided by five great mountain chains, the risks in the communications with France through rugged provinces inhabited by the tenacious Basques and Catalans, the difficulty of holding down the fertile south, so as to ensure a revenue, while making head against the English in the west and the guerrillas everywhere,—these obstacles and problems

alone would have retarded a permanent conquest, even in the
face of a commander of ordinary talents; and Wellington
possessed a combination of gifts—political tact in dealing with
his allies, prudence in husbanding resources, and discernment
when to strike quick and hard—possessed by no one of the
French Marshals, except perhaps Soult.

At the opening of the Peninsular campaign of 1810 the
position was, in brief, as follows. Suchet's bold and skilful
attacks were reducing most of the rugged province of Catalonia,
which a British force might have easily kept from his grasp.
Soult with 65,000 French had overrun the fertile province
of Andalusia and driven the Spanish Junta with its army into
the island which protects Cadiz (Feb. 1810). This great seaport remained the national capital as long as Madrid was
held by King Joseph's forces. In the north the French were
investing Astorga and Ciudad Rodrigo, when Masséna, Prince
of Essling, took command of an army of 86,000 men largely
composed of troops victorious in Germany, with orders to "drive
the leopards into the sea." The speedy success of Soult in
Andalusia and the formidable invasion of Portugal threatened by
Masséna quickly reduced Wellington to the defensive. In the
opinion of our allies and foes alike, he was guilty of deserting
the Spanish general who attempted a brave but unavailing
defence of Ciudad Rodrigo. Its surrender (July, 1810) and
the explosion of a powder magazine at Almeida, laid open the
northern road into Portugal, and the allies retired down the
valley of the Mondego. The slowness of Masséna's pursuit
gave Wellington the opportunity of massing some 50,000
Anglo-Portuguese troops on the heights of Busaco. The
French commander, though informed by Marbot that there
was a road which turned that strong position, yet persisted in
the front attack which Ney had first advised. His rashness
led to a severe defeat. Three brave attempts by about 60,000
French veterans to storm the heights were repulsed with the

loss of 4,500 men (Sept. 27, 1810). The moral effect of this battle was most important: the inexperienced Portuguese troops gained confidence: the British Ministry, long wavering before the attacks of a strong peace party, was encouraged to persevere with the war; and the disputes between Masséna and his generals were so envenomed by disaster as to paralyse French efforts at Torres Vedras. In a strategic sense the battle of Busaco was useless. Wellington's chief aim was to collect the allied resources within those famous lines; while Masséna's true course of action was shown by the ease with which he turned Wellington's position at Busaco by the flank march previously urged on him. The French now occupied Coimbra, but allowed Wellington to retire unmolested within the lines of Torres Vedras, taking with him or destroying the supplies of the country north of these defences. They consisted of an external and weaker line of works nearly 30 miles long from the sea to the Tagus, following the course of the mountains; a stronger inner line roughly parallel to the first; and a third at the mouth of the Tagus merely designed to cover a forced embarkation if the second line were pierced: 150 redoubts with 600 cannons crowned the most important positions; a flotilla on the Tagus protected the allied right; and the presence of 70,000 regular troops and 50,000 irregulars, under Wellington's supreme command, promised a desperate resistance of this the chief refuge of the cause of national independence. The peninsula of Lisbon, the island on which Cadiz stands, and the fortresses of Badajoz, Elvas, Gibraltar, and Tarragona, were the only strongholds on the Continent which defied Napoleon's domination. Considering the excellence of the French spy system, it is extraordinary that Masséna should only have heard of the existence of Wellington's lines of defence five days before he came in sight of them. His numerous delays had enabled the defenders to strengthen the outer line with walls and abatis of trees; and

Ney and Reynier now flatly refused to move their corps
against positions stronger than that of Busaco. Rains of
tropical violence and the difficulty of gaining food from districts which Wellington had cleared of its resources, decided
Masséna after a few vain attempts to retire to Santarem.
There he exhausted the country without gaining the reinforcements which he requested; for Soult, though ordered to
reinforce him from Andalusia, stopped to reduce Badajoz, an
act of disobedience which brought the severe censure from
Napoleon—"Soult gained me a town and lost me a kingdom."

Unable to gain a hold on the left bank of the Tagus, Masséna's army was at last forced (March, 1811) to retreat. The
most pertinacious of Napoleon's marshals was foiled by the
skilful defence of Wellington, whose firmness had infused vigour
into the wavering councils of Westminster, and had silenced
the factious opposition of the Portuguese Regency at Lisbon.
His tactics had, it is true, entailed terrible sufferings on the
Portuguese people and vast expense to the British treasury to
feed the multitudes of civilians within the lines; but few will
now deny that the cause of European independence was worthy
of these sacrifices.   Portugal, the very ground on to which
Napoleon had once hoped to lure the English in order to
defeat them, was freed from the French with a loss of 30,000
to their effective strength. Ney had been removed from
his command for disobedience, and Masséna's reputation
gained at Zürich, Genoa and Essling, was clouded over by a
final and well-deserved disgrace for his failure at Busaco and
Torres Vedras.   This signal reverse, the first unretrieved
disaster to Napoleon's arms, aroused secret feelings of hope
among German patriots.   After the gloom cast over Germany
by the death of the heroic Prussian Queen Louisa (July, 1810)
came the news of Wellington's successful resistance.   "In my
intercourse with the farmers of North Germany (wrote Arndt)
I awoke such romantic interest in the great Englishman and in

the Spanish leaders, that whoever possessed a flock of merino sheep named the finest wether after one of them."

The events of 1810—1811 indeed proved that Napoleon's endeavour to control from Paris the actions of King Joseph and his marshals in Spain only hampered their movements and embittered their disputes. The French Emperor grumbled at the expense of the war in Spain, where the scanty resources had long been exhausted by plunder and requisitions. He often threatened to annex to his Empire all the land between the Pyrenees and the Ebro in compensation for the subsidies which he had frequently to send to Madrid; and he sometimes even menaced his brother with the annexation of the whole of Spain, offering to give to him the still more precarious dignity of King of Portugal. On his side Joseph had numerous causes of bitter complaint against Napoleon. He rightly argued that no king could gain the confidence and respect of so proud a people as the Spaniards, who was not invested with all the attributes of royal power. His letters contain frequent protests against the entire subservience to which he was subjected by the Emperor, who seemed intentionally to degrade him in the eyes of his new subjects. He complained bitterly that the almost unlimited powers of the French Marshals in their respective provinces reduced his authority to a mere shadow; that they intercepted his revenues, and ravaged the country to support their troops. Hence the prospects of reconciliation were indefinitely postponed, the treasury at Madrid was depleted and the administration was crippled at its source. In March, 1811, Joseph sent the following pathetic letter to Berthier :—" The troops in my service have neither been clothed nor paid for eight months. The contractors have just taken all the objects of value which still remained in the palace at Madrid, and I have been obliged to strip the chapel. Two of my Ministers have been reduced to asking me for rations for their families. This I was obliged to refuse, as all the other civil servants would have made the same demand. My ambassador in Russia is a bankrupt: the one in Paris died in the greatest poverty, and I live here in the ruins of a great monarchy."

Joseph's trusty adviser, Miot de Melito, had several times urged him to resign his crown as a final protest against the dictatorial pretensions of his brother; and now, oppressed by defeats and the imminence of bankruptcy, he hurried to Paris to gain better conditions or to abdicate (April, 1811). Both efforts failed; and with a monthly subsidy of £20,000 and the promise that the army of the centre should be under his immediate control, he was cajoled back to the unreal splendours of Madrid. The annexation of Catalonia to the French Empire in the spring of next year showed how little the king's plea for the appearance of independence was respected by his brother; and the Cadiz Cortès mocked at Joseph as being "more than ever a puppet."

The campaigns of 1811—1812 in Spain must be briefly summarised here. An attempt by Graham to turn the French lines menacing Cadiz led to the brilliant but fruitless victory at Barosa (March 1811). The French still kept their strong positions opposite Cadiz. After the bloody battle of Fuentes d'Onoro (May, 1811) had been lost by the French entirely owing to the jealousies of their marshals, they retired on Salamanca; and the interest centred in the operations around Badajoz. Soult, advancing to raise the British siege of that fortress, was confronted by Beresford at Albuera, and the most desperate battle of the whole war was finally decided by the stubborn valour of the British infantry (June, 1811); but all Wellington's skill failed to reduce Badajoz, the siege of which was soon raised by Soult and Marmont. The same month saw Suchet's capture of the Catalonian fortress of Tarragona; and that intrepid general by the end of the year conquered most of Valencia. "Had Wellington then retaken Badajoz and Ciudad

Rodrigo (wrote Napier of this campaign) he would have gloriously finished the fourth or defensive epoch of the war; but, being baffled partly by skill partly by fortune, factiously opposed by the Portuguese Regency, thwarted by the Spanish Government, only half supported by his own cabinet, and pestered by the follies of all three, he was reduced to seeming inactivity, while the French added Tarragona and the rich kingdom of Valencia to their conquests." That the spirit of the north, however, was unbroken by defeat, was shown by the Spaniards seizing the fortress of Figueras, and by their incessantly harassing French communications. "The enemy (wrote Macdonald) were ubiquitous, and yet I could find them nowhere, though I scoured the whole of Catalonia." The famous guerrilla chief Mina was especially famed for his daring exploits, in one of which he liberated 1,100 Spanish prisoners near Vittoria, capturing their French escort. The general trend of events in Spain, however, distinctly favoured the French until 40,000 of their seasoned troops were withdrawn for the Russian campaign, their place being taken by younger soldiers. Even then, so vast were Napoleon's resources that when he was preparing to humble the Czar, nearly 300,000 French troops maintained his authority beyond the Pyrenees; and Joseph was able to enlist several thousand Spanish levies from the docile inhabitants of the south. The futility, however, of his efforts to stamp out resistance in the north and centre is strikingly illustrated by some incidents narrated by the young Duc de Broglie in his Memoirs. He was attached to the staff of Marshal Bessières, who had full military authority in Leon and Old Castille, and wielded it less harshly than some other French Marshals. Yet, because the town of Valladolid had not furnished the supplies requisitioned for his army, the marshal imposed a fine of 1,000,000 reals (about £10,400). Towns and villages which were suspected of reinforcing the guerrillas were closely watched; persons who were absent from home without leave for more than three days suffered confiscation of their property; and the relatives of guerrillas were held responsible for their acts. In spite of all this severity, or perhaps because of it, the French could not, except in large numbers, venture far beyond the walls of Valladolid with impunity; and Broglie compares Bessières' whole position with that of a "terrorist on mission."

Wellington began the operations of 1812 by a successful dash on Ciudad Rodrigo (Jan.); and the southern road into Spain was laid open in April by the storming of Badajoz with a desperate courage, sullied by the ferocity of the British soldiers in their hour of triumph. But Wellington was recalled to the north by a move of Marmont into the Mondego valley, whence that marshal had promptly to retire on Salamanca, and finally beyond the Douro. After receiving reinforcements, the French commander suddenly crossed the river, thereby menacing Wellington's communications; and a race ensued over the open plains of Leon to seize or save the important position at Salamanca. Eager to press his advantage by intercepting the British retreat on Ciudad Rodrigo, Marmont swung round his left wing far away from his main force posted near the Arapeiles hills. Wellington saw his chance. The French left was crushed by Pakenham's brilliant charge. Marmont was badly wounded, the French centre after a desperate resistance was driven from one of the Arapeiles, and only the approach of darkness, the skill of their General Clausel and the abandonment of Alba Castle by the Spaniards saved them from complete disaster (July 22). As it was, this battle cost the French about 7,000 killed and wounded with as many prisoners, and led to their temporary abandonment of nearly half of Spain; for Wellington, after pursuing Clausel's shattered forces through Valladolid, turned south to overthrow a smaller army under King Joseph which was to have reinforced his presumptuous marshal. The king at once retreated through Madrid towards Valencia, ordering Soult's army to join him there to effect the recovery

of his capital, which had enthusiastically welcomed the English
deliverers. Soult reluctantly abandoned the twenty lines of
entrenchments opposite Cadiz, the arsenal of Seville, and the
other fruits of his splendid conquest of Andalusia which for two
years had been Joseph's chief support. In the opinion of the
French historian Thibaudeau, the disaster at Salamanca was the
chief cause of the ultimate loss of Spain to Napoleon. Certain
it is that the drooping spirits of the Spanish patriots were
everywhere revived; while the British Government, just then
distracted by the war lately declared by the United States, was
encouraged not to relax its efforts in the Peninsula. Wellington's laurels were, however, to be dashed by an important
check. His deficiency in artillery occasioned the failure of five
assaults on the castle of Burgos, gallantly held by the French;
and the concentration of their armies of the south and centre
compelled him to withdraw his forces from Burgos and Madrid
towards Ciudad Rodrigo, where his wearied troops went into
winter quarters (Dec. 1812)—an opportune and skilful retreat,
offering a signal contrast to that of the Grand Army from
Moscow.

The influence of this sanguinary struggle on the political
life of Spain presents some features of interest. The Spanish
Cortès, or Parliament, which met at Cadiz (1810), not far
beyond the range of the French cannon, was mainly elected
by refugees who claimed to represent towns or districts of
Spain occupied by the invaders; and its tone was that of the
tumultuous democracy of Cadiz. While its blustering incom-
petence paralysed military operations and aroused Wellington's
anger and contempt, the Cortès also confirmed the colonists in
their desire for independence from the old oppressive colonial
system, and alienated the sympathies of the royalists and
clericals, who had the support of nearly all the Spanish
peasantry. In its anxiety to obliterate the memory of Napoleon's programme of social reforms proclaimed at Madrid in

Dec. 1808, the Cortès proceeded to an hysterical imitation of the French Constituent Assembly of 1789. It proclaimed freedom of the press, forbade its members to receive any office, pension or reward, abolished the Inquisition, and began to encroach on the executive powers of the Regency which was striving to govern in the name of Ferdinand VII. Quickly developing its democratic ardour, the Cortès gained as signal a triumph over the more moderate party of Spanish reformers, as the French National Assemblies had won over the Left Centre in 1789—1792. The leader of what may be called the Spanish *Feuillant* party was the able and statesmanlike Jovellanos, whose position in Spanish politics was somewhat analogous to that previously occupied by Pombal in Portugal and by Turgot in France. He was a reforming statesman, sincerely attached to the philosophical doctrines of the eighteenth century, which he had long sought to carry into effect by royal decrees. Thus, when he was appointed Councillor of State by Charles III in 1794, he endeavoured to avert the bankruptcy which threatened to overwhelm Spain, by proposing that the property of the titled clergy should no longer be exempt from taxation; and though he was disgraced and was banished to the mountains of his native province of Asturias for making so sacrilegious a proposal, yet through the pressure of events the tax was imposed somewhat later. In 1799 his services were again required and he was appointed to the Ministry of Justice, soon to be banished again owing to the persistence with which he urged reforming projects on the Court. After the fall of Godoy in 1808, he became a member of the Central Junta, which, two years later, had to give way to the Cortès. In the Junta, Jovellanos and the party of moderate reform had carried their point that nobles and titled clergy should form a higher Chamber, while deputies of the untitled clergy and Commons should form a second Chamber. But this compromise, which had been vainly urged by Necker, Mounier and others at

Versailles in 1789, was now equally distasteful to the democrats of Cadiz. For at this time everything English was abhorrent to the fervent patriots in the Cortès and in the political clubs of Cadiz ; and the term *Inglesimo* was the height of opprobrium. To the excitable Spanish imagination, chafed by frequent disputes with the English commanders whom they ever suspected of treachery, and fanned to fever heat by intemperate newspapers and pamphlets, the moderation of Jovellanos seemed akin to treason ; and in a popular rising of November 1811 he was put to death by the so-called patriots. Had his advice been followed, first by reactionary rulers and now by headstrong revolutionists, the course of Spanish politics might have been far more tranquil. As it was the Spaniards rushed from one political extreme to another so inconsiderately as to postpone to our own days any approach to orderly constitutional government.

In 1811 the Cortès decided to apply to military hospitals the funds of religious orders, abolished torture, as well as all the old feudal and seigneurial rights or *banalités* over ovens, mills, forests, fishing, &c., together with every sign of vassalage. Declaring that "sovereignty resided essentially in the nation," it next proceeded to draw up a Constitution, modelled on that of France in 1791. Legislative power was to reside in the Cortès along with the king, who was left nominally with the control of the executive ; but his functions were as carefully restricted by one omnipotent Assembly as those of Louis XVI after 1791. The Cortès was to be elected every two years by universal suffrage for equal electoral districts ; it could not be dissolved by the king and his veto was merely suspensive, being valid only through two sessions and lapsing if the measure was carried in a third. The king was to name his Ministers, but they remained responsible to the Assembly, which also fixed his civil list every year. The provincial and parochial administrations were to be modelled on the French Departmental System, with the addition of a plan for public education; and yet the Roman Catholic faith was to be the only one tolerated by the State. Improving on Robespierre's motion of 1791, the Cortès declared that deputies of one Assembly were ineligible for the next; and crowned its work with the order that no alteration in this Constitution of 1812 was to be made within eight years.

The victory of Salamanca released the dreamers of Cadiz, and, bringing them into contact with central and northern Spain, produced sharp conflicts between Jacobins and 'serviles.' Galicia and the Basque provinces at once rejected this central-ising constitution. Indeed the strifes between the Cortès and the clerical party nearly led to a civil war, and brought Welling-ton almost to despair. Placed by the Assembly in supreme command of all the Spanish troops (Oct. 1812), he was more than once on the point of overthrowing it, and wrote to the British Government to ask whether it would approve of such a step being taken as a last resort. So narrow was the balance between success and failure in the Peninsula. Certainly nothing but his "long enduring blood" and his military genius could have snatched victory from defeat in every one of the years 1809—1812.

It is, however, a task as profitless as it is easy to criticise the false steps in the first wild rush for political freedom where the very idea was a novelty. A less superficial view of the Tyrolese and Spanish struggles against foreign usurpation, and of the legislative efforts of Stein and the Cadiz Cortès, reveals the fact that the spirit and the principles of 1789 were now being effectively used by two great peoples to sap the founda-tions of the Napoleonic domination.

The position of Italy in the European system of States was throughout this era almost entirely one of passivity. Napoleon's conquests had given to the long-divided Italians some approach to social equality and political unity; and though the French domination eventually aroused much discontent, yet the benefits conferred by Napoleon's sway partly counterbalanced the sacrifices entailed by the conscription and by his commercial system.   With the exception of France, no land benefited so much as Italy by his splendid activity in organisation.   Hence, the nationalist reaction, which was to have so potent an influence on the history of Spain and Germany, acquired no very decisive activity in Italy, at least until the year 1814.   The sentiment of Italian nationality was not at first unfavourable to the great warrior, whose vigorous blows awakened it from the torpor of centuries.

As has been incidentally mentioned, Napoleon had in 1808 annexed the eastern and northern parts of the Papal States to the kingdom of Italy.   At the same time Rome was occupied by a French force, and the Pope was kept almost a prisoner in the Castle of St Angelo, while the cardinals were either arrested or dispersed throughout their dioceses, and the papal troops were enrolled in the French army.   In May 1809, when Napoleon seemed compassed with difficulties in Germany and when French supremacy in southern Italy was menaced by the landing of an Anglo-Sicilian force, the Pope appeared to sympathise with the Emperor's foes.   This was sufficient to precipitate the long impending catastrophe. An Imperial decree proclaimed the deposition of the Pope from his temporal power in the following words—"Charlemagne, my august predecessor, in conceding certain domains to the bishops of Rome only assigned them as fiefs, and Rome did not cease to form part of his Empire."   Under this flimsy pretext, which is devoid of any historical justification—for Karl the Great was not master of Rome, when he accepted the Imperial crown at Leo III's hands—the temporal power of the Papacy was abolished, and the last independent State in Italy ceased to exist.   It was in vain that Napoleon sought to disguise this act of spoliation by a misleading reference to a dim and distant past.   Men saw that in this extinction of the temporal power and of the sole surviving ecclesiastical State, he was recurring to the policy of the Directory in its most aggressive phase. Against the proclamation that Rome was henceforth a free and imperial city, Pius VII was preparing to protest by a bull of excommunication against the Emperor, when he was arrested by the French general Miollis and hurried northwards, to be long kept under restraint at Savona. When the negotiations for the Austrian marriage seemed to assure Napoleon's domination in Europe, the conqueror ventured on the final step by definitively incorporating Rome and its environs in the French Empire (Feb. 1810). The Eternal City was declared to be the second city in Napoleon's dominions; and the Charlemagne legend was further kept up by the bestowal of the traditional title, King of Rome, on the Emperor's son and heir.

French rule at Rome soon bore witness to the vigorous and enlightened policy of the Emperor, which did so much to palliate the violence of his methods of acquisition. At Rome as elsewhere we remark Napoleon's determination to effect a beneficent blending of the new and the old, or, as he himself once happily phrased it, to endeavour to harmonise Gothic institutions with the spirit of the nineteenth century. This was observable both in the intellectual, material and political spheres. The ruins of old Rome were to some extent cleared of the accumulations of rubbish which obscured their grandeur, and every care was taken there and elsewhere in Italy to preserve those monuments of the arts and the relics of antiquity which the rapacity of the French had left in their historic surroundings. The material prosperity of Italy was furthered by the institution of funds for the encouragement of agriculture and the industrial arts. A canal was cut to facilitate transport between Lake Como and the Adriatic Sea, the ports of Venice and Genoa were enlarged and fortified, and high-roads were improved. Napoleon also laboured hard to uproot clericalism from the former Papal States. The number of bishoprics was stringently reduced, and ecclesiastical discipline was to a large extent assimilated to the system then established in France. The administration of the Cardinals, almost mediaeval in its character, gave place to the vigorous organisation of a modern State; and central and southern Italy, even under the blighting reaction which followed the overthrow of Napoleon's sway, never quite lost the effects of the beneficent impulse which his master-mind imparted.

In spite of these undeniable benefits, Italy was by no means contented under the French supremacy. In the south, despite the benefits of Murat's rule, there were many attempts at insurrection, which were fomented by the emissaries of the former Bourbon rulers. Owing to the presence of an English force under Lord Bentinck and the protection of English cruisers, the Bourbons not only maintained themselves in the fertile island of Sicily but frequently threatened descents on the mainland. The republicans of southern Italy were dissatisfied with Murat's autocratic rule; and many of them, withdrawing to the fastnesses of the Abruzzi, founded or greatly extended the activity of the secret associations of the Carbonari. The Bourbons intrigued with them so as to increase the difficulties of the Neapolitan Government; but, down to 1813, Murat succeeded in repressing most of the attempts against his authority. By completing the abolition of feudal customs and introducing modern methods of administration, he effected much for the social and material welfare of his kingdom.

It was in the more commercial and industrial north, however, that the pressure of Napoleon's Continental System began to be felt most seriously; and the discontent arising from material need was there augmented by the attachment to the traditions of municipal freedom which have always distinguished the northern parts of Italy from the more docile and backward south. The men of Venice, Genoa, Milan, Turin and Brescia could look back on a splendid past, rich in memories of local freedom and industrial supremacy. It was little to them that Napoleon promised to renew these ancient glories, when their industries were ruined by the decrees dated from Milan and Fontainebleau, and when their harbours were almost deserted owing to the operation of the Continental blockade. In reading the usually prosaic records of commercial transactions, one is startled by finding such incidents as the following. Owing to the prohibition of all intercourse with England, two parcels of silk sent from Bergamo to London were smuggled, one by way of Smyrna, the other by way of Archangel, to their destination: the former took one year, the latter two years, in the wanderings necessitated by Napoleon's decrees.

Though Eugène Beauharnais endeavoured as far as possible to mitigate the hardships of such a *régime*, and honestly strove to promote the welfare of his subjects, yet the material pressure caused by Napoleon's great commercial experiment and by the constant drain of men to fill the ranks of his armies, naturally sowed broadcast the seeds of discontent. The promise of political liberty and representative government which had been made in 1797 to the Cisalpine Republic, had soon been found to be illusory; and the system of rule which after 1808 prevailed throughout Italy, was an autocracy concealed under the thinnest of disguises.—"Such was the state of Italy (wrote Bourrienne concerning the year 1809), that I have been informed by an individual worthy of credence, that if the army of the viceroy Eugène, instead of being victorious, had been beaten on the Piave, a deeply organised revolution would have broken out in Piedmont, and even in Italy, where, nevertheless, the majority of the people fully appreciated the excellent qualities of Eugène. I have been also credibly informed that lists were in readiness, designating those of the French who were to be put to death, as well as those by whom the severe orders of the Imperial Government had been mitigated, and who were only to be banished."—If this was the state of public feeling in a realm which had reaped many benefits from the French supremacy, and where the viceroy was beloved, the exasperation against Napoleon in Spain and Germany may be faintly conceived.

CHAPTER X.

The Wars of Liberation.

"The life of peoples cannot be summarised in the lives of a few individuals; for the bond uniting them to peoples has never been discovered."—Count Tolstoi.

That Napoleon must ultimately have succeeded in subduing the Spanish Peninsula, if he could have bent all his vast resources to that struggle, can only be denied by those who believe that one British soldier was worth some indefinitely large number of French. If the Emperor's policy had been such as to admit the evacuation of all central Europe and northern Italy by his troops, even the mythical British infantryman would probably have been outnumbered. With Napoleon in command the ridge of Busaco would have been turned, and the lines of Torres Vedras pierced. Considering the enormous difficulties of Wellington's position, it is no slur on his genius to assert that he must have succumbed to the Grand Army, if led by Napoleon in person, and not enfeebled by the mistakes and jealousies of his marshals.

But the fundamental blunder of the Emperor's policy was that he aroused the irreconcilable hatred of the Spaniards at the very time when he was already burdened with the vast problem of shutting out from the Continent the manufactures of Great Britain and the colonial products of which she had the monopoly. His Continental System could only succeed by being enforced on the whole of the Continent. A puncture at any one point must produce a general collapse of his commercial experiment. The connection between his economic system and his seizure of Portugal, which in its turn lured him on into the policy of Bayonne, has been already explained; and it is also obvious that his annexation of Holland, the North Sea coast and Lübeck had no other motive than that of ensuring the complete control of those important centres of commerce. The Spanish War, even after Torres Vedras, was indeed only one of his many Herculean efforts against the many-headed hydra of British commerce; and he felt himself unable to leave Paris, where he could best supervise the whole course of the general struggle. Not only in Germany but also in France itself there were ominous signs of discontent. To a deputation of merchants, who came in the summer of 1811 to ask for relief from the many grievances under which they groaned, Napoleon replied as follows : "Commercial relations with England must cease, I tell you plainly, gentlemen. Merchants who have business to wind up, or capital to withdraw, should do so as soon as possible....I shall remain armed in order to carry out my decrees and resist the attempts of the English in the Baltic. Some fraud exists still, but it shall be completely crushed."—The distress caused by the recent sharp rise of prices in France (the cause of which has been explained in the preceding chapter), was intensified by the increase of taxes necessitated by the warlike preparations which occupied the latter half of the year 1811, and by the heaviest drain of all, the blood tax. It had become customary for the conscription to be levied one year in advance of the legal age; and owing to this illegality, to the annexation of the North Sea coast, and also to the detestation of military service in Spain, the number of refractory conscripts was ever on the increase, rising in 1811 to the enormous total of 40,000. Light columns were organised to chase deserters and—as General Foy remarked—"to compel the French to become conquerors." The religious discords with the Pope had the further effect of re-opening the wounds temporarily healed by the Concordat; and the uneasiness in France was so general that a new war of conquest might well have seemed desirable to divert attention from internal and economic difficulties and rekindle the warlike ardour of her people.

As has been already remarked, Napoleon cherished the belief that an alliance either with Russia or Austria was a sufficient guarantee to his supremacy on the Continent. The irritation caused by the marriage negotiations has also been described. At the close of 1810 came a far more serious affront. Napoleon's annexation of Oldenburg, to whose Duke Alexander's elder sister had been so promptly betrothed after Erfurt, warned the world of the probability of a rupture between the allies of Tilsit. That treaty (as the Czar reminded the Courts of Europe in a circular despatch of March, 1811) guaranteed the possession of Oldenburg to its lawful sovereign. "What value,"—continued the Russian note—"could alliances have, if the treaties which cemented them did not hold good?" It is true that offers were made to give compensation to the dispossessed duke; but that could only be in Germany, which was equally at the mercy of Napoleon's statecraft; and the incident revived all the Czar's indignation at encroachments which promised to thrust Russia from all participation in European affairs.

Recurring to his early friendship with the Polish Prince Czartoryski, who when in office had always extolled the good faith of England as contrasted with the unscrupulous aggressions of Napoleon, the Czar at once wrote asking him to sound the feelings of the Poles in the Grand Duchy of Warsaw, and to ascertain the possibility of enlisting them on the side of Russia, if they were assured of the "certainty of their regeneration." With a rising of the Poles and the Prussians against Napoleon, the Czar hoped to meet him at least on equal terms. Czartoryski's reply was discouraging. The Poles felt gratitude to Napoleon for what he had done for them; their 20,000 troops serving in Spain were so many hostages in his hands, and his constant success fascinated their ardent imaginations; finally they would be satisfied with nothing less than the complete reunion of their ancient dominions, with outlets for trade (Danzig here is hinted at), and the restoration of the constitution of 1791. To this Alexander rejoined (Jan. 31, 1811) that he proposed to reconstitute the whole of Poland with the rivers Dwina, Beresina and Dnieper as frontiers, and a liberal constitution; Austria was to be provisionally offered Wallachia and Moldavia as far as the Sereth in compensation for her retrocession of Galicia to the Polish realm. "It is beyond a doubt" (continued the Czar's letter) "that Napoleon is striving to provoke Russia to a rupture, hoping that I shall make the mistake of being the aggressor. This would be a great blunder in present circumstances; but if the Poles would join me, that would put an entirely new face on the matter. Being reinforced by their 50,000 men, by the 50,000 Prussians who could then also join me without risk, and by the moral revolution which would infallibly result in Europe, I could advance to the Oder without striking a blow." But these secret overtures which the Czar urged his friend to make at Warsaw, were unsuccessful. The Poles adhered to Napoleon's fortunes,—a resolve as disastrous as the trust reposed in him by his other faithful allies, the rulers of Denmark and Saxony.

The fundamental cause of the war of 1812 still remains to be noted. It was the Czar's refusal to adhere to the later and more stringent developments of the Continental System. Not content with insisting on the exclusion of British ships and wares from Russia, Napoleon in a letter of Oct. 16, 1810 had requested Alexander to seize in Russian harbours the neutral ships—they were mostly American—which brought colonial produce, inasmuch as this was undoubtedly of British origin. "The blow to England (wrote Napoleon) will be terrible; for all these goods are to the account of the English. It depends on your Majesty to secure peace or to lengthen out the war. Peace is, and must be, your desire. Your Majesty is certain that we shall attain it, if you confiscate these 600 ships with their consignments. Whatever papers they carry, and under whatever names they disguise themselves—French, German, Spanish, Danish, Russian, or Swedish—your Majesty may be sure that they are English." The Czar, however, refused to go beyond the terms of the treaty of Tilsit and, by confiscating ships which were undoubtedly neutral, to violate the principle that the flag covers the goods, for which Russia had contended against England in the Armed Neutrality Leagues of 1780 and 1800. In his anxiety to strangle English trade, Napoleon was requiring his ally to adopt measures as arbitrary as those ever asserted by the mistress of the seas. Annoyance at the Czar's refusal was undoubtedly a secondary cause of the annexation of Oldenburg to the French Empire. Even before hearing of that sinister event, Alexander had shown his concern for the dearness of colonial wares in his own Empire, by issuing a ukase (Dec. 31, 1810) which facilitated the entry of those much needed goods; while it virtually excluded wines and other expensive products of France, the entry of which was thought to be injurious to the 'balance of trade' and the chief cause of the alarming depreciation of Russian paper money.

From this time a breach between these potentates was almost inevitable. In fact, during a conversation with Metternich in the previous September Napoleon had said—"I shall have war with Russia on grounds which lie beyond human possibilities, because they are rooted in the case itself"; and on the same occasion he confidentially offered in case of a war to give up to Austria her Illyrian provinces in exchange for Galicia, the addition of which to a regenerated Poland would gain him the enthusiastic support of that unhappy people. Napoleon, however, did not carry out this statesmanlike project, and when once embarked in the war he could not afford to alienate Prussia and Austria in return for Polish support. Thus on both sides the question of Poland was left in abeyance, each Emperor desiring to gain its support, and yet dreading to precipitate a conflict by pronouncing irrevocably for its re-establishment. The question thus turned on the Continental System, as to which the two potentates could not come to any accord. Napoleon desired to impose it in all its rigour on Russia and Sweden, in order to bring England on her knees; whereas these Powers, urgently needing colonial produce, refused to deny themselves the comforts of life, when Napoleon by his secret licences infringed his commercial edicts whenever the needs of his Government demanded it. In this momentous dispute Great Britain had been a most interested but still a passive spectator. "No indication," says M. Vandal, "permits us to suppose that this conspiracy (i.e. of Alexander against Napoleon) had been formed by connivance with England." But so far from having conspired against Napoleon, the Czar had endeavoured to observe the Treaty of Tilsit; and there is distinct evidence to prove that both potentates entered the arena reluctantly and only under what they conceived to be the pressure of events. Napoleon felt confident that by sealing up the Baltic against British goods, he would assure our ruin, which he thought to be imminent, and so bring about a general peace; while Alexander was not loth to decide a contest which he considered inevitable, while 300,000 of Napoleon's troops were still engaged in the Peninsular War.

The diplomatic and military preparations for the war occupied the greater part of 1811 and the spring of 1812; and in the endeavours to form coalitions the balance of success was on Napoleon's side. The Poles, as we have seen, refused

Alexander's secret overtures and remained true to the French alliance. Austria at first declared for armed neutrality; but Napoleon had no wish to leave an armed neutral in his rear; and the marriage alliance was found to entail its responsibilities, when he required and obtained the assistance of 30,000 Austrians to protect his right flank in Volhynia. Still more important, however, for the success of his preparations, was the concurrence of Prussia; for Danzig, with its French garrison and governor, was to be the chief base of supplies, his "Paris in the East." His troops still occupied the Prussian fortresses on the Oder as well as Berlin. Even that did not seem sufficient guarantee against a desperate national rising; and in Sept. 1811 he wrote to Davoust, who was marshalling some 100,000 troops on the Elbe, to be ready to seize the fortress of Spandau if necessary. But Frederick William III was not cast in that heroic mould which could do and dare everything for national independence even against hopeless odds; and he refused to stir without far stronger succours than Alexander could promise. As for help from England, the utmost that the patriotic Hanoverian Louis Ompteda had been able to obtain was a consignment of arms now on shipboard in the Baltic, with the offer of the English fleet as a last refuge for the king. In such desperate straits Frederick William was justified in rejecting Gneisenau's plan of a people's war against Napoleon, which he returned with the written comment—"very good as poetry." Finally Napoleon brought the Berlin Court to a treaty (Feb. 24, 1812), which marked the surrender of Prussia's resources into Napoleon's hands for all his wars except those in the south of Europe: 20,000 of her troops were to aid him in the coming war beyond the Niemen: the Grand Army was to traverse Prussia at her expense; and no levy of Prussian troops was to be made in its rear. This treaty seemed the death blow to the hopes of German patriots. Scharnhorst, Gneisenau, and von Boyen resigned their offices rather than serve under Napoleon. Gneisenau departed to join the Germans who with Stein were striving to strengthen the Czar's resistance. An envoy was secretly sent from Berlin to St Petersburg to explain that Prussia's action against the Czar was due solely to compulsion from Paris, and that by enticing Napoleon into the heart of Russia his ruin might be ensured, if a skilful defensive campaign were persevered in by Alexander's generals. A somewhat similar explanation was given by Austria of her ostensible hostility.

Napoleon's important diplomatic successes placed virtually the whole resources of Europe from the Pyrenees to the Carpathians, from Naples to Königsberg, at his disposal; and yet, by enabling him to begin his campaign at the Niemen, and impelling him into the heart of Russia, they ultimately served but to magnify his disaster.

His endeavours to secure the neutrality of Sweden and the active assistance of the Turks were unavailing. The Porte remembered his sudden change of front at Tilsit, and turned a deaf ear to his promise that the recovery of the Crimea should be the reward of an offensive alliance against the Czar. English and Russian diplomatists also persuaded the Turks that the union of all the Continent under Napoleon's sway was now more to be dreaded than Muscovite ambition, that Turkey existed only owing to the divisions and jealousies of the Powers; that, finally, it was her best policy to make peace with Russia, retaining Moldavia and Wallachia, which the Czar's troops had virtually conquered. By the politic Treaty of Bucharest (May 28, 1812), which gained for him the rich land of Bessarabia, Alexander now restored to the Porte two provinces which he could not have retained in face of the French invasion, and soon set free his army on the Danube for the defence of the Ukraine.

The conclusion of a Russo-Swedish alliance was still more advantageous for Alexander. The Court of Stockholm had in 1810 favoured the choice of Napoleon's Marshal Bernadotte for the eventual succession to its throne, as cementing anew the old friendship between France and Sweden, and on his side Napoleon was not altogether loth to see this strange event; for—as he said to Metternich—"A French marshal on the throne of Gustavus Adolphus is one of the finest tricks anyone could have played upon England." Alarm and indignation were loudly expressed both at London and St Petersburg. It was groundless. The Swedish choice had fallen upon that one of all the French marshals who was on the worst terms with the Emperor. Able in command, skilful in intrigue, and far more ambitious than Moreau, Bernadotte after his opposition to the *coup d'état* of Brumaire had been saved from disgrace only by his marriage to a sister of Joseph Bonaparte's wife. Many causes of irritation had embittered his relations to the Emperor; and the somewhat grudging consent of the latter to his acceptance of the reversion to the crown of Sweden gave this ambitious man a personal reason for resisting Napoleon's overbearing policy towards his adopted land. On his way to Stockholm he had been warned by Bourrienne at Hamburg that the Continental System would entail ruin on Sweden, and that his best policy would be to trade with England and brave the Emperor's wrath. He followed the advice. Napoleon had in the early part of 1810 given back Swedish Pomerania and Rügen to the Court of Stockholm as the price of its accession to his commercial system; but when it steadfastly refused to submit to an entire exclusion of colonial goods, he in Jan. 1812 invaded that province, as a pledge for the execution of his decrees. Whether from personal hostility to Napoleon, or from a desire to secure his position in Sweden by an independent and patriotic policy, Bernadotte accepted the challenge thus thrown down; and on March 24, 1812 a treaty of alliance was signed between Sweden and Russia, by which the former Power took for the third time a prominent part in the struggle against revolutionary France, on the understanding that it should gain Norway.

The events in Spain, Sweden, Turkey, and the exhaustion of France by a commercial crisis and a severe dearth weighed for a time on Napoleon's spirits. He finally decided, however, that the war was an inevitable part of his system for the acquisition of a general peace, and that his new dynasty, the outcome of a revolution, could never be secure while any of the old reigning families held a position of such power as that of the House of Romanoff. It was in vain that his Ministers, except the obsequious Maret, Duc de Bassano, who nominally controlled the Department of Foreign Affairs, protested against a war which violated all the principles of sound policy. They ineffectually urged on him the imprudence of engulfing half a million of men in the wastes of Lithuania, while at least half that number must be kept amidst the mountains of Spain, and they pointed out that a disaster beyond the Niemen would certainly entail a rising of Central Europe in his rear. Mollien reminded him of the embarrassment of his finances, only to be crushed by the characteristic reply—"Because they are embarrassed, they need war"; and the Emperor proceeded to amuse his Minister with an estimate of the rich gains which he would reap by requisitions in Russia, and by the sale of her timber and salt. The remonstrances of his advisers were unavailing, though they probably contributed to strengthen his desire to save appearances by sending pacific overtures to the Courts of London and St Petersburg. The negotiations at the former capital broke down as speedily as those in 1810 which they resembled in their general tenor. Napoleon offered to England proposals for peace on the basis of '*uti possidetis*,' which the English Government refused, unless Ferdinand VII were restored to the throne of Spain. At St Petersburg also the French overtures were no better received, Alexander finally requiring the entire evacuation of Prussia and Swedish Pomerania by Napoleon's troops, and a reduction of the French garrison at Danzig. He consented, however, to accept an indemnity for his brother-in-law, the dethroned Duke of Oldenburg, and even to renew commercial relations with France, but not so far as to exclude English goods so thoroughly as Napoleon's economic experiment demanded. It is, therefore, evident that though personal grievances and rivalry entered into the dispute, its main cause was the secession of Russia from the Continental System.

The march eastwards was begun without any formal declaration of war. At Dresden Napoleon held a reception (May, 1812) of the Emperor of Austria, the King of Prussia and his other German allies, in the hope that this display of his vast resources would intimidate his foe; but neither there nor at Wilna nor Smolensk did he receive the expected submission. At Dresden he incidentally remarked to Metternich that he would not venture further than Smolensk in that campaign, but would re-organise Poland and Lithuania, and if necessary advance in 1813 quite to the centre of Russia. " My enterprise is one of those of which the solution is to be found in patience."

On June 24, amidst strains of music and with shouts of martial ardour, three immense columns rolled towards the Niemen, which they crossed near Grodno and Tilsit; and by the end of the month 325,000 men had entered the Czar's dominions. Other forces, following as rear-guard and reserves, raised the total numbers to more than 600,000 men. The composition of this host reflected the cosmopolitan character of the Emperor's sway. About 250,000 were French, 147,000 were Germans from the Confederation of the Rhine, 80,000 Italians, led by Eugène and Murat, 60,000 Poles, besides Illyrians, Swiss, Dutch, and even a few Spaniards and Portuguese, while Prussians on its left and Austrians on its right were to guard its

flanks. The army had not therefore that homogeneity which
rendered the campaigns of Austerlitz and Jena so decisive.

Its first columns found no enemies but the almost tropical
heat of a Russian midsummer, a violent thunderstorm and
torrents of rain. The rough tracks were at once cut up by
the passage of the artillery and vast convoys of stores; and
it soon became apparent that the most perfect organisation
could not keep the Grand Army supplied with food. In vain
had East Prussia and parts of Poland been swept clear of carts
and horses. The horses began to die from the excessive toil
and from diseases caused by rank grass, some 10,000 succumbing between the Niemen and Wilna, so that a French general
coming up with reserves declared that the track of the Grand
Army resembled that of a defeated foe. The desire of surprising the Russians while they were scattered over a front of
eighty leagues spurred forward Napoleon, and only by speedy
retreat were the defenders saved from a military disaster; but
the haste of the invaders entailed serious consequences. The
regular commissariat system broke down from the outset. The
vast supplies collected at Danzig and Thorn could never be
hurried up in time to relieve the wants of the main army, which
therefore maintained itself almost entirely by plunder and
requisitions. So customary had this become as to lead up to a
calculation that the invading army should not exceed one tenth
of the invaded population, if it were to subsist in comfort on
the fruits of their toil. Such methods, highly serviceable in the
campaigns of Marengo, Ulm and Jena, were less practicable
in Spain, and now broke down hopelessly in the wastes of
Lithuania, where the resources had been already depleted by
the retreating Russians. Halting for a few days at Wilna to
rest his wearied troops, Napoleon endeavoured to enlist the
inhabitants of the old Lithuanian capital in his service by
cautious half promises which would not alienate Prussia and
Austria.

We have seen throughout this work how divulsive an influence the partitions of Poland exerted on the solidarity of the Eastern Powers. The Valmy campaign had been decided by the fears and cupidity of Vienna and Berlin as to a second partition, quite as much as by the bravery of Kellermann's levies. Poland, Bavaria, or Hanover had hitherto dissolved every compact of the Powers and left Central Europe a prey to Napoleon's concentrated strength. By reviving the ancient kingdom of Poland it was now possible for him to gain an ally in the East, and to thrust back the Czar's rule beyond the Dnieper and the Dwina; but, hampered as he now was by a dynastic alliance, he could not, as after Jena, boldly appeal to Polish sentiment. Now he could only deal in half promises which were nullified by the devastations of his troops. To a deputation of Poles and Lithuanians who came to Wilna to request the restoration of the old Polish realm, he replied, "If your efforts be unanimous, you may cherish the hope of compelling your enemies to recognise your rights....To this it is my duty to add, that I have guaranteed to the Emperor of Austria the integrity of his dominions, and that I cannot sanction any movement tending to disturb his peaceable possession of the Polish provinces which remain to him." This diplomatic reply chilled the ardour of the Poles and Lithuanians; and the nomination of seven grandees to form a provisional government under French supervision was his sole encouragement to the Polish patriots who in the Diet at Warsaw had lately declared for the restoration of their realm in all its extent. His appeal for a national rising to throw off the Russian yoke met with a timid response when it was known that a Lithuanian noble coming at the head of his vassals had been maltreated and robbed of everything by Napoleon's South-German troops.

There is, indeed, no sure proof that the restoration of Poland, which some historians assert to have been the real aim of Napoleon's expedition, was ever seriously entertained by him after the

Austrian alliance became the keystone of his policy. Passing from his utterances on this subject to the far safer testimony of his actual preparations, it appears certain that Napoleon had neither expected nor desired a general levy of these oppressed people. "What proved (says Marbot) that the Emperor's only aim in invading Russia was to re-establish the continental blockade was, that he had made no provision for arming and equipping the troops which the Poles were to raise." He trusted to his enormous superiority in regular troops, among whom were already some 60,000 Polish regulars. It is further pointed out by the young Duc de Broglie, who was then serving in the French Embassy at Warsaw, that Napoleon in his brief stay there had "drenched with cold water" the deputies of the enthusiastic Polish Diet; that he had chosen as his ambassador the Abbé de Pradt, who had been one of the butts of the French Court; that finally the Polish contingents in the Grand Army were kept separate and were not massed together under the command of that able and brilliant soldier, Prince Ponia-towski, as would have been the case if Napoleon had desired to revive their national feeling.

The general plan of campaign was to separate by a rapid incursion the Russian forces which had been stationed north and south of Wilna. The former had been thrown back on the Dwina, along which river several engagements took place, generally in favour of the French. The southern portion under Bagration was to be kept severed from the northern by a vigorous march of Davoust and Jerome Bonaparte on Minsk. With superior numbers and the advantage of the central position Napoleon trusted to end the campaign by a few vigorous blows on the upper Dwina and Dnieper. Davoust nearly succeeded in intercepting Bagration and his 45,000 Russians in the marshes west of the R. Beresina; and he asserts that only the disobe-dience of Jerome Bonaparte to his orders saved the South-Russian force from a disaster. Napoleon dismissed his brother and allowed him to return to his amusements in Cassel; and Bagration by a wide détour finally succeeded in joining the main body of Russians. Meanwhile their northern army under General Barclay de Tolly, a general who nobly sustained the bravery and prudence of his Scottish ancestry, had retreated towards Smolensk, leaving a corps to oppose the advance of St Cyr and Macdonald north of the Dwina. Pursuing Barclay as far as Witepsk, Napoleon was there forced, by the fatigue of his men and the utter exhaustion of his horses, to call a halt, exclaiming—"Here I must stop, refresh my army and organise Poland. The campaign of 1812 is finished: that of 1813 will do the rest." Had he now confined himself to his original intention of consolidating his conquest of Poland and Lithuania, the history of the world would have been different; but the prospect of maintaining for nine months a cautious defensive chafed his ardent spirit; and the difficulty of feeding and keeping under control his murmuring allies seemed greater than that of snatching the flower safety out of the nettle danger.

Massing his columns for a vigorous offensive, he pushed on swiftly for Smolensk, the fortress on the Upper Dnieper which barred the entry to Russia Proper. The news that Bagration and Barclay were there effecting a junction promised the decisive engagement which he had long been seeking. His troops sustained heavy loss in an attack on the holy city. The Russian resistance was, however, only intended to gain time for a retreat and the destruction of shelter and all possible supplies. In the night Barclay fired the city in several parts and protected by the flames withdrew his rear-guard (Aug. 18). Vainly did Napoleon seek to hide his chagrin under a violent tirade against Russian cowardice. His trustiest advisers, seeing the true position of affairs, counselled a halt within the charred ramparts of Smolensk, and pointed out the danger of engulfing himself amongst the fanatically hostile people of Russia. Outwardly Napoleon appeared to yield; but the news of St Cyr's victory at Polotsk over the Russians on the Dwina, and of a victory of the Muscovite horse over some of his own cavalry brigades, again seemed to promise a more enterprising spirit among his foes. By his acts he belied his words. He placed his two most daring chiefs, Murat and Ney, in command of the advanced guard; and they, rightly construing the Emperor's inclination, brought on an engagement on the Moscow road, ending in another barren victory for the invaders. But where was this campaign to cease? So far from availing anything in that vast land, each triumph increased the difficulties and distress of the victors by drawing them further than ever from their base, amidst a people impalpable and invincible as the air. The recent ratification of the treaty between Alexander and the Sultan had set free another Russian force to menace Napoleon's rear; but, measuring events only by the success of the Grand Army, he trusted to his ever increasing reserves and to his Austrian and Prussian allies temporarily to guard the rear, while he sought peace by the overthrow of the host in his front. To those who at Smolensk had reminded him of the pitiful state of his army, he had replied—"It is dreadful, I know: at Wilna half of it were stragglers; now they form two-thirds: there is therefore no time to be lost: we must extort peace: it is at Moscow." The Emperor had indeed observed that only the prospect of a great battle held together the weary ranks and kept them from the dissolution which a long halt ever produced.

The Russians on their side beheld his rapid advance with dismay. Unable to see the wisdom of Barclay's Fabian policy, they were enraged at the surrender of Lithuania, and of holy Smolensk, to a foe whom they detested as Antichrist; and since the junction of Bagration's force with that of Barclay the dissensions in their councils had risen to such a pitch that the cautious leader was at last accused of treason by his head-

strong colleague. The strife was assuaged by the appointment
of the old fighting general Kutusoff, reared in Suvóroff's school,
as generalissimo; and near the R. Moskwa and the village of
Borodino the Russians prepared to contest the approach to
Moscow. Their forces crowned a semicircle of hills, the right
of which was protected by a ravine. Near their centre rose a
hill which they strengthened by a formidable redoubt; and earth-
works defended their more accessible left. The presence of
about 130,000 men and 400 cannon on each side foreboded
a contest more sanguinary even than that at Wagram. On his
part Napoleon did not allow his joy at the prospect of the
pitched battle which he had been chasing from the Niemen to
the Moskwa, to outweigh his prudence; and owing to an
internal ailment, increased by his chagrin at the news of Salamanca, and inflamed by the first chills of autumn, he even
displayed a degree of caution which lost a great opportunity at
the end of the day (Sept. 7). By noon the divisions of
Murat, Davoust, and Ney had pierced the Russian left and
taken two of the redoubts; but the second Russian line twice
restored the balance of the fight, and only the havoc wrought
by the French artillery among the dense masses on the ridge
checked their advance. In this critical position Napoleon
refused repeated requests that his famous Old Guard should
move forward to threaten in its rear the shattered Russian left;
and the chance of rolling in the enemies' line on the ravine
on its right had to be abandoned by his incensed marshals.
Meanwhile the Russian right and centre had long maintained
a desperate fight, finally decided by a dashing charge of the
French cavalry into the rear of the great redoubt; and when
beaten from these heights, the defenders stoutly rallied
on a second ridge, thereby covering their retreat from the
bloodiest day's fight of all the Napoleonic wars. The battle of
Borodino or the Moskwa must indeed be called rather a
disaster than a victory for the Emperor; for it reduced his

force by 30,000 and depleted his ammunition, while the losses of the defenders were not much greater.

It cannot be proved that Moscow was the goal at which Napoleon had all along aimed, though secret advice from Berlin had reached the Czar that Napoleon would strike at the old Muscovite capital. Indeed, he was too great an adept in the complex and ever shifting game of war, to bind himself rigidly to plans, subservience to which has often led to great disasters. His great art, in which he excelled all the captains of ancient and modern times, consisted in his fertility of conception, his eagle glance which divined the weak point of his enemies' position, and the astonishing energy with which he compelled all circumstances to give effect to his fundamental maxim—"at the critical time and place to bring an overwhelming force to bear on the foe." These qualities, seen at their best in his Italian and German campaigns, had impelled him on his disastrously victorious career to Smolensk and Borodino. He had at the outset burst through the too extended line of defence and, pushing on his main army between their severed forces, had compelled these to converge at an acute angle if they were to reunite at all. Their junction at Smolensk and retreat along the Moscow road led him to pursue the victory which ever eluded his grasp, until it was seized amidst the slaughter of Borodino. It was the desire to destroy or capture the main Russian army which chiefly dictated the advance towards Moscow, though he also hoped that the occupation of that holy city would overawe the impressionable Czar and his superstitious subjects. But, that he was led on more by military than by political considerations is proved by his hesitations at Wilna, Witepsk, and Smolensk, as also by the frequency of his earlier assertions that he would not emulate the fortunes of Charles XII. And yet now his successful strategy had lured him on to an enterprise which yielded up as hostages to fortune far vaster forces than were embarked in the adventurous campaign of Pultowa. Strange examples of the Nemesis which overtakes great warriors when they cease to be statesmen! The valour of his veterans, wielded by his own genius, had at last yielded Napoleon the coveted victory, with Moscow and peace and plenty as the expected reward.

Such were the feelings which inspired Napoleon's weary troops as they gazed on the gilded cupolas of Moscow. Some of the veterans had heard his inspiring reminder that forty centuries looked down on them from the heights of the Pyramids. The ancient Muscovite capital, so they were now assured, was to be the goal of their wanderings, and its capture the prelude to a general and enduring peace. Great was their leader's chagrin when no request for an armistice, no deputation of obsequious citizens came forth to entreat his clemency: greater still the dismay of his troops at finding its streets nearly deserted. The policy of removing supplies and population before the advance of the foe, so successfully adopted by Wellington before Torres Vedras, had been carried out by Barclay and Kutusoff on Napoleon's line of march through Russia Proper. Moscow was to be the crowning example of this mode of warfare. Hatred and fear of the French as infidels and ruthless plunderers, had aided the governor, Count Rostopchin, in depopulating the capital and preparing for a general conflagration. Whether this terrible act was entirely the work of Russian incendiaries, or whether, as some of their writers aver, it was caused by French and Polish pillagers, it is at any rate certain that flames burst forth at several places on the night of Sept. 14, and, fanned by the equinoctial gales, raged for five days. That this event had less effect on his fortunes than has been commonly believed, is evident from the fact that the Grand Army remained in Moscow for a whole month afterwards, in spite of some further isolated fires, and that at the final council of war at Moscow one of his advisers strongly urged the advisability of wintering at Moscow. The chief difficulty was not the lack of shelter but the increasing scarcity of food for men and horses.

The arrival of stragglers and considerable reinforcements almost made up the gaps caused by the Battle of Borodino; but how were the 110,000 combatants, 20,000 sick and wounded, and the horses for 550 cannons and 2000 waggons, to be fed from an almost desolated district? In vain did Napoleon offer personal security and high prices to all peasants who would bring corn and hay. Their fanatical animosity against the French would have forbidden intercourse, even if the few who ventured had not been despoiled by pillagers; and distant forays were often attended with losses. Kutusoff, after abandoning Moscow, had occupied the south road to Kaluga, guarding thereby the more fertile south and the arsenal of Toula, and giving time for recruits and volunteers to throng to his ranks. His threatening attitude sufficed to deter Napoleon from a march on St Petersburg, against which all his marshals protested. By a tacit agreement there seemed for a time to be a suspension of arms between the Russians and the outposts of Murat; and it is said that the imposing presence and headlong courage of this great cavalry chief so impressed the Cossacks, that some of them even expressed a wish to have him as their hetman. Among the many strange results of the revolutionary wars none is more remarkable than the bewildering eminence to which many soldiers of fortune had risen. A Corsican *caporal* seemed about to reduce Russia to her limits under Peter the Great: the son of a lawyer at Pau was assuring his accession to the throne of Sweden: and the son of an inn-keeper at Cahors had sabred his way to that of Naples, and was now for a brief space eclipsing the Czar's lustre in the eyes of the Cossacks of the Don.

For a month the army remained in and around Moscow, its leader still clinging to the hope that Alexander would give way as he had done after Austerlitz and Friedland; but that monarch, surrounded by a devoted people who detested the principles of the French Revolution, now rejected overtures, the acceptance of which would have cost him his throne. The successes of Wellington in Spain, intercourse with the rugged personality of the German exile Stein, and the impression caused by deepened religious convictions, concurred to fortify a will which had been gaining in solidity since the days of Tilsit; and the mental instability on which Napoleon chiefly reckoned had now been replaced by a fixed determination to effect that liberation of Europe which had been the Czar's youthful dream in 1804. Just as Napoleon's military genius had led him into his present dilemma, so now his presuming on Alexander's lack of determination sealed his own doom.

He was also outmatched in cunning. Kutusoff feigned the utmost concern at the results of the war, and a belief that his master would lend a ready ear to overtures for peace which Napoleon proposed to send to St Petersburg (Oct. 6). A reply could not be expected for a fortnight; and before that time elapsed, the informal armistice between Kutusoff and Murat was broken by a sharp conflict in which the French advanced guard lost severely (Oct. 17). The Emperor saw that he had been duped; and, to make the most of the open autumn weather, he two days later moved his army secretly by the new road to Kaluga, hoping to avoid Kutusoff's forces. But the march was encumbered by a barbaric profusion of plunder; the Russian scouts were active, and Kutusoff seized a strong post at the town of Malo-Jaloslawitz. By the gallantry of the viceroy Eugène and his Italian troops this position was carried, only to disclose the foe drawn up in forest passes which Bessières, the Commander of the Guard, declared to be impregnable. In an agony of distress Napoleon saw his progress by the southern route to Smolensk completely blocked, and the devastated line of his advance alone available. With hearts foreboding disaster, and hard pressed by elated foes, his men turned northwards, and skirted the ghastly field of Borodino. Not all the skill and tenacity of Eugène and Davoust could avert heavy losses from the rearguard at Wiasma (Nov. 3); and the miseries of the retreat were infinitely increased by the tardy advent of sharp wintry weather. "Up to Nov. 6"—says General Gourgaud, a more trustworthy historian of the campaign than the melodramatic Ségur—"the weather was fine, and the cold much less than it was for some months in the Prussian and Polish campaigns of 1806—1807." As it is stated by Napier (to say nothing of less accurate panegyrists of Napoleon) that the Emperor's enterprise, "the grandest and most provident, the most beneficial ever attempted by a warrior statesman," was foiled by "the fires and snows of Moscow," and that he was "vanquished by the elements," the following official record of the numbers of his main army, apart from the reserves and the forces on the Dwina and in Volhynia, should be carefully noted. The number of effectives after the hardships and desultory fighting in Lithuania had shrunk to 182,000, and before the battle of Borodino to 133,000; on the departure from Moscow, inclusive of reinforcements, it stood at 107,000; and after the affair at Wiasma, but *before any snow or severe cold set in*, only 55,000 men and 12,000 horses were fit for active service.

Now was seen the horrible truth of the warnings given at Moscow by Russian prisoners—"In a fortnight your nails will drop off, and your weapons will fall from your benumbed and half-dead fingers." Henceforth man's attacks were feeble compared with the ceaseless rigour of Nature. Kutusoff, in very pity for his own men as well as for the foes, desired to leave the rest to winter; but his ardent lieutenants desired to destroy the whole of the Grand Army, and their Cossacks completed its miseries. The pitiful pretext that the retreat was a move to join St Cyr's army on the Dwina and threaten St Petersburg was no more heard at Napoleon's head-quarters;

and the hope that cantonments at Smolensk and Witepsk would afford shelter was soon to vanish. The standards were generally abandoned by Illyrians, Germans, and Italians—in fact by all who had no interest in a war the motives of which had ever seemed mysterious. The Poles, brave in fight but addicted to marauding, had ceased to hope for the restoration of their country and gave themselves up to despair or to plunder. The advanced columns swept the country of supplies and fuel, thereby increasing the miseries of the rear-guard, which was already sufficiently harassed by the Cossack lances. For in the horrors of a rout the fierce passions aroused by war are seen in all their hideousness, unveiled by the glamour which disguises them in a victorious advance. In place of regiments there were now generally seen bands of stragglers, kept together only by self-interest or skill in foraging; and these thrust back into the cold outsiders who sought to share the scanty meal or fire. But amidst this unarmed, half-clothed and frost-bitten rabble the heroism and fertility of resource of the French veterans stood out in brilliant relief. When Davoust's and Eugène's corps were exhausted by service as rear-guard, they were reinforced by that of Ney, "the bravest of the brave." The stores at Smolensk were of little service, for they were pillaged by the first comers; and the retreat was nearly intercepted by a sharp attack of the Russians at Krasnoë which completely cut off the rear; but Ney, after blowing up part of the ramparts of Smolensk, fought his way through throngs of Russians, crossed the Dnieper on insecure ice, and with the loss of his cannons and stores rejoined the main force (Nov. 20).

It was of little avail that the remains of what had been the Grand Army were now succoured by the reserves under Victor, and by St Cyr's troops which had been successfully repelling attacks of the Russian army of the Dwina; for the Austrians under Schwarzenberg had suffered, or rather, had been powerless to prevent, 60,000 Russians from the south passing northwards, taking up a position on the R. Beresina, and so threatening to cut off the survivors of the Grand Army. To secure the passage of that river General de Marbot's dismounted troopers vainly strove to seize and hold the only bridge against the Russian batteries. With the destruction of the bridge the last hope of the French seemed to have vanished; for owing to a partial thaw the ice would not bear the passage of an army. Napoleon, however, lured the enemy down the stream by a feigned march, while his brave engineers toiled for six or seven hours to construct two light bridges higher up, over which Napoleon and most of his effectives passed unmolested; but such was the confusion that few timely efforts were made to get the waggons and stragglers over while the enemy was absent. Finding out their mistake, Tchichakoff and Wittgenstein now advanced up both banks, and though stoutly repulsed at most points, their fire finally told with fearful effect on Victor's rear-guard and the crowd of stragglers who now rushed for the two bridges still remaining (Nov. 28). The breaking of one of these under the cannon, the agonised struggles of camp-followers and regulars, horse and foot, to gain or to keep a foothold on the few frail planks, under a hail of grape-shot that continued far into the night, presented an accumulation of horrors under which the stoutest hearts gave way to wild panic; and the final burning of the bridge to cover the retreat left a crowd of stragglers to the mercy of the pursuers.

Still, the *élite* of the army maintained a bold front, while the few remaining squadrons protected the Emperor in hollow square whenever the line was threatened by Cossacks. Thus in comparative safety the retreat dragged on its weary course; for the Russian regulars were too exhausted by cold and hunger to venture on serious attacks. On Dec. 5 Napoleon suddenly left the relics of the Grand Army, with orders to rally and resume the campaign at Wilna; while he secretly hurried on to

Paris to organise new forces and intimidate Prussia and
Austria. Meanwhile the survivors, paralysed by a return of
the intense cold, when halting at Wilna for rest and supplies,
were menaced by a small force of Cossacks under the adventurous leaders Platoff and Tettenborn. Storming the gates at
dawn, the latter struck such terror into his foes that they fled
instantly, leaving 6,000 prisoners, 24,000 wounded in their
hospitals, and nearly all the remaining cannons and stores
(Dec. 9). This was the last blow. Five days later the rear-
guard of 1,000 armed men under the dauntless Ney protected the miserable remnant of 20,000 stragglers who tottered
across the Niemen, over which five months before more than
half a million of men had passed to gain for the Emperor his
final triumph. And yet so vast were his resources, so trans-
cendent his genius, that after a disaster which completely
eclipses all others in the history of civilised nations, he was
still able to bring up half a million of soldiers and fiercely
assert his domination from the Oder to the Ebro[1].

Macdonald, with 20,000 Prussians and a few South Germans and Poles, had been hastily recalled from the siege of
Riga by the news of the catastrophe. Had these Prussians
and Schwarzenberg's Austrians in Podolia been aware of the
completeness of the disaster, the relics of the Grand Army
would have been as completely in their power as Darius was
in that of the Greek mercenaries at the bridge over the Danube
when he fled before the Scythian horsemen. But in the modern
instance the decisive news came barely in time, even if there
had been any leader bold enough to paralyse the brain of
Napoleon's military system by the capture of his marshals.
Their sole danger therefore was from Platoff's Cossacks, who

---

[1] According to the tables given by Gen. Chambray in his history of
the campaign, 20,000 survivors assembled behind the Vistula in Jan. 1813
out of the 505,000 men who had waged the main campaigns on the Upper
Dwina and beyond the Dnieper.

began to harass the retreat to Königsberg. Meanwhile Macdonald by a skilful retreat broke through the Russians and
crossed the Niemen at Tilsit, expecting General Yorck with
a considerable number of Prussians to follow. On the last
day of 1812 the hasty march of the Prussians from his head-
quarters to rejoin their comrades warned the French leader of
their total defection; and he himself barely escaped with his
remaining regiments to Königsberg.

On the previous day the Prussian general Yorck had taken
the momentous step of accepting the overtures of the Russians
that the district between Memel and Tilsit should be considered
neutral, and held as such by the Prussians, who were not to
serve against the Russians for two months. In a strict sense
Yorck's act was treason against his sovereign; and it was quite
possible that Frederick William might screen himself from the
Emperor's vengeance at the expense of his general. Yorck
hinted at this when he exclaimed to his enthusiastic officers,
" It is very well for you to talk : but my old head feels loose
on my shoulders." There was another danger, that the
Russians after losing fully half their troops in the past campaign would not venture beyond the Niemen and bind
themselves to another coalition. General Kutusoff pressed
this view on the Czar ; but, fortunately for Germany, Alexander
listened to the promptings of Stein and other German patriots,
as well as of his own generous nature, and decided to become
the liberator of Europe. He knew that Napoleon's character,
even his fundamental policy, must impel him to wipe out the
memory of his disaster. Prudence therefore dictated an attack
when the French military system was for the time paralysed,
and northern Germany was eager to cast off its chains. If the
French were not pursued beyond the Vistula, Napoleon would
reassemble the forces of Germany, compel the Court of Berlin
to hold to its compact, and Russia would again have to face
the forces of western and central Europe. It was therefore the

best way of defending Russia to appeal to the national hatred of the Germans against Napoleon, and to carry the war beyond the Elbe. As for the King of Prussia and his minister Hardenberg, they could be trusted to join the national cause when it was safe to do so, and in the meantime to wear the mask skilfully.

The need of forcing Frederick William's hand now explains the strange course of events. Russian troops began to occupy Prussia Proper; and on Jan. 18, 1813, Alexander commissioned Stein to act provisionally as governor of East and West Prussia, and to collect the revenues and arm the Landwehr and Landsturm, in the name of *the Czar.* Thus the preparations for the German War of Liberation were begun by a Prussian general and a German exile, both of whom were technically guilty of high treason. The Provincial Estates of East and West Prussia in their session at Königsberg (Feb., 1813) overlooked the illegalities of the position and enthusiastically greeted Yorck's words "I hope to beat the French wherever I meet them; and if we are too much outnumbered, we shall know how to die with honour." Frederick William, after launching against Yorck an order for trial by court-martial which was never carried out, now took the significant step of withdrawing from French influence at Berlin to Breslau, where the patriotic feeling ran as high as at Königsberg; and finally by the vigorous action of the Czar and Stein a Russo-Prussian treaty of alliance was signed at Kalisch (Feb. 27, 1813), which is of great importance as marking the second step (the treaties of 1805 having been the first) towards the reconstruction of Europe.

The Czar, desirous of reigning as constitutional King of Poland, refused the preliminaries which would have restored to Prussia Warsaw and other spoils gained in the second and third partitions. In place of that proposal, a clause was finally inserted that Prussia "shall be reconstructed in the statistical, geographical and financial proportions conformable to her

extent before the war of 1806." She was to receive her
compensations in North-Germany (excepting the ancient possessions of the House of Hanover) so as to give her "the
unity and compactness necessary for constituting an independent State": in particular she was to acquire on the east a
frontier which both in a military and geographical sense would
connect West Prussia with Silesia. This treaty vaguely foreshadowed the changes of the future, viz. the move westwards
of Prussian and Russian influence, the former Power thenceforth becoming almost entirely Germanic, while the Czar's
influence was for the first time to be extended beyond the
Vistula into the very heart of Europe.   Furthermore, Prussia's
renunciation of all claims on Hanover facilitated the accession
of England to this, the fourth great Coalition.   The signature
of this important treaty had been hurried on by the imperious
action of Stein ; and Prussia and Russia passed from a state
of war to a close alliance as quickly as had been the case with
Britain and Spain five years previously.   Both alliances were
pushed forward and cemented by statesmen, Canning and Stein,
who lent their great powers to change the war of the governments to a union of the peoples; but in 1813 as in 1808 the
address of statesmen, and even the determination of the Czar,
would have been of little avail but for their co-operation with
an irresistible impulse, the longing of an oppressed nation to
cast off an alien yoke.

The complete failure of Napoleon, in spite of his unvaried
military successes, to extort peace at Moscow has been already
referred to the invincible repugnance of the Great-Russians to
the character of his rule.   The passionate devotion to the Czar
expressed by nobles and merchants in meetings at Moscow, and
their readiness to sacrifice their wealth for the common cause,
had a less demonstrative but more effective counterpart in the
quiet but stubborn resolve of the peasants and serfs to have no
dealings with the invaders.   The principles of 1789 which had

been Napoleon's best ally in his campaigns from Arcola to
Jena, were as powerless at Moscow as they had been at Cairo.
The Russian social system, based on the Mir or village community, and cemented by devotion to the Czar, offered, it is
true, one weak place to its assailant, the custom of serfdom;
but the Czar had effected in 1803 some important ameliora-
tions in the lot of the serfs; and these were, besides, too
ignorant to understand any proclamation of freedom at the
hand of Napoleon, whom they detested as an infidel and a
sacrilegious plunderer.   There was therefore no solidarity of
interest between Napoleon and the inhabitants of Great Russia;
and to his tardy recognition of this fact the disaster of 1812
must be chiefly ascribed.   In West and South Germany, on
the contrary, his rule had directly or indirectly conferred
many benefits, abolition of serfdom, immunity from feudal
dues, some approach to personal and religious liberty and
social equality.   France was for some time looked upon as the
champion of the lesser States against the rapacious designs
of Austria and Prussia; and but for the material pressure
of the Continental System it is scarcely probable that the
Confederation of the Rhine would have been dissolved in a
single campaign.   Napoleon, indeed, still disposed of more
strictly German troops than Prussia and Austria when united
could bring against him; and only by degrees did the confederate troops rally to the national cause.   The decisive part in
this great struggle was therefore played by Prussia.

In that unhappy land the name of Napoleon was associated
with no reforms : these had been quietly carried out in the
teeth of his opposition by Stein, Scharnhorst and Hardenberg.
French supremacy only meant to the Prussian people the occupation of the capital and the chief fortresses at their expense,
the sequestration of their revenue for the payment of an elastic
war indemnity, the limitation of their army, the ruin of foreign
commerce, and finally the systematic plundering of their towns

and villages during the passage of the Grand Army. So intense and widespread was the hatred of French domination that pity alone seems to have preserved from popular vengeance the bands of frost-bitten survivors who in Jan. 1813 crept towards the ramparts of Thorn and Danzig. French influence was not more alien to the oriental fatalism of Moscow and the intense national pride of the Spaniard, than to the spirit of regenerated Prussia. The cabals of the French or aristocratic party at Berlin were now powerless against the tide of popular feeling. Staunch adherents to the old régime, like Yorck and Blücher, were at one with the innovators Stein and Scharnhorst; and there was but one fear, that Frederick William's prudence would postpone the struggle against Napoleon. Some ardent civilians had long been preparing for a national German rising against Napoleon. The enthusiastic patriot Karl Müller had even bought weapons and ammunition and had arranged plans of attack on the French garrisons; and it is stated by Louis Ompteda that if Frederick William had much longer delayed he would have been overthrown by a revolution begun by the people and the army. The identity of feeling between ruler and subjects was now, however, assured. Indeed, the delay was only due to the king's desire to gain some guarantee from his ally for the future position of Prussia; and regret can scarcely be felt for Frederick William's circumspection, inasmuch as it yielded the initiative in the proclamation of war to a professor.

While it was still doubtful against whom the volunteers, just called for by royal proclamation, were to serve, Steffens, Professor of Physics in the new University of Breslau, called on the students to enlist for a war *against Napoleon.* It was responded to with ardour. A similar zeal was shown by the youth of Berlin and Königsberg Universities, and even Halle, Jena and Göttingen were left almost deserted by the rush of students to join the muster at Breslau. The gaps still left by exemptions from regular service were more than made up by the throngs of volunteers. Scharnhorst's plan of a Land-wehr and Landsturm as second and third lines of reserve, was now carried into effect (March 17): the 150,000 men who had passed through the ranks in his short service system now came forward; and Prussia stood forth a nation in arms, organised even more completely than France after Carnot's *levée en masse.* The enthusiasm of France in 1793 was now rivalled by the superhuman efforts and sacrifices of Prussia in 1813. Old men brought their all for the support of regiments of volunteers, officials renounced their salaries, and sixteen workers in a Silesian coal-mine, as the results of their toil overtime, brought 221 thalers (£33) to equip their comrades for the war: women brought their jewels, and one girl, whose flowing locks were her only wealth, shore them off to lay on the altar of the Father-land. The gifted young poet Körner came from a life of rich promise at Vienna to serve in the famous Lützow brigade, and sealed with his life's blood his devotion to the cause of German freedom. His warlike songs, with those of Rückert, Kleist, and others, breathed the passions pervading young and old, rich and poor, which found their fullest expression in Arndt's "What is the German's Fatherland?"—that trumpet-call rallying the Germans of the west and south to the one national cause.

On his side Napoleon determined to maintain his grip on Spain, Germany and Prussia, as if he had not lost half a million of men and the districts east of the Vistula. "If I begin by giving up towns," he exclaimed, "they will end by demanding kingdoms." Such was his force of will, and so great was his confidence in the policy of never acknowledging an error and never receding a single step, a policy which often accelerates the progress of the victor but generally ends in irretrievable disaster.

Events in France might well have led him to compromise. Towards the close of October, 1812, a General Malet, with two other officers of strong republican opinions, by means of forged documents had succeeded in leading some troops to seize the Minister and Prefect of Police, Savary and Pasquier. A little more and he would have seized other ministers and proclaimed the republic. The success which for an hour or two favoured this foolhardy attempt, caused an uneasy feeling, which was vastly increased by the news of the Emperor's disaster in Russia; but when he suddenly appeared in Paris and appealed in his misfortunes to the nation, French generosity was touched, and no open opposition was offered to his design of a campaign on the Oder. By calling out all disposable troops and some 100,000 National Guards, as also by anticipating the conscription of 1814, he hoped to have nearly 500,000 troops without counting his armies in Spain. The Emperor's uneasiness as to the state of public opinion in France was, however, betrayed by a singular action. He charged the Prefect of each Department to enrol a hundred young men of the best families as guards of honour, not only because he desired to reinforce his cavalry by some 10,000 men, but chiefly because these guards would be hostages for the loyalty of their families. As Mollien naïvely remarks—"Napoleon was sceptical as to the value of devotion on word of honour, and desired another guarantee." Not a voice was raised by the servile Senate and Corps Législatif against the renewal of offensive warfare, though there was much discontent in the south and west of France and a slight revolt in the newly annexed German lands. It was left for the most independent of his advisers, such as Caulaincourt and Talleyrand, to counsel negotiations with the Powers; but the utmost concession which the Emperor would make was that he would request the intervention of his father-in-law, the Austrian Emperor, with the offer of a few shadowy concessions to the Czar; but, as will shortly appear, the Court of Vienna was now prepared to play a much more active part in the restoration of the equilibrium of Europe, than that which Napoleon desired to assign to it. As to French finances, they were to be strengthened by selling for the benefit of the exchequer the domains of parishes or communes, at least those which were let out on lease; and in spite of Mollien's protest against this act of confiscation, it was carried out—a strange corollary to the policy of confiscation begun in Nov. 1789.

When his government was reduced to these straits, it is surprising that Napoleon did not frankly accept the offer of mediation which his father-in-law sent from Vienna; but he spurned this suggestion as an infraction of the Franco-Austrian alliance of 1812, which he tardily endeavoured to cement by promising to Francis I the restoration of Illyria and acquisitions in Silesia and Poland, if he would place 100,000 men in the field against the Russians and Prussians. It was not, however, to the interests of Austria that French supremacy should again be assured; and when her intervention was nominally accepted but virtually rejected, she concluded a secret convention at Kalisch (March 29) with the Czar, whereby his troops were to be allowed to enter Cracow. Poniatowski's Poles were thus compelled to fall back on the province of Galicia and pass westwards, giving up their arms until they had passed through the Austrian dominions. Unable to draw the Emperor Francis from his present attitude of armed neutrality, Napoleon thought to avert his eventual hostility by conferring the Regency of France on Marie Louise, which would also be some safeguard against any enterprise like that of General Malet. This was almost the only precaution which Napoleon took on the resumption of the war; and even his panegyrist, Thiers, considers his uncompromising attitude as great a disaster as the Russian campaign itself.

Napoleon, on leaving the Grand Army, had entrusted the command to Murat, King of Naples; but that dashing soldier, ill-adapted for conducting a retreat and anxious for the security of his throne, abruptly left the army and hurried to Naples, throwing the command on the shoulders of the viceroy Eugène. The latter, after strengthening the French garrisons in the fortresses on the Oder, fell back on Berlin; and when unable to hold the capital, he retired to Wittenberg, trusting to the line of the Elbe as a defence against the victorious allies. The Russians, after helping to free Berlin, threatened this great natural barrier on Eugène's front as also at Dresden and Hamburg.

The citizens of this famous old Free City were too much exasperated against French rule to wait even for the approach of the Cossacks led by the adventurous Tettenborn. A riot occurred at the Altona gate on Feb. 24 owing to the harshness of the French customs' officers in searching every one who entered the city. The mob disarmed the guard, tore down the octroi palisade and imprisoned all the French in the town. Tettenborn, after persuading or compelling the Duke of Mecklenburg to withdraw from the Confederation of the Rhine, entered Hamburg (March 18) amidst unbounded enthusiasm. —" None had ever seen (wrote Varnhagen von Ense) such an outpouring of passionate joy, nor were Germans deemed capable of so much emotion: the people even went so far as to kiss the Cossacks' horses in their excess of rapture." Tettenborn, a native of Hamburg, though now serving under the Czar, at once declared it a free port, ordered the seizure of all French property and handed over to the city the goods in the customs' house valued at £60,000. A levy of troops called the Hanseatic Legion was held there as at Lübeck and other towns which now revolted against French rule; but the fortunes of the Hanse Cities rose and fell with the main current of events higher up the Elbe. Vandamme retook Hamburg at the end of May, and Davoust was able to renew his despotic sway in Hamburg up to the end of the year.

Though this campaign in North-Germany was of merely secondary importance, it furnished many incidents, which served to illustrate the character of the whole struggle. An attack of the enemy on Lüneburg threatened to dash the hopes of its citizens for the long-desired independence; but as the French were about to shoot those who had most prominently sympathised with the patriots, the advent of a Russo-Prussian force aroused the inhabitants from the depths of despair to transports of joy, and compelled Napoleon's troops to evacuate the town. There, and indeed everywhere throughout Germany, the depth of popular feeling may be measured by the ardour shown by non-combatants, and especially by women. That faculty of inspiring men to the fray and of restoring the fortunes of an unequal contest, which Caesar and Tacitus described as a characteristic of the women of ancient Germany, was once again called forth at many crises of the War of Liberation; and the exalted patriotism which Schiller had portrayed as the formative influence in the life of his noblest female character, Gertrud, now nerved many a town and district to more desperate and persistent efforts. It is related that when sympathy was offered to an old woman for the loss of her cottage by fire in an engagement, she exclaimed, "Well, let it burn, if it will get the French out of the place more quickly." Some girls emulated the example of the Maid of Saragossa. In the fight at Lüneburg, a girl distinguished herself by the coolness and daring with which she braved the bullets of the foe in order to carry ammunition to her countrymen; and later on a warlike maiden succeeded in enlisting as a volunteer, and in concealing her identity, which she only revealed when she lay dying of a wound.

The position at the opening of the campaign of 1813 was briefly as follows. Napoleon's garrisons still held the fortresses of Danzig, Thorn, and Modlin on the Vistula, Stettin, Cüstrin and Glogau on the Oder, Spandau, Wittenberg and Magdeburg on the Havel and Elbe; but the capture by the allies of Hamburg and Dresden had weakened his main line of defence.

Macdonald had given the sensible advice to evacuate the fortresses on the Vistula and Oder and concentrate all forces on the Elbe. Had this been done Napoleon would have had a great superiority of force. As it was, he had to rely mainly on the young conscripts lately raised in his Empire, who, with all their bravery, could not move with the speed and steadiness of the veterans lost in Russia, or even of those now blockaded in Polish and Prussian fortresses. He was also rather deficient in artillery and very weak in that terrible cavalry whose charges had so often decided and crowned his greatest triumphs. At the close of April, 1813, both sides marched towards the fertile plains of Saxony, which contest with those of the Low Countries the claim to be the battle-ground of Europe. Napoleon, as usual, marched his troops at a rate which outstripped all the efforts of his commissariat department; and their wants were satisfied partly by requisitions but still more by plunder. According to von Odeleben, a Saxon officer in his army, the wantonness of the pillage exceeded anything which had yet been seen.—"To set fire to a house or a village through negligence was an act entirely unnoticed. The cursed *c'est la guerre* was an excuse for everything." Such conduct, it is true, lightened his commissariat and accelerated the advance, but it also added fuel to the hatred long nursed by the peasants of Germany, and ensured the defection of the Saxons and Bavarians at the first possible opportunity. In fact, the King of Saxony at first declared himself friendly to the allies; and only the sudden irruption of Napoleon's troops kept him to the French alliance.

The first pitched battle of 1813 was fought near the village of Lützen, the scene of the last and greatest victory of Gustavus Adolphus. Napoleon was marching his troops, only one-third of whom were French, towards Leipzig, when near Lützen and Gross Görschen they were attacked on their flank by the allies (May 2). Drawing back and reforming his lines,

Napoleon for a time was forced to maintain the defensive, and Ney's young conscripts at first gave ground to the Prussians. Never did Napoleon show greater anxiety as to the issue of a battle, exposing himself to fire, and riding to animate his troops when ordered up for the attack. The key of the French defence was so seriously threatened that only the arrival of Eugène's and Macdonald's corps, and a charge of the Young Guard supported by the fire of 60 cannon, restored the balance of the fight. Finally a second great column of attack broke the centre of the allies and compelled them to fall back; but Napoleon's lack of cavalry prevented any pursuit; and as night fell a squadron of the allied horsemen by a brisk attack nearly swept off the Emperor and his staff. It is claimed by German historians that if the first attack had been more vigorously delivered by Wittgenstein, or that if at the crisis of the fight the allied cavalry and part of the Russian reserves had been launched against the foe's right flank, victory must have been assured. As it was, the Prussians had captured 800 prisoners and 5 cannons without losing any; but the gallant Scharnhorst received a wound which soon proved fatal. The retreat of the allies eastwards laid open Dresden to Napoleon; thereby assuring the wavering fidelity of the Saxons, and regaining the whole line of the Elbe. He now sent Ney and Victor northwards to threaten the Prussians and Swedes near Berlin; for Bernadotte had brought 25,000 Swedish troops, in order to earn the prize of Norway promised by Alexander the year before. The main body of the allies had retired on Bautzen, where they again sustained a defeat from the Emperor's forces (May 20, 21); but the determination of their officers and soldiers was seen not only in a stubborn defence, but in their orderly retreat and the complete success of an ambush which they laid for their pursuers and the capture of 11 cannon and many prisoners. Napoleon, however, succeeded in carrying the war into Silesia; and at the beginning of June his left was near Glogau, his centre occupied Breslau, and his right threatened Schweidnitz.

The prospects of the allies looked black indeed. The prudent Barclay, lately appointed commander-in-chief of the Russian forces, knew that his men were greatly disorganised and declared that he must retreat into Poland. Ammunition was running short: the fortress of Schweidnitz was untenable, and a reinforcement of 20,000 Silesian Landwehr was useless because their muskets hastily bought in Austria had no touch-holes bored. With the greatest difficulty Barclay was dissuaded from a retreat beyond the Oder by the argument that the allies could at least hold out for six weeks in the fortresses of Silesia and in the mountains which separate that province from Bohemia: and that if he retired into Poland, Austria would certainly withdraw her promise of acceding to the coalition in six weeks' time if Napoleon rejected her armed mediation.

On his side the French Emperor had offered the allies a truce which they now (June 4) gladly accepted as being the only means of keeping their armies near together and close to the Bohemian frontier. Napoleon seems to have considered that the gain of time would enable him to bring up new levies from France, to add to his weak and overworked cavalry, and to threaten Vienna from his Illyrian provinces. He also hoped that two victories would assure the fidelity of his father-in-law, as that of Lützen had won him the reluctant support of the Saxons; and he naturally expected the discouragement of the Czar and Frederick William to lead to the peace which was freely discussed at their head-quarters; but here again he omitted from his reckoning the unquenchable hatred of the Prussian people. The fear that the armistice would lead to a dishonourable peace roused the fierce resentment of the patriots. It was nothing that the French were threatening even Berlin itself. Karl Müller called the people to go forth like the Helvetii and burn what they left behind; and inspired by the examples of Saragossa and Moscow, he exclaimed—"Let us learn as the Russians did, first to go round and burn, and then find for ourselves poison and dagger as the Spaniards did. Against those two peoples alone could Napoleon's troops effect nothing." With such a spirit pervading the peoples, a second Tilsit was impossible.

In striking contrast to this reckless determination to do and dare all for the Fatherland, stands the cool and calculating diplomacy of the Court of Vienna. As far back as Sept. 1810 Metternich had foreseen that the impending conflict between France and Russia would "ensure a decisive importance for Austria's opinions during the war and at the end of it." Amidst the disasters of the 1812 campaign the Austrian Government had quietly drawn back Schwarzenberg's corps on Cracow without offering any opposition to the victors. The prospect of regaining access to the sea by the recovery of the Illyrian provinces became more remote with every French victory, and Metternich now decided that the hour had come for Austrian intervention. The terms which Austria offered to Napoleon were the partition of the Grand Duchy of Warsaw between Russia, Prussia and Austria; the restoration of the Illyrian provinces to Austria with a good frontier towards Italy, and the renunciation by France of her German provinces beyond the Rhine.

All Metternich's actions were adroitly designed to make the weight of Austria tell most fully in the balance of power. Proceeding to the allied head-quarters in Silesia he was received by Alexander with the mistrust which since 1806 had arisen between him and the Court of Vienna; but the skilful diplomatist soon convinced him that Francis I meant well for the allied cause.—" If Napoleon declines our mediation the truce will come to an end and you will find us among the number of your allies : if he accepts it, the negotiations will most certainly show Napoleon to be neither wise nor just, and then the result will be the same." Having received a pressing message from Napoleon to go to Dresden, Metternich proceeded thither (June 26) to be greeted by these menacing words—" So you too want war : well, you shall have it. I have annihilated the Prussian army at Lützen : I have beaten the Russians at Bautzen : now you wish your turn to come. Be it so : the rendezvous shall be in Vienna. Men are incorrigible. Experience is lost upon you...." Metternich remarked that peace rested with him ; but the Emperor re-torted that he, the child of fortune, could not give up one handbreadth of soil—" My reign will not outlast the day when I have ceased to be strong and therefore to be feared." Later on, in a fit of rage at being told that his soldiers were boys and the last that France could give him, he flung his hat into the corner and declared that a man such as he did not concern himself much about the lives of a million of men. " The man is lost," was Metternich's reply to the French generals who crowded around him after this memorable interview hoping to hear news of the assurance of peace.

A singular concurrence of events during the armistice served to strengthen the allied cause. On June 14th and 15th Great Britain signed at Reichenbach conventions of alliance and subsidy with Prussia and Russia, whereby these Powers agreed to keep on foot at least 80,000 and 160,000 men re-spectively, receiving for the current year the sums of £666,000 and £1,133,000. Subsequently it was also arranged that England should support a German legion of 10,000 men serving under the Czar. In this convention, which was ratified with some additions in the following September, the Court of Berlin definitely renounced all claims on Hanover. The course of the reaction against Napoleon was thus marked by the recurrence to a diplomatic situation somewhat similar to that of Bartenstein in the spring of 1807. But Napoleon's

position was in reality far more perilous than that from which
the lightning stroke of Friedland had delivered him. The need
of complete accord between the Powers, if they were to make
head against the French Emperor, had been well learnt during
six years of disunion and humiliating subservience. Austria
was now ready to accede to the alliance from which she had
so unaccountably turned away in the spring of 1807; and
Wellington's sword was now thrown with overpowering effect
into the wavering balance of European affairs. His decisive
triumph at Vittoria (June 21) had a marked influence on the
negotiations at Dresden.

On June 30 Napoleon acquiesced in Austria's mediation,
and the armistice was prolonged to August 10. That Power
had, however, signed a treaty with the allies at Reichenbach
(June 27) pledging herself to join them with 150,000 troops if
Napoleon did not accede to her conditions as stated above;
and so far had the rivalry of Austria and Prussia vanished in
their misfortunes, that Austria in the negotiations with Napoleon
then pending, insisted on the restoration of Prussia to the
place of a great Power, little thinking that half a century later
she would be ousted from Germany by the very State which
she now helped to re-create. To face this formidable coalition, the only ally which Napoleon could gain was Denmark.
The Court of Copenhagen, knowing that Bernadotte, Crown
Prince of Sweden, had joined Russia and England, on the
understanding that the kingdom of Norway should be the price
of Swedish assistance to the allies, saw safety only in a close
union with Napoleon—a decision which was to prove fatal to
Danish interests in the near future. The French Emperor,
however, made great and finally successful efforts to gain active
assistance from his brother-in-law Murat, who had retired in
high dudgeon to Naples at the close of 1812. He also called
Fouché back to favour to fathom "this infernal Austrian
negotiation which is slipping through my fingers."

Into the details of the negotiations at Prague it is unnecessary to enter. With a natural feeling of resentment at the return which Francis was giving for the care lavished on his daughter at Paris, and with a magnificent confidence that his genius would conquer as at Austerlitz and Wagram, Napoleon refused, until it was too late, the Austrian terms that would have reduced his eastern boundary to the Rhine[1].

When the armistice ceased on Aug. 10 Napoleon's position was but little stronger than at its commencement, while that of the allies was vastly more commanding. Bernadotte with 25,000 Swedes reinforced the Prussians at Berlin and brought the strength of the northern army to 150,000 men. The accession of Francis I to the coalition gave the allies the help of a great Austrian army led by Schwarzenberg, who with Russians and Prussians now began to threaten Napoleon's flank from the vast natural bastion formed by the mountains of Bohemia. Blücher's army in Silesia had also been nearly doubled in strength, and mustered nearly 100,000 strong. To oppose these there were the corps of St Cyr, Vandamme and Poniatowski, in all about 100,000 men, watching Bohemia; as many under Macdonald in Silesia; 75,000 menacing Berlin; 50,000 held as a reserve by Napoleon himself; beside Bavarians on the Inn and Eugène's troops in Italy watching the Austrians on the Danube and the Drave respectively. From her central

[1] The treaties which built up the fourth great Coalition were (1) Russia and Sweden, March 24, 1812: (2) Russia and Prussia at Kalisch, Feb. 28, 1813: (3) England and Sweden, March 3, 1813: (4 and 5) Conventions of subsidy and alliance between England and Russia and Prussia at Reichenbach, June 15, 1813: (6, 7 and 8) Definitive Treaties of alliance between Austria and Russia and Prussia at Teplitz, Sept. 9, 1813: (9) Preliminary treaty of alliance between England and Austria at Teplitz, Oct. 3, 1813. In Oct.—Dec. Austria also made treaties of alliance with Bavaria, Saxony, Würtemberg, Baden, Hesse, &c. It will be noticed that as in the second and third Coalitions, Russia and Sweden took the initiative, and that England was one of the later signatories.

position Austria was thus able to threaten Napoleon and his allies in Saxony, Bavaria, North-Italy and Illyria. Though the French Emperor had regained for himself the central strategic position of Saxony, yet over the whole area of the war the advantage of position lay with Austria; and the diplomatists of Vienna were thus able in the approaching collapse of French supremacy to substitute Austrian predominance in the affairs of Germany and Italy. Such were the interests involved in this vast struggle. The allies had in all nearly half a million of armed men in Central Europe; while Napoleon's slight numerical inferiority was counterbalanced by the vigour and unity of action inspired by one master mind. After twenty years of almost constant war the forces of every people in Europe except the Turks were confronting each other on the banks of the Oder and the Elbe, the Ebro and the Bidassoa.

Keeping with the reserves at about an equal distance from his three main armies, Napoleon heard of the incursion into Saxony of the allied Grand Army led by Schwarzenberg, Barclay and Kleist, which drove in St Cyr's outposts on Dresden. Hurrying up for the defence of the Saxon capital, which he had formed into a vast fortified camp, Napoleon repelled the attack and occupied the hills south of the city. Reinforced during the night by Marmont and Victor, he on the next day resumed the offensive, and a dashing charge of Murat's cavalry cut up the Austrian left and gained a complete victory (Aug. 27). Swift concentration of troops had once more gained a victory over the allies, who owing to divided councils and a defective intelligence department had not enough troops close at hand to repel so vigorous an attack. They left ten battalions and a vast number of cannon and stores in the hands of the victors. For skill of combination before the attack, and the vigour of its execution, the Battle of Dresden deserves to rank among Napoleon's greatest victories,

and refutes the assertions often made as to the decay of his
powers. He fell in the plenitude of his vigour before forces
which no one man could overcome. The pursuit of his beaten
foes was partly paralysed by news of Macdonald's defeat on the
previous day; and he left without due support a strong column
led by Vandamme, which attempted to seize a pass of the Erz-
Gebirge at Kulm and so cut off the retreat of the allies.
A Russian corps, soon reinforced by Austrians, obstinately
contested Vandamme's advance, while a body of Prussians
closed in on his rear. Caught in a trap such as had long
ago been fatal to the Romans at the Caudine Forks, all
Vandamme's troops except a few horsemen had to lay down
their arms (Aug. 30). This blow, which cost Napoleon 15,000
men in killed and prisoners, had been closely preceded by
even worse disasters to his cause. Oudinot's advance on
Berlin had been checked by the allies at Gross Beeren; and
though Bernadotte desired to retreat and abandon the capital,
a battle had been forced on by the determined Prussian
General von Bülow which ended in the defeat of the French
(Aug. 23). Three days later a more decisive victory was won
by the allied army in Silesia led by the gallant old Blücher.

This veteran of over seventy years of age brought the skill
and experience gained under Frederick the Great to rebuild
the fortunes of Prussia. After the disaster of Jena his tenacious
resistance at Lübeck together with that of Gneisenau at Kolberg
stood out in bold relief amidst the tame surrenders of other
Prussian generals. He had lived on for revenge. Arndt
describes him during the weary years of subjection to the
French, as often spending the heavy hours in lunging with his
sword at an imaginary foe, calling out—Napoleon ! Nothing
is more astonishing than his vitality. His limbs were fine and
round as those of a youth. The upper part of his face seemed
to Arndt a fit abode for the gods, curiously blended with lines
about the mouth and chin which betokened the "cunning of

the hussar." Such was old " Marshal Forward " who was now to lead the army of Silesia from the Oder to the Seine. At the outset this army was pressed back by Macdonald from Goldberg; but it fiercely assailed that marshal's forces as his lieutenants (against his orders, he states) were leading them over the flooded stream of the Katzbach on to a plateau sodden by the rain. The French were hurled back in wild confusion (Aug. 26), and in the disorder of a protracted retreat left 18,000 prisoners and 103 cannon in the hands of Blücher's troops. In September another of Napoleon's best marshals suffered defeat. Ney was beaten at Dennewitz by the northern allied army (Sept. 6).

Thus, on the whole, Napoleon had only maintained his ground at his centre of operations in Saxony, while his lieutenants had been badly beaten in Brandenburg, Silesia and on the confines of Saxony. The way was thus opened to strike a blow at his centre, Dresden, or to cut off his communications with Erfurt and the Rhine. The latter alternative was chosen ; and the allies prepared to effect the long desired junction of their forces. Blücher and Schwarzenberg again advanced on Saxony, but retreated when Napoleon opposed them in force. When reinforced however by 50,000 reserves from the east, the allies appointed Leipzig as their rendezvous. By a daring flank march, Blücher led his troops through Bautzen, crossed the Elbe near Torgau, and, constructing an entrenched camp, waited for Bernadotte's army of the north. The allied movements were, however, much hampered by the tardiness of the Swedish Crown Prince, who was justly suspected of only joining in the campaign in order to dethrone Bonaparte and take his place. At any rate, he did as little as possible against the French.

Meanwhile Napoleon had been losing much precious time in efforts to invade Bohemia; but the difficult passes of the Erz-Gebirge were found to be impenetrable; and in the time thus allowed Blücher with Bernadotte in his rear was beginning to threaten Leipzig from the north, while the Grand Army advanced against that city from the south. Leaving Murat to defend Leipzig against the main army of the allies, Napoleon hurried northwards to overthrow Blücher, who foiled his aim by a wary retreat, thereby enabling the allies on the south to press Murat back. Alarmed for the safety of Leipzig, the Emperor determined to rejoin the King of Naples and accept the battle to which the skilful movements of Blücher and Schwarzenberg had reduced him. The position was unfavourable. At his back was an unfortified city the inhabitants of which were eager for his overthrow. In case of a retreat westwards there was but one important bridge over the R. Elster; and by a strange oversight Napoleon gave no definite orders for the construction of temporary bridges. Thus commenced the greatest series of battles ever fought at any one place, in which about half a million of men were finally engaged.

On the first day (Oct. 16) the allied Grand Army failed to hold against Napoleon three villages which it had captured, still more to cut off his communications on the west. Napoleon, in fact, hoped by hurrying Marmont's army from the north side to gain a complete victory; but his marshal was there fiercely assailed by Blücher and finally had to abandon the village of Möckern. This defeat compelled Napoleon to draw in his own army nearer to Leipzig, and he vainly sent a request for an armistice. On the 18th Murat, supported by Napoleon and the Old Guard, maintained an obstinate resistance to the overwhelming numbers of the Grand Army; but the French defence on the left wing was endangered by the desertion of 3600 Saxons and Würtembergers. Only the speedy arrival of Napoleon and his Old Guards prevented an immediate collapse at that point. Meanwhile Bernadotte's tardy approach was threatening an even

worse disaster to the French, and with more energy on his
part their retreat could have been cut off. As it was, they
only had ammunition left for two hours more, and finally fell
back into the crowded streets of Leipzig amidst terrible confusion. A slight wooden structure over the Elster broke down,
and while the stream of fugitives was still surging across the
only other bridge, a premature explosion cut off the rear-guard
which had been bravely defending the suburbs. A few, among
them Macdonald, escaped by swimming or by felled trees;
many more were drowned, including the gallant Poniatowski,
who had received his marshal's baton but three days before;
and thousands were made prisoners. In all Napoleon lost on
those three days 300 cannon, 45,000 men killed, wounded or
prisoners, besides leaving 23,000 in the military hospitals. But
the freedom of Germany, which was fully assured by this gigantic
conflict, had been dearly bought. The allies had sustained
still heavier losses in the field and were in no condition for
a vigorous pursuit. Beset by typhus fever and harassed here
and there by light troops, the remains of Napoleon's army
plodded through the miry lanes of Saxony and Thuringia, past
Lützen, Auerstädt, and Erfurt, once the scenes of victory and
splendour and now of a hurried and disastrous retreat. Still,
the sunset of his fortunes was gilded by some acts of generosity
worthy of the new Charlemagne. He had forbidden his
generals to set fire to the suburbs of Leipzig, though the allied
advance would have been thereby retarded. In the hapless
city he had bidden his unwilling ally the King of Saxony to
make the best terms he could with the allies; and he permitted
the rest of the Saxon troops to join the national cause, against
which they had throughout the campaign unwillingly fought.
The Bavarians had allied themselves with Austria a week
before Napoleon's disaster; and their troops vainly sought to
cut off his retreat at Hanau; thereafter he finally led about
70,000 men across the Rhine (Nov. 1—2), and returned

to Paris as in the previous winter with a loss of nearly half a million of men.

Meanwhile Tettenborn, when driven from Hamburg by the French, had captured Bremen by a *coup de main*; and after Leipzig he was there reinforced by Bernadotte. The allies were able also to help a general popular rising against the French in Holland, and despatched troops against the Danes in Holstein. The latter came to terms with the allies; and Bernadotte reinforced by 10,000 Danish troops began to march towards the lower Rhine. With the exception of Davoust's entrenched position at Hamburg, French rule suddenly shrank within the limits gained by the revolutionary armies under Jourdan and Kléber. The garrisons imprudently left in Polish and German fortresses also began to surrender—Danzig (with the wrecks of Napoleon's Russian army and 1300 cannon), Modlin, Zamosk, Stettin, Torgau, Erfurt, &c.: Dresden, Küstrin, Wittenberg and Magdeburg held out through the winter; Hamburg and Glogau until the following autumn. The results of the campaign showed that though the possession of fortresses may be very important, it can rarely reverse the effects of a decisive defeat in the open field, and that after a great military disaster such as Leipzig, it may prove, as at Metz in 1870, to be merely a trap for their garrisons. In all about 190,000 men were cut off from France by the results of the battles near Leipzig.

Side by side with the collapse of his vast military effort, Napoleon's political supremacy in Germany and Italy fell with a rapidity which revealed its hollowness and artificiality. The Austrians had easily regained Illyria and Dalmatia, where they were generally welcomed. Jerome Bonaparte's rule in Westphalia vanished like a dream, and the imposing Confederation of the Rhine dissolved at the first touch of the allied arms. What would replace it?

We have already noticed the commanding influence of

Austria on the course of events, enhanced by Metternich's skilful diplomacy. That statesman now used all his powers to counteract the efforts of Stein and other friends of liberty to gain free institutions for Germany. He had vainly endeavoured to dissuade the Czar from handing over to that zealous patriot the provisional administration of the liberated German lands, and now set himself to curb the "revolutionary aims" of young Germany and assure the future supremacy of Austria by treaties with the States seceding from the Confederation of the Rhine. The first of these treaties had been with Bavaria (Oct. 8), which was secured in "the full and entire sovereignty of all its States, towns, domains," with a secret reservation that Austria was to gain a good military frontier on the side of Bavaria and Tyrol. These terms, acceded to by the other allies, assured to Bavaria the formerly Prussian lands of Baireuth and Anspach, as well as the numerous Free Cities and knightly domains seized in 1803—1806. In this treaty as in many others—22 were signed in a single day at Frankfurt—the allies restored lawful princes to their States, largely increased as these were at the expense of church lands and the estates of the Imperial Knights; and the princes were invested with "unreserved sovereignty."

In two respects these arrangements were fatal to German liberty and unity. They abandoned the principle of subordination to some central authority, which had existed in name down to 1806 and since then in stern reality, to Napoleon; and the perpetuation of the French Emperor's policy of mediatisation aggrandised the middle-sized States and so vastly enhanced the difficulties of future unification. For the present Metternich sought solely to secure the supremacy of Austria by diplomatic bargains which would ensure the support of the German princes. Thus, amidst all the efforts made by the people of Germany, their desires for liberty and effective unity were ignored.

The Austro-Bavarian treaty also gave the Emperor Francis a commanding influence over the destinies of Italy. A secret clause gave him permission to send his troops into Tyrol. Eugène's positions in Venetia were thus turned, and he was soon unable to hold the line of the Adige against the invaders. Italy was in a weak and distracted state. She had poured forth her best blood for Napoleon on the battle-fields of Germany, Russia and Spain, while the pressure of his Continental System had ruined her industries and effaced the memory of his earlier reforms and public works. He had awakened, without satisfying, the sentiment of Italian nationality; and at every blow dealt to French supremacy north of the Alps, there were ominous reverberations throughout the Peninsula, which revealed the stifled discontent of all republicans and of the partisans of the fallen dynasties.

The people were, however, united only in the wish to throw off Napoleon's yoke. On all else they were divided. The old bands of the *sanfédists*, together with the Carbonari of the south, declared for the return of the Bourbons; while some generals in Murat's army, among whom was Pepe, plotted to gain a constitution similar to that enjoyed by Sicily under its English protectorate. Republican, Austrian, and Papal intrigues or plots completed the confusion. For a time Murat, who again abandoned Napoleon's fortunes, endeavoured to come to terms with the Austrians and with Lord Bentinck, the English commander in Italy. He desired, in fact, to be recognised by the allies as King of Italy, and, declaring for the independence of the Peninsula, he occupied Rome, Ancona and Bologna. This weakened Eugène's defence of Lombardy, which was further compromised when Bentinck with an Anglo-Sicilian force, landing in Tuscany, declared that fertile land freed from the French empire, and occupied Genoa. Eugène, finding his position untenable, finally (April, 1814) concluded an armistice with the Austrians, by which his French troops were allowed to return to France. Murat soon afterwards abandoned the hope of becoming king of all Italy, and retired to Naples.

The Leipzig campaign, therefore, swept away the political results of all French victories gained since Bonaparte's first appearance as a general in the Italian riviera. But in the spheres of intellectual and social development, the mighty impulse given by the French conquests could not disappear. Their influence lives on to-day in the ideas, customs and laws of Holland, Switzerland, Italy and Germany; and among the most important, if less evident, results of Napoleon's triumphs must be remembered the strong desire for effective national unity aroused in the breasts of Germans and Italians, finally to be consummated at Königgrätz and Sedan.

Compared with the momentous issues decided on the plains of Saxony, the expulsion of the French from Spain was an event of secondary importance. In fact, as soon as Napoleon was menaced by the fourth great Coalition he virtually decided to abandon Spain. Had that been done promptly, the presence of 200,000 more tried troops in Saxony would have been fatal to the allies; but Napoleon's desire to hold as much ground as possible from the Douro to the Vistula was to lose him everything.

The importance of Wellington's Salamanca campaign in showing the completely artificial character of Joseph Bonaparte's rule in Spain, has been already explained; and though the English commander had finally to retreat to Ciudad Rodrigo, it was only before a concentration of French armies which lost them the wealthy province of Andalusia. The numbers of the French party, which up to the middle of 1812 had been slowly increasing, were winnowed by failure and still more by the news of the Russian expedition. At once Napoleon began to recall the flower of his armies in Spain, to form a nucleus for the young levies who were to maintain his cause in Germany; and

Joseph found himself in May 1813 with rather less than 200,000 effectives, including the reserves at Bayonne. Of these 68,000 were needed by Suchet to hold down the warlike North-east, while 20,000 under Clausel were chasing Mina's guerrillas in Navarre and Aragon, with what success may be judged from his final assertion that it would take 50,000 troops three months to crush the Spaniards of the North. This single fact will suffice to refute the sneers which many English writers, including Napier, level at the partisan warfare. It not only disconcerted French plans by the capture of despatches, but compelled Joseph's troops to scatter in mobile columns, thus leaving far fewer men to concentrate against Wellington.

The king, in fact, now found it impossible to hold Madrid, and retreated towards Burgos, there collecting about 55,000 men at the beginning of June. Wellington, after many difficulties with the Cortès and the insubordination of the Spanish and Portuguese troops, assumed the offensive with about 90,000 men, of whom rather more than half were British. Aided by the guerrillas of the North and assured of supplies from the Asturian ports, he began what has been well called the march to Vittoria. Pushing French detachments beyond the Tormes and the Douro, he kept extending his left wing so as to outflank Joseph's army, thus winning many strong positions, including the castle of Burgos. The French fell back on the upper Ebro, where they were again outflanked by Wellington's superiority in numbers and tactics. The king had sent an urgent order to Clausel to cease chasing Mina's guerrillas and come to his help; but not more than 14,000 men were available, and they were not to arrive until all was over. Rolled back by Wellington's left, the French concentrated in good positions west of Vittoria, their left and centre crowning hills in front of which flowed the R. Zadora, while their right wing was far in the rear on the other bank of that river, guarding the bridge to the north of the town. Marshal Jourdan, the chief of the king's staff, desired to retreat to stronger positions, but he was overruled on the ground that Clausel was approaching Vittoria and that it would disgrace 70,000 trained troops to abandon Spain without fighting a battle.

The king and Jourdan showed a strange lack of energy. They neglected to strengthen their front by breaking the bridges, and Vittoria was so blocked by waggons as to hamper any backward movement. Their hope of Clausel's arrival was also disappointed by Wellington's vigorous attack with 83,000 British, Portuguese and Spanish troops (June 21). General Hill, after two hours' obstinate fighting, drove the French left from its strong position on the heights of Puebla, while Wellington's centre crossed the bridges and carried the hills in the teeth of deadly volleys from infantry and artillery. "The terrible fire from our battery (wrote Miot de Melito) could not arrest the advance of the English, and we observed the intrepidity of that advance with irresistible admiration." The French fell back on a second range of heights, which they defended with desperation; but their line of retreat was by this time seriously menaced by Graham's persistent and finally successful attacks on their right wing. Late in the afternoon his horse cut off the retreat by the direct road to France, while other squadrons threw into wild disorder the main body of French in the crowded streets of Vittoria. Artillery-men cut the traces, and the army fled in utter rout by the eastern road towards Pampeluna, leaving behind 151 cannon, all the ammunition, the baggage, and the treasure chests of the army, besides all the property amassed by King Joseph, his generals, officers and civilians during five years of warfare, plunder and extortion. The completeness of the victory surprised even Wellington himself. Clausel hastily retreated and finally regained France; but Suchet, though pressed by Mina's guerrillas in the north and an Anglo-Sicilian force in the south, long held out in Catalonia; and the obstinate defence of the French garrisons at Pampeluna and San Sebastian retarded Wellington's progress. The rest of Spain was, however, irretrievably lost to Napoleon at Vittoria.

On receiving at Dresden news of that disaster, the Emperor at once ordered King Joseph and Marshal Jourdan to retire to country-seats in France, where they were to live in seclusion. He also promptly selected Soult, Duke of Dalmatia, as the leader best able to oppose Wellington; but the marshal's ambitious wife strongly opposed his acceptance of a post "where nothing is to be got but blows." Her protests to Napoleon were cut short by the incisive statement that woman's province was to obey her husband and a marshal's duty was to obey his Emperor; and Soult, with his duchess, was hurried off with orders to defend the Pyrenees inch by inch. Rallying the French forces, he boldly assumed the offensive, in the endeavour to succour Pampeluna and San Sebastian, and was with difficulty beaten back from before the former fortress (July 27—30) and from the crags and defiles of the Pyrenees. Only the astonishing hardihood of the British infantry, and the thirst for vengeance of Wellington's Portuguese and Spaniards, could so speedily have driven their foes from a succession of natural ramparts, and finally from strong entrenchments on the precipitous bank of the Bidassoa. On his side, Soult showed how quickly an able general can rally troops disorganised by disaster, and amply justified the Emperor's recent choice. Junot, Victor, Ney, Masséna, Bessières, Marmont, Clausel, and Jourdan had come out of the ordeal of conflict with the great British leader, with reputations dimmed if not completely eclipsed. It was reserved for Soult to show that glory could be gained even in a series of reverses, when these were inflicted by Wellington and his Peninsular veterans.

The surrender of the French garrisons in San Sebastian and Pampeluna, on the last day of August and October respectively, removed the last obstacles to Wellington's invasion of France.

When Napoleon was fighting his way back to the Rhine, nothing remained to him in Spain except a few positions held for a time by Suchet in Catalonia; and in the spring of 1814 the only results of his Spanish policy were the devastation of the Peninsula, the loss of fully 200,000 of his best troops, and a secure foothold gained by Wellington on the soil of France itself.

CHAPTER XI.

THE RECONSTRUCTION OF EUROPE.

"Thou might'st have built thy throne
Where it had stood e'en now: thou didst prefer
A frail and bloody pomp, which Time has swept
In fragments towards oblivion."—SHELLEY.

TALLEYRAND, with a perspicacity which was not blinded by all the splendours of the Erfurt interview, had there confidentially remarked to the Czar, that all the conquests beyond the Rhine, Alps and Pyrenees, were the work of Napoleon, not of France, and that she must inevitably lose them in course of time. The remark, which as regards Italy and Germany, must have seemed in 1808 to be a prophecy of the remote future, is interesting as showing that at least one prominent Frenchman was not so fascinated by Napoleon's genius as to lose the sense of historic perspective or overlook the silent but resistless forces which tend to re-adjust the equilibrium of States or peoples. The birth of some great idea, the spread of a vivifying belief, the advent of some mighty organizer or warrior, has temporarily bound together and spurred on even scattered tribes to subdue the inert masses of half the known world. But the very force of the impact in course of time evokes energy, if only that of sheer despair. The peoples subdued or menaced with subjection are thrown back on the firmest centres of resistance; their faith becomes fiercely militant, and the military reaction calls forth a Tancred, a Cœur de Lion, and the Cid.

Revolutionary France was raised to unparalleled power by a singular concurrence of all the above-named factors of national greatness. The growth of the democratic idea, and fervent belief in Rousseau's gospel of social equality, endowed her with latent energies soon to be called into unexampled activity by her two great organizing powers—the Committee of Public Safety and Bonaparte. It has been briefly shown in this work, how the French armies, warring against effete systems, retained their revolutionary ardour, even after that had spent itself at Paris amidst the degrading strifes of factions. What must have been the strength of the prime impulse and the thoroughness of organization, if when Paris was weary of interminable wars, Napoleon's eagles still could wing their flight to Cadiz and Moscow? Those two names, however, recall the fact that military triumphs which overleap the bounds of racial solidarity, and war against the sympathies or material interests of the conquered, cannot be long maintained against the earthquake shocks of some impulse originating in the popular consciousness or against the denuding influences of time.

These two potent influences are ever at work in history as in the physical world, the volcanic process tending to form a great State along the lines of least resistance, whereupon it is immediately subjected to the denuding effects of war and diplomacy, or of the constant strivings of the human race for the fittest conditions of existence. The weathering-away process is the more usual—witness the gradual dissolution of the Angevin dominions in France, of the Holy Roman Empire, and of the Turkish power in south-eastern Europe. The formative process in the history of States (especially when it is of the volcanic rather than of the sedimentary character) is naturally far more concentrated and interesting. The climax of interest is of course reached whenever an internal popular impulse is developed by some great genius to an abnormal power or intensity. It is for this cause that the revolutionary and Napoleonic era exhibits triumphs so astonishing, followed by overwhelming disasters. It is essentially cataclysmic. The democratic movement, which under a Carnot, Kléber, or Moreau, might possibly have touched Vienna, Berlin and Rome, was carried by Napoleon's determination to conquer England upon the Continent, to the banks of the Guadiana and the Moskwa. The rebound, the rising of the nations against an Imperialism that had become intolerable, was proportionately the more violent. It swept away, not only his conquests over the bitterly hostile peoples of Russia, Prussia and Spain, but also his rule in Germany and Italy, lands which had at first welcomed the principles of 1789.

The reaction of the peoples and their rulers against Napoleon, intensified by their dread of leaving him in power, was now threatening the limits of revolutionary France. Even the tide of military events, from Valmy to Friedland and back again from Baylen to Waterloo, bears witness to the truth of the statement that the real boundaries of a nation are not marked by its political limits but by the sphere of its intellectual and spiritual attraction. To the discerning eye, the confines of France in 1789 were far wider than those of Napoleon's Empire when it stretched to the Baltic and the Adriatic. At the earlier date her ideas were permeating the world. In 1812 the growth of the national principle was already threatening to drive her back within her strictly historical limits; and it is significant that the attitude of the Prussian and German patriots was now distinctly more aggressive than that of their governments.

At the time when the allied sovereigns at Frankfurt were offering Napoleon the Rhine, the Alps and the Pyrenees as the boundaries of his Empire, Arndt issued his important pamphlet—"The Rhine a German river, not Germany's boundary"—which had a marked influence on public opinion and even on the diplomatists at Frankfurt and Châtillon. But the rising tide of German nationality was beginning to alarm the sovereigns. They were inclined to disregard a public opinion which they regarded as revolutionary; and peace would probably have been assured but for Napoleon's determination not to accept it in the midst of defeat.

It is a wide-spread and very natural error to suppose that Napoleon's fall was due to the snows of Russia and the rising of Central Europe. Both notions are incorrect. The Emperor boasted to Metternich that he had spared Frenchmen in the Moscow campaign and made other peoples bear the brunt of it. As a matter of fact, his losses of French troops there were less than those caused by the constant drain of the Spanish campaigns. The results of the war of 1813 were far more serious; but at most they only shattered his supremacy in Germany and Italy, and reduced him to limits which Louis XIV's arms had never been able to gain. The Moscow expedition had lost him only some of the results won at Friedland and Wagram; and the Leipzig campaign after all only limited France to what she had virtually gained by 1795. The great majority of Frenchmen now longed for a peace which would assure to them the quiet possession of what the revolution and its armies had won. Fouché wrote to Napoleon from Rome at the close of 1813, warning him of the magical effect of the word *independence* throughout Italy, and begging him to content himself with the "natural frontiers" of France. A similar wish was loudly expressed even in Napoleon's Court.

By a strange coincidence the very same offer was now distinctly sent by the allied sovereigns from Frankfurt. There was a strong peace party among the allies. Indeed, but for the death of Kutusoff in the spring of 1813 it is doubtful whether the Russian army would have advanced beyond the Oder; and it is certain that the Czar was now satisfied with freeing Europe as far as the Rhine. Frederick William, of a disposition naturally hesitating and rendered more so by years of calamity, had no wish to venture everything in a campaign beyond the Rhine. The Emperor Francis, seeing Illyria, Tyrol, and northern Italy virtually in his power, did not wish to press his son-in-law further; and Lord Aberdeen, England's representative at the allied head-quarters, declared—" England is satisfied; for the power of France is now reduced within legitimate bounds; and this is all that England ever desired." The allies therefore drew up the famous offers of peace to Napoleon (Nov. 9, 1813), leaving to his Empire the ' natural boundaries' of France, the Rhine, the Alps and the Pyrenees: the unconditional independence of Germany and Spain must be acknowledged; Italy and Holland must be independent of France, but their form of government and the Austrian boundary in Italy were to be determined by negotiation. England was prepared to offer great sacrifices for peace on these terms and to abandon most of her maritime claims. A congress was to assemble at some town east of the Rhine, to adjust these and other questions.

Extraordinarily favourable though these terms were to a sovereign who had recently lost two immense armies, Metternich rightly judged that Napoleon would refuse them, and the sovereigns did not suspend the march towards the Rhine. The French Emperor consented (Nov. 16) to negotiate, but only on the general principle of the equilibrium of the Powers, and gave no definite assent to their terms as a basis for negotiations. On the contrary the *Moniteur* bristled with warlike articles; and the instructions given to Caulaincourt, his new Minister of Foreign Affairs, prove how wide an interpretation Napoleon gave to the phrase 'natural boundaries':

the *têtes de pont* east of the Rhine were to remain in French hands, and also a considerable part of Holland: a federal constitution for Germany was objected to, and Jerome was to retain his kingdom of Westphalia or gain compensation in Italy. Even before this virtual rejection of the allied terms, Napoleon's ambiguous attitude had strengthened the war party at Frankfurt; and when it heard of Wellington's successes in the south, the revolt of Holland against Napoleon's rule, and the surrender of French garrisons in Germany, there was little prospect of similar terms being again offered to the once redoubtable foe.

It is difficult fully to fathom Napoleon's reasons for not frankly and unreservedly accepting those conditions. It is stated by the Baron de Vitrolles, who was soon to play so important a part in the restoration of the Bourbons, that the air of uncertainty and extreme moderation in the allied governments amidst a triumph for which they were not prepared, and their offering terms instead of dictating them, encouraged Napoleon to hope for the dissolution of the coalition, or that one French victory would gain him much better conditions. The Frankfurt terms were, however, not much less favourable than those to which he had, when too late, acceded at Prague just after the lapse of the armistice. It is possible, indeed, that in his remorse at having acceded to that suspension of arms, so fatal to his fortunes, he had now steeled himself to the conviction that all signs of moderation, whether in himself or his foes, were proofs of weakness. His other illusion, that a new dynasty could not survive a confession of weakness which might be borne with impunity by an old reigning family, had twice been disproved by the state of public opinion in France. Malet's venture was made before the news of the evacuation of Moscow had reached Paris. After two fatal campaigns there was no attempt to dethrone Napoleon; and most Frenchmen would have hailed with joy the return to the natural frontiers as a pledge of a peaceful policy.

But the voice of France now rarely reached the Emperor's ears, and he remained in the illusion that she was entirely devoted to his cause so long as he gave her glory and victory. The campaign of 1814 was to show that he singularly overlooked the real strength of his position—viz. that he was the sole effective guardian of the material and social gains effected by the Revolution. All the rest, the boasts of military honour and glory, were now mere idle talk to all save a few infatuated devotees and the veterans of his army. As for his other assertion, that the allies wished to humiliate France and that he must win a victory in order to conclude an honourable peace, it was skilfully refuted by a declaration which the allies drew up at Frankfurt (Dec. 1) and caused to be circulated throughout France:—"The Powers confirm to the French Empire an extent of territory such as France has never had under her ancient kings; for a brave nation does not lose its rank because it has in its turn sustained reverses in the course of an obstinate struggle in which it has fought with its usual bravery"; and the public offer to the French people of the 'natural boundaries' would, it was hoped, sever the cause of France from the policy of Napoleon.

Another incident might surely have given him pause. The *Corps Législatif*, usually so obsequious, voted by a majority of four to one (Dec. 29), an address urging him to declare that he "would give to Europe and the world the assurance that he continued the war only for the independence of the French people and the inviolability of its territory"; and it prayed him to "guarantee the rights of freedom, security of property, and to the nation the free exercise of its political rights." Napoleon's only reply was to order the prorogation of the Assembly, the destruction of the address, and to launch a tirade against the authors of the address as bad men "in the pay of England." In fact, his whole attitude at the close of 1813 gives some colour to the charge that he was not altogether averse from war, as tending to stifle political agitation in France and rally around him all who were interested in maintaining the material gains of the Revolution.

He made an effort to detach Spain from the allies by a treaty with the captive Ferdinand VII (Dec. 11, 1813), offering to restore to him his throne, on condition that all British troops evacuated Spain. Ferdinand adroitly referred him to the Spanish Cortès, which honourably refused to treat apart from the English Government. Consequently Wellington's base of operations in Spain remained unshaken, and he was able to advance towards Orthez. The sternness with which he checked plundering by his troops, even by the insubordinate Spaniards, made a good impression on the French peasantry; and an official letter from Bayonne declared that the good order which he maintained did Napoleon's cause more harm than ten battles.

The decisive blows were, however, to be struck in the valleys of the Marne and Seine. In spite of the opposition of the Czar, therein influenced by his old tutor Laharpe and another Swiss democrat, General Jomini, it was decided not to observe the neutrality of Switzerland, which had been violated by Napoleon for ten years past. The allied Grand Army, some 250,000 strong, therefore passed the Rhine at Basel, and, proceeding to turn the strong defensive line of the Vosges, finally debouched on the plateau of Langres and menaced the lines of the rivers which there have their source. A detached column also marched on Geneva and threatened Lyons. On the first day of 1814, Blücher led his Silesian army of about 90,000 men across the Rhine at three points between Mannheim and Coblentz; while the allied army of the north, under Bernadotte and von Bülow, began somewhat later to threaten the Belgian Departments. With the allied forces under

Wellington and others in Italy and North Germany, the whole forces opposed to Napoleon promised to exceed 600,000 men, among whom were Rhenish Confederation troops which had previously fought for him.

To oppose these masses the French had scarcely 250,000 men ready to take the field; but a *Senatus-consultum* ordered the enrolment of 300,000 unmarried men, though the conscription had already been rigorously pressed. It was found that the conscripts of this time, having been born during the Reign of Terror, were distinctly below the average strength; yet it was on these that France now mainly had to rely. Napoleon, however, still had the advantage of the central position, which Carnot had turned to such account in 1793: he also rightly counted on the presence of invaders on the 'sacred soil' to still all divisions, while these would increase among the allies as they advanced nearer to their goal. The densest masses of invaders were also mainly Austrians and Confederate troops of indifferent quality, and were handled by Prince Schwarzenberg, who had little confidence in himself, and was constantly hampered by the pacific leanings of the Emperor Francis. The northern army was reorganizing in Holland. For the present, therefore, only the Silesian army was to be met, and its junction with the Grand Army on the Aube prevented at all costs.

The first events were in favour of the allies. Blücher's rapid and unexpected advance deprived the French of the two strong lines of the Moselle and the Meuse, the fortresses on which rivers he left detachments to observe or besiege. When his columns reached Brienne without serious resistance (Jan. 26), and were not very far from Schwarzenberg's vanguard, the campaign seemed, in a strategical sense, decided. He was soon undeceived. Napoleon, rallying the French forces which had been falling back, drove a Prussian column from St Dizier, and on Jan. 29 hurled back another part of the Silesian army at Brienne, where as a youth he had first studied the art of war; but, on receiving reinforcements from the Grand Army, Marshal 'Forward,' with about 85,000 men, resumed the offensive, and inflicted on Napoleon's 40,000 a decisive defeat at La Rothière, capturing 3,000 prisoners and 73 cannon (Feb. 1).

The completeness of the success was in one sense a misfortune. Young officers invited each other to dinner in the Palais Royal in a week's time. Blücher himself, regarding the victory as decisive, desired to march on Paris by way of Châlons; while the Czar and the Emperor Francis, not desiring too complete a triumph of the Prussian arms, began to withdraw the support of the Grand Army, and recommended a leisurely march on Paris, chiefly by way of Troyes. A force of 12 Cossack regiments was to keep the two chief armies in touch. It was urged at the allied head-quarters that this division of forces was necessary to secure provisions; but General Müffling states in his memoirs that even then it appeared a device for delaying operations so as not to cut off Napoleon from the means of concluding peace in the Congress at Châtillon, where negotiations had been opened; and that the prospect of Blücher's army gaining possession of Paris evidently aroused the jealousy and fears of the two Emperors. Indeed, when Blücher had nearly traversed the plains of Champagne, an order came from the Czar that his forces were not to enter Paris before the arrival of the sovereigns; and at the same time a corps was withdrawn from his command. Strange to say, the sovereigns of Austria and Prussia suspected the Czar of desiring to place Bernadotte on the throne of France, or, as being easier and more conformable to the spirit of the times, of favouring a return to a moderate republican government; and they even entered into a secret treaty (Feb. 14) for garrisoning Paris equally, lest the Czar should perpetrate a republican *coup d'état.*

Owing to these dissensions, all touch was lost between the Grand Army on the Seine and the forces of Blücher and Yorck in the Marne valley. The latter were, on Feb. 5, between Sézanne and Châlons, and appeared to have interposed a wedge between Napoleon's army retreating from Troyes, and Macdonald's forces near Épernay; but the Silesian army, in its effort to cut off Macdonald's direct retreat on Paris by the Marne valley, left its columns at intervals of more than a day's march, and thus dangerously exposed to a flank attack from the south. Napoleon, ever apprised by his marshal of the enemy's movements, seized the opportunity. Marching by miry cross-roads from Nogent northwards, he fell with about 30,000 troops on Blücher's severed corps and completely defeated them at Champaubert, Montmirail, Château-Thierry and Vauchamps (Feb. 10—14), inflicting total losses of more than 15,000 men and 50 cannon. These French victories in the Marne valley had a far more important effect than that of throwing back the shattered Silesian army on Châlons. They raised the spirits of the young French conscripts and strengthened the wavering belief in the Emperor's invincibility. Not a *vivat* had greeted him ten days before on his entry into Troyes. The citizens would supply nothing except on compulsion. A considerable number of the troops—6,000 it was said—deserted there. Napoleon himself was for some hours deeply depressed. He complained in his letters that his troops were nearly starving, and authorised Caulaincourt provisionally to accept the allied terms; while to his brother Joseph, who was aiding the government at Paris, he sent orders (Feb. 9) to have everything removed from Compiègne and Fontainebleau which would serve as a trophy for the enemy. Not only was the devotion of his soldiers beginning to cool, but the wealthy and mercantile classes were almost to a man hostile. The Duc de Broglie states that the audience at one of the Paris theatres hissed off the stage a play ordered by the Imperial police, which in one scene represented the Cossacks plundering and burning a French village. Nevertheless, the alienation of urban feeling only served to show more clearly what was the central support of the imperial edifice. Except in the royalist west and south, the peasants still looked on the Emperor as the guarantee for their tenure of lands confiscated during the revolution. In regard to the material interests of the peasantry, he was still the crowned Jacobin guarding the agrarian conquests of 1789 against a return of the Bourbons and the *émigrés*.

This feeling was strongest in the centre and east of France, where feudalism had been most oppressive; and the allied reinforcements on their march were now often harassed by National Guards and popular risings. The spirit of his troops had also been restored by the recent victories. The terrible cry 'Vive l'Empereur' again menaced the invaders; and the spirit of Valmy seemed to animate the young conscripts who daily came to fill the ranks. Still more important was the arrival of two divisions of infantry and one of cavalry, which he withdrew from Soult's army at the beginning of February. He would have fallen again on Blücher's army at Châlons, but for news that the allied Grand Army was now threatening to overwhelm the divisions of Victor and Oudinot, which he had left to guard the Seine valley; and the war, strategically the most interesting of all Napoleon's campaigns, except perhaps those of Italy and Waterloo, became more than ever a struggle for the possession of the roads leading down the Seine, Aube and Marne towards Paris, on which the two chief rivers converge.

The student will here observe the immense defensive importance of a broad and deep river. It is in some respects a better military defence than a mountain chain. The approach of the enemy can be observed more readily. There are few chains which are not penetrable by numerous defiles; and the invaders, if defeated, can find refuge in them or on the slopes.

The passage of the Alps by Hannibal and Napoleon illustrates
the practicability even of a vast range of mountains to armies
led by great commanders; and the battle of Kulm in 1813
shows how a retreating foe may rally in a defile and restore
the fortunes of the war.   On the other hand, the passage of
a river or marsh in front of undefeated enemies is one of the
most hazardous of military movements.   Its successful per-
formance by Marlborough at Blenheim, and by Wellington
above Oporto, ranks among the great achievements of modern
times; whereas neglect of due precautions in this operation
led to the disasters of Austerlitz, Friedland, and the Katzbach, beside vastly increasing the losses at the Beresina and
Leipzig.   Indeed, the whole course of Napoleon's defeats may
in a military sense be summarised thus, that after losing
successively the lines of the Niemen, Vistula, Oder, Elbe,
Saale, Rhine, Moselle and Meuse, he was now using all the force
of his genius and indomitable will to hurl back the Silesian
and Grand Armies on the further banks of the Marne and
Seine.

In the former of these efforts he seemed to have almost
succeeded, when he was recalled by the news that part of the
Grand Army was advancing on Paris by the Seine valley.
Retracing his steps, the Emperor hurled his compact forces on
them and at the close of a sharp engagement at Montereau
drove them in much confusion across the river and seized
the bridge before it was cut by the enemy (Feb. 18).   The
allies, taught by these severe lessons, saw the need of concentration; and, as after Ligny and Quatre Bras, foiled
Napoleon's efforts at separating them, by a concentric retreat.
The Grand Army retired towards Troyes to re-organise, while
Blücher promised to support them near that town with an
army now strengthened by the arrival of reserves.   But more
important than the accession of numbers was the undaunted
bearing of the veteran Field-Marshal, whose spirit now, as in

June 1815, only seemed to rise higher with defeat. All his energy was now needed to re-invigorate his staff and the allied sovereigns.—"In what a position were we on Feb. 22 (wrote General Müffling) as compared with the 2nd! Now fugitives, avoiding a battle with Bonaparte who had probably only half our numbers."

Remembering the advantages gained by the armistice of the previous summer, the allies now tried to gain time for further reinforcements from Germany, by sending overtures for an armistice to Napoleon, which he refused. A true view of the situation should have convinced Napoleon that his brilliant resistance had amply satisfied the honour of France and retrieved the glory of his arms, that when the northern allied army was beginning to appear on the arena, the psychological moment had arrived for accepting any terms not absolutely humiliating. But, either from alarm at the discontent in Paris, or from an exaggerated estimate of his recent successes[1], or because the portentous triumphs of his earlier days had ingrained in his masterful nature a confidence which absolutely excluded the thought of ultimate failure, Napoleon

---

[1] This alternative may be supported by a few extracts from his letters to King Joseph at Paris. Feb. 11 (after Montmirail) "The army of Silesia has ceased to exist. I have completely routed it."—Feb. 15 (after Vauchamps), "The peasants have picked up here on the battle-fields more than 40,000 muskets."—Feb. 18 (just before Montereau), "The enemy is now in a very different position from that which he occupied when he made the Frankfort proposals: he must now feel almost certain that few of his troops will recross the frontier."—Feb. 19, "As soon as the allies heard that I had forced the bridge of Montereau, they ran away as fast as they could. Their whole army is terrified."......"I have ordered General Maison to collect the garrisons in Flanders, to march towards Flanders and resume operations."—At the same date he expresses to Eugène the hope of preserving Italy and making Murat change sides. At that time von Bülow was at Mons in great force, and Eugène was barely holding his own.

once more let slip, until it was too late, an opportunity for a peace which the allies offered and for which France herself had long been sighing.

As has been noticed, negotiations between Napoleon and the allies had been resumed at Châtillon on Feb. 5 ; and at that time of his despondency after la Rothière he had given to his envoy Caulaincourt, Duc de Vicenza, almost *carte blanche* provided he brought the negotiations to a happy end and saved Paris from occupation. The apparently decisive results of the first great battle far within the limits of ancient France, the news of Murat's defection from the Emperor, the arrival of the English Foreign Minister, Lord Castlereagh, with the welcome news of the determination of his government to persevere with the war in the South,—all these influences concurred to raise the expectations of the allies ; and they firmly declared that they would treat with France in the name of Europe as forming a single entity. At the second sitting of the Congress it was resolved to demand that France should return to her pre-revolutionary frontiers with a few exceptions determined by mutual convenience. To this Caulaincourt took exception, seeing that his government had stipulated for the Frankfurt terms of Nov. 1813 as the basis for the present negotiation ; and he stated that though the Emperor was ready to make the greatest sacrifices, he would demur to the limits of the old monarchy.

We learn from Napoleon's secretary M. Fain, his indignation at these terms—"What can I answer to the republicans in the Senate when they demand from me their Rhine boundary? God keep me from such disgrace. Tell Caulaincourt that I reject such conditions. Rather will I endure the worst evils of war." Nerved by desperation, he flung himself on the Silesian and Grand Armies with the surprising results previously described. At one time Macdonald's troops advanced so near Châtillon that the allied envoys threatened to break up the Congress, and Caulaincourt had to beg the French Marshal to retire. Nevertheless, the allies refused to give way on the chief points at issue, while Caulaincourt, pursuant to Napoleon's temporising policy, avoided any definite rupture of the negotiations.

On Feb. 17 the allies presented to the French pleni-potentiary the draft of a treaty nearly identical with that which ultimately became the basis for the reconstruction of Europe; and, when it was obvious that Napoleon would not accept these terms, the allies formed by the Treaty of Chaumont (March 1) a Quadruple Alliance which cemented, far more intimately and definitely, the compacts framed at Teplitz in the previous summer. Each of the four Powers now agreed to keep 150,000 men on active service for the war against Napoleon. England consented to furnish subsidies to her three allies at the annual rate of £5,000,000 to be equally divided; and she was left free to substitute money, if the number of her troops could not be made up to the required total. The treaty was to hold good for twenty years. It was also secretly agreed that Germany was to form a federal State.

As for the negotiations at Châtillon, they were protracted to March 20, without any result; and it was not until the allies were marching victoriously on Paris that Napoleon decided to accept their terms. As in 1813, he let the time for negotiation pass by, and only gave his assent when it was too late.

The recent defeats had only served to cement the union between the allies and to defer their jealousies until victory had fully crowned their arms. Two days previously fortune had again deserted Napoleon's cause. At Bar-sur-Aube, the Russian commander Wittgenstein had administered a severe check to the French, while at the same time Wellington, after passing the Gave at Orthez, drove his able adversary Soult

from strong positions north of the town. The French marshal's retreat eastwards uncovered Bordeaux, to which great
city Wellington was invited by a strong royalist party among
the citizens. Beresford was despatched thither with light
troops; and, supported by their presence, the Duc d'Angou-
lême, eldest son of the Comte d'Artois, entered the city, and
there proclaimed Louis XVIII as king (March 12).

Events marched still more swiftly in the north. The corps
of von Bülow and Wintzingerode were threatening Paris on the
north-east; and as early as Feb. 25 Blücher had formed the
daring and eventually successful plan of leaving Napoleon to
follow the Grand Army, while he himself marched towards the
capital, arranging with Wintzingerode for a junction at or near
Meaux on the Marne. Pushing the small corps of Marmont and
Mortier down the Marne, his vanguard sustained a check from
them near Meaux; and he soon gladly learnt from Tettenborn's
Cossacks that Napoleon, suddenly awakened from his dream
that the allies were retreating on the Rhine, was marching
north in hot haste to prevent his junction with the northern
army. This would give time for the Grand Army to threaten
Paris from the Seine valley, while he and von Bülow menaced
it from the Soissons road. In a strategic sense, therefore,
Blücher's march resembles his famous flank march before
Leipzig, which had the effect of gradually bringing irresistible
forces to bear on the objective of the whole campaign—in this
case Paris. The prospects of the allies were improved by the
somewhat tame surrender of the fortress of Soissons by a
French general, and there Blücher and von Bülow effected the
desired junction, forming an array of 110,000 Prussians and
Russians with 500 cannon (March 4). The assertion of
Napoleon's panegyrists that the surrender of Soissons ruined
his campaign is a gross exaggeration. The junction of forces
was the decisive event, not the capture of a third-rate fortress.
Behind the old walls of Soissons there were but 20 cannon

and about 1000 troops; and many of these were disabled before
the commandant surrendered with the honours of war. Besides, if the place was of such extreme importance, why was it
left with a feeble garrison and deficient ammunition? Had it
held out for some days longer, the issue of events could hardly
have been very different; for there were other points at which
a junction could have been effected. Blücher was about to
throw bridges across the Aisne when he heard of the surrender.

By threatening the allied flank and communications,
Napoleon transferred the contest to the plateau of Craonne,
where a desperate conflict ended in his favour. The allies fell
back on the strong defence afforded by the natural citadel of
Laon surrounded by wide plains; weakened by dissensions
more than by defeat, they there awaited the attack of half
their numbers. On the first day of battle at Laon (March 9)
the French maintained an equal contest even against these
odds; but at nightfall, the allies carried out with startling
success an attack on the wearied French and threw Marmont's
wing into utter rout. The temporary illness of Blücher and
fear of Napoleon kept the allies from pushing the pursuit.
Deep depression reigned in Napoleon's camp. He had failed
to drive the allies back on Belgium; and the sole result of
these battles on the Aisne seemed to be the loss of about
15,000 men. Any other commander, on the news that
Schwarzenberg was marching down the Aube, would have
judged that enough had been done to save honour; but Napoleon, in his determination not to yield to the allied terms,
preferred to struggle on against hopeless odds, and led his
weary troops by way of Soissons (which had been easily retaken), hoping to surprise the allies. He succeeded at Rheims,
where he routed a Russian division (March 16). This led him
to persist in rejecting the allied terms; and he marched southwards in the hope of catching the Austrians napping. A hasty

concentration of Schwarzenberg's marching columns sufficed to avert defeat.

Napoleon, mistaking these movements for that retreat on the Rhine which ever dominated his imagination, was ordering a march eastwards on Vitry to hasten their retreat, when his columns were menaced near Arcis, the birthplace of Danton. While part of the French were pressing on to Vitry, others were slowly and methodically attacked at Arcis by vast masses of the allies who, if effectively handled, ought to have captured them (March 20, 21). As it was, the French rearguard suffered heavily; and, as Napoleon's movements towards the Marne had uncovered the road to Paris, the Czar and his Staff officers formed the surprisingly daring resolve to march on Paris, leaving behind a light corps as a screen to their movements. Blücher's approach southwards supported them on their right, and in a rapid march the combined forces overthrew Marmont's and Mortier's corps at la Fère Champenoise, capturing thousands of prisoners and all Napoleon's reserve ammunition and stores. Meanwhile the French vanguard severed Schwarzenberg's communications on the upper Marne and captured its baggage, pontoons, and even some of the couriers and diplomatists at Chaumont. Thus the campaign presented the unexampled scene of simultaneous attempts upon the hostile rear, Napoleon hoping to relieve his garrisons in the east, to excite a popular rising in that quarter, and to intimidate the nervous Austrian commander; while the allies were resolved to dictate terms of peace at Paris. The French Emperor was committing the same blunder as at Smolensk, Moscow and Leipzig, that of underrating the energy and courage of his foes. Alone among his staff he did not suspect the truth. Near Vitry on March 27, Macdonald brought him a bulletin of the allies with the news of la Fère Champenoise. Napoleon's disbelief in its news was strengthened by a curious misprint, March 29 for March 26; but when later on Drouot and Macdonald pointed out from internal evidence that the battle had been fought on the earlier day, he proceeded to St Dizier to learn the truth, and so lost some more precious hours, while the vanguard of the allies was coming within sight of the spires of Paris.

At last it had come to this. The Parisians, who in 1792 had been in a frenzy of rage and terror at the capture of Verdun, were now by this strange series of events suddenly confronted with the forces of Europe thundering at their gates. The capital was even more defenceless than when Brunswick's manifesto had aroused the courage of desperation. The lassitude which always follows years of purposeless war, had now produced a wide-spread desire for the acceptance of any honourable terms. There was now no *levée en masse*, still less any threat of massacring the royalists who listened eagerly for the Prussian cannon. What was the inner cause of this striking change in public opinion? Mainly this; that Napoleon, who in 1799 had seemed about to consolidate and guarantee the political liberties of France, had finally gagged and enchained them; so that the chief desire of the urban population of France was to shake off his yoke as a preliminary to some other political experiment. And yet the Parisians revolted at the thought of a foreign occupation, which their city had not known since the days of Jeanne d'Arc. Some attempts at barricades were made, but to save the honour of Paris, not to maintain the rule of Napoleon. Few were nerved by this last sentiment except possessors of confiscated lands, the men implicated in the revolutionary excesses, officials, soldiers, and all whose interests were bound up with the Emperor's rule.

In the absence of the Empress-Regent, who had departed for Blois, Joseph Bonaparte published a bombastic call to arms, which was signally stultified by facts; for there were hardly weapons sufficient for the 13,000 National Guards of

Paris ; but the presence of more than 25,000 troops of the line under Marmont and Mortier, besides Invalides and pupils of the military schools, promised a defence sufficiently prolonged to ensure succour from Napoleon. Whether from fear of his arrival or from desire of avoiding a further effusion of blood, the allies issued a proclamation urging Paris to follow the examples of Bordeaux and Lyons—the latter had been surrendered by Augereau to the Austrians—and so hasten the advent of peace. It was in vain. At dawn of March 30, the allies began to march on the villages east of Paris, while others guarded the Fontainebleau road by which Napoleon was known to be hurrying to the rescue of his capital. For hours the combat raged in and around the village of Pantin ; and when the arrival of the Silesian army on the north brought the number of assailants up to fully 60,000, the Czar sent overtures to Joseph Bonaparte for a suspension of hostilities and the surrender of Paris. The Emperor's elder brother was not cast in that heroic mould which would gladly have defied the forces of combined Europe even amidst the ruins of Paris. The prospect of a bombardment and of street-fighting between 100,000 enraged combatants dismayed his imagination ; and though the relieving army was known to be near Fontainebleau, he shortly after midday gave directions to Marmont and Mortier that if they were unable to hold their positions, they might enter into negotiations with the allied commanders, and then retire on the Loire. At the same time Blücher's troops began to assail the heights of Montmartre and were about to carry the summit when news of the armistice arrived. Nevertheless, the fierce veteran at once ordered 84 cannon to be placed there to command Paris. Beaten back on the east side after desperate fighting, Marmont about four o'clock judged that the claims of honour were satisfied, and that he might now sue for an armistice to save Paris the horrors of a bombardment. The French troops were withdrawn into

Paris, which they were forthwith to evacuate. Joseph had departed from Paris immediately after giving his message to Marmont.

Meanwhile Napoleon, after awaking from his cherished illusion that the allies were retreating on the Rhine, rushed with his troops from Vitry to save the capital. Near Corbeil he hears of its surrender, and breaks into bitter taunts against his brother and generals. Still he is for a last desperate dash, to arouse and arm Paris against her captors. The sight of Mortier's vanguard in retreat recalls him to his senses; and he spends the night in a hostel, some fifteen miles south of Paris, gazing at his maps and plans—only to hear in the morning that the allied sovereigns are entering Paris. The imperious will, till then unsubdued by disaster, breaks down for a while, only to re-assert its force in conferences with his marshals at Fontainebleau. Berthier, Ney, Lefebvre, Oudinot, Macdonald, and others there insisted that the troops—even the Guard— were weary, famished, longing for peace, and determined not to expose Paris to the fate of Moscow. Macdonald showed him a letter from General Beurnonville, a member of the Provisional Government just formed at Paris, declaring that the allies would not treat with Napoleon and that France was to have a constitution like that of England. This was decisive. " Very well, gentlemen," said Napoleon, "since it must be so, I will abdicate....Will you accept the King of Rome as my successor and the Empress as Regent?"—They all assented. He began to write his act of abdication. Even then the indomitable resolve flashed forth in a hasty last appeal—" Nonsense, gentlemen, let us leave all this alone, and march tomorrow. We shall beat them." The protest of Macdonald and the silence of the rest spoke the feelings of generals and soldiers; and Napoleon felt himself powerless.

Such was the strange end of this brilliant campaign, in which the genius of one man had long held at bay three armies, each stronger than his own. And yet, such is the confused turmoil of war in which the greatest commanders at times grope but blindly, that the greatest master of the art of military concentration finally left his capital exposed to an overwhelming attack; and by an equally singular *contretemps* it was reserved for his once vacillating eastern rival to propose and deal the final stroke. By a singular Nemesis, too, the destinies of France and Europe lay for a few critical hours in the hands of Joseph Bonaparte, whose bourgeois qualities seemed designed by nature as a necessary foil to the commanding gifts which she had lavished on the second brother; and, as if to crown this chapter of paradoxes, Napoleon's abdication was finally assured by mingled advice and compulsion from the very marshals whose fortunes he had created.

As we have seen, the allies had only recently contemplated the deposition of Napoleon. After Leipzig they had offered him the Rhine boundary: after La Rothière they offered the limits of 1790; and, even when fortune had again smiled on their arms at Bar-sur-Aube, the Quadruple Alliance cemented at Chaumont (March 1) ostensibly proposed to leave Napoleon in possession of pre-revolutionary France. But even then there was a secret though powerful impression among the Prussian, Austrian and English diplomatists that so daring a genius could not be left in limits which would cramp his energies, and that a peace " founded on legitimism " would alone be durable. Events were to justify the former belief as signally as they falsified the latter.

This impression was deepened by the confident declaration (March 11) of the Baron de Vitrolles, spokesman for the French royalists, to Metternich—" There will be no peace with Buonaparte, and there will be no France without the Bourbons." Metternich objected that the allies saw no signs of attachment to the old dynasty, and that they would act against the law of nations if they imposed it on France.

Vitrolles maintained that when Napoleon's power was broken, the free opinion of France would declare for the Bourbons. The Czar, however, remained as before opposed to the return of the Bourbons; and though he had now renounced the idea of Bernadotte's accession, yet he still (March 17) was persuaded that a wisely organised Republic would be the best for France. Vitrolles' skilful representations to the allied sovereigns and diplomatists after the rupture of negotiations at Châtillon first prepared them for a declaration that they would reject all further overtures from Napoleon. The first public declaration of the allies that they would not treat with Napoleon or any member of his family was after their triumphant entry into Paris. They also promised to respect the limits of ancient France such as it was under the legitimate kings, as well as to recognise and guarantee the constitution which the French people should adopt. The Senate was consequently invited to designate a provisional government.

Up to the last exciting weeks, the very existence of the Bourbons had been almost forgotten by young France. The name Louis XVIII had for years past conjured up visions of a figure dimly flitting from one asylum to another in the far north, and occasionally uttering academic protests against the usurpations of his all-powerful rival. The recent proclamation of Louis XVIII at Bordeaux had first brought into prominence the possibility of a Bourbon Restoration, which a few weeks before would have seemed a theme of merely antiquarian interest. Even now the cries at Paris were "Down with Napoleon"—"No conscription"—"No consolidated duties"; but few were raised for the Bourbons. A small informal meeting of nobles and wealthy men had, it is true, voted for the restoration of Louis XVIII, but the proposal was viewed with indifference or aversion by the mass of the people. Once more, as in 1791, 1795 and 1799, it was evident that the task of construction would be infinitely more difficult than the ever inspiriting efforts for demolition; for the portly old gentleman who had spent nearly a quarter of a century in exile since the fateful night of Varennes, though surpassing his unfortunate brother in ability, commanded little of the sympathy enjoyed by Louis XVI.

The entry into Paris of the Czar and the King of Prussia—Francis I was at Dijon—revealed the existence of a small but vociferous party of royalists who distributed white cockades to the few who cared to don the Bourbon colour. The attitude of the many was that of resignation, curiosity, or, at most, of joy at the tardy advent of peace. Warned that the Élysée was mined, the Czar occupied Talleyrand's mansion; and this skilful diplomatist now played a momentous part in the affairs of France and of Europe. Having convinced himself that "under the Bourbons France would cease to be gigantic, in order again to become great," he now persuaded his illustrious guest that, to form a durable government, it must be based on a principle. That principle was legitimism. Its outward manifestation was Louis XVIII. The wily diplomatist had touched the Czar's weak side in his appeal to a principle. There was no more talk of a French Republic, still less of Bernadotte, whose threats of leading his troops against the allies if they restored the Bourbons seemed to unmask his designs in undertaking the war. Talleyrand forthwith convened the Conservative Senate, whose duty was to safeguard the constitution which at every crisis it had violated. It was now again true to its past. Though less than half its numbers were present, it appointed a provisional government in place of Napoleon, who was deposed from his throne and from the exercise of all his powers (April 2).

In vain did Napoleon send Ney, Macdonald, and Caulaincourt as his commissioners to urge that Marie Louise should be allowed to act as Regent for the King of Rome. Even Austrian diplomacy rejected a plan which a few days previously would have been welcomed by all the allies. Their determination was strengthened by the defection of Marmont, whose generals led the French vanguard within the allied lines (April 5). Marmont's excuse for desertion was the need of rescuing France from needless dangers; but she rejected the excuse and branded his name with infamy. The allied positions south of Paris were sufficiently strong to have defied the power of Napoleon had all his troops advanced to renew a hopeless fight; but even on April 6 he had endeavoured for the last time to rouse his marshals to an onset. They stoutly refused. The superhuman pertinacity of his will furnishes the best, indeed the only, excuse for Marmont's defection, and for that of Ney which speedily followed. At last, on final pressure from his marshals, Napoleon put an end to the suspense of the world by signing (April 11) the Act of Abdication for himself and his son; and after a thrilling scene of farewell to his "children"—the Old Guard—he departed for Elba, which the Czar had suggested as a fit abode. Only the presence of a Russian escort saved him from massacre at Orgon by a mob of royalists, whose rancorous hearts were untouched by the sight of fallen greatness. The story that he attempted to poison himself before leaving Fontainebleau, probably arose from his having taken a heavy dose of opium to secure much needed repose. Had he intended suicide, he would surely have committed it when surrounded by the rabble of the Rhone valley. His indulgence to Marie Louise was requited by her desertion of him; and he never saw her or his son again.

The last act of the war was a bloody and not very decisive engagement between Wellington and Soult at Toulouse (April 10). During his hasty retreat on Carcassonne, the French marshal heard that peace was now secured; and the English general finished on the upper Garonne the campaigns begun at the mouth of the Mondego.

Meanwhile at Paris the ardent royalists were urging the return of Louis XVIII without conditions; but Talleyrand and the Senate were equally determined to have the following guarantees for constitutional government—two Chambers, a Ministry responsible to them, a Budget subject to the control of the Chambers, liberty of the press and of public worship, admissibility of all Frenchmen to all employments, &c. The Comte d'Artois was persuaded by the Czar to acknowledge these principles of a Revolution which his youthful follies had done so much to provoke, and was declared lieutenant-general of the kingdom, until his elder brother, now called to the throne, should have acceded to the Constitutional Charter.

In this capacity the Comte d'Artois signed (April 23) Conventions with the allies which were ratified in the Treaty of Paris (May 30, 1814). The allies now granted conditions of peace slightly more favourable than those offered to Napoleon in March. Instead of fixing the limits of France as in 1790, those of 1792 were now conceded. This implied the retention by France of the County of Avignon, as also of Salm, Montbéliard, and the district connecting Landau with Alsace. On the other hand it severed from France all the gains of the revolutionary and Napoleonic wars except Mühlhausen and the districts around Philippeville, Saarbrücken, Annécy and Chambéry. If France lost heavily on land, she regained most of her colonial possessions. Perfidious Albion yielded up all the French colonies conquered by her, except Mauritius, the Seychelles, Tobago and St Lucia. The French coast claims on Newfoundland were also recognised by us. France regained Guadaloupe from Sweden and her part of Guiana from the Portuguese, ceding however to the Spanish Government the part of St Domingo which had belonged to Spain before the Treaty of Basel. After twenty years of war, which added about £600,000,000 to the National Debt, some discontent was very naturally felt in England at the magnitude

of the restitutions to our late foe; but Lord Castlereagh replied
to some strictures in Parliament on this subject that it was
desirable to give France an occupation for the time of peace:
—"It is better (he said) for France to be commercial and
therefore pacific, than a warlike and conquering State."

This naïve confession may be commended to the notice of
the class, still numerous, it is to be feared, on both sides of the
Channel, who can see nothing in English policy from 1793 to
1815, save perfidious and violent attempts to seize the trade of
the world and destroy the liberties of France. That the war of
1793 was to some extent a war of principles has been admitted:
that it was so after 1803 has been refuted; and it has been
abundantly shown that English maritime domination was as
distinctly an engine of war, as Napoleon's conquest of the
Continent was an attempt to humble the mistress of the seas.
French declamation against the greed and perfidy of England
is therefore no less irrelevant than the complacently insular
explanation that Napoleon's march to Moscow was solely due
to his overweening ambition. Both combatants played desperately for enormous stakes, and their methods are open to
severe censure. That Napoleon would have granted peace
and prosperity to Europe if he had conquered, is quite
probable. It is certain, however, that England's ultimate
triumph—due to the fact that she had the resources of the
tropics at her back, while Napoleon's policy finally outraged
the sentiments and wants of millions—was followed by the
restitution of most of her conquests and the abandonment of
her chief maritime claims.

It is interesting to observe that in the Anglo-French
additional articles to this Treaty, efforts were strenuously
made by Castlereagh to procure the abolition by France of the
trade in slaves; and also to gain a promise of a commercial
treaty between the two nations. Both questions were, however, adjourned.

The surrender of nearly all the conquests made in the revolutionary and Napoleonic wars, seemed an unspeakable ignominy to the generation of Frenchmen who had been nurtured on the phrase 'natural boundaries'; and the cession of 53 fortresses with some 12,000 cannon, involved by the return to the limits of 1792, was felt by ardent royalists as a terrible blow to the restored dynasty. The shrinkage of the Napoleonic Empire into the kingdom of France severed from her rule 15,300,000 Italian, German, Flemish and Dutch subjects; but, except in Western Savoy, very few French-speaking people were transferred to an alien rule. Indeed, the France of Louis XVIII, as contrasted with that of Louis XVI, gained districts with nearly half a million souls. Yet the vastness of the immediate loss very naturally obscured these slight gains on the old historic limits. The allies imposed no war indemnity on France; and most of the objects of art taken from the various cities of Europe were left at Paris. Among the few which were reclaimed in 1814 was the Victory of the Brandenburg Gate at Berlin, which was received by the Berliners with unbounded rejoicings. The debt still due from Prussia to France since 1807 was of course cancelled.

Hard though these conditions seemed to the French, they can scarcely be considered so, when the magnitude of the allied efforts and the completeness of their triumph are duly considered. Talleyrand, Louis XVIII's Minister of Foreign Affairs, was severely blamed for signing such a treaty, and was indeed accused of being bribed into it. His refutation is complete and crushing. He shows in his Memoirs and Appendices that two-thirds of the French army were prisoners, and half of Napoleon's empire in the hands of foreign troops; further, that the Emperor himself when he heard of the march of the allies on Paris, despatched Caulaincourt to accept their conditions: finally, that now in the complete helplessness of France, better terms were finally gained by the restored dynasty than Napoleon could have obtained at the close of the last campaign. These facts were not known to the multitude; but they absolve the allies from the charge of trampling remorselessly on France in her helplessness, and of imposing a weak dynasty in order to plunder her of the natural boundaries. The Rhine boundary was lost by Napoleon at and after la Rothière; and his own ruin was assured by the pertinacity with which in August 1813 and March 1814 he held out against the offers of the allies until after the definite rupture of negotiations.

Sufficient has also been said to disprove the charge that the allies forcibly imposed the Bourbons on France. On the contrary, they viewed this alternative with suspicion, they were virtually forced by Napoleon's obstinacy to depose him, and then they left French opinion to decide on its form of government. The Restoration was brought about by the energy of the French royalists, the skill of their spokesmen, Vitrolles and Talleyrand, and by the vote of the Senate. Among those who voted for the deposition of Napoleon were some men prominent in the earlier part of the Revolution, Roger Ducos, Grégoire, Kellermann, Lanjuinais, Serrurier, &c.; and these men in deposing the Emperor must have known the truth of Talleyrand's words to the Czar, "Either Bonaparte or Louis XVIII, Sire: anything else is an intrigue."

Limits of space preclude any account of Louis XVIII's measures during the first restoration. His speech at the opening session of the Chambers showed what a gulf yawned between the ancient régime and the new order of things. The phrases—"The Charter granted (*octroyée*) by us," "The nineteen years of our reign"—jarred on the ears of the young generation; and the Charter itself, though granting most of the points required by the Senate, limited the franchise to citizens who paid 300 francs a year in direct taxation. Even in the later days of the Empire, the pretence of universal suffrage had been kept up; and the present limitation of the franchise to about 80,000 persons was felt as a direct contravention of one of the chief principles of the revolution. Some features of the imperial régime were continued under Louis XVIII. The king alone was to propose laws, though the Chambers might supplicate him to do so. The Senate was to consist of members nominated for life by the king; and its debates were to be secret. The Charter also declared an amnesty for all past acts except those of the most prominent regicides; and it proclaimed in unmistakable terms the inviolability of all lands and property gained during the confiscations of the revolution. The apprehensions, however, of the holders of confiscated lands were soon re-awakened by the increasing arrogance of the old nobles and by the demands of their journals that confiscated lands should now revert to their ancient possessors. A project for indemnifying these men was proposed by Macdonald to the Chamber of Peers; but such a torrent of claims flowed in that the matter had to be adjourned owing to the embarrassment of the finances, and only the few national domains which remained unsold were restored to their former landlords. With this slight exception, the agrarian settlement was postponed, and was not solved until the reign of Charles X.

Other questions, such as an attempted limitation of freedom of the Press, irritated public opinion. The slights inflicted on old soldiers, and the honours showered on all who had intrigued for the royalist cause, disgusted all who during the Empire had seen honours bestowed according to genius and deserts. "The Court (wrote Marshal Macdonald) was daily losing ground in public opinion. It seemed as though the Ministry and their agents were vying with each other as to which should give proof of the greatest folly, and the *entourage* of the King, as to who should exhibit the greatest haughtiness and conceit."

Equally precarious was the situation in Central Europe. Throughout this work I have insisted on the divulsive effect on the first three great coalitions of the jealousies and rivalries of the Powers concerning Poland, Bavaria, and Hanover. Each of these questions was worth an army to France. Only the crushing weight of Napoleon's domination hushed the quarrels about those States. Not till Prussia was entering on the death-grapple with her foe in 1807 and 1813, did she renounce those claims on George III's Electorate, which would yield to her the line of the Weser and the fortress of Hameln as the western bulwarks of her power. That question had at last been set at rest by the treaty of Teplitz (Sept. 1813). The Leipzig campaign had also shown to the Austrian Government the possibility of outflanking Eugène's positions in Venetia, if it came to a close understanding with Bavaria. Here again, then, it was antipathy to Napoleon and desire for complete preponderance in distracted Italy, that led the Hapsburg Emperor to renounce designs on Bavaria which had for a generation past weakened the Germanic system; and the Austro-Bavarian Treaty of Oct. 1813 cleared away the chief elements of discord in South Germany. There still remained, however, the eternal Polish problem, and the closely allied question of the future of Saxony, not to speak of the reconstruction of Germany, Italy, and the Netherlands.

The re-construction of Europe at the Congress of Vienna presented, indeed, the vastest political problems ever approached by statesmen and diplomatists. Imagine the soil of a continent rent by subterranean convulsions and desolated by floods, till the old land-marks had well-nigh disappeared, and some conception may be formed of the political confusion of Europe in the summer of 1814. It is not surprising that the most meritorious attempts at reconciling the rights of property with the public welfare should have failed to please the old proprietors and also to meet the claims of the many.

Still less is it to be wondered at that the occasion yielded a rich harvest to many an adroit pilferer.

Amidst the hurly-burly of war three important compacts had been struck—those of Kalisch, Teplitz, and Chaumont. Of their clauses only the following need be recapitulated here as bearing on the negotiations at Vienna. At Kalisch Prussia had been promised by the Czar an eastern frontier adapted to connect the province of West Prussia with Silesia—a phrase capable of very wide interpretation: for his losses in the east, Frederick William was to receive compensation in North or West Germany, so as to bring his realm to the position it held before 1806. The Treaty of Kalisch therefore foreshadowed that western extension of Russian and Prussian power which was ultimately to place the middle course of the Vistula and the Rhine in their keeping.

The Teplitz Treaties stipulated that after the dissolution of the Rhenish Confederation, the German rulers of the lands between Prussia and the Rhine should enjoy "full and unconditional independence." In vain did Hardenberg, Stein and the Prussian patriots oppose this clause as being fatal to any effective union of Germany. Stein submitted a plan for two great German federations, Prussia heading the North and Austria the South. Metternich, however, desired by friendly compacts with the other German Governments to assure Austrian supremacy, and also to postpone any attempt at a popular federal constitution for which the Prussian patriotic party was striving. Instead of Joseph II's revolutionary and aggressive policy, Austria now aimed at heading a sort of Fürstenbund or League of Princes, which would keep "the revolution" in check and quietly pave the way for Hapsburg predominance in German affairs. Treaties with Bavaria and the other German States (Oct.—Dec. 1813) assured the triumph of Metternich's policy. At Châtillon and Chaumont (March 1814) it was resolved that the States of Germany should be independent but united by a federal bond.   The Treaty of Paris (May 30, 1814) also stipulated that the part of Italy which did not fall to Austria should be composed of sovereign States : that Holland under the restored House of Orange should receive an accession of territory, the lands between the new limits of France and the Rhine being named as compensation for Holland, Prussia, and the smaller German States.   Genoa, which had been occupied by English troops, was to strengthen the reconstituted kingdom of Sardinia ; and the return of the Pope into possession of the Papal States was acknowledged by the Powers, in spite of the annoyance of Austria, which had hoped to gain those important territories.   A secret understanding was arrived at by the Powers forming the Quadruple Alliance, that France was not to interfere in the pending territorial changes.

Beside these compacts of primary importance there are others which also influenced the transactions at Vienna, and must therefore be briefly noticed here.   Both from Russia and England the assurance had been given to the Court of Stockholm that Norway should be the reward of Swedish help in the struggle against Napoleon.   When Denmark was overwhelmed by Bernadotte's forces in Holstein, she concluded the Treaty of Kiel (Jan. 1814) by which England promised her good offices to obtain for the Danish realm a fit indemnity for the loss of Norway.   Sweden ceded to Denmark Rügen and Swedish Pomerania ; but by a complicated series of exchanges they ultimately went to Prussia, Denmark taking Lauenburg.   Great Britain retained Heligoland as well as the Danish fleet captured in 1807—thereby refusing to make reparation for that high-handed action.   It is true that after the Danes had rejected the final offer of England to regard the fleet as a pledge, it was taken as a prize of war ; but its restoration at the general peace was nevertheless morally binding.

During a visit of the allied sovereigns to London it was

decided (July 1814) that Belgium should form the addition to Dutch territory foreshadowed in the Treaty of Paris. An illusory attempt was made to safeguard the interests of the Belgians in this artificial arrangement, which avowedly aimed at building up a barrier state on the north-east of France. A month later England agreed to restore to Holland the Dutch colonies (all of which had been conquered) with the very important exceptions of the Cape of Good Hope, Demerara, Essequibo and Berbice. England, however, agreed to pay a sum not exceeding £3,000,000 towards the fortification of the frontier fortresses in the south of Belgium.

The Austro-Bavarian alliance was strengthened by a secret Convention (June 1814) transferring nearly the whole of Tyrol, Vorarlberg, Salzburg, and the Inn-viertel to the Hapsburg dominions; while Austria ceded in return Würzburg (held by her Arch-Duke Ferdinand), and promised to secure for Bavaria as much land as possible on the left bank of the Rhine. The retention by Bavaria of Anspach and Baireuth—formerly Prussian principalities—was also tacitly agreed on, as in the preceding treaty of Oct. 1813.

Treaties between Spain and the Powers recognised the restoration of Ferdinand VII as King of Spain and its colonies. Some States also yielded to English solicitations for the abolition of the traffic in slaves. "There is hardly a village (wrote Castlereagh to Sir H. Wellesley in Spain) that has not petitioned on this subject: both Houses of Parliament are pledged to press it; and the Ministers must make it the basis of their policy."

Such was the general condition of European affairs before the commencement of the Congress of Vienna (Nov. 3, 1814). The visit of Alexander and Frederick William to London had revealed sharp differences between the Czar's opportunist Liberalism and the desires of the English Government to support legitimist claims. Moreover, ever since the violation of Swiss neutrality, there had been a personal feud between the Czar and Metternich, which was to develop into a life-long struggle ending in the complete success of the diplomatist. In 1814 the victory was in the main to Alexander. "I shall keep what I hold :...I have given Saxony to Prussia : Austria consents : " such were his menacing words to Talleyrand, the plenipotentiary of France. Alexander's determination to keep all, or nearly all, the Grand Duchy of Warsaw, was supported by the pleadings of Laharpe and Czartoryski that he would resuscitate the Kingdom of Poland. Prussia, in return for sacrificing two-thirds of her former Polish lands, was determined to have the whole of Saxony besides a great gain of territory in western Germany. Austria and England were strongly opposed to the extension of the Czar's power beyond the Vistula ; while France, Austria and Bavaria equally objected to the extermination of the Kingdom of Saxony as fatal to the balance of power in Germany. Austria, France, and Great Britain were, therefore, naturally opposed to the Russo-Prussian claims. Wellington himself, writing from Mons in August 1814, had advocated an understanding between England and France as safeguarding the interests and even the peace of Europe. Castlereagh also favoured an understanding with our late foe as a check to "improvident schemes and undue pretensions."

It is evident, then, that the desire for accord existed at Downing Street; and that Talleyrand's claim in his letters to Louis XVIII, of having formed that *entente cordiale,* is exaggerated. Indeed, he was at first filled with the usual French belief in the utter selfishness of British policy, as contrasted with his own edifying advocacy of "principles"; but the first few weeks at Vienna sufficed to reveal the difference between Castlereagh's tone and that of the three Continental Powers, especially Russia and Prussia. There was thus once again a possibility of that Anglo-French alliance which Voltaire and Adam Smith had advocated, for which

Pitt and Fox, Mirabeau and the youthful Talleyrand, had used their gifts of eloquence and statesmanship, only to see their hopes vanish before the aggressive claims of the Jacobins and the rampant militarism of the Napoleonic régime. After more than twenty years of bitter hostility between the two nations, the disciple of Mirabeau now again began to realise the practicability of that alliance which his master probably inculcated on his death-bed, and which he himself vainly strove to effect in the autumn of 1792.

To so dextrous a diplomatist as Talleyrand it was not difficult to reveal the hollowness of the accord between the four other great Powers. His skilful refutation of their claim to be "allies" as against monarchical France, and his disavowal of all the compacts made before the Congress, speedily lifted France from the depths to which Napoleon's obstinacy had hurled her. Threats that France must be made to feel some of the hardships which the Napoleonic arms had inflicted on Prussia and other lands, were deftly parried by the legitimist shield: France had returned to her lawful sovereigns and to her historic limits:—"We Frenchmen must be good Europeans. France ought to demand and does demand nothing, absolutely nothing, beyond a just re-division (of Europe) among the Powers, i.e. the balance of power." This last principle of policy, which has long been regarded as the climax of artificiality and yet was so natural as a protest against the predominance of France, was defined to mean—"a combination of the rights, the interests, and the relations of the Powers among themselves, by which Europe seeks to ensure (1) that the rights and possessions of a Power shall not be attacked by one or several other Powers: (2) that one or several other Powers shall never attain to domination over Europe: (3) that the combination adopted shall render difficult or impossible a rupture of the established order and of the tranquillity of Europe." Talleyrand's adroit acceptance of the very claims

for which the Powers had since 1805 been persistently con-
tending, completely enfiladed the allied position, the climax
of diplomatic comedy being reached when he blandly insisted,
in spite of the impotent protests of some of the plenipotentiaries,
that the Congress should be held according to the principles of
international law[1].

The two burning questions at the Congress which nearly
involved Europe in a general conflagration, were those of
Poland and Saxony. The King of Saxony had since Tilsit
held the Grand Duchy of Warsaw, which the Czar was now
determined to revive as a Kingdom of Poland, subject to some
cessions to Prussia. Even so the Court of Berlin dreaded such
an extension of the Czar's power, and regarded the possession
of the whole of Saxony as inadequate compensation for the
loss of the lands around Warsaw. England and Austria
for a time persuaded Prussia to protest against the Czar's
Polish claims, but pressure which the Czar put on Frederick
William and through him on his plenipotentiary, Hardenberg,
renewed the Russo-Prussian accord (Nov. 6). Theoretically,
the most skilful way of countermining their claims would have
been for England and France to protest against the two last
partitions of Poland, which the former had never acknowledged,
and to have declared for the complete independence of Poland
as in 1791 ; but that was felt by Castlereagh and finally by
Talleyrand to be impracticable, and after admitting the principle of partition there was no valid argument against the
Czar's claim that in return for his immense services to the

---

[1] Matters of general concern were settled in a Commission of the Great
Powers. German affairs were to be adjusted in a separate Commission
in which Austria, Prussia, Bavaria, Würtemberg, and Hanover (*not*
Saxony) were represented. The reconstruction of Germany is treated very
briefly here, as it forms the subject of another volume of this series, "The
Foundation of the German Empire, 1815—1871." This volume will also
contain a map of Central Europe after 1815.

European cause he must have the lion's share of the Duchy of Warsaw.

In that case, Prussia insisted on obtaining Saxony, the administration of which, hitherto in the hands of the Russians, was now by the Czar's orders transferred to the Berlin Government. This arrangement, acquiesced in conditionally for a time by Austria and England, was strongly opposed by France, Bavaria and the German Princes, who signed a protest that "without a free and independent Saxony, there is no stable federal Germany." Metternich and Castlereagh were also brought by Talleyrand to see the importance of keeping Saxony with strength little impaired; and the conclusion of peace between Great Britain and the United States (Dec. 24, 1814) on the basis of the *status quo ante bellum*, left the former free to take a firmer tone in European matters. The dislike of our Prince Regent and all German princes to Prussian predominance also helped to range England side by side with France, Austria and the German States, who cloaked their fears of Prussian aggrandisement under their professions of horror at the spoliation of a king. The work of the Congress, wrote Talleyrand to Castlereagh, was to close the Revolution and restore the lawful sovereigns—a perfectly unwarrantable assumption: all but one of the revolutionary dynasties (he referred to that of Murat) had vanished: all but one of the old reigning families, that of Saxony, had been restored: it remained for the Congress to show its devotion to principles by dethroning the usurper, and restoring the much persecuted King of Saxony to his governing powers. European Liberalism also protested against a plan which would hand over the Saxons to an alien rule. On the other hand there certainly was some feeling in Saxony in favour of union with Prussia, as a step towards that unification of Germany which had nerved the Germans to the efforts of 1813. "The far-sighted and energetic spirits (wrote Varnhagen von Ense) were all on the side of Prussia." The splendid efforts which speedily raised her from an abyss of degradation to heights never reached even by Frederick the Great, her new institutions, and the seemingly sure prospect of Parliamentary Government, aroused the eager hopes of all Germans who longed to sweep away the barriers raised by feudality and particularism, and to unite with the one German State which appeared able to guarantee the safety and liberty of the Fatherland. Following the general lead of Stein, this "unitarian sect," as it was sneeringly called by Metternich, urged that the Saxons did not form a nation, that their absorption by Prussia would powerfully aid the work of German unification, to which the middle-sized States then, as ever, formed the chief obstacle, and that the Saxon King's opposition to the national cause, and his faithlessness to Austria in 1813, justified his complete deposition. A suggestion that the king should receive as compensation some German lands west of the Rhine, was objected to as certain to create a satellite of France on Germany's weak side.

Thus raged the diplomatic contests, aggravated by the haughty tone of the Czar, which so annoyed Castlereagh as to evoke from him the declaration that England would not accept laws from anybody. The Powers began to arm as if for war; and Talleyrand attained a brilliant diplomatic triumph by the formation of a secret compact between England, France and Austria, to which Bavaria, Hanover and the Netherlands soon acceded, for resistance to the Russo-Prussian demands. Whether French soldiers would have fought side by side with English and Austrians, or the British Parliament would have sanctioned a war for this purpose, is at least problematical; but the compact enabled Talleyrand to boast to Louis XVIII that the coalition against France was dissolved for ever, and that she now had alliances which she could hardly have hoped to gain in fifty years. Further, he was at once admitted to all the conferences of the Great Powers. Satisfied with his success, and unwilling to push his sovereign into an unpopular war, Talleyrand now abated his claims, as did all parties in the dispute. Alarming news of Bonapartist intrigues in France and Italy helped on the solution of the Polish and Saxon difficulties. Metternich showed the danger of dethroning the Saxon King and giving him lands on the confines of France, and now offered that Prussia should take rather more of Saxony than had lately been conceded. The Czar consented to leave the fortress of Thorn to Prussia; and to calm the fears of Austrian military authorities, the important city of Cracow with its district was to remain a free Republic. The Liberal principles of the Czar were emphasized in a clause that all parts of Poland as it was before the partitions should enjoy " a representation and institutions" which should ensure the preservation of their nationality."

As regards the Saxon question, Castlereagh finally persuaded Austria and France to concede not only the fortress of Wittenberg but that of Torgau to Prussia, thereby safeguarding the southern approaches to Berlin. She was also to acquire the more thinly peopled half of Saxony, with 850,000 inhabitants, on the north, east and west, reducing that kingdom to its present extent.

On the side of Poland, Prussia regained from her spoils of the second and third partitions only Danzig, Thorn and the province of Posen ; but by her great gains in the west (noted below [1]) she became the chief purely Germanic power, and stood forth as the natural protectress of the

---

[1] Her former lands west of the Elbe, the Alt-Mark, with Magdeburg, Halle, Erfurt, Eichsfeld, Paderborn, Minden, Münster, and Clèves, returned to her sway, beside other lands which helped to build up the present Westphalian and Rhenish provinces. On the other hand she sacrificed Anspach and Baireuth to Bavaria, and Hildesheim and East Frisia to Hanover—now made a kingdom.

weaker German States not only against Russia but also against France. Strange to say, she viewed with apprehension the acquisition of the Roman-Catholic Rhenish Province, so long subject to France, as entailing great difficulties and expenses for defence. On their side, the French diplomatists regarded it as a triumph to maintain the independence of the richer half of Protestant Saxony, and to yield to Prussia the population of the Rhine lands, which she would assimilate with great difficulty. Both sides then failed to discern that the guardian of the Rhine would naturally become the champion of Germany against France. It is difficult, indeed, to see how German unity could have been accomplished, had the allies acceded to Hardenberg's plan of acquiring all Saxony and indemnifying its king with lands west of the Rhine, and Bonn as his capital. The duc Pasquier at that time saw the advantages of having a firm foe to Prussia established in that commanding position; but the French diplomatists in their excessive zeal for the legitimist cause, preferred to maintain the Saxon Government in Dresden and Leipzig in order to trim the balance in German affairs. Events were to show that in this respect Talleyrand, Metternich and Castlereagh were Prussia's best friends; for the efforts to defend her long and straggling frontiers braced her to the contest which ended in the annexation of the intervening German States, and the consolidation of that unity for which Germany was not fully prepared in 1815.

A question discussed at great length in the Congress was the compensation to Bavaria for her cessions to Austria and for her efforts in the allied cause. Mainz, the key of Germany on the west, was coveted by her; and Austria, according to treaty promise, endeavoured to procure that stronghold for her satellite; but it was felt to be too important a fortress for a growing State like Bavaria to hold, and with its adjoining land was assigned to Hesse-Darmstadt, subject to its being garrisoned by Prusso-Austrian troops as a federal fortress. The claims of Bavaria to the lands about Hanau, Frankfurt, Fulda and Mannheim were set aside, as tending to sunder southern from northern Germany; and she was finally limited to gains which formed approximately her present territories. As these were neither conterminous nor so extensive as she had hoped for, the seeds of dissension were thereby sown between her and Austria. Hesse-Cassel and Oldenburg were revived in nearly their old extent; as also were the Free-Cities of Hamburg, Lübeck, Bremen and Frankfurt, now the only survivors of the 51 which existed in 1789. The 12 Imperial villages had of course been entirely absorbed. The shocks of revolution had completely shattered the rights of the petty 'immediate' princes, and had also blotted out from the map of Germany the 73 ecclesiastical States or domains which had governing powers. The concentrating tendencies of this era may be summed up in the statement that of about 300 sovereign States existing in Germany at the death of Frederick the Great, only 39 remained at the fall of Napoleon to build up the new Germanic Confederation.

While these and other territorial changes were approaching a settlement, startling news arrived which promptly hushed all minor differences. The last faint possibilities of war between the Powers vanished when it was known that Napoleon had eluded the vigilance of French and English cruisers off Elba and was sailing northwards. Talleyrand at once remarked that he would land in Italy, then in a ferment of agitation; but Metternich shrewdly conjectured that Paris was his aim.

Three landings of Napoleon Bonaparte on the Provençal coast will serve to remind posterity of the vicissitudes in his extraordinary career. In the spring of 1793, after the expulsion of his family from Corsica, he lands in France to carve his way by his sword, either in the service of the Sultan, of the English East India Company, or of the regicide republic. The autumn of 1799 sees him disembark at Fréjus, after almost miraculously escaping Nelson's cruisers, to be enthusiastically greeted as the conqueror of the East and the only possible saviour of France. And now on March 1, 1815 he lands near Cannes with about a thousand men to rouse France against the Bourbons and emigrant nobles.

The people of Provence were deaf to his appeals, but the potency of his fascination over the army was at once evident. Many of the soldiers in garrison at Antibes climbed down the ramparts to join their Emperor. His activity and skill were phenomenal. He baffled the designs of the authorities for his capture by a speedy détour through the difficult mountain-road to Grenoble, thus avoiding the lower Rhone valley, the ardent royalism of which he had reason to remember. Proclamations scattered among the people aimed at reviving the old illusions, that he was in 1814 conqueror at all points and only the treachery of Augereau at Lyons and Marmont at Paris thwarted the complete success of his movement for cutting the communications of the allies. "Soldiers! we have not been beaten. Two men, who rose from our ranks, betrayed our laurels, their country, their prince, their benefactor." —"Your general, called to the throne by the choice of the people, and raised on your shields, has come back to you: come and join him.—The eagle with the national colours will fly from steeple to steeple right to the towers of Notre Dame."

To the citizens he protested the right of each country to have the ruler that it chose, and to reject a rule forced on it by foreigners. The splendour of his personality hid from the general eye the unreality of these claims, and France threw herself at his feet as readily as in 1799. The garrison of Grenoble, when ordered to capture the Emperor in the interests of France and of peace, marched to fulfil its duty. Muskets were raised to fire, when Napoleon, opening the well-known grey over-coat, exclaimed "Let him among you who wishes to kill me, fire." What else could the generous French soldiers do than cheer for the Emperor and mount the tricolour cockades long carried in their knapsacks! This dramatic scene decided the whole course of events. Napoleon's Guards afterwards assured Macdonald that, had they been fired upon by the Grenoble garrison, they would have laid down their arms and retired home, since most of them had come with him to France only to escape from the weary exile at Elba. As it was, the gates of Grenoble were now pulled down by the excited citizens and Napoleon entered in triumph. At Lyons Macdonald's ardent appeals to the royal troops to join in a cheer for the king were answered by stony silence. Officers and soldiers alike were disgusted with the shower of honours to emigrant nobles and *chouans*, and the neglect of services rendered on many a famous battle-field. The Comte d'Artois hurriedly left Lyons escorted by a single trooper, and Macdonald with one general barely escaped from the town which in 1793 had fought desperately for the royalist cause.

Events now rapidly trended in the direction of burlesque. Ney had declared that Napoleon ought to be brought back in an iron cage. He promptly took all his troops, the chief remaining support of the Bourbon throne, over to the Emperor. At Paris nothing was heard but loud protestations of loyalty to the king, while measures were secretly taken to ensure favours from the usurper on his arrival. At a royal session of the Senate, the Comte d'Artois and his sons threw themselves into the king's arms, swearing fidelity to the Charter which they detested. Louis XVIII declared that he would die on his throne in defence of his people: four days later he hurriedly left Paris for Lille and Ghent. Finally, on the night of March 20 Napoleon, escorted by a vast torchlight procession, entered the Tuileries amidst a delirium of excitement.

The glamour of this transformation-scene failed to impose on the minds of the thinking few. They besought the soldiers and people not to plunge Europe again into a war which was inevitable with Napoleon on the throne. The chiefs of the constitutional party, Lainé, Lafayette and others, pointed out the securities for liberty and peace which Louis XVIII's Charter and general policy assured. It was in vain. Napoleon or his partisans skilfully proclaimed that he intended to follow a pacific policy, that he had a friendly understanding with Austria, that he came to restore liberty and prevent the return of the old feudal dues. What did soldiers and peasants care for the tame constitutional rule of the Bourbons, and Talleyrand's diplomatic triumphs at Vienna? They saw only the insolence of the emigrant nobles and their avowed intention of recovering their old lands.

In some respects, then, this startling revolution resembled that of 1789. Fear of a return to the old abuses, at any rate when the Comte d'Artois should mount the throne, was the most potent motive with civilians. But, though in part a social and agrarian revolution, it yet bore a closer resemblance to that of Fructidor than to the essentially popular movements of 1789. After all it was in the main the work of the army. The return of a quarter of a million of soldiers imprisoned in England, Spain, Russia, and Germany would at any time have been a formidable danger to a new government. To the Bourbons it was fatal. Still, it is only fair to say that with such materials the work of building up a firm government was almost impossible. The example of Imperial Rome exhibits the difficulties of staying the course of revolutions begun by the Praetorians, save by the advent of some general with commanding powers or by the destruction of the disturbing elements. Unfortunately for France, the return of the great general involved war with Europe.

Napoleon's sincerity in his professions of a pacific policy has been hotly discussed. In a striking address he spoke of having heard at Elba, as in a tomb, the voice of posterity.

he protested that he now desired peace, that although he would never have signed the peace of Paris, yet he would faithfully observe it: that the repose of a constitutional king would accord with his declining years, and that his sole desire was to *save the Revolution*. The value of these declarations was unfortunately lessened by his previous conduct. When menaced by the forces of united Europe in the heart of France, when scarcely 100,000 wearied troops followed his eagles, he had persisted in his refusal to accept the historic limits of France, until the time for negotiations had passed. Even before their rupture he wrote to his brother Joseph (Feb. 18, 1814) "If I had signed peace on the terms of the ancient limits, I should have rushed to arms in two years, and I should have told the nation that I had signed not a peace but a capitulation." When he penned those words three-fourths of his veterans were in the power of the allies. Is it conceivable that now, when he had the prospect of speedily forming a great army, he would have renounced for ever the hope of regaining those natural frontiers, the loss of which the French regarded as a national disgrace? Was it possible for the guardian of the revolution to abandon the conquests of Jourdan and Kléber? The question, if regarded in a broad spirit, i.e. in regard to the dominant sentiment in France and Germany, reveals an inherent antagonism respecting the ownership of the Rhine Province. That the French army would of its own initiative have attempted to regain the natural frontiers, is highly probable; for it never regarded itself as beaten in fair fight even in 1812—1814. That peace could not have lasted long must be conceded even by those who believe in Napoleon's pacific professions. The advent of the great warrior precipitated a perhaps inevitable struggle, rendering it short, dramatic and decisive; for if on the one hand Napoleon's return restored to France the greatest captain of modern times, the fear of his prowess at once banded the rest of Europe against her.

Talleyrand's skilful work of dissolving the coalition against France was swept away in a moment; and the Powers at Vienna declared (March 13) that in violating the Convention which established him at Elba, Napoleon placed himself outside the pale of civil and social relations, and was an enemy and disturber of the repose of the world. This stern denunciation would, it was hoped, stay his progress to Paris. It had no such effect, except on the few Frenchmen whose heads were not turned by the excitement of that stirring march. Napoleon on his side cherished the illusion that the Powers were on the point of fighting about Saxony; and he strove to sow further dissensions by sending to the Czar a copy of Talleyrand's secret compact against Russia and Prussia. Alexander contented himself with embarrassing Metternich by showing him the full copy, and then burnt it with the words "Let us forget all that: the question now is to overthrow our common enemy." A treaty of alliance was signed among the Powers (March 25), each agreeing to send 150,000 men to secure his deposition and effectual banishment. On the ratification of this treaty a declaration was added by Great Britain, with the warm approval of the Czar, stating that she did not bind herself to procure the restoration of the Bourbons. In spite of this reservation the British Government was subjected to sharp censure in Parliament for binding the country by treaty without consent of the nation. In regard to constitutional right, the censure was just; but the further declaration of belief by the Opposition in Napoleon's professions of peace betrayed a singular credulity. The Ministerial contention that to let him consolidate his power would only aggravate an inevitable struggle, was consonant with all past experience.

The other Powers acceded to the British declaration concerning the Bourbons; and all the European States, including Switzerland and Denmark, joined the league against Napoleon. Under a show of paternal compulsion Marie Louise with her son remained at Vienna, beguiled by the prospect of the Duchy of Parma for herself. Eugène also continued his residence at Vienna, but without any hopes of retrieving a brilliant past.

Napoleon's efforts to reconcile the constitutional and old Jacobin parties to his rule met with little success. The royalist resistance in the west and south was repressed without much difficulty; and an Additional Act, which promised to crown the Imperial edifice with the long delayed pinnacle of political and civic liberty, gained some approval. A compromise was necessary, though it accorded ill with his own ideas of sovereignty. Shrewd observers like Caulaincourt remarked that even so he did not give the liberty which France expected, that his habits of demanding entire obedience frequently carried him away, and that in fine "he was not in his own saddle." These were the opinions of his Foreign Minister, an outspoken but trusty friend. For the rest, he made Davoust Minister of War, Carnot Minister of the Interior, and for Police he had to put up with that time-serving intriguer, Fouché, who in his new capacity carefully sounded the ground at Vienna in his own interests, and further remarked to Pasquier that when once Napoleon had departed for the war, the constitutionalists would be masters at Paris! Suspecting that the ground beneath him was mined, Napoleon desired an imposing display of devotion to his cause, so as to "nationalise the war," as Talleyrand phrased it.

The Additional Act, drawn up by Benjamin Constant the leading constitutionalist and friend of Mdme. de Staël, but amended in some points by Napoleon, granted a freer representation to France than that accorded by Louis XVIII's Charter. Nominees appointed for life and with hereditary functions were to form the Chamber of Peers. The Chamber of Deputies was to consist of deputies elected directly by electoral colleges, themselves chosen by adult Frenchmen:

it could be dissolved by Napoleon provided that another was convened in six months. Liberty of the press was fully accorded; but the proposal to prohibit confiscation was thwarted by Napoleon himself. The Additional Act failed to satisfy the zeal for liberty which had lately burst forth with redoubled energy after the long restraints of imperial despotism. In a plébiscite it was accepted by 1,300,000 votes, but the vast majority did not go to the urn—a striking contrast to the enthusiasm of 1799 and 1804. Now, the Emperor's promises of liberty were no more believed by the constitutionalists and old Jacobins, than were his pacific professions by the rest of Europe,—a terrible Nemesis which blighted what was at least an interesting experiment.

Once more, in this phase of the Revolution, the attempts at reconstruction revealed differences and discords, which lay hid amidst the dramatic scenes of destruction. A *Champ de Mai*, an imposing scene which aimed at recalling the Federation Festivals of 1790—1792, excited the enthusiasm of the soldiery as the eagles were entrusted to their keeping; but it aroused the discontent of all friends of liberty at a renewal of imperial pageantry. So wide-spread were the murmurs that Fouché, his Minister of Police, ventured to privately advise the Emperor to proclaim his son Napoleon II and retire to America. The new Chamber of Deputies now took an almost menacing tone. The Girondin Lanjuinais was chosen its president, and his words with those of Lafayette soon warned Napoleon of the determination to have done with the old imperial régime. The very name 'Additional Act to the Constitutions of the Empire' was interpreted by friends of liberty as a sign that Napoleon's views on government had not changed. The Vendéans were still in arms in the west; and disquietude gained ground at the Tuileries as it appeared that France was torn by dissensions, while the forces of united Europe were marching against her. A furious proclamation by the Prussians suggested a further comparison with the events of 1792. But how different the position of the European peoples now! Years of disaster had brought temporary accord between governments as also between rulers and subjects ; and the national hatreds against Napoleon now rendered a military promenade, like that of Custine to Frankfurt, an utter impossibility.* Amidst general forebodings in France, the Emperor alone remained unshaken, ever buoyed up by his indomitable will, and displaying a confidence which might be called sublime but that it again entailed a useless effusion of blood. After further troubles with the deputies he departed for the Belgian frontier, trusting by sheer force of military genius to hurl back his foes, and as at Marengo and Austerlitz to bring the monarchs of Europe and the republicans of France alike submissive to his feet.

Napoleon's three last campaigns exhibit a fierce concentration of effort. That of Russia dragged its weary length through half a year. The freedom of Germany was decided in four months' fighting. The overthrow of the French Empire was assured in half that time ; and the attempt at its reconstruction was baffled in the most exciting trilogy of war which the world has ever witnessed. No three days of human history have called forth so perennial a flood of discussion and dispute as those which hurled the Emperor from his throne ; but into the controversies which still rage around many of their incidents, it is both undesirable and impossible to enter at length.

On June 15 the allied generals were only beginning to concentrate their troops ; and as these were dispersed over nearly all the space between Mons, Namur and Brussels, they were quite unprepared to render mutual support. Blücher's unrelenting energy brought together most of his men between Ligny and Charleroi, while Wellington's scattered forces were uniting more slowly. This remissness of the British commander has exposed him to just and merited censure. A speedier concentration of the allied forces would have gained them the defensive line of the Sambre with its bridges at and near Charleroi. Napoleon had rightly judged that Blücher, with his dashing "hussar spirit," would concentrate his men more speedily than the cooler and more methodical Wellington; and in his Memoirs he claims it as his intention to strike first at the Prussians and then at the Anglo-Dutch forces, thus forcing them on "divergent lines of retreat." The two allied armies were exposed to the same strategic movement which in 1796 hurled back the Austrian and Sardinian armies from the Apennines on Milan and Turin respectively. Here, in his last campaign as in his first, Napoleon hoped to defeat his foes in succession and drive them back on their ultimate bases of operation, in this case Wesel and Antwerp respectively. But years of disaster had taught the allies the absolute need of close and effective support; and, as in 1813—1814, Napoleon's blows only served to weld their cause into a firmer unity.

If the allies are open to criticism for their slackness in face of a foe who had often decided a campaign at the first blow, yet on the other hand some of Napoleon's arrangements have been censured quite as sharply. It is true that he lacked the support of many of his ablest Marshals. Masséna and Moncey were effete; Berthier was detained in Germany, where he met a violent death; Macdonald, Marmont, Oudinot, St Cyr and Victor remained true to the royalist cause; Augereau's services were rejected as those of a traitor; Mortier fell ill; Clausel was holding down the royalist South; Suchet was awaiting the advance of the Austrians and Russians on the east, and Brune was skirmishing with the Austro-Sardinian forces in the Maritime Alps. But the Emperor made the singular mistake of condemning two of the ablest of his Marshals, Davoust and Soult, to positions which afforded no fit scope for their ability, energy, and tenacious courage. To the former, in spite of his remonstrances, was confided the command of Paris; while Soult had to replace Berthier in the merely executive duties of Chief of the Staff. Moreover, only at the last moment did Napoleon entrust Ney with any command, as if to mark his distrust of him, after that Marshal's early defection to the royalists; and it was not until the first shots had been exchanged at Charleroi, that Grouchy, essentially a cavalry general, was placed in command of the right wing of the army, in spite of Soult's protests.

To this strange redistribution of duties must be mainly attributed the extraordinary blunders which brought the campaign to so speedy a conclusion. With 124,000 highly trained troops and 340 guns swiftly approaching two armies still partly in their cantonments, Napoleon might have hoped for another Ulm. Certain it is that his own energy was at this time but slightly impaired by the internal disease which had troubled him once before, in 1812. For vigour of conception and swiftness of execution his first blows in 1815 recall the days of Marengo and Eckmühl. Blücher's army numbered about 120,000 men, nearly all Prussians, and mostly animated by their leader's hatred of Napoleon; but even among his troops there was a strong French feeling in the Saxon and West German contingents. Wellington headed a motley array of 31,000 British troops, 29,000 Dutch-Belgians, 22,000 Hanoverian-Brunswickers, 6,000 King's German Legion, &c.—in all about 93,000 men. Such a force was necessarily wanting in cohesion, while the fidelity of the Belgians was deservedly questioned. Most of the British and Hanoverian troops had never stood fire before, a fact which condemned the Duke to defensive tactics. His army could therefore be little more than the pivot on which that of Blücher moved. Against such armies Napoleon might hope to hurl his 124,000 French veterans with every hope of success. The results of his secret and speedy advance were at once apparent. On June 15th he drove the Prussian vanguard from Charleroi, pushing it back on the road leading to Fleurus and Ligny, while Ney gained possession of the high-road to Brussels as far as Frasnes, within three miles of Quatre Bras. It is claimed by many writers who desire to throw all the blame of Napoleon's disaster on his lieutenants, that Ney had received a verbal order to seize this important post; while in reply it is urged that Ney's troops had had a very long march ending with an engagement, and were unsupported by Count d'Erlon's corps, which was far in the rear. Had Ney seized this important position on the 15th, it is improbable that Blücher would have accepted battle next day at the exposed position of Ligny.

Even as it was, though Napoleon's aim of driving back the Prussians out of touch with Wellington had not been realized, yet the communications between the allied armies were seriously menaced by the triumphant French advance, for which both Blücher and Wellington were unprepared. The latter, who was not informed of Napoleon's attack on Charleroi till the evening of the 15th, was not shaken in his belief that the French main advance would be by way of the Mons-Brussels road to cut off his communications with the sea; and yet, when it was of the highest importance to ascertain Napoleon's plans, the Duke thought it not incompatible with his duties to attend the Duchess of Richmond's ball at Brussels. Indeed, it was in contravention of Wellington's first orders, that the Prince of Saxe-Weimar occupied the important position at Quatre Bras with Dutch-Belgian troops; and, but for his promptitude, that post would have been occupied without fighting by Ney. Riding hastily to the front on the morning of the 16th, Wellington gave to Blücher a promise of support in case he himself was not attacked in force, cautioning Blücher however against accepting battle in so advanced a position and on a slope so exposed to the French cannonade. The statement of most Prussian writers that he gave an absolute promise of support, is quite without foundation.

The military position at noon of the 16th was briefly

as follows.   Blücher with about 80,000 troops, of whom about
one-third were Landwehr, held a strong but exposed position
on a slope extending between Ligny and neighbouring villages,
where he intended to defend his communications with the
fortress of Namur on the east, and the Namur—Quatre Bras
road in his rear, which still provided access to Wellington's
vanguard.   Bülow's corps was far away in the rear.   The
British troops were beginning to approach Quatre Bras.   Their
presence in force would have relieved the pressure on Blücher's
exposed right, only some five miles distant from the Dutch-
Belgian brigade; but for a long time Wellington could scarcely
hold his own.   On his side Napoleon with 67,000 men hoped
to cut off Blücher's right in St Amand by an attack on the
Prussian centre at Ligny; and he ordered Ney, after seizing
Quatre Bras, to march on the Prussian rear and help in
capturing the whole of its right wing.   The Emperor, however,
under-estimated Blücher's forces.   Ney's operations were
clogged by the tardy advance of d'Erlon's corps in his rear;
and this delay, due to friction and mistakes in Ney's newly
constituted staff, saved the allies from serious disaster.

With only half his full forces, the French Marshal began
his attack on Quatre Bras about two o'clock, when scarcely
any British troops were there.   The Dutch-Belgians fell back
after a creditable resistance, until the arrival of the Duke of
Brunswick's brigade and Picton's division restored the fight.
Even so, the superiority of the French in cavalry and
artillery wrought havoc among the allied infantry; and only
the gallantry of the 42nd and 44th regiments withstood an
attack on flank and rear by the French lancers.   The rout
of some Dutch-Belgian and Hanoverian Landwehr regiments
left the issue doubtful even late in the afternoon when Wellington had a superiority of numbers.

Meanwhile Napoleon, on hearing the first sound of Ney's
cannon, had begun to assail the Prussians.   After a fierce

cannonade and charges on the villages of St Amand and Ligny which at first were bravely repulsed, he was ready to commence the decisive move of his Guards on Blücher's centre, when Vandamme reported the approach on his flank of a hostile force. The combat slackened for nearly two hours, until the approaching column was ascertained to be the belated corps of d'Erlon, which, when marching to reinforce Ney, had been ordered off to join Napoleon by a special despatch from the Emperor. After this long delay about seven o'clock the Old Guard was launched against Ligny, with decisive effect. Blücher, coming up from St Amand, where he had presumed the supreme struggle would be, was overthrown and much hurt in one of a series of cavalry charges, and was saved only by the skill and courage of his *aide-de-camp*, who skilfully concealed him until a charge of Uhlans brought rescue to their chief. Indeed such was the tenacity of the Prussian troops that after a loss of 15,000 killed and wounded they retired under cover of the darkness and in good order, beating off the onsets of the French horse. The delay in Napoleon's final attack, caused by d'Erlon's unlucky corps, saved Blücher from protracted pursuit. The same cause had hampered Ney's operations. He has been severely blamed for leaving a whole corps more than two hours in his rear, but he is not responsible for its deviation towards Napoleon's army. Imperiously re-calling it to his own command when it was about to turn the Prussian flank at St Amand, he yet derived no succour from it; and thus 19,000 troops were left oscillating between two battles and taking part in neither.

Their weight, if thrown into the wavering balance at Quatre Bras, must have been decisive. As it was, the gradual arrival of British reinforcements decided that bloody contest in favour of the allies. Kellermann's cuirassiers were not brought into action until the British and German infantry were so well posted as to beat back the hero of the Marengo charge with crushing loss; and after six hours of desperate fighting Ney was eventually driven back on Frasnes with the loss of 4,000 men, Wellington's losses, however, being even heavier. Among the slain was the gallant Duke of Brunswick, the hero of the attempt of 1809. The allied success at Quatre Bras was rendered fruitless by the Prussian reverse at Ligny; and the Anglo-Dutch forces fell back promptly on the Waterloo position.

The fate of the campaign now depended on the vigour of Napoleon's pursuit and the direction taken by Blücher's forces in retreat. Over-estimating the importance of his victory, or fatigued by his great exertions—he had travelled from Paris and fought a great battle in five days—Napoleon delayed striking at Wellington's exposed forces, or following up the retreating Prussians. This remissness, so unlike his conduct after Jena, lost him all the fruits of his victory, and gave the Prussians the opportunity of retreating on a line parallel to the Quatre Bras—Brussels high-road.

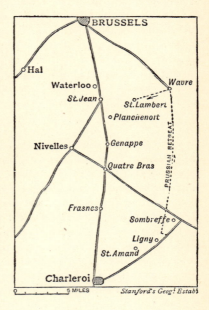

A partial reconnaissance ordered by Soult early on the 17th seemed to indicate that the Prussians were retreating eastwards towards Namur, their immediate base of operations. So strong was Napoleon's belief in this, the natural move of a beaten

army, that not till noon did he order Grouchy with 33,000 men
to pursue Blücher's forces. In vain did the Marshal—he had
lately received his baton—remark that his troops were wearied,
that the Prussians had 18 hours' start, and that the direction of
their retreat was not known. Napoleon soon repeated his commands more explicitly; for in the meantime news had arrived
that 20,000 Prussians were near Gembloux. Grouchy accordingly received written instructions (now known in their entirety)
to explore in the direction of Namur and Maestricht, and find
out whether Blücher's forces "are separating themselves from
the English or whether they are intending still to unite, to
cover Brussels or Liège, and to try the fate of another battle."
Grouchy did not start till 2 P.M. on June 17. Rain began to
fall heavily, so retarding his progress that twelve hours elapsed
before he found out definitely that the Prussians had marched,
not south-east towards Namur, but northwards to Wavre.

The credit for the initial move in this direction belongs to
Gneisenau, and is consonant with his undaunted spirit. Yet
even he hesitated in taking the decisive step of abandoning
the Prussian communications with the Rhine, and boldly
joining Wellington at the first opportunity. It was the septua-
genarian Blücher, weak and bruised from his fall at Ligny,
who took the responsibility and therefore deserves the credit
for this final resolve. The student will observe that, whereas
up to 1809 the defeats of the coalition forces became disasters
owing to want of persistent mutual support, from 1813 and
onwards the allies clung together as the only means of safety.
Their concentration near the Bohemian frontier of Silesia after
the defeat at Bautzen, Blücher's flank marches from Silesia
to join von Bülow on the Elbe, and again in 1814 from the
Seine to join him on the Aisne, foreshadowed the prudently
daring movement which assured the final triumph at Waterloo.

On Wavre, therefore, the Prussians began to concentrate;
and the arrival of Bülow's and Thielemann's fresh corps

XI.] *The Reconstruction of Europe.*

brought the Prussian forces up to 90,000 men. News of this was sent to Wellington, who replied that he would accept battle at the Waterloo position if one Prussian corps were sent to support him. At 3 A.M. of June 18 he received the definite offer of help from Blücher, who promised that Bülow's corps should march off at dawn. Thereupon the Iron Duke resolved to accept battle at Mont St Jean, trusting in the bravery of his British and German troops and the strength of the position to repulse an army which excelled his own in cohesion, experience, and numbers. Nevertheless, owing to the Duke's inability to support the Prussians at Ligny, there seems to have been in Blücher's staff some fear that Wellington would retreat on Brussels and leave his allies exposed. At any rate, it was not till they heard the welcome sound of the cannon at Waterloo, that any vigorous attempt was made to advance. The same winged messenger should have reminded Grouchy that the spirit at least of his instructions (part of which he afterwards suppressed) required a half-left turn to intercept any flank march of the Prussians towards Waterloo. A warm remonstrance to this effect by General Gérard only confirmed him in his belief that he ought to attack the Prussians at Wavre. He did so, gained his point, and lost the campaign.

Wellington's position at Mont St Jean extended along the ridge of a slope at the back of which ran a rough road, while further in his rear were the village of Waterloo and the forest of Soignies. The front of his right flank was strengthened by the château and wood of Hougomont, his centre by the spacious farm-buildings of la Haye Sainte, commanding the Brussels high-road. A shallow valley separated the allies from the rather higher ridge east and west of la Belle Alliance along which extended Napoleon's imposing lines. To confront 72,000 French, of whom 15,700 were cavalry, Wellington could muster only 67,000, of whom not quite 24,000 were

British; and he had only 156 cannons against the enemy's
246. But his skilful arrangement of most of his troops behind
the brow of the ridge screened them from the terrible losses
of the Prussians on the St Amand-Ligny slope. The Iron
Duke's tactics offered throughout the day a masterly defence
against foes whose effective strength for the first four hours
of fighting was nearly double his own. Only one error in his
dispositions has been remarked, viz. his leaving 18,000 men
at Hal so far away to the west, as to be useless on the day
of battle. By that time it was fairly obvious that Napoleon
was attempting to crush the allies in succession, not to sever
the English communications with the sea.

The Emperor's delay in beginning the battle until nearly
noon has been sharply criticised; but it was necessary for the
movements of his formidable cavalry and artillery to let the
ground harden after 16 hours of heavy rain; and if, as seems
certain, the Prussians deferred their march from Wavre until
the cannonade was heard, the delay had none of the decisive
consequences which have often been stated. The ardour
of the French troops converted what was intended to be a
subordinate attack, that on the wood and mansion of Hougomont, into a fierce and prolonged contest; but this advanced
post was stubbornly held by the English Guards and their supports throughout the day against double their numbers. The
key of the British position was, however, la Haye Sainte, held
by part of the King's German Legion. After a cannonade from
the overwhelming French artillery, which decimated an exposed
Dutch-Belgian brigade, the Emperor was about to order an
attack in force on the allied left centre, when he observed
troops far away towards Wavre. The uncertainty was ended
by the capture of a Prussian hussar who was bearing to Wellington news of von Bülow's advance. Soult thereupon, just
after 1 P.M., added a postscript to a despatch urging Grouchy
"not to lose an instant in approaching and joining us, and to

crush Bülow whom you will catch in the very act"; but this order did not reach him till 6 P.M. In Grouchy's defence it is urged that an earlier despatch approved of his movement on Wavre. But this did not reach him till 4 P.M., up to which time he alone is responsible for not moving against the flank of the Prussians and striving to stop their march.

For the present, Napoleon was satisfied with detaching some light cavalry to the right, and sending repeated messages to his Marshal, all of which reached him too late. Evidently, however, Ney's attack on Wellington's centre must be pushed home with irresistible force; and this apparently accounts for the denseness of the columns hurled on Wellington's right. A persistent attack in that formation against foes disordered by a severe cannonade had rarely failed to secure the victory, as at Wagram, Borodino, Lützen, and Ligny; and the criticism lavished on the unusual massiveness of the columns seems irrelevant. They actually mounted the crest and their menacing appearance sufficed to break up the Dutch-Belgians in their front but there the French masses were received by a withering fire from Picton's division; this was in part being overborne when a charge of the 'Union Brigade' rolled the columns down the slope with heavy losses. As the French cuirassiers advanced against Wellington's centre they met the fearful shock of Ponsonby's household brigade and fled in confusion; while the Scots Greys, Inniskillings and Royal Dragoons hustled and completed the rout of d'Erlon's columns, which lost in all some 3,000 prisoners and two eagles.

The 'Union Brigade,' pursuing its furious career, rode up the French slope, sabred the gunners and disabled many cannon; but the hostile cavalry, previously inactive, now rode them down, inflicting severe losses in their retreat, until the French lancers themselves received prompt punishment.

Thus to and fro swept the tide of battle for the first three hours, the advantage being in the main with Wellington. The artillery fire was now redoubling in intensity, a sure prelude to another attack in force, this time by the chief mass of the French cavalry on Wellington's right and centre. The French tactics here too have been severely criticised; but Napoleon's belief in the power of cavalry was justified by all previous experience; and his surmise that Wellington's untrained troops were demoralised by the hail of grape-shot was correct. Moreover, at la Haye Sainte a Hanoverian regiment had been completely dispersed by his cuirassiers—the only success there gained by his troops. These grand cavalry charges may also be defended as a speedy though wasteful method of snatching at a victory which was rendered more and more doubtful by the slow but steady approach of the Prussians on the French right flank. After giving a general assent to the employment of his cavalry against Wellington's squares, Napoleon about 4.30 P.M. strengthened his right at Planchenoit then menaced by von Bülow's corps; while Ney for two hours hurled his heavy cavalry against Wellington's right centre. The Duke's dispositions to meet these living avalanches are worthy of all praise. Sheltering his squares behind the crest of the slope from the hail of grape-shot which preluded each onset of the horsemen, Wellington left his artillery alone exposed to view. The cannoneers, after dealing death among the approaching squadrons, unlimbered their guns and ran for shelter to the squares. These defied all the efforts of the chivalry of France, which swerved from them and vainly sought to cleave an entry. Foiled at the very time when they imagined themselves masters of the ridge, the successive waves of cavalry surged back again, hard pressed by the allied horsemen or galled by shot and shell. Though again and again the French brigades enveloped the British and German squares and apparently carried the position, yet no French infantry was at hand to maintain the ground won, nor could the allied cannons be carried off, and neglect to give due support to these cavalry charges seems to be Ney's chief blunder on that day. The exploits of the French horse at Marengo, Jena, Eylau, the Somosierra, Borodino, and Dresden—the last of which perhaps inspired Ney's tactics— could not be repeated on the ridge of Waterloo, and by 6 P.M. the French cavalry was exhausted. During the same critical time a French infantry attack on la Haye Sainte was again steadily repulsed by the King's German Legion; and at 6 Wellington's position was intact[1].

Napoleon's chief blunder on the 18th seems to have been his neglect to oppose any but a few light troops to the Prussian vanguard when crossing the defile below St Lambert; but he thought that Grouchy would come up and take the enemy in the rear. About 4.30 von Bülow deployed his troops on the French flank; and an hour later, after sharp fighting, 30,000 Prussians gained a hold on the outskirts of Planchenoit; but Lobau's corps and the Young Guard drove them out for a time until reinforcements arrived. This temporary diversion of French infantry to face the flank attack, probably accounts for its lack of due support to the cavalry and to the second great onset on la Haye Sainte. But the battalions of the German Legion, which for seven hours held this exposed post, had at last exhausted their ammunition, and shortly after 6 their few survivors retired to the allied lines. Had Ney possessed sufficient reserves of infantry and cavalry, Wellington's centre might now have been pierced. The shattered allied lines there and on the right were for some time in the greatest danger, and only the tact of Wellington and his staff in drawing in supports from his

---

[1] Mr Ropes, in his careful and exact review of the Waterloo campaign, follows Charras in stating 4 P.M. as the time when la Haye Sainte was finally taken. This, however, must refer to a temporary lodgment gained by the French. The evidence of Kennedy, staff officer of the division so seriously menaced, and the Journal of the King's German Legion, seem to show that it was not completely taken till 6 P.M. But Judge O'Connor Morris in the *English Historical Review* for Jan. 1895, fixes the time earlier.

extreme wings, sufficed to make good the fearful gaps. All three armies were in a critical position; and Napoleon, feeling the pressure of von Bülow's renewed attack on Planchenoit, was convinced that only a supreme effort of his Old Guard could win the day. That was still possible; for not more than 35,000 Prussians as yet menaced him, and Wellington had scarcely so many trustworthy troops still available.

About 7 o'clock the Emperor hurled against Wellington's right centre six battalions of his Guard, supported by masses of infantry. These veterans of the revolutionary and Napoleonic wars, led by Ney in person, supported by horse artillery and their sharp-shooters, steadily mounted the slope. The leading part of their column was plied with a destructive fire from Napier's guns and from a Dutch-Belgian battery, while the line of Maitland's Guards shattered their front. Halkett's two regiments on their flank crushed every attempt at deploying, and an advance in line rolled the veterans down the slope in complete disorder, as the second part of their great column marched up to retrieve the fight. This fared even worse. Galled in front by a steady cannonade and volleys of musketry, it was charged on the flank by Colborne's 52nd regiment, and driven in utter rout into the valley. The other French troops fell back, and Wellington, feeling the touch of Ziethen's Prussians on his left, gave to his troops the long desired order for a general advance. His wisdom in holding back the British horsemen was now manifest. The brigades of Vivian and Vandeleur did fearful execution among the disordered French; and the Emperor, in his fallacious bulletin, ascribed the loss of the battle to these effective onsets of the British horse. That these, supported by a general advance of the allies, drove back the wrecks of the French squadrons and two reserve battalions of the Old Guard, cannot be questioned. Yet it would be disingenuous not to recognise the importance of the Prussian share in this momentous victory. Wellington's final advance would have been most hazardous had not Ziethen's fresh corps then hurled itself on the French right. The invincible energy of Blücher, von Bülow, Ziethen, and their devoted troops overcame the serious obstacles to the advance, and launched in all some 41,000 men against the French. Yet so stubbornly did the Comte de Lobau defend Planche-noit that not till after the final advance of Wellington's line was it yielded to von Bülow's men. Then all was panic and disaster on the road to Charleroi, and under the protracted pursuit of the Prussians—their revenge for Jena—the French fled beyond the Sambre with the loss of all their artillery, ammunition and stores. Napoleon himself escaped capture only by precipitate flight. Had he fallen into the hands of Gneisenau's troopers, they would have shot him on the spot.

The tactics of Napoleon and Ney have been severely censured, as always happens after disaster. To the present writer they do not appear to differ materially from the Emperor's usual method of freely sacrificing his men in order to wear away and confuse his foes at all points until the final blow could be delivered with crushing effect. To launch heavy columns of attack after the enemy had suffered from the first onsets and crushing cannonade, had till then almost invariably won the day against continental foes. These tactics were foiled by the tenacious defence of Hougomont and la Haye Sainte and still more by Wellington's dextrous use of the brow of the ridge to screen his troops from the tempest of iron and to hide his defensive moves. Time after time did the French horse and foot mount the slope in triumph, only to be shattered by volleys from the squares or from the thin red lines which mangled their front and then charged with the bayonet. Tactics which had succeeded elsewhere were baffled by the natural strength of the position, by the invincible courage and steadiness of Wellington's best troops in meeting the columns with an outflanking attack in line, and by the deadliness of the

British musketry fire, which had been proved in every battle from Corunna to this final contest. Colonel Tomkinson, in his recently published diary of the campaigns of 1808—1815, points out the advantages of the line formation for experienced and steady troops against a massive column. This can only move slowly and emit a scanty fire, while the lines can destroy the head of the column, harass its flanks, and complete its disorder with the bayonet. These tactics, employed with decisive effects at Albuera and other battles of the Peninsula, received their final and most dramatic illustration on the slopes of Mt St Jean, where the veterans before whom Europe had trembled for the last decade were broken by less than their own number of British regulars. On the other hand, the fearful losses of the allies, amounting to more than one-fourth of the British troops and the King's German Legion, with 6,700 Prussians, bespeak the vigour of the French attacks. How Wellington could have held his ground, had Grouchy marched against the Prussian flank, and so secured for Napoleon's army freedom to act in front, it is difficult to conceive. Yet, however severe the blame which may be lavished on Ney and Grouchy, a considerable share of it must rebound on the Emperor, who at a few hours' notice assigned duties to these Marshals for which they were not well suited. Even before his defeat at Dennewitz, Ney's splendid fame was that of a desperate fighter and gallant corps leader, rather than that of a skilful tactician; while on Grouchy, known till 1815 only as a dashing cavalry general, devolved a task which called for some strategic insight. Had their places been filled by Soult and Davoust, justly renowned for their combination of skill and tenacity, the issue must have been different.

Attempts have often been made to account for the disaster by the decay of Napoleon's bodily and mental powers. It is true, of course, that he did not display the freshness and clearness of conception of his Italian campaigns, and that the fatigues caused by his multifarious energy at Paris and by the lightning strokes with which he astonished the allies, somewhat told on a frame which had lost the elasticity of youth; but the endeavour to exhibit the commander as oppressed by bodily torpor at the crisis of his destinies, is a ludicrous distortion of facts. Whatever hesitation he displayed in the middle of the battle was due to the unexpected success of Wellington's defensive tactics, to the delay in Grouchy's fulfilment of his own reiterated orders, and to the increasing vigour of the Prussian attack. Enough has been stated above to prove that the errors on the French side were due, not to the Emperor's obesity, but to the somewhat strange redistribution of duties which accompanied the hasty reorganization of his vast and complicated engine of war.

Napoleon's main army now presented the scene, unparalleled except at Jena, of an army of veterans utterly broken up in a single day. Grouchy, after beating the Prussian rear-guard at Wavre, hastily fell back on Namur. Thence he retired to Dinant, Rheims, and Soissons, where a feeble attempt at resistance was offered. In fact, the triple line of fortresses which had foiled the allies in 1793–4 now scarcely delayed their conquering march. Meanwhile at Paris the Emperor was endeavouring to invest himself with dictatorial powers. Carnot also urged the necessity of declaring the country to be in danger, and of rousing the people against the allies. But the spirit of 1793 had vanished. Fouché skilfully maintained in the Imperial Council the need of relying on the Chambers, not on a dictatorship which would dissolve them. Cajoling the Bonapartist deputies with the hope of a proclamation of Napoleon II as a last resort, the *quondam* regicide now began to weld together parties against the Emperor. It was also reserved for the earliest hero of the revolution to deal a blow at the pretensions of its last and greatest dictator. Lafayette brought forward and carried a series of propositions that the independence of the nation was menaced, that whoever attempted to dissolve the Chamber was guilty of high treason and that the Ministers must repair to its sittings. These and other signs convinced Napoleon that his work was done, and he a second time abdicated in favour of his son Napoleon II, with the noble parting injunction—"Let all unite for the public safety, in order to remain an independent nation." Strange to say, the act of abdication was written by his brother Lucien, who had helped him to power in 1799; and it was opposed in the Council of Ministers only by Carnot, who in 1804 had left France rather than acknowledge the Empire.

At the end of June the allies were before Paris. Some combats ensued in the neighbourhood, Blücher's troops driving the French from Sèvres, and occupying the commanding plateau of Châtillon, while Wellington threatened the capital from the north. The news of the Austro-Russian advance and the departure of Napoleon for the coast, facilitated the conclusion of an armistice which was drawn up at St Cloud, July 3; and five days later Louis XVIII re-entered Paris. On that same day Napoleon embarked on a frigate at Rochefort, intending to sail for the United States; but being watched by British cruisers he placed himself under the protection of the captain of H.M.S. Bellerophon. In pursuance of the declaration of the allies at Vienna, the fallen Emperor was finally conveyed to St Helena. After his refusal to abide by the Elba compromise, and the fearful effusion of blood which occurred in the Hundred Days, the need of some such final decision must be manifest to all but the devotees of hero-worship. The special malignity which some writers discern in England's action (e.g. Dumas, who describes it as that of Judas to the new Saviour of mankind) is solely the result of a vivid imagination. The recent treaty between the Powers bound them to prosecute the war until Bonaparte was put

"absolutely beyond the possibility of exciting further troubles."
Nevertheless his influence was not to end; for the tales of the
indignities which he suffered, as concocted by his followers,
Las Cases and Montholon, helped on the growth of a new
Promethean legend, which was to have a strange influence on
Europe in 1848—1870.

The world now needed first and foremost some security
for peace. This was the chief reason for restoring the phlegmatic and unwarlike Louis XVIII to the throne. Fouché
himself entered into intrigues so as to press on this solution
of the problem; and in spite of the former declarations of
the allies, they now insisted on the restoration of Louis XVIII,
who announced from Cambrai that he came to interpose himself a second time between the allies and the French armies.
Certainly, under no other rule than his could France have
escaped heavy losses of territory to the Powers, especially to
the incensed Prussians. With the greatest difficulty Blücher was
dissuaded by Louis XVIII and Wellington from blowing up
the *pont d'Iéna*. The irate veteran at Wellington's banquet
in Paris proposed as a toast—"May the diplomatists not spoil
with their pens what the soldiers have won with their swords";
and this expressed the general resolve of the Prussian government, army and people that France must be punished by the
cession of Alsace-Lorraine to the Fatherland. Some of the
German newspapers even stated that France must now be
partitioned to reduce her to the weakness from which Germany
had lately been rescued. It is recorded, indeed, by the duc
de Pasquier, the new French Minister for the Interior, that
had Napoleon remained at large, France would have been
subjected to some such treatment. Now that he was on his
way to St Helena, such a proposal lost all validity. Nevertheless, a strong claim was made by Prussia that Alsace-Lorraine
should revert to Germany. "Not till then (so ran the Prussian
Declaration) will France find herself in her true line of defence,
with the Vosges and her double line of fortresses from the

Meuse to the sea; and not till then will France remain quiet." Even Metternich, the champion of old dynasties, now declared that the offensive power of France must be reduced by the cession or demolition of all her first line of fortresses, i.e. from Lille to Strassburg, while Stein suggested that Alsace-Lorraine should be ruled by an Austrian Archduke. There is much to be said in support of these claims both from the standpoint of historic right and of temporary expediency. Those lands had been German, and Prussia's demand for a better boundary for her distant Rhine Province was in a military sense incontestable. Her army had suffered severely, and after a triumph more decisive than Jena, she might reasonably expect a territorial gain half as large as that wrung from her at Tilsit. Finally, her plenipotentiaries Hardenberg and Humboldt declared that, as the forbearance of the Powers towards France in 1814 had only led up to the Hundred Days, it was now necessary to employ sterner measures and to prefer the safety of Europe to the prestige of the Bourbons.

Against these arguments drawn from past and present conditions, the Governments of Great Britain and Russia urged the necessity of founding peace on a lasting basis. In a statesmanlike Memoir of Aug. 11, Wellington set forth the impolicy of so exasperating French public opinion as to mar the settlement. Granting that that land was still left " in too great strength for the peace of Europe," he yet pointed out that " revolutionary France is more likely to distress the world, than France, however strong in her frontier, under a regular Government; and that is the situation in which we ought to endeavour to place her." The views of the Czar were analogous, viz. that the allies should endeavour to strengthen as far as possible the cause of constitutional monarchy in France, not to enfeeble it by demanding territorial cessions which would wound the national pride; and that only so could the European equilibrium be assured. It was further pointed out that Germany under an almost nominal form of union such as that now proposed, would be far too weak to hold Alsace-Lorraine against the bitter hostility of France. Had German unity been effected in 1815, it is probable that these provinces would then have been detached from France.

The final success of the Anglo-Russian arguments led to the terms of the Treaty of Paris (Nov. 20, 1815), whereby France was to recede within her limits of 1790, surrendering to the Netherlands the districts around Marienburg and Philippeville, to the Prussian Rhine-Province part of the Saar valley, to the Bavarian Palatinate Landau and its environs, and to the Kingdom of Sardinia Chambéry and Annecy. Allied troops to the number of 150,000 were to occupy the French fortresses of the east and north for a time not exceeding five years, and France was to pay a war indemnity of 700,000,000 francs (about £28,000,000). The Powers likewise stipulated that the French army was to be temporarily disbanded, and that all the works of art and literary treasures seized by the French, " contrary to every principle of justice and to the usages of modern warfare," should be restored to their rightful owners.

For the second time, then, the desire to establish the Bourbon rule saved France from the vengeance of German patriots, and averted from her the application of that undisguised force by which Prussia had been nearly crushed out of existence at Tilsit. That France was completely at the mercy of the allies, and could have been partitioned, is indisputable. A mere relic of her army remained, while nearly a million armed men lived on her from July to November; but it was to the interest of Russia and England to respect her historical boundaries in the interests of orderly government. Had the French royalists and Charles X exhibited similar moderation, their rule might have become far firmer than ever that of Louis XVI had been. France, it is true, continued to chafe at the settlement of 1815; but the verdict of time has on the whole justified the wisdom of the compromise as regards her frontiers on the east and north.   Certainly, history records no instance of efforts so great ending with victory so complete, yet crowned with such self-abnegation, as the efforts of Great Britain during the Hundred Days.   After spending enormous sums on her own troops, and subsidising all the allies, she gained nothing which had not been virtually decided before the adjournment of the Congress of Vienna.   Weak and tardy in her first opposition to the Jacobin designs on Holland, she had at last won the decisive triumph on the scene of her earlier reverses; and after long stemming the tide of French conquests, she now, with the help of the Czar, set limits to the westward rush of the nationalist reaction, which threatened to overwhelm France.

In its effect on the map of Europe the democratic impulse may be compared to a mighty tidal wave which, sweeping on from the Seine to the Tiber, the Tagus and the Moskwa, produces a reflux as powerful in its ultimate effects.   When the old limits are reached, the spectator can at once discern the mighty work of levelling, simplification and destruction of effete or artificial barriers accomplished in the interval.   European affairs, mostly arranged by the Congress of Vienna at the time of Napoleon's entry into Paris, were soon settled after his abdication.   My task will be completed by a brief survey of the political and social changes effected in this great formative period of our modern world.

After an unparalleled dilation and contraction of influence, France in Nov. 1815 returned almost exactly to her frontiers of 1790, having absorbed and assimilated the small fragments of foreign States within her frontiers.   A similar process is observable in her political and social institutions.   The revolution found her a monarchy strangely hampered by the complicated political and commercial rights or privileges of the provinces; it left her a strongly centralised State wherein all the functions of government were clearly defined by the Charter. Indeed, the collision between Rousseau's theories and the old monarchy ended by vesting the latter with powers not much less than those claimed by Louis XVI in his Royal Session of June 23, 1789. The chief difference was revealed in the first article of the royal Charter—" The French are equal before the law, whatever may be their title or rank." The principles of civil equality and religious liberty were now frankly accepted by Louis XVIII ; and the chief social and political results of the revolution were to survive the royalist reaction of 1824—1830.

The changes effected in the Germanic system were analogous to those in France. The frontiers of the new German Confederation (1815—1866) were almost the same as those of the old Empire which it was intended to replace, except that Savoy and the Austrian Netherlands (save Luxemburg), together with a few outlying districts, had now fallen away from the old connection. As has been previously indicated, the shocks of this terrible epoch had been fatal to nearly all the small States and Free Cities, and only 39 sovereign States survived, while the larger States, Austria, Prussia, Bavaria, Hanover, &c., now possessed more compact territories than ever before. Austria gave up her distant and scattered Flemish and Swabian possessions, but vastly increased and consolidated her lands by the absorption of Salzburg, Trent and other bishoprics, as also by the recovery of Milan, Mantua, Venetia, Istria and Dalmatia, besides gaining Ragusa and Cattaro. She now ceased to touch France and to be the natural champion of Germany on the west ; but her vast gains in Italy were none the less a challenge to France, and were destined to renew the strife of centuries in that unhappy land. For her losses in Poland, Prussia gained largely in Saxony and the Rhine lands, her growth following the general trend of military events westwards in the final campaigns against Napoleon. Though Austria retained her old position of supremacy in the Germanic system, yet these territorial changes bequeathed to Prussia the burden of defending Germany against France ; and the events of half a century later were to solve the question of German dualism in favour of the Power which successfully grappled with its heavy responsibilities.

The Federal Constitution was soon seen to be little more than a Fürstenbund, a league of the Governments, impotent to secure unity in internal affairs, and apparently designed for the suppression of liberty in the several States. After heroic efforts in the cause of national independence and political liberty, the general failure of Germans to secure either of these aims aroused bitter discontent against the rulers who now, except in the south, evaded their promises of constitutional government. On social matters, here as elsewhere, the influence of the French domination was more abiding than on constitutional forms. In very few strictly German States was serfdom re-established. With few exceptions the social results of the Germanic revolution survived in all the lands between the Rhine and the Niemen ; and the Napoleonic code of laws long remained in force in the German provinces west of the Rhine.

In Italy the same general results are still more observable, viz. the permanence of most of the social reforms brought by the French occupation, but an approximate restoration of the previous boundaries and forms of government. Murat's final efforts to arouse a national feeling in his favour had failed because they had been ambiguous and ill-sustained. His General Pepe declared that a bold proclamation of a national war against the Austrians would have rallied 60,000 men to his standard. As it was, he was soon overwhelmed in a brief campaign in the Papal Legations and fled to France (May 1815). In the autumn a final madcap attempt to wrest the crown from the Bourbons resulted in his capture and execution. Between the Austrians in the north and the Bourbons in the south, Italy was now a prey to a calamitous and bloody reaction, which caused Murat's rule long to be regarded with regret. "Within the space of ten years (wrote General Pepe) we had made more progress than our ancestors had done in three centuries. We had acquired the French civil, criminal and commercial codes. We had abolished the feudal system, and justice was administered with improved methods." The same regrets were felt throughout Italy. Her old republics, except that of San Marino, had disappeared, that of Genoa being incorporated with the Kingdom of Sardinia, while Venetia formed part of Austria's Lombardo-Venetian Kingdom. Modena was restored to the House of Este, and Tuscany to the Austrian Archduke Ferdinand, while Marie Louise gained Parma for herself, though not for her son. The Ionian Isles, formerly belonging to Venice, were now declared a free and independent State under the protectorate of Great Britain, which had wrested them from France in 1809—1814. The temporary administration of Sicily and Genoa by Lord Bentinck accentuated the contrast presented by the now unfettered rule of the Spanish Bourbons and the House of Savoy respectively; and though in both cases the English Government had given promises more or less binding for the continuance of popular liberties, it allowed them to be trampled on with impunity. Hence Sicily and Genoa were in the van of all the insurrectionary movements of the years 1820 —1860. For the present, Italy was too exhausted to offer any resistance to her domestic tyrants or to the Austrians encamped in her northern and central fortresses; but, as in Germany, the new groupings of the population under the French supremacy had aroused that sentiment of nationality which was finally to achieve the unification vainly attempted in 1815.

As Sardinia was strengthened to form on the side of Italy a barrier State against France, so too the House of Orange received an important aggrandisement in the Belgian Provinces, holding the old barrier fortresses against her on the north-east

—an artificial arrangement which ignored the differences of language, religion and sentiment between Dutch and Belgians. As a set-off to the loss of their German lands, the younger branch of this family received the Duchy of Luxemburg, for which the King of the Netherlands was to have a vote in the German Confederation. Luxemburg was to rank, with Mainz and Landau, as a federal fortress.

The course of the reaction in Spain merits little attention. In May 1814 Ferdinand VII had been received with tumultuous acclaim by the people of Madrid, and perceiving the slight support accorded to the democratic Constitution of 1812 he speedily annulled it and resumed the royal powers in their entirety. It was in vain that our envoy Sir H. Wellesley protested against the wholesale arrests of the Spanish Liberals and the restoration of the Inquisition. English appeals for the abolition of the slave trade met with no better result. After a heedless rush into advanced democracy Spain relapsed into a mediæval policy which spared only some of the agrarian reforms of the years 1809—1811. The restoration of the House of Braganza in Portugal ultimately led to similar proceedings in that country.

At the other extremity of Europe the cause of national independence was compromised by the forcible union of Norway with the Swedish Crown. Instead of gaining the complete independence which they desired, the Norwegians now had to accept a distasteful connection, owing to the assistance of Sweden and the hostility of Denmark to the allied cause in 1812—1813. Norway was virtually the exchange for Finland, ceded by Sweden to the Czar in 1809; and, as has been noticed above, the small duchy of Lauenburg was finally the meagre compensation awarded to the Danish Crown for the loss of Norway.

Strange to say, it was in Poland that the cause of liberty and independence seemed to have suffered least in 1815.

True to his early promises of reigning as constitutional king of Poland, Alexander granted a constitution to his new realm similar to that established in France by Louis XVIII's Charter, with the proviso that all officials should be Poles and that Polish should be the official language. "The general impression (wrote Czartoryski at Warsaw) at the promulgation of the Constitution has been as favourable as could be desired....Its principles have attached the people to your Majesty." The joy was brief. The arbitrary proceedings of the Grand-Duke Constantine, Russian commander in Poland, soon overrode the new popular liberties; and the Poles, whose lot presents some curious parallels to that of France in 1791, 1807 and 1815, were ten years later to see their charter set aside by the unbending autocrat Nicholas. Every revolutionary outbreak in France sent a thrill through oppressed Poland. Its sole effect was to rivet tighter the Muscovite chains; and the chief result of Alexander's Polish policy was to introduce the Czar's power into the heart of Europe.

For the rest, the Congress of Vienna declared the perpetual neutrality of Switzerland (now reorganised in 22 cantons), and affirmed the principle of the free navigation of rivers, and of the abolition of the slave trade. The chief obstacle to British efforts for the complete vindication of this last great principle, was the determined opposition of our late allies, Spain and Portugal.

Such were the general results of the revolutionary era. The conflicts which unhappily burst forth between democracy and the old Governments produced approximately the results which two such dissimilar thinkers as Burke and Robespierre had foretold as certain to be entailed by a warlike policy. After the dictatorial actions of the secret committees had saved social equality at the expense of political liberty, it was not difficult for a young genius who combined all the gifts which France then so urgently needed, to impose his will on her, and through her on Europe. But the second of these dictatorships signally reversed many of the cherished aims of the earlier revolutionary thinkers and statesmen. In place of that federation of small friendly republics wherein Rousseau foresaw a new and peaceful future, there sprang Minerva-like from the revolution a military Empire which imposed laws on Europe and drove the peoples into revolt. It is impossible to over-estimate the disasters to the cause of political liberty from its close association with an aggressive policy. The Girondin War of 1792, so fatal to the Constitution of the previous year, and the war policy of 1793 which involved all Europe in flames, threw back the cause of freedom in France for more than half a century, and extinguished the last hopes of Polish independence. Of the principles of 1789 France in 1804—1814 retained only social equality, which Napoleon safeguarded at the expense of liberty and the fraternity of nations. Lafayette scarcely exaggerated when in 1815 he described him as "the greatest foe, considering his circumstances, which liberty ever had." The task of reconciling the often conflicting claims of liberty and social equality has ever been found most difficult, even in times of profound peace; and to the inexperienced legislators of France success was perhaps impossible amidst the storms of popular tumult. The revolution produced no leader except the great Mirabeau who was capable of preventing the fatal divergence of those principles, which began after his death. Thenceforth the revolution lost all solidarity of aim, and its difficulties were vastly enhanced by the inflexible rigidity of Girondin and Jacobin policy both at home and abroad. All the tenacious mental characteristics of the young Corsican *caporal*, and his early training in the civil strifes of Ajaccio and Paris, unfortunately tended in the direction of a military autocracy such as the policy of France increasingly required. Throughout this work an attempt has been made to exhibit the direct descent of the Napoleonic régime from that dictatorship of 1793–4 which naturally resulted from the warlike policy of the Girondins and Jacobins.

In the sphere of social equality, however, Napoleon remained to the end a true democrat. Side by side with his work of destruction, he will always be remembered as having consolidated or founded the social and agrarian systems of France, Italy, Belgium, Holland, Switzerland and Germany; while his invasions virtually compelled the legislators of Prussia and Spain to adopt a similar policy. This is his true glory, that even amidst the tempests of war, his matchless genius for organisation quietly laid the foundations of the chief social systems of the Continent.

After the cause of social equality had been carried by the French arms as far as the Niemen, the nationalist reaction against the Napoleonic domination began to gather strength. In Germany, and to some extent even in Spain, the desire for national independence linked itself with the cause of popular liberty; and the spirit of 1789 thenceforth inspired the coalition far more than the Napoleonic armies. The allied cause, however, suffered no less than the earlier democratic impulse from its close association with the exploits of generals and the bargains of diplomatists; and the conflict of two principles not necessarily opposed resulted in a curtailment of popular liberties which left Europe maimed, exhausted, and in a state of arrested development.

APPENDIX I.

A LIST OF THE MOST ACCESSIBLE AND TRUSTWORTHY WORKS DEALING WITH THIS PERIOD.

(Limits of space preclude any attempt at forming a complete bibliography. An asterisk is affixed to the foreign works which have been translated into English.)

THE FRENCH REVOLUTION (PART I. 1789—1799).

A. HISTORIES:—

Sorel's *L'Europe et la Révolution française*: also the works of Carlyle, Fyffe, Häusser, Louis Blanc, Mallet, *Mignet, Morse Stephens, Oncken, Quinet, *Sybel, and *Taine. *Le Règne de Louis XVI* (1774—1789) by Droze. *L'Ancien Régime* by *Tocqueville and *Taine. *Dix Ans de Paix armée* (1783—1793) by the Viscount de Barral-Montferrat. *La France en 1789* by Boiteau. *Le Comité de Salut Public* by Gros. *L'Histoire de la Terreur* by Mortimer-Ternaux. *The Cambridge Modern History* (vol. VIII).

B. BIOGRAPHIES:—

Marie Antoinette by M. de la Rocheterie: *Mdme. de Lamballe* by M. Bertin: Voltaire, Diderot (2 vols.), Rousseau (2 vols.) by Mr John Morley, and his articles on Turgot, Condorcet, Robespierre, &c. in his Miscellanies: *Correspondance de Mirabeau et la Marck* edited by Bacourt: *Mirabeau et la Constituante* by Reynald: *Mirabeau* by Mézières: Dumont's *Souvenirs sur Mirabeau*: *Étude sur Madame Roland et son temps* by Dauban: *Madame Roland* by Miss Mathilde Blind: *Les Femmes célèbres de 1789—1815 et leur influence dans la Révolution* by Lairtullier: *Portraits de Femmes* by Sainte-Beuve: *Condorcet* by Robinet: *La Vie privée de Danton* and *Le Procès des Dantonistes* by Robinet: *Marat* by Chèvremont: *Robespierre* by Hamel: *St. Just* by Hamel: *Hoche* by Rousselin: *Kléber* by Ernouf: *Marceau* by Johnson: *Dubois Crancé* by Jung: *Mémoires sur Carnot* by his son: *Bonaparte et son temps* by Jung: the monographs of Chuquet; *Robespierre* by Belloc.

C. The chief Memoirs dealing mainly with the years 1789—1799 are those of Bailly, Barbaroux, Barère, Bertrand-Molleville, Beugnot, Bouillé, Brissot, Buzot, *Mdme. de Campan, des Cars, Chevernay, Cléry, Dumouriez, Ferrières, Mdme. de Genlis, Lafayette, Latude, *Mallet du Pan, *Pasquier, Pontécoulant, Mdme. Roland, Mgr. de Salomon, Thibaudeau, Thiébault, Mdme. de Tourzel, Mdme. de Staal-Delaunay, and Weber. The travels of Arthur Young in France (1787—1790), the journal of Forster of Mainz, and the Correspondence of A. Miles also throw valuable light on this period.

D. Of the many Essays and miscellaneous works on this period the following may be noted:—Burke's *Reflections on the French Revolution* with Mackintosh's reply, *Vindiciae Gallicae*: Mdme. de Staël's *Considérations sur la Revolution française*: Helen M. Williams' *Sketches of Manners &c. in the French Republic*: Aulard's *Études et leçons sur la Révolution française*: Aulard's *Le Culte de la Raison et le Culte de l'Être Suprême*: Aulard's *Les Orateurs de la Constituante, Les Orateurs de la Législative et de la Convention, La Société des Jacobins*, and *Recueil des Actes du Comité de Salut public*: Morse Stephens' *Orators of the French Revolution*: Oscar Browning's *Varennes and other Essays*, and his edition of Earl Gower's *Despatches from Paris*: Croker's *Essays on the French Revolution*: Alger's *Englishmen in the French Revolution* and *Glimpses in the French Revolution*: Dickinson's *Revolution and Reaction in Modern France*.

THE FRENCH REVOLUTION (PART II. 1799—1815).

A. HISTORIES:—

Bignon, Capefigue, Fyffe, *Lanfrey, Morse Stephens, Oncken, Thibaudeau, and *Thiers. Sorel's *L'Europe et la Révolution Française* (Parts V—VIII). Captain Mahan's *Influence of Sea Power on the French Revolution and Empire.* *The Cambridge Modern History* (vol. IX).

B. BIOGRAPHIES:—

Fournier, *Napoleon der Erste*: Roloff, *Napoleon*: J. H. Rose, *Life of Napoleon I* (2 vols.): Sloane, *Life of Napoleon* (4 vols.). *Talleyrand* by Lady Blennerhassett and by Mc'Cabe. *Joséphine* and *Napoléon et sa Famille* by Masson. *Les Rois frères de Napoléon* by Ducasse. *Ney* by

Rouval, *Soult* by Combes, *Davoust* by Vigier : *Vandamme* by Ducasse : *Maret* by Ernouf : *Les Diplomates Européens* by Capefigue : *Mme. de Staël* by Sorel and by Lady Blennerhassett.

C. The chief Memoirs dealing mainly with the years 1799—1815 are those of the duchesse d'Abrantès, * Bausset, Joseph Bonaparte, Lucien Bonaparte, Jerome Bonaparte, * Bourrienne, Broglie, Chaptal, Chateaubriand, Drouet (Comte d'Erlon), Fain's *Manuscrit de 1812—1814*, * Fouché, * Guizot, Hyde de Neuville, * Macdonald, * Marbot, Marmont, Masséna, * Méneval, * Miot de Melito, Mollien, * Pasquier, Pingaud, Puymaigre, * Mdme. de Rémusat, Rochechouart, * Savary, * Ségur, * Talleyrand, and Vitrolles.

D. Among the many miscellaneous works dealing with this period the following may be named :—Roederer's *La première et la seconde Années du Consulat* : * Saint-Amand's *La Femme du premier Consul* : Mdme. de Staël's *Dix Années d'Exil* : Ernouf's *Les Français en Prusse* (1807— 1808) : Ernouf's *Souvenirs d'un officier polonais* : * Mdme. Durand's *Napoléon et Marie Louise* : Vandal's *Napoléon et Alexandre* : Houssaye's *1814* and *1815* : Coquelle's *Napoleon and England* : J. H. Rose's *Napoleonic Studies* : Lord Rosebery's *Napoleon, the last Phase* : R. C. Seaton's *Napoleon's Captivity in relation to Sir H. Lowe*.

Napoleon's correspondence, though far from complete, is the best authority for his policy. Part of it has been edited by Captain Bingham in a spirit hostile to Napoleon. Louis Bonaparte's *Des Idées Napoléoniennes* (1839) and the late Prince Napoleon's *Napoleon and his Detractors* are official presentations of the Napoleonic legend.

GREAT BRITAIN (1789—1815).

HISTORIES :—

Massey's *Reign of George III* : James' *Naval History*. *The Political History of England*, vol. XI (1801—1837).

BIOGRAPHIES :—

Pitt by Lord Stanhope and by Lord Rosebery : *Fox* by Lord J. Russell and by Hammond : *Canning* by Temperley : *Wellington* by Sir H. Maxwell : *Life of Nelson* by Captain Mahan (2 vols.) : *Addington* by Pellew : *Castlereagh* by Alison : Brougham's *Historical Sketches of Statesmen of the Time of George III* : *Craufurd and his Light Division* by Rev. A. H. Craufurd : *Life of Sir R. Wilson* : *Diary of Sir J. Moore* (ed. by Maurice).

MEMOIRS, CORRESPONDENCE, AND MISCELLANEOUS WORKS :—

The Wellington Despatches : Castlereagh's Memoirs and Correspondence: the Correspondence of the first Earl of Malmesbury : the Correspondence of James, first Earl of Charlemont (vol. II) : the Correspondence of A. Miles : the Correspondence of the Right Hon. George Rose : Memoirs and Correspondence of Collingwood.

Beamish's *History of the King's German Legion,* and the Memoirs of Kincaid, Sir G. Napier, *Ompteda, Capt. Patterson, and Col. Tomkinson, illustrate the course of the wars of 1808—1815. The Waterloo Campaign may be studied in the works of Siborne, von Ollech, Ropes, and in the Waterloo Letters, Kelly's *The Battle of Wavre* and Mercer's *Journal.*

Tooke's *History of Prices,* many pamphlets in the *Pamphleteer,* and the works of Cobbett, will illustrate the economic and social conditions of the time.

GERMANY.

HISTORIES :—

*von Sybel, Häusser, Duncker, Oncken's *Das Zeitalter der Revolution, des Kaiserreiches, und der Befreiungskriege*: Treitschke's *Deutsche Geschichte im neunzehnten Jahrhundert* (vol. I) : Perthes' *Politische Zustände und Personen in Deutschland* (1795—1813) : Beitzke's *Die Freiheitskriege* (1813—1814) : *Kriegsgeschichte der Jahre* 1813—1814 by Müffling and by Plotho : Cathcart's *Commentaries on the War in Russia and Germany* 1812—1813 : Krones' *Geschichte der Neuzeit Oesterreichs*: Beer's *Zehn Jahre oesterreichischer Politik* (1801—1810) : Léger's *Histoire de l' Autriche-Hongrie*: Coxe's *Memorials of the House of Austria*: Schöll's *Congrès de Vienne* : Pflugk-Harttung's *Napoleon I. Das Erwachen der Völker.*

BIOGRAPHIES :—

Stein by Pertz and by Seeley : *Blücher* by Scherr and by Blasendorf : *Yorck* by Droysen : *Gneisenau* by Pertz : *Scharnhorst* by Lehmann : *Schill* by Bärsch : *von Bülow* by Varnhagen von Ense: See too *Stein* by Lehmann : *Hardenberg* by L. von Ranke : *Queen Louisa* by Mary Moffat.

MEMOIRS :—

*Arndt, von Boyen, Hardenberg, *Metternich, *Müffling, *Christian Ompteda, Louis Ompteda, *von Odeleben, *F. Perthes, Radetzky, Steffens, Stern, *Varnhagen von Ense.

The political pamphlets of Arndt, Gentz, Karl Müller, Fichte's *Reden an die deutsche Nation* and Freytag's *Bilder aus der deutschen Vergangenheit* (vol. IV) give many details of German life and thought.

ITALY.

The history of Signor Botta on the French domination in Italy needs to be corrected and supplemented by the critical works of Peschieri and Parenti, as well as by the histories—Franchetti's *Storia d' Italia dal* 1789 *al* 1799, De Castro's *Storia d' Italia dal* 1799 *al* 1814, Tivaroni's *Storia critica del risorgimento italiano* (vols. I—II), Vimercati's *Histoire d' Italie de* 1789 *à* 1863, Turotti's *Storia delle armi italiane dal* 1794 *al* 1815, Carutti's *Storia della Casa di Savoia durante la revoluzione e l' Impero francese,* Lumbroso (Giacomo) *Roma e lo Stato romano dopo l'* 89, Colletta's *Storia del reame di Napoli dal* 1734 *al* 1827. *Marie Caroline* by Helfert and by Bonnefons.

MEMOIRS :—

Alfieri, Azeglio (Massimo d') *I miei ricordi* (vol. I), Balbo (Cesare) *Autobiografia,* Bigarré, du Casse's *Mémoires d' Eugène,* Leopardi (Monaldo) *Autobiografia,* *Macdonald, Melzi (Duca di Lodi), *Miot de Melito, *Pepe, Thaon de Revel, Thiébault, and Zucchi.

SPAIN.

Baumgarten's *Geschichte Spaniens seit* 1789: Napier's *History of the Peninsular War*: Wellington's Despatches. Arteche y Moro, *Guerra de la Independencia*: Oman, *History of the Peninsular War* (In progress).

The Memoirs or Diaries of Broglie, Kincaid, *Marbot, Marmont, *Miot de Melito, Sir G. Napier, *Ompteda, Captain Patterson, Soult, Colonel Tomkinson, and Beamish's *History of the King's German Legion,* deal with parts of the Peninsular War. See too, the Memoirs of Foy, Harris, Jourdan, Macdonald, Simmons, and Suchet.

RUSSIA.

Bernhardi's *Geschichte Russlands* (vol. I, 1814—1831): Rambaud's *Histoire de Russie*: Vandal's *Napoléon et Alexandre*: Tatistcheff's *Alexandre I et Napoléon*: *L'Histoire de l'expédition en Russie* by the Count de Ségur, and a damaging criticism on this work by General Gourgaud : also the accounts of the 1812 campaign by Cathcart, Chambray, Clausewitz, Marbot, and Wilson. See too H. B. George, *Napoleon's Invasion of Russia,* and Fabry, *Campagne de Russie.*

Memoirs by *Prince Czartoryski, Eugen von Würtemberg, Eugène de Beauharnais, Bourgogne, Fezensac, Gouvion St Cyr, Labaume, Oginski, Porter, Rapp and Toll.

THE SCANDINAVIAN COUNTRIES.

HISTORIES:

Boyesen's *History of Norway*; Dunham's *History of Denmark, Sweden, and Norway*: Fryxell's *History of Sweden* : Bain's *History of Denmark, Norway and Sweden from* 1513 *to* 1900: Pingaud, *Bernadotte, Napoléon et les Bourbons.* Schefer, *Bernadotte Roi*, Touchard-Lafosse, *Histoire de Charles XIV* (*Bernadotte*).

HISTORIES OF TREATIES.

The collections of Clercq, Duteil, Neumann, Garden and Martens, and Koch and Schöll's *Histoire des Traités entre les Puissances de l'Europe,* 1648—1815.

APPENDIX II.

LIST OF THE CHIEF APPOINTMENTS, DIGNITIES AND HONOURS &c. BESTOWED BY NAPOLEON.

[An asterisk is affixed to the names of his Marshals.]

* Augereau. Duc de Castiglione.
* Bernadotte. Prince de Ponte Corvo.
* Berthier. Chief of the Staff. (Prince de Neufchâtel.) Prince de Wagram.
* Bessières. Duc d'Istria. Commander of the Old Guard.
  Bonaparte, Joseph. (King of Naples.) King of Spain.
  „   Louis. King of Holland.
  „   Lucien. Prince de Canino.
  „   Jerome. King of Westphalia.
* Brune.
  Cambacérès. Arch-Chancellor. Duc de Parma.
  Caulaincourt. Duc de Vicenza. Master of the Horse. Minister of Foreign Affairs (1814).
  Champagny. Duc de Cadore.
  Chaptal. Minister of the Interior. Comte de Chanteloupe.
  Clarke. Minister of War. Duc de Feltre.
  Daru. Minister of War. Comte.
* Davoust. Prince d'Eckmühl. Governor of Hamburg.
  Drouet. Comte d'Erlon.
  Drouot. Comte. Aide-Major of the Guard.
* Duroc. Duc de Friuli.
  Eugène (Beauharnais). Viceroy of Italy.

Fesch (Cardinal).   Grand Almoner.
Fouché.   Minister of Police (1801—1810).   Duc d'Otranto.
Jomini.   Baron.
*Jourdan.   Comte.
*Junot.   Duc d'Abrantès.
*Kellermann.   Duc de Valmy.
*Lannes.   Duc de Montebello.
*Lefebvre.   Duc de Danzig.
*Macdonald.   Duc de Taranto.
Maret.   Minister of Foreign Affairs (1811—1814).   Duc de Bassano.
*Marmont.   Duc de Ragusa.
*Masséna.   (Duc de Rivoli.)   Prince d'Essling.
Miot.   Comte de Melito.
Mollien.   Comte.   Minister of the Treasury.
*Moncey.   Duc de Conegliano.
Montholon.   Comte.
*Mortier.   Duc de Treviso.
*Mouton.   Comte de Lobau.
*Murat.   (Duc de Berg.)   King of Naples.
*Ney.   (Duc d'Elchingen.)   Prince de la Moskwa.
*Oudinot.   Duc de Reggio.
Pasquier, Duc de.   Prefect of Police.
*Poniatowski.
Rapp.   Comte.
Rémusat.   Chamberlain.
Reynier.   Duc de Massa.
Savary.   Duc de Rovigo.   Minister of Police.
Sébastiani.   Comte.
*Sérurier.
*Soult.   Duc de Dalmatia.
*St Cyr, Marquis de.
*Suchet.   Duc d'Albufera.
Talleyrand.   Minister of Foreign Affairs (1799—1807).   Grand
        Chamberlain (1804—1808).   Prince de Benevento.
*Victor.   Duc de Belluno.

[Grouchy received the Marshal's staff in 1815.]

INDEX.

i/m
9/= Nel
10/30